THE WHICH? GUIDE TO AN ACTIVE RETIREMENT

THE WHICH? GUIDE TO AN ACTIVE RETIREMENT

CONSUMERS' ASSOCIATION

Which? Books are commissioned and researched by
Consumers' Association
and published by Which? Ltd,
2 Marylebone Road, London NW1 4DF

Distributed by The Penguin Group:
Penguin Books Limited, 27 Wrights Lane,
London W8 5TZ

First edition September 1993
Reprinted September 1994
Second edition May 1995

Copyright © 1993, 1994, 1995 Which? Ltd

British Library Cataloguing in Publication Data
Consumers' Association
Which? Guide to an Active Retirement:
Positive Steps to a Secure Future
I. Title
646.7

ISBN 0-85202-541-6

Cover photograph by courtesy of ACE/Bill Bachmann

No part of this publication may be reproduced or transmitted in any form or by any means, electronically or mechanically, including photocopying, recording or any information storage or retrieval system, without prior permission in writing from the publisher. This publication is not included under licences issued by the Copyright Agency.

Typeset by Litho Link Ltd, Welshpool, Powys, Wales

Printed and bound by Firmin-Didot (France)
Groupe Herissey
N° d'impression: **30729**

ACKNOWLEDGEMENTS

Financial editor: Jane Vass

Other contributors: Jonquil Lowe; also Anthony Bailey, Jane Bell, Amanda Bristow, Dr Steve Carroll, Philip Cullum, Bill Evans, Amanda Jarvis, Avril Rodway, Tess Sullivan, Roger Taylor, Diana Vowles, Virginia Wallis, Cat Weakley

Original index: Marie Lorimer, updated by George Bennett

Typographic design: Paul Saunders

OTHER BOOKS FROM CONSUMERS' ASSOCIATION

120 Letters That Get Results
How to make a complaint and demand redress

The Which? Guide to Home Safety and Security
An indispensable guide to protecting yourself and your property

The Which? Guide to Giving and Inheriting
The most tax-efficient ways to pass on money, property and other valuables (England and Wales)

Wills and Probate
How to make your will and how to administer the estate of someone who has died, without employing a solicitor (England and Wales; plus a brief explanation of the main differences in Scotland)

What to Do When Someone Dies
Dealing with the practical arrangements that have to be made after a death (England, Wales and Scotland)

Understanding HRT and the Menopause
Managing 'the change' with or without hormone replacement therapy

Caring for Parents in Later Life
Essential advice on the practical, financial, legal and emotional issues

All these books and many others are available from bookshops, and by post from Consumers' Association, Castlemead, Gascoyne Way, Hertford X, SG14 1LH. Access/Visa card-holders can phone free on (0800) 252100 to place an order.

Contents

Introduction																										9

PART 1: PLANNING AHEAD
1 Retirement in the distance										13
2 Retirement on the horizon										19
3 Coping with sudden retirement							24

PART 2: YOUR FINANCES IN RETIREMENT
4 Planning your income												31
5 Planning your spending											42
6 Balancing your income and spending				52
7 Pension from an employer scheme						70
8 Personal pension plans											89
9 Financial support for the family						109
10 Investments																	119
11 Getting financial advice									142

PART 3: WORKING IN RETIREMENT
12 Deciding to carry on working							159
13 Getting a new job													167
14 Starting your own business								179

PART 4: TAX AND RETIREMENT
15 The basics of tax													195
16 Tax if you carry on working								215
17 Tax and investments												235
18 Tax and your home													246
19 Dealing with the tax authorities					253

PART 5: YOU AND YOUR HOME

20	Where to live in retirement	265
21	Buying and selling	273
22	Moving home	290
23	House insurance	298
24	Security and safety in the home	307

PART 6: DAY-TO-DAY LIVING

25	Basic utilities	321
26	Know your rights	331

PART 7: MAKING THE MOST OF YOUR LEISURE

27	Getting around	353
28	Holidays	365
29	Enjoying your leisure	376

PART 8: THE GOOD HEALTH GUIDE

30	Healthy eating	387
31	Exercise	400
32	You and the National Health Service	409
33	Health problems	426
34	Caring for elderly parents	466

PART 9: WILLS AND INHERITANCE

35	Making your will	489
36	Inheritance tax	507

Addresses	522
Index	532

INTRODUCTION

Whatever it was that shaped your working life – paid employment or running your own business – the transition from working to not working will benefit from careful planning, and it cannot start too soon. Retirement is a time for redefining priorities, for taking new opportunities, for re-structuring routines. But whether retirement has come sooner than expected or at the long-appointed time, three factors will largely determine your ability to enjoy it.

Money: nothing is more important than ensuring in advance that you'll have sufficient funds to keep your home in good order, to enjoy everyday life and leisure, and to bolster you against the ravages of inflation or unforeseen expense.

Health: keeping yourself fit and eating well, recognising problems at an early stage and knowing where to turn to for help if necessary should be priorities at any age, but are especially important as you get older.

And home: the years shortly before retirement are an excellent time to review your domestic arrangements. Do you want to live in your present house or flat for evermore or is there a danger that it could become a millstone? Now is the time to make a realistic assessment of the options available to you.

All these topics – and many more besides – are covered in detail in *The Which? Guide to an Active Retirement*. You will certainly want to maximise your income, whether from pensions built up over the years or from other sources; you may even want to start a business; and you might well want to sharpen up your plans for passing on your money in the most tax-efficient way. You may wish to get involved in voluntary work, or put more time into interests which previously had to play second fiddle to your job. And you may need at some point to get help in arranging for the care of elderly relatives.

Whatever it is that you hope to gain from this new phase of your life, *The Which? Guide to an Active Retirement*, drawing on the knowledge and experience of a team of *Which?* experts, will help you take positive steps to a secure, happy and fulfilling future.

PART 1

PLANNING AHEAD

CHAPTER 1

Retirement in the distance

If you are already struggling to reconcile the demands made on your purse and energies by a family, a mortgage and a job, then planning for retirement may be low down the list of your priorities. However, although there are some last-minute things you can do to ensure an active and happy retirement, it is easier if you can start to think and plan some years in advance.

When to start planning

The days are gone when you could be reasonably sure of your retirement date years in advance. There has been a general trend in the UK to people stopping work (voluntarily or involuntarily) at earlier ages, with only 35 per cent of people aged 60 to 64 working in 1994, compared to 66 per cent in 1971. For example, if you're employed by a major employer which offers a good pension scheme and which is trying to slim down its workforce, you could be offered early retirement at 55 or even earlier. That won't, of course, necessarily mean the end of working altogether, and if you're self-employed or working in a more flexible and individual field, you may never 'retire' at all.

But whenever you eventually stop work, it can take years to build up an adequate income for your retirement. So, however far away from retirement you are, the first thing to think about is your pension.

Will your pension be enough?

The state retirement pension on its own does not provide a reasonable income in retirement and, whatever the political developments, it is difficult to see how this could be reversed by the time you retire. It is forecast that by 2030 there will be 2.4 people aged 20 to 65 to each person over 65, compared to the current ratio of 3.7 to one now. However, you may also qualify for an income from the State Earnings Related Pension Scheme (SERPS). See **Chapter 4** for a detailed explanation of state pensions. Some women will also be affected by the change in their state pension age from 60 to 65. This will be implemented gradually, starting in the year 2010 – for more information see page 36.

> **TIP**
>
> You may have opted out of SERPS. However, as you grow older this becomes less attractive, so check now whether it is time to opt back in – see page 78.

The limited level of state pension puts more onus on you to save for your retirement. The most obvious – and usually most suitable – way of doing so is either through an employer pension scheme or through your own personal pension plan, if you're self-employed or not a member of an employer scheme. **Chapter 7** covers employer schemes, and **Chapter 8** personal pension plans.

The most an employer scheme can give you (to comply with Inland Revenue rules) is two-thirds of your final salary on retirement. Since a typical scheme will give you a percentage of your final salary for each year of membership, each year you put off joining will haunt you as a reduced pension in retirement – although (within limits) you can make additional voluntary contributions to make up for lost time.

EXAMPLE

Ian joined his current employer, and its pension scheme, when he was 21. He's now 35: normal retirement age in his employer scheme is 60 for both men and women, but there is a clear trend to earlier retirement and he expects to go at 55. That would give him 34 years of membership and since his pension scheme pays one-sixtieth of final salary for each year of membership he should get a pension of 34/60 times his final salary. Assuming his salary remains at £25,000, that would give him a pension of just over £14,000.

However, Ian's case is not entirely straightforward. He left his employer when he was 31, rejoining the company (and the pension scheme) two years later. The pension scheme took his previous years of membership into account, but that two years' break would knock his pension down to 32/60 of £25,000, i.e. just over £13,000. So he's making additional voluntary contributions to make up for the lost years, in order to get as near as possible to the 2/3 of final salary, which is the maximum pension allowed – £16,666.

A personal pension plan is 'money purchase', which means that instead of being linked to your salary your contributions are invested on your behalf, and you have your own 'pension fund' which is used to purchase you a pension on retirement. The earlier you contribute, the longer your money has to accumulate, as Table 1 shows.

Table 1: How much to invest in a personal pension plan?

	Monthly contribution (after tax relief at 25%) needed for:		
Man £	Age	Woman £	Age
52	24	67	19
97	34	126	29
200	44	262	39
540	54	709	49
To get a pension of £10,000 a year at age	65		60

Source: Legal and General

Note that Table 1 makes standard assumptions laid down by regulators: it assumes that your pension fund grows at a steady rate of 6 per cent a year, and that a set amount of charges and expenses is deducted by the company. You might be lucky enough to choose a plan which performs very much better than this, or a company which has much smaller charges. This would compensate you to some extent for investing for a shorter period. The converse is equally true: you also run the risk of picking a company whose investments plummet, or whose costs soar. But it is investment performance that has the most dramatic effect. A 12 per cent growth rate, for example, would cut the contribution needed from a 35-year-old man from nearly £100 to around £25. Investing for a longer period at least offers a chance for the inevitable peaks and troughs to be evened out over time.

Other ways of investing for retirement

Pension contributions have the advantages of receiving tax relief at your top rate, and of growing in a tax-free fund. But unless you are leaving an employer scheme after less than two years of membership, you cannot usually get your money back until retirement date (though this is not necessarily when you stop working). So you will probably want to keep your options open for at least some of your disposable income. You may want some available before retirement to support a child through college or university, to help pay for a wedding or because you are worried about possible redundancy. In this case, see **Chapter 10** for suitable investments.

A warning against inflation

Even if inflation runs at only 2.5 per cent a year, £1,000 left in a building society will be worth only £781 after 10 years, in terms of its purchasing power, and £610 after 20 years (ignoring any interest received). To look at it another way, thirty-six years ago *Which?* magazine collected the prices of some common groceries. Table 2 shows the prices of those items in 1958 and 1994. Although the average rise in these prices has been only 5.4 per cent a year, you can see that the overall increase is dramatic.

The whole basket of groceries shown in Table 2 would have

Table 2: Prices of selected groceries compared, 1958 and 1994

Item	1958 price old money s d	1958 price new money p	1994 price p	Total change %
Tinned steak	2/6½	12.7	97	664
Tinned herrings in sauce	1/10½	9.4	56[1]	496
Tinned baked beans	9½	4.0	25	525
Tinned spaghetti (large)	1/8½	8.6	27	214
Tinned tomato soup	10	4.1	33	705
Tomato ketchup	3/7	17.9	93	420
Salad cream	3/2½	16.1	74	360
Instant coffee (small)	6/1½	30.7	169	450
Tea	1/11½	9.7	70	622
Self-raising flour	1/11½	9.9	72	627
Madeira cake mix	1/1½	5.6	53	846
Porridge oats	1/11	9.7	97	900
Corn flakes	2/3	11.3	102	803
Marmalade	1/8	8.3	79	852
Apricot jam	1/5	7.2	68	844
Jelly	1/7	7.9	59	647
Orange squash	3/3	16.3	79	385

Adjusted to reflect quantities in which items sold in 1994.
[1] 1993 price

cost £1.89 (£1/17/9½) in 1958. You would need £12.53 to buy the same items in 1994. Another way of viewing this is to consider the effect which the price rises have had on your income (assuming that you spent your income on that same basket of groceries): looked at this way, the buying power of £1 in 1958 had fallen to just 15p by 1994.

Not only do you have to ensure that the money earmarked for your retirement keeps pace with inflation until you stop work, but you also need to think about how your income will keep pace with inflation after retirement. This can make planning your pension somewhat complicated. **Chapters 4 to 6** give more guidance on budgeting in retirement.

Taking care of your family

As well as laying the foundations for a secure financial future in retirement at this stage, you should also review your will, or make one if you haven't already done so. Otherwise, your money may not go where you want it to and sorting out your affairs on your death may take longer than it need. **Chapter 35** gives more information.

You should also consider life insurance. If you have any existing policies, when do they mature? If you haven't got any, should you buy one now before your age pushes the cost up? **Chapter 9** may help you decide.

CHAPTER 2

RETIREMENT ON THE HORIZON

As you come up to retirement, it's time to check how much pension you will have and to take any last-minute steps to boost your retirement income. But retirement is about much more than money, and it's worth preparing yourself emotionally, perhaps by attending some sort of pre-retirement course. You should certainly be doing all this during the five years before retirement, but many people say they would have benefited more had they had appropriate information and an opportunity to think about retirement even earlier.

CASE HISTORY

About three years before he retired, Mr Duncan attended a very useful pre-retirement course at the local technical college. It lasted five days, including two half-days on finance. Among the 100 pages of handouts received was a budget sheet. Using this, Mr and Mrs Duncan kept records of their spending for the three years running up to retirement so that they could see where the money was going, and they gradually reduced their expenditure to the after-tax amount of their pensions. As a result there was no sudden reduction in their standard of living when they retired.

*The addresses and phone numbers of organisations marked with an asterisk can be found in the address section at the back of the guide.

Checking up on your pensions

State pensions
Ask the Department of Social Security (DSS) for a forecast. To do this, get form BR19 from your local Benefits Agency (or DSS office – see under Benefits Agency or Social Security in your phone book), complete it, and send it off to the Retirement Pensions Forecast and Advice Unit at the address shown on the form. Allow several weeks for a reply.

Employer pensions
Contact the administrators of any schemes to which you have belonged. You should find the appropriate person to contact on literature you've been sent about the scheme; otherwise contact the personnel department for help. If you've lost touch with a scheme, there is a Registrar of Pension Schemes★ which runs a free tracing service. If you have difficulty getting information from scheme managers the Occupational Pensions Advisory Service★ may be able to help.

Personal pension plans
These include plans used to contract out of the State Earnings Related Pension Scheme (SERPS) and Free-Standing Additional Voluntary Contribution schemes. Ask the pension provider for a benefit statement and information on options you have. Again, the Registrar of Pension Schemes★ may be able to help if you have lost touch.

Remember, though, that in most cases, you will be given only an estimate of your future pension. For example, the pension from a personal pension plan will depend both on the plan's investment performance and on annuity rates when you retire, which affect the amount of pension your pension fund will be able to buy. Note too that the forecast of any SERPS pension is based on assumptions different to those used by pensions salespeople when estimating the possible benefits you might get by contracting out – see **Chapter 7** – so don't compare these two types of forecast.

Virtually all personal pension plans invest your money in a unit-linked fund, and its value can bounce up and down in line with investment performance. If you want to reduce the risk of your investment falling in value before retirement, now might be the time to start to transfer it to one of the less risky investment funds, such as a 'cash' or 'deposit' fund.

Boosting your pension

If you're in an employer scheme
All employer schemes must give you the option to make Additional Voluntary Contributions (AVCs) to boost your retirement benefits. Alternatively, if your scheme is a poor one, you may prefer a 'Free-Standing' scheme (FSAVC) from a life insurance company or other pension provider. See page 83 onwards for more on these options.

If you're not in an employer scheme
You can take out a personal pension plan, or, if you already have one, increase your contributions to it. You can contribute more than the normal maximum allowed by the Inland Revenue once you are over a certain age (which depends on when you started your plan). You can also pay in more than normally allowed if you have not contributed the maximum possible in previous years. See page 101 onwards for more information.

Should you repay your mortgage?

Before you use any lump sum received on retirement to pay off your mortgage, you need to consider how much you owe, how interest rates on borrowing and investing compare, and how much access to a loan you might need in future. You should also consider your tax position: see **Chapter 18**. Paying off your mortgage means losing mortgage interest relief which you will not be able to get again unless you move. However, the value of this relief has dwindled, since you get it on only the first £30,000 of your mortgage and the rate of tax relief has fallen to 15 per cent from 6 April 1995. It's certainly worth paying off enough to bring the mortgage down to £30,000, and possibly more, providing you're not going to need ready access to the money.

Don't forget, if you have an endowment mortgage, that you can pay off the amount you owe your lender while still keeping up the endowment policy. This is often well worth doing, particularly if you have a 'with-profits' policy (where you get regular bonuses which, once added, can't be taken away). As much as 60 per cent of the total return from a with-profits policy may come from the terminal bonus which you get only when the policy matures, so it's worth hanging on for that.

Cutting other running costs

Chapter 6 explains how to balance your income and spending. But things you can do now to reduce your outgoings later include:

- Improving insulation – draughtproofing single-paned windows and external doors yourself will cost about £50 for an average-sized house, but could save you up to about £44 a year.
- Replacing your car, washing machine or other such goods for models which are more economical to run.
- Checking that your bank and credit card accounts are ones with low charges.

Preparing yourself emotionally

Some people see retirement as a happy release, for others the end of work seems the end of their useful life. People may have no friends outside work and may have simply no idea what to do with themselves all day. Added to this may be financial worries.

It may help to reduce stress when you do retire if you can 'wean' yourself off work gradually, by working part-time. And, although it may take some self-discipline, consider starting now some of those activities you've always looked forward to taking up in retirement, such as a hobby or sport, voluntary work or further education. A pre-retirement course is a good opportunity to air any worries about the emotional and financial implications of retirement.

Pre-retirement courses

These are run by commercial companies such as insurance companies, voluntary organisations, companies which provide courses for their own employees, and local authorities (though the number of authorities able to do this has reduced significantly over the past 10 years). They can be free to the individual or cost several hundred pounds; take up a few hours a week at the local college or be combined with a week's holiday in Devon; be run by experienced lecturers with relevant qualifications or – since there is no recognised form of vetting – people with none.

The Pre-Retirement Association* publishes an invaluable guide to the 250 or so course providers currently operating; the 1994-5 edition costs £8.50, but individuals can get extracts for specific regions for 50p. Questions to ask both yourself and course organisers include:

- What do you want from the course? Hard factual information, or an opportunity to think more generally about retirement? Can you influence the course content?
- Who will be running the course? What qualifications do they have? Is anybody giving financial information authorised to provide independent financial advice (see **Chapter 11**)?
- What will be expected from you? Can you bring your partner?
- What background material will be provided?
- How many participants will there be, and what is their background likely to be?
- How much does it cost and what does this include (particularly if it is a residential course)?

*The addresses and phone numbers of organisations marked with an asterisk can be found in the address section at the back of the guide.

CHAPTER 3

COPING WITH SUDDEN RETIREMENT

You may find yourself effectively retired, because of redundancy or ill-health, before the date you had anticipated. If so, the reason you leave work could make quite a difference to both your rights and your finances.

Early retirement

Benefits from your state retirement pension – or a personal pension plan taken out purely as a way of contracting out of the State Earnings Related Pension Scheme (SERPS: see page 39) – can't be drawn before state pension age.

Employer pension schemes usually allow early retirement, though the minimum age at which the Inland Revenue allows you to draw a pension is normally 50 (or, in a few cases, 45 for women). For schemes set up before 14 March 1989 the Inland Revenue also scales down the maximum pension the scheme can offer. In practice employers are likely to be less generous than the Inland Revenue allows, though if the employer is slimming down the workforce, better terms than normal might be offered.

If you have a personal pension plan, unless you are in one of the occupations listed on page 100, the earliest age at which you can draw a pension is 60 for plans started before 1 July 1988, 50 for other plans (though you can transfer to a plan with the younger age). But drawing your personal pension early means the amount you get will probably be smaller than if you had contributed until the planned pension age, when your money would have had longer to grow. Some pension providers may also impose early retirement penalties.

Early retirement on health grounds

Although you can't get a state retirement pension early, you may get other state benefits, for example incapacity benefit, or disability living allowance if you need help with personal care and getting about. For guidance on the state benefits available if you are sick or disabled see Social Security leaflet FB28 or phone the Benefits Enquiry Line on 0800 882200.

There are no Inland Revenue limits on the age at which you can draw an employer pension on health grounds, and the limits on amounts are relaxed. Each employer scheme will usually set its own conditions, which may be more rigorous than the Inland Revenue rules (though possibly more generous than those on voluntary early retirement).

If you have to retire because of ill-health, you can draw a pension from a personal plan at any age, though again the amount is likely to be smaller than it would have been had you contributed to the plan until your planned retirement date.

You may also have some relevant insurance. Permanent health insurance, bought yourself or as a perk from your employer, will pay out an income if you are unable to work due to ill-health or disability, but usually stops at retirement age. Credit insurance covers loan payments for you if you can't make them yourself because of sickness, accident or redundancy, but often only for one to two years.

Note that with all the options above, definitions of 'ill-health' will vary, and you are likely to need medical evidence.

Compulsory redundancy

For losing your job to be classed as redundancy, normally your job must have disappeared; it is not redundancy if your employer immediately takes on a direct replacement, though it will not matter if they are recruiting more workers of a different type, or in some other location (unless your contract could have required you to move there).

If it is classed as redundancy you get certain rights (unless you are self-employed) on some fixed term contracts, or in some occupations. Chief among these rights is statutory redundancy pay for anyone who has been employed continuously by the employer for at least two years. If the employer cannot pay, the state may make the payment on the employer's behalf. The legal minimum (the employer may pay more) is:

- for each complete year in which you were between 18 and 21, half a week's pay
- for each complete year in which you were between 22 and 40, one week's pay
- for each complete year in which you were between 41 and 64, one and a half week's pay.

The maximum number of years taken into account is 20 and the maximum payment is £6,150. However, you have no legal entitlement to redundancy pay if you are 65-plus or over the company's normal retirement age, and your entitlement is reduced after your 64th birthday. For how redundancy pay is taxed, see page 201.

You may also have the right to reasonable time off, with pay, to look for another job or arrange training; a right to a minimum period of notice, and, if there is a recognised trade union whose members are affected, a minimum period of consultation. See the leaflets available from your JobCentre (in the phone book under 'Employment Service') or phone the redundancy payments Helpline on 0800 848489.

Voluntary redundancy

You may get a better deal for volunteering; another incentive might be if you could qualify for early retirement as well. But be careful. Your employer may be entitled to offset part of your pension payment against the redundancy payment. Although redundancy won't lead to disqualification for receiving unemployment benefit because you left your job voluntarily, any non-statutory redundancy or ex gratia payment may affect your entitlement. Volunteering for early retirement may also have an effect (and your pension may reduce your benefit – see below).

Also, credit insurance usually covers loan payments on compulsory, but rarely voluntary, redundancy.

Making the best of redundancy

Your employer may be prepared to negotiate. As well as negotiating on pay, ask about extending perks: you may be able to continue to qualify for the company's private medical insurance scheme, or discounts on the company's products. Consider asking your employer to pay for counselling or financial advice, but check what strings are attached, particularly whether the adviser represents only one company or is fully independent. **Chapter 11** should help.

Unfair dismissal

Your company should follow some consistent procedure before dismissing staff, and these procedures may be set out in company disciplinary or redundancy selection procedures. If these procedures aren't followed, or if you believe you were unfairly dismissed or selected for redundancy, you can take your case to an independent industrial tribunal, providing you have the qualifying length of service – 2 years' continuous service with the employer. You must do so within three months of the dismissal. If you believe you have been selected because of race or sex or for trade union reasons, there is no qualifying length of service. Applying to an industrial tribunal is free and legal representation is not essential. The leaflet *Industrial Tribunals Procedure* is available from Employment Service offices (listed as such in the phone book).

Unemployment benefit

You can get unemployment benefit for up to a year: amounts for the year from 6 April 1995 are £46.45 a week plus £28.65 for a dependent partner, £58.85 plus £28.65 for a dependent partner if you are both over state pension age. But you must have paid enough National Insurance contributions and be actively seeking work, and you can't get the benefit at the same time as state retirement pension. And, if you're 55 or over and get more than £35 a week (before tax) from an employer pension scheme or personal pension, your benefit will be reduced by 10p for every 10p over the £35 limit. DSS leaflet NI230 gives more information. Note that your unemployment benefit can be affected by payments such as an award from an industrial tribunal, some ex gratia payments, pay in lieu of notice or payments from an employer pension scheme: see DSS leaflet NI12.

Always sign on as unemployed the first day you leave work, even if you won't qualify for benefit. This means that you should get National Insurance credits in order to protect your rights to benefits (or pensions) in future. Men aged 60 or over don't need to sign on, as they get credits automatically.

If you don't qualify for unemployment benefit, or are on a low income, you may get means-tested benefits such as Income Support. See page 67 for where to get more information, or ring Freeline Social Security on 0800 666555. From April 1996, unemployment benefit will be replaced by Jobseeker's Allowance. This will cut to six months the period during which your benefit depends on your National Insurance contributions, after which your benefit will be means-tested.

Coping emotionally

Loss of a job is rated as one of the most stressful events that you can experience. Warning signs that you may be under more stress than is good for you include changes in eating or sleeping patterns, or an increase in smoking or alcohol intake. One of the most obvious early signs of stress to look out for in another person is an intensification of personality traits. For example, a defensive person may become suspicious, a careful person overmeticulous. To reduce stress, try to find ways of replacing the social contact and discipline of a job, for example by keeping to a daily routine, taking regular exercise or taking on voluntary work. It might help to talk things over with your GP.

PART 2

YOUR FINANCES IN RETIREMENT

CHAPTER 4

PLANNING YOUR INCOME

When you retire, there are four main sources of income which you may rely on:

- state pensions and state benefits
- private pensions either from employer schemes you belonged to while working or from personal pension plans you took out
- interest and other income from investments and savings
- pay or profits from work you continue to do after retirement.

Incomes of people retired now

In 1993, nearly half of all retired households relied mainly on the state pension and/or other state benefits for their income. Of these, nearly 60 per cent of one-person households had to live on a before-tax income of less than £70 a week (£3,640 a year), and 40 per cent of couples lived on less than £113 a week (£5,876 a year). If you want to enjoy a reasonable standard of living in retirement, it is clear that you cannot rely just on the state – you need income from at least one of the other sources as well.

The average weekly before-tax income of a retired household in 1993 was £181.52 (£9,439 a year). The pie chart below shows where this income came from.

The older retired, on average, manage on less than the more recently retired: average before-tax income in households where the head is aged 75 or over is just £152.96 a week (£7,954 a year), compared with £216.72 a week (£11,269 a year) for households where the head is aged 65 to 74.

There are four main reasons for this age discrepancy. Firstly, older retired people are less likely to work. Only 6 per cent of their income comes from wages, salaries and employment, against nearly 15 per cent for the younger retired. The second reason is that the very elderly are less likely to have had the opportunity to build up pensions privately during their working lives, so they will more often be among those who are mainly dependent on state pensions and benefits. In addition, they will have been largely excluded from the earnings-related part of the state pension scheme (see page 39) which started up only in 1978. And lastly, unlike state pensions, other sources of retirement income often don't hold their value in the face of inflation, so what may have started out many years ago as a healthy income could now be worth much less.

Average weekly income of a retired household

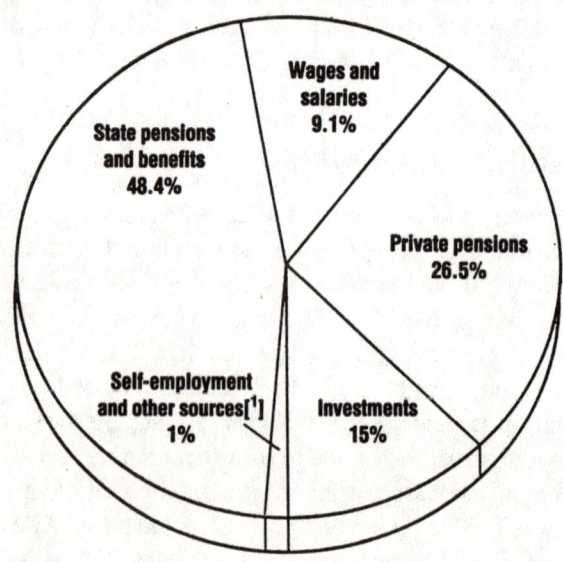

Source: Family Spending, HMSO, 1994, Table 8.5.
([1] Self-employment 0.6%, other sources 0.4%)

The effect of inflation

Inflation and retirement income

If your income doesn't rise as fast as the prices of the things you need or choose to buy, you will be able to afford less and less of those things as time goes on. Inflation in the UK is usually measured as changes in the Retail Prices Index – this is based on a varied basket of goods and services weighted to reflect the spending patterns of the population as a whole (and so doesn't necessarily reflect the spending of retired people). The rate of inflation can vary enormously: back in 1975, it was running at a yearly rate of 27 per cent – in other words, prices were rising by more than a quarter over the space of just one year; but in June 1993, inflation fell to a low point of just 1.2 per cent a year.

However, even a very modest rate of inflation can have a huge impact on prices over time. Table 1 shows the impact which various rates of general inflation would each have on £1,000 of income over time.

Table 1 shows that if you had an income of £10,000 at the start of your retirement at the age of 60, say, its value would have fallen to just £360 by the age of 95, assuming inflation averaged 10 per cent a year. And, even if inflation averaged only 3 per cent a year throughout your retirement, the buying power of your £10,000 would have fallen to £3,550 – just a third of its original value.

So, when you plan your retirement, it is essential that you think about what impact inflation may have over the years. Either you need pensions or other income which will increase year by year with inflation, or you need to set aside some savings, or other sources of income, to boost your income later in retirement. See **Chapter 10** for more on investing in retirement, and **Chapter 12** for working in retirement.

Inflation and retirement savings

It's not just in retirement that you need to keep an eye on inflation. It will also affect the amount you need to accumulate to provide your eventual pension. Suppose you are 55, currently

Table 1: How inflation reduces your income

After this many years:	... the buying power of £1,000 of income would fall to this much, if the average yearly inflation rate was:				
	3% £	4% £	5% £	7% £	10% £
1	971	961	952	935	909
2	943	925	907	873	826
3	915	889	864	816	751
4	888	855	823	763	683
5	863	822	784	713	621
10	744	676	614	508	386
15	642	555	481	362	239
20	554	456	377	258	149
25	478	375	295	184	92
30	412	308	231	131	57
35	355	253	181	94	36

earn £30,000 a year and hope that your personal pension savings will provide a retirement income of £15,000 a year, in terms of today's money. It might be estimated that you'd need a pool of £150,000, in today's money, to provide that pension. But, even if inflation averages a modest yearly rate, £150,000 will be worth less by the time you come to retire, so how much will you need to have saved by then to provide you with the equivalent of £15,000 a year in terms of future money values?

Table 2 suggests the answer. It shows, given different rates of inflation between now and retirement, how much money you would need in future for it to be worth the same (in terms of what you can buy with it) as £1,000 today. For example, if inflation averaged 3 per cent a year over 10 years, you would need £1,344 at that time to be worth the same as £1,000 today. This means that, in the example above, you would need a fund of 150 × £1,344 = £201,600 at the age of 65 to provide a pension of £20,160, which would have the same value as £15,000 in today's money. And, if inflation averaged 10 per cent a year instead, you would need a fund of 150 × £2,594 = £389,100.

It's important to be aware of the impact of inflation on the amounts you need to save. Many projections of the money which a pension plan will provide are given in terms of future money without being adjusted for inflation. You might be tempted to think that being a half-millionaire by the time you retire will mean being rich, but your 'riches' may not buy very much by then.

Table 2: What you need to keep up with inflation

After this many years:	you would need this much money for it to buy the same as £1,000 today, if the average yearly inflation rate was:				
	3% £	4% £	5% £	7% £	10% £
1	1,030	1,040	1,050	1,070	1,100
2	1,061	1,082	1,103	1,145	1,210
3	1,093	1,125	1,158	1,225	1,331
4	1,126	1,170	1,216	1,311	1,464
5	1,159	1,217	1,276	1,403	1,611
10	1,344	1,480	1,629	1,967	2,594
15	1,558	1,801	2,079	2,759	4,177
20	1,086	2,191	2,653	3,870	6,727
25	2,094	2,666	3,386	5,427	10,835
30	2,427	3,243	4,322	7,612	17,449
35	2,814	3,946	5,516	10,677	28,102
40	3,262	4,801	7,040	14,974	45,259
45	3,782	5,841	8,985	21,002	72,890
50	4,384	7,107	11,467	29,457	117,391
55	5,082	8,646	14,636	41,315	189,059
59[1]	5,720	10,115	17,790	54,156	276,801

[1] The maximum period for which pension savings can be left invested is from age 16 to age 75 – i.e. 59 years

What the state provides

It is likely that you'll qualify for some pension from the state when you reach pension age. The main advantage of state pensions is that they are fully inflation-proofed, in line with prices, both during the time you are building up an entitlement to them and while they are being paid out. The drawback is that state pensions are low and insufficient, on their own, to support a comfortable lifestyle.

However, state pensions can be a useful backbone for your retirement income which you should supplement through your own additional savings. To work out how much extra pension income you'll have to plan for, you'll first need to know roughly how much income you can expect from the state.

There are two main state pensions: the basic pension and pension from the State Earnings Related Pension Scheme (SERPS).

How much basic pension?

In the year from 6 April 1995, the full state basic pension is £58.85 a week (£3,060.20 a year) for a single person. A married couple get more – up to £93.35 a week (£4,854.20 a year). If both husband and wife qualify for a basic pension in their own right they can get a maximum of 2 × £58.85 = £117.70 a week (£6,120.40 a year) between them.

You build up your entitlement to basic pension by paying National Insurance contributions throughout your working life. If you have not paid enough contributions for a full basic pension, you may still qualify for a reduced-rate pension. But it is possible to pay too few contributions to qualify for any pension at all.

How you qualify for basic pension

In the context of state pensions, 'working life' is officially defined. Generally, it means the tax years from the one in which you reach the age of 16 to the last tax year before you reach state pension age.

For women born after 5 March 1955, and for all men, state pension age is 65, giving a maximum working life of 49 years. If you are a woman and you were born before 6 April 1950, your state pension age is 60 and your maximum working life is five years shorter – i.e. 44 years. And anyone born before July 1932 may have a shorter than normal working life.

Women born between 6 April 1950 and 5 March 1955 are caught in a transitional period during which women's state pension age is being progressively raised from 60 to 65. To work out your state pension age, take age 60 and add to it one month for each tax month (or part tax month) that your birthday falls after 5 April 1950. A tax month runs from the sixth day of one month to the fifth day of the next month.

You need to have paid National Insurance contributions for about 90 per cent of the years in your working life in order to qualify for the full basic pension and you need to have paid contributions for about a quarter of those years in order to receive any basic pension at all. In between those limits, you qualify for basic pension at a reduced rate. Table 3 gives a guide to how much basic pension you'll get if you have a standard working life of 44 years or 49 years.

You generally pay National Insurance whenever you are working – either as an employee or while self-employed or in a partnership. Table 4 shows the type of contributions that you pay. Only complete tax years of contributions count – so, for example, a year in which you were self-employed and paying National Insurance for 36 weeks but travelling abroad for the remaining 16 weeks will not count towards your pension unless you choose to make voluntary payments of National Insurance for the 16 weeks.

Table 3: How much basic pension?

If you've paid National Insurance contributions for this many years . . .	You'll get this percentage of the full basic pension . . . Women born after 5 March 1955 %	Women born before 6 April 1950 and all men %
9 or less	0	0
10	26	0
15	39	35
20	52	46
25	65	57
30	77	69
35	90	80
40	100 [1]	91
44	100	100 [2]

[1] The full pension for a woman with a working life of 44 years is payable if she has 39 or more years of contributions.

[2] The full pension for a man or woman with a working life of 49 years is payable if they have 44 or more years of contributions.

If you're not working

In some non-working situations, you will qualify for National Insurance credits which are the equivalent of contribution payments in your record for basic pension purposes. You qualify automatically for these credits when:

- you're unemployed and have 'signed on'
- you're a man or woman with a pension age of 65 who is aged over 60 and unemployed (regardless of whether you have 'signed on')
- you're claiming sickness benefit
- you're a woman claiming maternity benefit
- in the tax years in which you reach ages 16, 17 and 18, if you

Table 4: Types of National Insurance contributions

Type of contribution	Description	Can it count towards your pension?
Class 1 Full-rate	Paid by employees, including company directors[1], but not people earning less than a 'lower earnings limit'	**YES**
Reduced-rate ('small stamp')	Paid by some married women and widows – they can choose to switch to full-rate	**NO**
Class 2	Paid by self-employed, but optional for people with profits below a lower limit and for some married women and widows	**YES**
Class 3	Voluntary – you choose to pay if you want to fill in gaps in your contribution record	**YES**
Class 4	Paid by self-employed on profits between lower and upper 'earnings limits'	**NO**

[1]Before 6 April 1975, company directors counted as self-employed

are in full-time education and were born after 5 April 1957.
- in tax years in which you take part in an approved training course (which doesn't include going to university), if you were born after 5 April 1957.

If you can't work because you are at home caring for children or other dependants (for example, an elderly relative) you may qualify for 'home responsibilities protection' (HRP). With this, you don't get credits for National Insurance but the number of years for which you need contributions in order to qualify for a given level of pension is reduced. You can get HRP only for full tax years – in the example above, if you had been self-employed for 36 weeks of the tax year but at home caring for your children for the remaining 16 weeks, the year would not count towards your basic pension unless you paid voluntary contributions during the 16 weeks. You get HRP automatically if you are receiving child benefit; in other circumstances, you'll usually need to claim it.

How much SERPS pension?

The State Earnings Related Pension Scheme (SERPS) provides pensions which are additional to the basic pension. You can build up a SERPS pension only if you're paying full-rate Class 1 National Insurance – so, if you're self-employed, unemployed or on low earnings you can't belong to SERPS. The amount of pension you eventually get is linked to your earnings (between a lower and upper limit) during part or all of your working life, which means that the amount of SERPS pension built up varies from person to person.

Even if you're eligible for the SERPS scheme, you may be 'contracted out' of it. This means that instead of building up SERPS pension, you are building up a pension which will be paid from an employer pension scheme (see **Chapter 7**) or a personal pension plan (see **Chapter 8**). In this case, either you and your employer will pay lower National Insurance contributions or part of your National Insurance payments will be returned by being paid into your pension scheme or plan.

The formula for calculating SERPS pension is complex – particularly as the rules were changed in 1988. But you don't need to work through complicated sums yourself because you can get a forecast from the Department of Social Security (DSS) of your SERPS pension based on your contributions to date and assuming you carry on contributing up to retirement. See page 20 for details of how to get this forecast.

Table 5 gives you an idea of the maximum SERPS pension you could get, depending on when you will reach state pension age and in terms of today's money. Once you start to receive your SERPS pension, it is increased each year in line with price inflation.

Table 5: How much SERPS pension?

Tax year in which you reach state pension age	Maximum SERPS pension in 1995 money Weekly amount
1995-96	£90
2000-01	£102
2005-06	£94
2010-11	£87
2020-21	£84
2030-31	£81
2040-41	£76

Graduated pension

There was an earlier state pension scheme related to earnings which ran from 6 April 1961 to 5 April 1975 and provides 'graduated pensions'. Unfortunately, the scheme was designed without adequate safeguards against inflation and the pensions it provides are now very small.

The scheme worked as follows. You paid different amounts of National Insurance depending on your earnings. The total you paid was divided into 'units' – for women, every £9 paid counted as a unit and, for men, every £7.50 counted as a unit. In the 1995-6 tax year, you get 7.64 pence in graduated pension for every unit. Graduated pensions are increased each year in line with the Retail Prices Index.

Information about your state pensions

The DSS runs a Retirement Pensions Forecast and Advice Service*, which can provide you with information about the basic, SERPS and graduated pensions you've built up so far, a forecast of the amount of state pensions you could build up by retirement, together with advice about any steps you could take now to increase your future pension (for example, making voluntary National Insurance contributions or switching to full-rate contributions if you currently pay at the reduced Class 1 rate). See page 20 for how to get hold of a statement and forecast.

If you have any other queries or problems about your state pension or National Insurance position, contact your local Benefits Agency (DSS office), preferably in writing – don't forget to put your National Insurance number on all correspondence. If you have a purely general query (i.e. one that can be answered without reference to the files for your specific case), try the DSS information service on Freephone 0800 666555.

CHAPTER 5

Planning your spending

It is probable that your income will be considerably less in retirement than it is while you are working, but this will not necessarily imply a lower standard of living once you retire, because your expenditure will also change. Spending on some items will fall or no longer be needed, but spending on other items will tend to increase.

Work-related expenses

If you go out to work every day, you'll be paying out for a range of work-related items. Unless you live close enough to work to be able to walk or cycle to the office, you'll probably be paying for bus or train fares or paying for petrol and a certain amount of wear and tear on your car. Some employers provide a company car and/or pay for the running costs of a car, in which case you may not be paying out directly, but you'll be paying some extra tax on the value the Inland Revenue thinks you're getting from this perk. Once you retire, you'll save on the fares or car costs associated with work.

Working away from home also means that you may be paying for lunch every day. This could be a costly item if you are buying expensive sandwiches or restaurant meals. On the other hand, your lunch may be cheap if your employer provides subsidised food in a canteen or through vending machines. You'll also be consuming various drinks throughout the day and, again, this can be a dear item if you have to buy them outside work or very cheap (or free) if your employer subsidises them. So the impact once you retire will vary.

You may also save on clothing costs once you stop work. An employer will generally provide any special uniform or protective clothing required, but many people simply need to look smart and must do this at their own expense. After retirement, you'll be able to please yourself regarding dress, which may mean you can rely on cheaper, more casual clothes.

You should not overlook the 'extras' associated with work – things like drinks after work with friends, contributing to birthday and leaving presents, taking part in sweepstakes, and so on. You will save these amounts once you retire. You might also now be paying out for a daily newspaper and, perhaps, for magazines to keep you abreast of current affairs or your specialist area of knowledge; once you retire, you might decide to have a paper less often or to take fewer journals. On the other hand, your workplace may give you access to newspapers and magazines which you wish to replace – at your own cost – once you retire.

While you are working, you'll be paying National Insurance contributions; these will cease once you retire, unless you are under state pension age and carry on with some work, or you're under age 60 and decide to pay voluntary contributions. You may also be paying into an employer-run pension scheme and these payments will cease once you retire.

If you work from home, retiring is likely to have less impact on your spending, but you should still have a realistic look at how your costs might change – for example, after retirement, you might go out more, which could mean paying less for heating and lighting at home. If you're self-employed or run your own company, then stopping work will clearly reduce your spending substantially; on the other hand, you may find that items you were once able to buy through your business (which probably meant claiming tax relief on them and possibly getting back the VAT) must still be bought after retirement but at the full cost.

Life insurance

When you are working, your employer may be providing you with free life insurance cover. Once you retire, you'll have to decide whether you still need life cover. Life insurance costs more as you get older, so this could be a hefty expense.

On the other hand, as you get older, your need for life insurance is likely to decline. Your greatest need for life cover is when you have children who are dependent on you. As your family grows up, you can cut back on that aspect of your insurance. However, you may still need cover to protect a dependent wife or husband and you should also consider the position of anyone else who may be financially dependent on you, such as an ageing parent. **Chapter 9** gives further information on life insurance.

You may find spending on life insurance increases later in life, if you expect to leave a reasonable estate when you die and wish to protect dependants from inheritance tax (see **Chapter 36**).

House and car insurance

You may be able to cut the cost of premiums for house insurance once you retire. Some companies recognise that elderly customers pose a lower risk because they spend more time at home, which tends to deter burglars. **Chapter 23** shows companies which either offer a discount to, or arrange special policies for, mature policyholders.

Car insurance also usually gets cheaper as you get older, and many companies offer particularly good deals if you are over 50 or retired. This is because, statistically, drivers over the age of 50 or so tend to have fewer accidents than younger people. To find out about special deals, ask two or three insurance brokers to get quotes for you. If you haven't had your own car insurance policy for some time (because you've had a company car, say), you may not qualify for a no-claims discount. Ask your employer for evidence of your claims record before giving up work: some insurers may be prepared to give you a discount on the strength of this.

Household expenses

If you've been buying your own home, by the time you retire you are likely to have paid off your mortgage or to have only a small loan outstanding. If you do still have a mortgage, see **Chapter 2** for the pros and cons of using some of your retirement or redundancy money to pay it off. If you rent your home, this expense may not be affected by retirement.

On retiring, many people take the opportunity to carry out major home improvements, such as replacing old windows or building a conservatory. Later in retirement, changes to your home may be necessary to help you cope with health problems (see **Chapters 20 and 34**). You'll need to consider how home improvements made at the start of retirement, or later on, are to be financed – for example, out of a lump sum from your pension scheme or plan, out of savings, or by borrowing.

If your home is usually empty every weekday while you're out at work, retirement may mean a significant change in your fuel bills. You'll probably be at home a lot more and so will need to have the heating on more often. In the winter months, you'll also be using the lights more. You may feel the cold more and need to have the heating at a higher temperature. Being at home more also means greater use of household appliances such as the kettle. (See **Chapter 25** for more on use of fuel.)

You may be reluctant to undertake big jobs around the house as you grow older, so you should consider allowing for the possibility of paying someone else to do decorating for you, say, and digging the garden once or twice a year.

Telephone bills

Once you're retired, you may find that phone calls you used to make from work are now made from home and you might find that you use the phone a lot more to keep in touch with friends you used to see through work. On the other hand, calls connected with work or to contact your working husband or wife may cease and you may prefer, once you have more time, to visit people rather than talk on the phone. So, you'll need to evaluate your own particular use of the phone and how this might change after retirement.

If you often make calls outside your local area, especially in the evenings and at weekends, you may save money by subscribing to Mercury. You still have a British Telecom (BT) bill for line usage, and local calls are likely to be cheaper with BT unless a local cable company is able to offer a more competitive local service. The Mercury service is now available to the vast majority of UK phone users – you dial 132 before the number itself (but you need to join the Mercury scheme first).

If your use of the phone is very low, you could save money by switching to BT's 'Light User Scheme' service. If, on the other hand, you find yourself using your phone more, both BT and Mercury offer schemes for private customers who use the phone a lot. For information on BT services phone 150, and for Mercury services phone 0500 500194.

Travel

Don't automatically assume that stopping work will reduce the miles you travel. You may have more opportunity to go out, so your travelling could increase.

If you currently have the use of a company car you will need to consider alternative arrangements after retirement. Buying, insuring and running your own car will be a significant extra expense. If you don't expect to use a car much, you might instead consider using public transport or taxis and, perhaps, hiring a car occasionally. But, undoubtedly, it's very convenient having your own car, and economical places to buy food, DIY items, furniture, and so on, are often only adequately accessible if you have a car.

If you and your husband or wife each run your own car now, you may find that after retirement you can cope perfectly well with just one, which would save you money. Similarly, if you currently have a large car, you may find that after retirement you'll be happy to run something a bit smaller – this could save on fuel and insurance costs.

Public transport is often cheaper if you are older or retired. For example, British Rail operates a Senior Railcard. You pay a modest lump sum for it but it gives you a one-third discount for a year on most rail tickets apart from journeys made at peak hours on weekday mornings. Similarly, many bus and coach companies offer cheaper tickets to older customers. Your local council should be able to give you details of concessionary travel schemes operating in your area – see **Chapter 27**.

Holidays and leisure

When retired, you're likely to have a lot more leisure time and one pleasurable way to fill this is to take more holidays. This won't necessarily imply increased spending, since you'll have the freedom to take holidays at off-peak times when travel and accommodation will often be much cheaper. There are also many special deals aimed at older people.

However, on the whole, you should allow for higher spending on leisure activities after retirement than before.

Spending on your health

When you reach the state pension age you'll be entitled to free prescriptions for medicines – assuming present rules continue. But, apart from that, it's sensible to allow for some increase in health-related spending during retirement. Short-term illness can strike anyone at any time, but Table 1 shows that men, in particular, are more likely to face a spell in hospital as they get older.

Table 1: Survey of in-patient stays in hospital, 1992

Age group	Percentage of people who had been a hospital in-patient in the 12 months before the survey	
	Men	Women
All ages	8%	11%
65 to 74	16%	11%
75 or over	18%	17%

Source: *General Household Survey* 1992, HMSO, 1994

It's worth bearing in mind that, if you have to stay in hospital for more than six weeks, your state pension is reduced (on the basis that the state is paying for your keep anyway). Since many of your household expenses will continue even if you are in hospital this could have a serious impact on your budget. You can find out more by reading leaflet NI9 *Going into hospital* available from your local Benefits Agency (address in the phone book). One way to overcome this problem might be to take out special insurance generally known as 'hospital cash plans'. These pay out a specified cash sum for each day that you are in hospital if you are admitted as an in-patient either for NHS or private treatment. You can get details from an insurance adviser or broker (see *Yellow Pages*).

Waiting to go into hospital might have an impact on your budget too. For example, waiting for a hip replacement operation could leave you with a serious mobility problem and the need to pay for extra help and home alterations. It is worth considering taking out private medical insurance (see **Chapter 32**), which would cover the cost of receiving private treatment, usually allowing you to avoid NHS waiting lists. Although this insurance can be costly when you are older, some policies limit the cost by paying out only if you'll have to wait more than six weeks for treatment on the NHS. However, many plans exclude 'pre-existing conditions' – problems you've suffered from before – and others include them only after, say, two years without problems.

If you're aged 60 or over, the premiums you pay for private medical insurance can qualify for tax relief at the basic rate. This relief is given automatically (even to non-taxpayers and 20 per cent taxpayers) through a reduction in premiums. If you currently get private medical insurance as a benefit through your job, you may be able to continue the cover at preferential rates once you retire – ask your personnel department at work to look into this for you.

As you get older, you may have to face some health problems. Four out of five men over the age of 85, and nine out of ten women, face some kind of mobility problem and nearly half of this age group is unable to go out alone. Even a minor long-standing illness may mean an increase in spending, if, for

PLANNING YOUR SPENDING

example, you need to pay for someone to help clean your home or do the shopping for you.

Table 2: Incidence of long-standing illness which limits activities, 1992

Age group	Men	Women
All ages	18%	20%
65 to 74	40%	38%
75 or over	49%	52%

Source: *General Household Survey* 1992, HMSO, 1994

Paying for care

For some people, it will eventually be necessary to move to a nursing or residential home. This could prove extremely expensive. **Chapter 34** deals with this in detail, but nursing and residential homes typically charge several hundred pounds a week. If your income is low and you have less than £8,000 of capital, your local authority may help with the costs of nursing in your own home or living in a residential or nursing home. But, if not, you'll need to meet these bills yourself.

Although it's depressing to think about serious illness or disability, it's a good idea to confront this possibility early on in your retirement and to consider how you would like to cope if you did become ill later on. There are four main options:

- You could meet the costs out of your income if this is high enough.
- You could meet costs directly out of your capital and, if this runs out, rely on your local authority to help.
- You could use some capital – possibly from the sale of your home – to provide an income which would cover the costs of nursing care or living in a home. Table 3 lists companies which offer investment plans specifically designed for this purpose.
- You could plan ahead by taking out 'long-term care insurance' now which is designed to pay out in future if you need nursing care at home or have to move to a

49

residential or nursing home. In the mid-90s, relatively few companies offer this type of insurance – the main players are listed in Table 3. The ways in which the plans work vary, but usually they will pay out only once you are unable to perform, say, two or three out of five 'activities of daily living (ADLs)' for yourself. ADLs include being mobile, being able to dress yourself, coping with the toilet and feeding yourself.

You can get details about the plans offered by the companies listed in Table 3 either by contacting a local branch (address in the phone book) or through an insurance broker or other financial adviser.

Table 3: Main companies offering long-term care insurance

Company	Name of Plan
Insurance plans you take out in advance	
Commercial Union	Well-Being Insurance
PPP Lifetime	Lifetime Care
MGI Prime Health	Home Healthcare
	Home Healthcare Plus
Scottish Amicable	Long-Term Care Bond
(Long-term care insurance is also sometimes offered as an optional extra with other types of insurance – e.g. critical illness cover)	
Plans where you use a lump sum to provide an income now:	
Eagle Star	Care Fee Payment Plan
Commercial Union	Continuing Care Plan
PPP Lifetime	Immediate Care Plan

CASE HISTORY

Mr Davis took early retirement at 55, after working 34 years with the same company. He had no outstanding debts and his mortgage had been paid off, but he disagrees with people who expect him to be in a good position financially to sit back and enjoy life now. 'There are, of course, some savings after retirement, in travelling costs and contributions to company pension schemes,' he says. 'But these are more than outweighed by a number of additional expenses, such as eating out more often, extra leisure activities, and far more use of my private car, petrol costs, and especially during the winter higher heating costs of my house, which are currently approaching £1,000 a year.'

CHAPTER 6

BALANCING YOUR INCOME AND SPENDING

In order to find out whether you expect to have enough to live on in retirement, you need to bring together your expected income and your likely expenditure. The Calculator in this chapter will help you to do this.

Using the Calculator

We recommend that you fill in the Calculator twice: first time around, consider your position at the start of retirement; second time, try to work out how your income and spending may square up ten years or so into retirement. This will help you to see, first, whether you're on track with your general retirement planning and, secondly, whether you need to take any extra measures to protect your position later on.

Fill in the Calculator in today's money. So, for example, if you expect to qualify for a full-rate basic pension from the state, put in the rate that's being paid now (see **Chapter 4**) – don't try to guess what it's going to be years ahead. Similarly, express your expected spending in today's money. Think about how much you pay now for various items and try to estimate the proportionate change in those expenses after retirement, but don't try to inflate them for future price increases.

If you are married, each of you should fill in the relevant column in the 'Income' section and work out your after-tax income separately (see **Chapter 15** for who gets the married couple's allowance). You can then add your two after-tax incomes together and complete the rest of the Calculator as a couple.

After-tax income

The Calculator first asks you about sources of taxable income. Then it guides you through a rough estimate of the tax you might pay on your income. It uses 1995-6 tax allowances and rates. Lastly, add on any tax-free income you expect to receive. Note that, for the sake of simplicity, the Calculator assumes that you and your husband or wife will be basic-rate taxpayers after you retire.

Your expenses

The Calculator asks you to estimate your spending under various categories. If a category does not apply to you, leave it blank. Use yearly amounts. In some cases, it asks you to fill in amounts you might save up to cover major expenditure, such as replacing your car or making home improvements. If you would pay for these out of capital that you've accumulated, leave the entry for savings for them blank, but bear in mind that if your capital had been producing investment income, then your income would fall after you had spent the capital.

The Calculator asks you about loan repayments that you make. Do not include credit card repayments here if you have already included your spending using the card under other headings – for example, if you usually buy petrol using your credit card, enter the amounts spent under petrol, not loan repayments. If you anticipate taking out a loan to buy furniture or a car, say, enter either the amount of the loan repayments or the amount spent on the item, but don't enter both.

Income versus spending

When you've filled in all the figures for income and spending, subtract total spending from total income. If the answer is a positive number, you are on course for a financially secure retirement. If the answer is negative, your income – on current plans – won't be enough to support the lifestyle that you want. See page 57 onwards for steps to remedy the situation.

The Retirement Calculator

		At the start of retirement		Ten years into retirement
	Your income	husband	wife	
A	State basic pension (full rate is £3,060 for the 1995–6 tax year) – see page 36	_____	_____	_____
B	Other state pensions and/or taxable state benefits – see Chapter 4	_____	_____	_____
C	Pension(s) from employer pension scheme(s) – see Chapter 7	_____	_____	_____
D	Pension(s) from personal pension plans – see Chapter 8	_____	_____	_____
E	Taxable income from investments; enter gross (i.e. before-tax) amounts – see Chapter 10	_____	_____	_____
F	Earnings/profit from work you do after retirement – see Chapter 12	_____	_____	_____
G	Other taxable income	_____	_____	_____
H	Taxable income – add A + B + C + D + E + F + G	_____	_____	_____
	Your income tax bill			
I	Personal tax allowance – see Chapter 15	_____	_____	_____
J	Any other allowances except married couple's (and related) allowances – see Chapter 15	_____	_____	_____
K	Any outgoings you pay gross (i.e. before deducting tax relief) – see Chapter 15	_____	_____	_____
L	Add I + J + K	_____	_____	_____
M	Deduct L from H	_____	_____	_____
N	If M is £3,200 or less, take 20% of M. If M is more than £3,200, write in £640	_____	_____	_____
P	If M is £3,200 or less, leave P blank. If M is more than £3,200, work out: 25% of (M − £3,200)	_____	_____	_____
Q	Add N + P	_____	_____	_____
R	If applicable, from Q deduct the married couple's (or any related) allowance restricted to 15 per cent – see Chapter 15	_____	_____	_____
S	Tax on your income. If R is 0 or less, S = 0, i.e. there's no tax on your income. If R is greater than 0, S = R	_____	_____	_____

		At the start of retirement	Ten years into retirement
		husband wife	
T	After-tax income – subtract S from H	_____ _____	_____
U	Any tax-free income (e.g. £10 Christmas bonus paid to state pensioners, proceeds from long-term life insurance) – see Chapter 15	_____ _____	_____
	Your retirement income	single person/couple	
V	**Total income in retirement** – add T + U, for both partners	_____	_____

Your expenses: living at home

a	Food shopping and household basics	_____	_____
b	Buying and repairing household equipment	_____	_____
c	Newspapers/magazines/books	_____	_____
d	TV licence/videos/music	_____	_____
e	Dog/cat/other pet	_____	_____
f	Clothes/shoes/cosmetics/hairdressing	_____	_____

Your expenses: living it up

g	Sports and hobbies: materials/lessons/other	_____	_____
h	Dining out/theatre/cinema/concerts/exhibitions	_____	_____
i	Holidays/holiday home/second home	_____	_____
j	Other indulgences (e.g. smoking, drinking)	_____	_____

Your expenses: transport

k	Costs of owning a car: tax/insurance/servicing/repairs/breakdown insurance	_____	_____
l	Renting a car: rental charge/insurance	_____	_____
m	Costs of running car: petrol/diesel/oil	_____	_____
n	Train fares/bus fares/coach fares	_____	_____
o	Other travel costs	_____	_____

Your expenses: home-related

p	Mortgage/rent	_____	_____
q	Repairs/service charge/decoration/furnishing	_____	_____
r	Buildings and contents insurance	_____	_____
s	Council tax/water rates	_____	_____
t	Gas/electricity/oil/solid fuel	_____	_____

		At the start of retirement	Ten years into retirement
		single person/couple	
u	Home help/window cleaner/other paid help		
v	Gardening		
w	Telephone		

Your expenses: health-related

x	Dentist		
y	Optician		
z	Hospital cash plan/private medical insurance		
aa	Long-term care insurance		
bb	Other health-related expenses		

Your expenses: caring for others

cc	Spending on children/grandchildren		
dd	Financial help for elderly relatives		
ee	Christmas/birthday/other presents		
ff	Gifts to charity/church collections		
gg	Protection-type life insurance – see Chapter 9		
hh	Other caring expenses		

Your expenses: saving and borrowing

ii	Saving to replace car/household equipment		
jj	Saving to finance home improvements		
kk	Saving to cover higher health spending later on		
ll	Other regular saving		
mm	Loan repayments (other than mortgage)		

Your expenses: other

| nn | Postage/stationery/other | | |
| W | **Total expenses** – add up all expenses a–nn | | |

Balancing income and spending

| X | Subtract W from V and enter at X. If X is 0 or greater, you should have enough to live on during retirement. If X is a minus figure, you will not have enough. Look at ways of increasing your income – see below | | |

Not enough income?

One way to cope with a shortfall of income in retirement would, of course, be to economise on your spending, but really this is not ideal. First, consider ways in which you could boost your income.

Your state pension

If you expect to have more than enough income at the start of your retirement but you are worried that you'll be short of money later on, you could consider putting off the start of your state pension in order to earn extra pension later.

At present, your state pension starts to be paid when you reach the age of 60 if you're a woman or 65 if you're a man. But you can defer your pension for up to five years and, by doing so, earn extra pension. There's more information on page 160.

Building up your own pension

If you're still some way from retirement, you have time to build up a pension income. **Chapters 7 and 8** describe how you can save tax-efficiently for retirement through an employer pension scheme or personal pension. Certainly, if you're not yet saving in this way, you should start as soon as possible. If you're already contributing through an employer scheme, have you thought about boosting this form of saving by making additional voluntary contributions (AVCs)? See page 83.

Other forms of saving

Even if you have time enough to build up a pension, you might be put off saving this way, for example because you can't generally get your money back before retirement. In this case, you could consider other forms of saving, such as through a personal equity plan, and **Chapter 10** looks at suitable investments.

If you are close to retirement, you may already have savings – or be about to receive a cash lump sum from a pension scheme or plan – which you could invest to provide you with extra income during retirement either straight away or later on. Once again, **Chapter 10** can guide you to appropriate investments.

Carrying on working

Retiring from your normal work doesn't mean you have to give up work altogether. State pensions and pensions from a pension plan or former employer scheme can all be paid to you even if you are still working. See **Chapter 12** for advice on working during retirement.

However, you would be unwise to *rely* on the possibility of working to supplement an otherwise insufficient retirement income. If you run into health problems, you might not be able to carry on working; you might have to give up work to care for your husband or wife or parent, say; and, if the economy is in recession, there may be no demand for your labour.

Income from your home

If you own your own home, it's likely to be one of your most valuable assets, but money tied up in your home can't help you pay the bills. If your home is large for your needs once you retire, you might consider moving somewhere smaller and, thereby, releasing some of your capital which you could then invest to provide an income. But think very carefully before taking this course of action: the change from working to retiring can be very stressful and moving to unfamiliar surroundings may make the adjustment even more difficult. See **Chapter 20** for points to consider before moving home in retirement.

One way to generate income from your home would be to take in a lodger. As long as you find a suitable person, this could also have the advantage of providing you with some help around the house with heavy jobs and some companionship. Under the Inland Revenue 'Rent-a-Room' scheme, you can earn up to £3,250 a year from letting out a room in your home (and providing associated services such as food and laundry) without having to pay any tax on the income. For more information see page 248.

BALANCING YOUR INCOME AND SPENDING

Home income plans
When you reach your seventies, it could be worth considering a home income plan. These come in a number of forms, but they are all made up of two parts: first the property is used to raise cash, and then some or all of the cash is used to provide an income.

In the safest and simplest type of scheme, you take out a fixed-interest mortgage for up to, say, 75 per cent of the value of your home. The proceeds of the mortgage are used to buy you an annuity, which will give you a regular fixed income for life. Interest on the mortgage (after basic-rate relief) and basic-rate tax on the annuity are deducted before you get the income (see page 250 for more on the tax implications). The mortgage doesn't need to be repaid during your lifetime: it is usually repaid out of the sale of the property on death.

You should avoid the following variations:

- With some schemes, the mortgage interest rate varies, so when interest rates are high, a lot of your annuity income will be eaten up by mortgage repayments.
- 'Roll-up' plans allow you to add the mortgage interest to your loan rather than paying it every month. The size of your loan will increase at an alarming rate, and you may be asked to pay off the interest once it rises above a certain level – if you can't pay, you may be forced to sell your home.
- Rather than buying an annuity, the mortgage proceeds may be used to buy investment bonds, which can go down and up in value. If the investment return is too small to pay both the interest and your income, then some of the capital invested in the bond may be used – so the remaining money will have to work even harder to make up this loss and still pay an income.

Another variation is a 'home reversion' scheme. With this, you sell all or part of your house, keeping the right to live there as a tenant for the rest of your life. You can then use the cash from the sale to buy an annuity. Reversion schemes are worth considering, since they provide a higher income than home income plans and don't have to be used to buy an annuity, but with most you don't benefit from any subsequent increase in value of the part of your home you sold.

Another alternative is to set up your own scheme. Several building societies will provide an interest-only mortgage but leave you to invest the cash released (though the warnings above on variable interest rates apply).

Home income plans can provide a useful boost to your income, but if you are considering one, it is essential to get the scheme vetted by your solicitor. Age Concern* also publishes a useful factsheet, which contains names of organisations that offer home income plans and home reversion schemes.

Aspects to look out for are:

- What happens if you want to move house – you may be able to transfer your scheme, providing your new home is acceptable to the lender.
- What happens if you want to sell up altogether, e.g. to move to a nursing home.
- What scope there is for increasing your income to counter inflation. Most home income plans give fixed income, but you may be able to borrow more to boost your income later.
- The effect on any state benefits. Means-tested benefits like income support will be reduced or lost altogether.

Help if your income is very low

If you are on a very low income, you may be eligible for social security payments from the state which aim to meet your basic living expenses, such as food, clothing, footwear, fuel and accommodation. Most of these benefits are not paid out automatically – you must claim them. It's estimated that up to 700,000 pensioners who are eligible to claim income support – the main benefit for people on low incomes – fail to do so.

What counts as a low income?

How low does your income have to be before you qualify for this help? There's no single answer to this. The main benefit you might be eligible for is income support. The government lays down minimum levels of income which people in different circumstances are deemed to need (called the 'applicable

BALANCING YOUR INCOME AND SPENDING

amount') and, if your income comes to less than the amount deemed applicable to you, you may be entitled to enough income support to bring you up to that amount. Note that if your only income is the state basic pension, it's likely that you will be eligible for some income support to top it up.

The applicable amount of income support will be made up of several elements:

- **The personal allowance** For the 1995-6 tax year, this is £46.50 a week for a single person (over the age of 24) and £73 a week for a couple (one or both over 18).
- **Personal allowance for a child** Extra amounts ranging from £15.95 to £36.80 in 1995-6 are payable for each child dependent on you – the amount varies according to the age of the child.
- **Premium payments** On top of the personal allowance(s), you may get a premium payment which reflects the extra income which a person in various circumstances is deemed to need. If you could qualify for more than one premium payment, you usually get just the highest one but, in a few circumstances, you may be eligible for more than one premium payment. Premiums which are particularly relevant to retired people are shown in Table 1.
- **Housing costs** Extra amounts may be payable to meet accommodation costs – for example, mortgage interest payments and some service charges – which will not be met through 'housing benefit' (see page 66).

The allowances and premiums are usually increased each April in line with the change in the Retail Prices Index over the year to the previous September.

The sum of allowances, premium payments and housing costs makes up the applicable amount; and whether you will receive the full amount, a reduced amount or nothing at all will depend on your income and capital.

The income limits

Income, for the purpose of calculating your entitlement to income support, is defined as money coming in from all

Table 1: Some income support premiums, 1995–6

Premium	Description	Amount in 1995–6
Pensioner premium	For pensioners aged 60 to 74	Single £18.60 Couple £28.05
Enhanced pensioner premium	For pensioners aged 75 to 79	Single £20.70 Couple £30.95
Higher pensioner premium	For pensioners aged 80 or more, or pensioners aged 60 or more and disabled	Single £25.15 Couple £35.95
Severe disability premium	For severely disabled people. This can be paid in addition to the higher pensioner premium	Single £35.05 Couple[1] £70.10
Carer premium	For people looking after someone who is disabled. This can be paid in addition to any other premium	£12.60

[1] Paid at the single person rate of £35.05 if only one member of the couple qualifies.

EXAMPLE

Rose is a fit 82-year-old and lives alone. She has virtually no savings and qualifies for a reduced state basic pension of just £15.31 a week. She qualifies for housing benefit (see page 66) to cover the rent for her council bungalow and is eligible for income support. The amount of income support she can get is calculated as follows:

Applicable amount:	
Personal allowance	£46.50
Higher pensioner premium	£25.15
	£71.65
less Rose's income	£15.31
Income support payable	£56.34

sources, for example, your state pension(s), pension from a previous employer, pension from a personal pension plan, any earnings from a job or business you run. Income doesn't include payments in kind, such as meals, or the repayment of expenses incurred while doing your job.

Some types of income are partially or fully ignored. For example, if you take in a lodger or sub-let part of your home, some of the money you receive is ignored. If, at the time you retire, you are still owed some pay by your employer, it will be ignored. If you work part-time, the first £5 of your earnings will usually be disregarded.

Any income you receive from savings or investments is also ignored, but instead you are deemed to receive a certain notional income from your capital (see below). If interest you get is re-invested it is deemed to increase the amount of your capital.

The capital limits

Your capital, for income support purposes, includes cash, bank and building society accounts, shares, unit trusts and any other investments you have. It doesn't usually include the value of your home if you own it, provided you are living there. Your personal possessions, such as furniture, car and so on, usually don't count as capital, and the surrender value of life insurance policies is generally ignored. If you run your own business, your business assets are not counted as part of capital for as long as the business is trading.

If your capital comes to £3,000 or less, it is ignored and will not affect your entitlement to income support – the limit applies to your joint capital, if you're a couple. If your capital amounts to more than £8,000, you will not be eligible for income support at all – once again, this limit applies to your joint capital if you are a couple. If you have more than £3,000 of capital but less than £8,000, you will be deemed to be receiving a set amount of income, as shown in Table 2 – this is called 'tariff income'. Your tariff income will therefore reduce the amount of income support to which you are entitled.

If you deliberately reduce your capital – by giving assets away to your family, say – in order to become entitled to income support or to increase your entitlement, you'll be treated as if you still have the capital. If, however, you have to run down your capital to meet your living expenses, once it falls below £8,000, you'll be able to claim income support.

Table 2: Income you're deemed to receive from your capital

Capital held by you, or by you and your partner	Assumed weekly income
£3,000.01 to £3,250	£ 1
£3,250.01 to £3,500	£ 2
£3,500.01 to £3,750	£ 3
£3,750.01 to £4,000	£ 4
£4,000.01 to £4,250	£ 5
£4,250.01 to £4,500	£ 6
£4,500.01 to £4,750	£ 7
£4,750.01 to £5,000	£ 8
£5,000.01 to £5,250	£ 9
£5,250.01 to £5,500	£10
£5,500.01 to £5,750	£11
£5,750.01 to £6,000	£12
£6,000.01 to £6,250	£13
£6,250.01 to £6,500	£14
£6,500.01 to £6,750	£15
£6,750.01 to £7,000	£16
£7,000.01 to £7,250	£17
£7,250.01 to £7,500	£18
£7,500.01 to £7,750	£19
£7,750.01 to £8,000	£20
over £8,000	You are not eligible for income support

Source: DSS leaflet IS20 *A guide to income support*

If you move to a home

Before 1 April 1993, the cost of accommodation and meals in a residential or nursing home, up to a maximum limit, could be met through income support and the normal rules about applicable amounts did not apply. This continues to be the case for people who were already in this position before April 1993.

For people on low incomes who move into homes from 1 April 1993 onwards, responsibility will rest with the relevant local authority instead of the Department of Social Security (DSS). For more information see **Chapter 34**.

If you go into hospital

If you have to go into hospital as an in-patient, your income support is unchanged for the first six weeks (though if you qualify for the severe disability premium or carer premium, this may stop after four weeks). After that, it's reduced.

If you're a single person, after six weeks, instead of the normal personal allowance and premium(s), you'll get a much lower hospital personal allowance. This is set at either 25 per cent or 20 per cent of the basic state retirement pension rate and is supposed to help you meet continuing household costs, such as water rates, standing charges for fuel and phone, and so on. The higher rate of 25 per cent is paid from your seventh week in hospital to week 52. If you're in hospital for more than a year, the allowance falls to the lower 20 per cent rate or less if the hospital manages your money for you or a doctor certifies that you're unable to use the allowance.

If you're a couple and only one of you goes into hospital, there's generally no change to your income support for the first six weeks. After that and up to week 52, your normal applicable amount less the lower hospital personal allowance applies. After 52 weeks, you and your husband or wife are each assessed separately for income support.

If you are a couple and you both have to go into hospital, there is no change to your income support for the first six weeks. From the seventh week to week 52, you get twice the higher hospital personal allowance, and after 52 weeks you are each assessed separately for income support.

Any housing costs which are normally met through income support continue to be met while you are in hospital for as long as you're responsible for them. But, if you're in hospital for more than a year or it becomes clear that you will be, the housing cost payments will usually stop. If your husband or wife or someone else continues to live in the home, they may be eligible to claim housing costs through their income support instead.

If you had been living in a residential care or nursing home before you were admitted to hospital, income support will meet any retaining fee charged by the home for the first six weeks; it will then meet 80 per cent of the fee for a further 52 weeks.

Other state benefits

If you're on a low income, you may be eligible for housing benefit to help you meet accommodation costs, such as rent. This is paid by your local authority. You may also qualify for Council Tax Benefit (contact your local authority).

If you get income support, you'll automatically qualify for cold weather payments – extra cash to help you meet higher fuel bills – if the average daily temperature in your area is at or below freezing for a week, or forecast to be so. You may also claim help with exceptional expenses, such as funeral costs, from the social fund. The social fund is also able to make interest-free loans to help you spread the cost of paying for an expensive one-off purchase, such as a washing machine. And if you need money urgently to meet your living costs or to buy some essential item, you may be able to get an interest-free crisis loan from the social fund. To find out about social fund payments and loans, contact your local Benefits Agency – in the phone book.

If you qualify for income support, you'll also be eligible for help with the cost of National Health Service (NHS) services. You'll get:

- free prescriptions (these will be free anyway if you've reached state pension age)
- free dental treatment
- free eye tests and money-off vouchers for glasses if you need them
- free NHS wigs and fabric supports (for example, to support your abdomen or spine)
- help with travel costs to and from hospital for NHS treatment.

How to claim income support

You will need to fill in a detailed claim form which you can get by writing to your local Benefits Agency or by filling in the form in DSS leaflet IS1 *Income support – cash help* which is available from Benefits Agency offices and many post offices. If you're not happy with the decision made in your case, you can ask for it to be reviewed or you can appeal (see Table 3 for useful leaflets to guide you through these procedures).

Payment will usually be by orders which you cash at the post office. If you already get a state retirement pension paid by order, you may get an order book which combines both benefits.

Table 3 lists DSS leaflets which may be useful if you're on a low income. You can obtain them from the local Benefits Agency office. Alternatively, many post offices, libraries and advice centres have these leaflets.

Table 3: Useful leaflets if you're on a low income

Number	Name of leaflet
IS1	*Income support – cash help*
IS20	*A guide to income support*
IS50	*Help for people who live in residential care homes or nursing homes*
SB16	*A guide to the social fund*
CWP1	*Extra help with heating costs when it's very cold*
NI260	*A guide to reviews and appeals*
NI246	*How to appeal*
D49	*What to do after a death*
P11	*NHS prescriptions*
D11	*NHS dental treatment*
G11	*NHS vouchers for glasses*
WF11	*NHS wigs and fabric supports*
H11	*NHS hospital travel costs*
CTB1	*Help with the council tax*

Borrowing

Clearly, borrowing to meet a permanent shortfall in income compared with expenses is not a sound policy and you should avoid this. But, if you need to buy a large item, it may make sense to spread the cost over a period of time by using credit or taking out a loan.

Some shops and sales outlets offer 0 per cent finance – often available, for example, when you buy a car or electrical goods. Check for any hidden charges, but in general this type of credit is a good deal, if you would have bought that car or electrical appliance anyway.

Avoid shop or store cards which operate like credit or charge cards – the interest rates on these are often extremely high. Normal credit card charges can also be high if you generally have an outstanding balance, but if you use them for borrowing over a short period they can be cost-effective and very convenient. If you pay off your credit card balance every month, the cost will be small – or even nothing at all if it's a card which doesn't levy an annual fee – and, used in this way, credit cards can be a relatively safe and convenient way of buying costly items.

Avoid going overdrawn on your bank account without notifying your bank first – this can work out very costly as you'll usually have to pay interest on the overdraft, charges for all your account transactions over a given period and extra fees for letters from your bank notifying you that you've gone overdrawn. If you can arrange an overdraft in advance this may be a reasonably priced way of borrowing, but your bank may try to persuade you to take out a personal loan instead – if so, check the cost carefully and compare with other forms of borrowing available.

In general, avoid loans secured on your home – they will generally be cheap compared with unsecured loans but, if you don't keep up the payments, you could lose your home. Also be wary of fixed-term loans for longer than you really need: lenders are entitled to charge early repayment penalties.

If your borrowing gets out of hand, don't be tempted to take out further loans to pay off creditors who are getting angry or threatening legal action. Get help at once – your local Citizens

Advice Bureau (see phone book) can help and some local authorities run debt advice agencies. National Debtline – phone 0121-359 8501 – may also help. Contact the organisations to whom you owe money and offer to pay back the borrowing or outstanding bills at a steady rate which you can manage.

CHAPTER 7

PENSION FROM AN EMPLOYER SCHEME

If you work as an employee, it's quite likely that your employer runs a pension scheme which you can join. If not, consider instead taking out a personal pension plan (see **Chapter 8**).

You don't *have* to join your employer pension scheme, but usually it will be a good way of saving for retirement because, once you join, your employer must pay in money on your behalf – you may also be required to contribute – and employer pension schemes qualify for special tax treatment:

- You and your employer get tax relief on the contributions you pay.
- The invested contributions build up tax-free.
- You can take part of the proceeds at retirement as a tax-free lump sum. (The rest must be taken as pension, which is taxable.)

Employer pension schemes generally provide a range of benefits other than just a retirement pension – for example life insurance and a pension for your widow or widower if you die – see **Chapter 9**. If these other benefits are useful for you, an employer scheme is likely to be more attractive than a personal pension plan, because you would have to pay in extra or take a lower pension at retirement in order to have these benefits included in the plan.

How much pension will you get?

This depends partly on what type of scheme is offered by your employer. There are two main types of scheme: final pay schemes and money purchase schemes.

Final pay schemes

This type of scheme is also called a 'final salary scheme' and is the most widely used type of 'defined benefit scheme'. They are not the most common type of employer scheme but more people are covered by them than by any other type, because large companies tend to offer final pay schemes.

With a final pay scheme your retirement pension is worked out according to a formula based on your pay at or near retirement and the number of years for which you've been a member of the pension scheme. For example, you might get a pension of one-sixtieth of 'final pay' for each year. One-eightieth of final pay per year is also commonly used.

'Final pay' will be defined in the rules of the scheme. 'Pay' may mean just your basic pay or it might also include bonuses, overtime, the value of some fringe benefits and so on. 'Final' may mean your pay on some specified date, your average pay over the last three years or the average of the best three years' pay out of the last ten before retirement, or some other definition.

EXAMPLE
Alan retired from a dairy company, part of a larger commercial group, after thirty-four years in the pension scheme. The scheme paid a pension at retirement of one-sixtieth of final pay for each year. Final pay meant the average of the best three years' pay out of the last ten, which worked out at £16,000 for Alan. His pension was calculated as follows:

$1/60 \times £16,000 \times 34 = £9,067$ a year.

The great advantage of final pay schemes is that you have a good idea in advance of roughly how much pension you'll get at retirement in terms of today's money. Moreover, you know that if your earnings rise then your expected pension will rise too, so your expected pension keeps broadly in line with inflation up to the time when you retire.

Money purchase schemes

These are also called 'defined contribution schemes'. Since many smaller companies, sometimes with only a few employees, as well as some large employers, run this type of scheme, money purchase schemes are very common.

With a money purchase scheme, your employer – and you too, if it's a contributory scheme – pay in contributions which are usually a set percentage of your pay. The contributions are invested to build up a fund, which is used at retirement to buy a pension. How much pension you get depends on 'annuity rates' at the time you retire. The 'annuity rate' is the rate at which insurance companies (or friendly societies) are willing to convert the lump sum which makes up your fund into a regular income for life.

So, the amount of pension you get from a money purchase scheme depends on four things:

- how much is invested
- how long the money is left invested
- how well the invested money grows
- annuity rates at the time you retire.

EXAMPLE

Sheila recently started work for a small engineering company with 25 employees. The company runs a money purchase pension scheme. To build up a retirement pension for Sheila, the firm pays into the scheme contributions equal to 10 per cent of Sheila's salary, and Sheila is required to contribute a further 5 per cent of her pay. This year, Sheila will earn £14,000, so a total of [10% × £14,000] + [5% x £14,000] = £2,100 will be paid into the scheme on her account.

The contributions which are paid in year by year are left to grow. If the £2,100 paid in this year grew by, say 1 per cent a year more than inflation until Sheila's retirement in 15 years' time, it would have grown to £2,438 in terms of today's money. If the annuity rate then were, say, 12 per cent, the £2,438 could be used to buy a pension of £292 a year.

Assuming the growth and annuity rates didn't change, each subsequent year's contributions would buy less than £292 pension because they would not have been invested for as long.

The drawbacks of a money purchase scheme are, first, that you can't accurately estimate how much pension you'll get at retirement either in terms of today's money or in terms of future money values. Also, although your contributions will generally increase in line with your pay, there are too many other unpredictable elements, so there is no link between the pension you're building up and inflation up to the time you retire.

Other types of employer scheme

Some employer pension schemes combine both final pay and money purchase elements – for example, you might get a retirement pension which was the best of a pension worked out according to a final pay formula and the pension which could be bought with the fund built up by investing contributions. These combination schemes are often referred to as 'hybrid schemes'.

Final pay schemes are not the only sort of defined benefit scheme. Other less common variations include:

- **Average pay schemes** These are similar to final pay schemes except that the pension formula is based on the average of your pay throughout the whole time you belonged to the scheme, not just pay at or near retirement.
- **Revalued average earnings schemes** With these, your pension is based on pay during the whole time you belonged to the scheme, but each year's earnings are increased in line with inflation up until retirement. Such

schemes can offer very good pensions, especially if your earnings peaked in mid-career rather than near retirement.
- **Salary grade schemes** You earn a set amount of pension for each year that your pay falls within a given band on the salary grid. The higher your earnings band, the more pension you 'earn'.
- **Flat rate schemes** With these, you get a fixed amount of pension for each year that you're in the scheme.

EXAMPLE

Janet earns £13,000 a year working for a publishing firm which runs a hybrid pension scheme (under which the final pay element is based on one-hundredths of final pay). She pays 3.5 per cent of her earnings into the scheme and the firm pays a further 11.5 per cent. She has been in the scheme for only three and a half years, but if she were to reach the age of 65 now and retire, she would receive the higher of a final pay pension worked out as follows:

$1/100 \times £13,000 \times 3½$ years = £455 a year

or of the money purchase pension which could be bought with the fund of £4,000 which has built up. This would be £420 a year. As the final pay formula produces the higher figure, she would retire with the pension of £455 a year.

Pension increases

If the scheme you belong to is contracted out (see page 78 onwards), at least part of your pension must be increased each year once it starts to be paid. Beyond that, schemes have not, in the past, been obliged to make pension increases, although most do. Increases may be guaranteed – e.g. inflation up to a maximum 3 per cent a year. Alternatively, they may be discretionary – this means that the scheme reviews the position each year (or less frequently) and decides what increase to make. Although discretionary increases are not guaranteed, they may be generous and worth more to you than a smaller guaranteed amount.

At the time of writing, a pensions bill was being considered by Parliament. If the proposals in it become law, schemes will have to increase pensions built up from some future date by inflation up to a maximum of 5 per cent a year. This will apply to your whole pension from an employer's scheme, not just any contracted-out pension.

Tax-free lump sum at retirement

One of the great advantages of employer pension schemes (and personal pension plans – see **Chapter 8**) over other types of retirement saving is that you can take part of the retirement proceeds in the form of a tax-free lump sum. With some schemes – particularly those covering people who work in the public sector, such as local authority employees and health service staff – you'll receive the tax-free cash automatically. With other schemes, you can choose either to take just a pension from the scheme or to swap part of the pension for a tax-free cash sum.

The rate at which pension is converted into lump sum by the employer scheme will depend on the rules of the scheme. At present, a man will give up £1 a year of pension for every £9 of lump sum and, a woman, £1 a year of pension for every £11 of lump sum. Women get a better deal, reflecting the fact that they tend to live longer, so each £1 a year of their pension is more expensive.

Lump sum or not?

If you have the choice about taking the lump sum, what should you do? The conversion of pension to lump sum is usually based on the life expectancy of an average man or woman. So, if your health is poorer than average, you'll probably be better off taking the largest lump sum that you can.

Even if your health is average or good the answer will often still be: take the cash. Obviously this will reduce the remaining pension to be paid from the scheme, but you need not end up with less retirement income overall. The pension is taxed; the cash lump sum is tax-free. Moreover, you can use the lump sum to buy an annuity (an income for life), the regular payments from which will count partly as taxable income but partly as return of your original investment. The capital element of a purchased annuity is tax-free, so the after-tax income from the annuity can easily come to more than the after-tax pension you gave up.

The conversion of pension into lump sum will take account of any other promised benefits being given up, such as guaranteed annual increases on the amount of pension swapped. However, if your pension scheme regularly increases pensions which are currently being paid but doesn't guarantee to do so, you should think carefully before deciding to swap pension for tax-free cash. The conversion rate will not usually take into account benefits which are not guaranteed so you would be giving up the probability of pension increases without receiving any compensation for this.

Note that, in most schemes, while taking a lump sum reduces your own pension, it will not reduce the amount of any widow's, widower's or dependants' pension payable if you died.

Limits on your pension and lump sum

Because pension schemes benefit from special tax advantages, the Inland Revenue places limits on the benefits which you can have from a pension scheme. Due to a series of changes to the laws concerning pensions, there are three different tax regimes which could apply to an employer pension that you've built up. The three regimes are shown in Table 1. In addition to the limits shown, under any of the three regimes, once pensions start to be paid, they can be increased each year as long as they don't exceed the maximum possible pension increased in line with changes in the Retail Prices Index.

The Inland Revenue limits are set in relation to final pay but this does not mean that they apply only to final pay schemes. In fact, the limits apply to most employer pension schemes – even money purchase schemes. They set an upper limit on the

Table 1: Inland Revenue limits on your pension and lump sum

Tax regime [1]	Limit on pension [2] at retirement [3]	Limit on tax-free lump sum at retirement [3]
Post-1989 regime Applies to: (a) a scheme set up on or after 14 March 1989; or (b) a scheme set up before 14 March 1989 but you joined on or after 1 June 1989; or (c) a scheme set up before 14 March 1989 which you joined on or after 17 March 1987 but before 1 June 1989, if you elect to be treated under the post-1989 regime	Two-thirds of final pay up to a maximum of £52,400 [4]	One-and-a-half times final pay up to a maximum of £117,900 [4]
1987-9 regime Applies to a scheme set up before 14 March 1989 which you joined on or after 17 March 1987 and before 1 June 1989 (unless you have opted to be treated under the post-1989 regime – see above)	Two-thirds of final pay	One-and-a-half times final pay up to a maximum of £150,000
Pre-1987 regime Applies to a scheme you joined before 17 March 1987	Two-thirds of final pay	One-and-a-half times final pay

[1] As well as the three categories of scheme listed here, it is possible for you to have joined a scheme after 1987 or 1989 but for the pre-1987 or 1987-9 regime rules to apply. This might be the case where, say, your employer's business had been restructured or party to a merger.

[2] This is the limit which applies if all your own benefits from the scheme are taken as pension. If part is taken as a lump sum (or certain other benefits), the maximum you can take as pension is reduced to less than the amount shown here.

[3] Under the 1987-9 regime and pre-1987 regime, these maximum limits apply at the normal retirement age for the scheme. Under the post-1989 regime, the limits apply at any age within the range 60 to 75.

[4] This is the limit proposed for the 1995-6 tax year. The limit is based on an 'earnings cap' – a ceiling on the amount of final pay which can be used in the calculation. The earnings cap is usually increased each year in line with the Retail Prices Index.

pension and lump sum which a scheme may provide but, in practice, most schemes provide less than the maximum benefits permitted.

Contracted-out pensions

Chapter 4 described the State Earnings Related Pension Scheme (SERPS). You may be 'contracted out' of SERPS through your employer pension scheme. This means that both you and your employer pay lower National Insurance contributions; you give up your right to build up SERPS pension for as long as you are contracted out and instead build up a pension in the employer scheme. Precisely what this means for your pension income overall depends on the way in which you are contracted out. (If you have belonged to more than one scheme and/or had a personal pension plan, you may have been contracted out on different bases at different times.)

Final pay schemes

If you are contracted out on a final pay basis (as will usually be the case if your employer runs a final pay scheme which is contracted out), your employer scheme is currently committed to pay you a defined pension at retirement called the 'Guaranteed Minimum Pension' (GMP). This is your employer's commitment in return for paying lower National Insurance contributions; your employer may or may not require you to make contributions towards the scheme to help meet the cost of providing the GMP.

Under the current system you cannot lose, if you're contracted out on a final pay basis. You can see why this is the case if you look at what happens when you reach retirement. The Department of Social Security (DSS) calculates the total SERPS pension which you would have received if you had not been contracted out; then it subtracts the GMP due from the contracted-out final pay scheme. The DSS then pays you whatever amount remains. So your SERPS plus GMP will always together equal the full SERPS pension you would have had if you had never been contracted out. After retirement, your employer scheme will increase your GMP by up to 3 per cent a year; the remaining amount required to increase your SERPS pension plus GMP in line with inflation is paid by the DSS.

However, at the time of writing, a pensions bill was being considered by Parliament and, if its proposals become law, contracted-out pensions from final pay schemes will be worked out under a new system. Your employer will be committed to providing a retirement pension which passes a test laying down how much pension builds up in relation to your earnings and length of time in the scheme. After retirement, the pension will have to be increased by inflation up to a maximum of 5 per cent a year. But there will no longer be any link with SERPS – for example, you would lose out if inflation was substantially more than 5 per cent a year for a prolonged period. Overall, you could be either better or worse off contracting-out under the new system.

The new system will not be backdated, so you may receive more than one type of contracted-out pension from the same scheme at retirement.

Money purchase schemes

If your employer scheme is contracted out on a money purchase basis, it is not committed to paying you a set amount of pension at retirement. Instead, it is committed to investing a given amount on your behalf. The amount is the savings which you and your employer make by paying lower National Insurance contributions – called the National Savings rebate – plus tax relief on your part of the savings. It is your employer that agrees to invest this sum – he may or may not require you to contribute towards the scheme.

With this form of contracting out, you may be better or worse off than if you had not contracted out. This is because the amount of pension which the invested National Insurance rebate eventually provides depends – like any money purchase pension – on how well the investment grows and on annuity rates at the time the pension starts to be paid.

After retirement, the scheme increases the pension which results from the invested rebates by up to 3 per cent a year.

Under the present system, the DSS will, through your SERPS pension, at least partially top this up if inflation runs at more than 3 per cent a year. If proposals being discussed by Parliament at the time of writing become law, this link with SERPS will be broken for contracted-out pensions built up after a given date. Under the new system, the scheme will increase your contracted-out pension by inflation up to a maximum of 5 per cent a year, but there will be no DSS top-up if inflation is greater than this.

As with final pay schemes, since the new system will not be backdated, you could receive contracted-out pension under both the old and new system from the same money purchase scheme.

Personal pension schemes

If your employer scheme is not contracted out, you can be a member of it and still contract out independently. You can do this by taking out a personal pension plan which is designed solely for contracting out. For details, see **Chapter 8**.

Should you contract out?

If your employer scheme is contracted out on a final pay basis, you'll be automatically contracted out. Under the current system it doesn't matter that this is the case since you can't lose by being contracted out on a final pay basis. Under the new system, the position will not be so clear-cut.

If your employer scheme is contracted out on a money purchase basis, you can't tell in advance whether this will be to your benefit or to your disadvantage. However, at present the National Insurance rebates for contracting out are the same for everyone, regardless of age and sex. This means that contracting out is likely to be a better deal for younger people (whose rebates can be invested for longer) and for men (who on average give up less SERPS pension given that they retire later and tend to live less long). If you are between 35 and 40 or so, contracting out may be a good idea. Much above those ages and, other things being equal, you would probably be better off belonging to SERPS.

PENSION FROM AN EMPLOYER SCHEME

You can contract out of SERPS and then, under current rules, contract back in when you reach the age at which SERPS is preferable. However, if your employer scheme is contracted out, you can't usually contract back into SERPS without leaving the employer scheme completely. If the scheme would provide a pension and other benefits, you should not leave it simply for the sake of contracting back into SERPS. It is vital that you look at the whole package of benefits that the scheme offers.

For guidance on whether to contract out using a personal pension plan, see page 95.

What you pay

Some pension schemes are 'non-contributory' in which case you pay nothing at all – your employer foots the whole bill for the scheme. However, most schemes are 'contributory' and you'll usually pay in a set proportion of your before-tax earnings – four or five per cent, say. Any contributions you pay qualify for tax relief at your highest rate.

EXAMPLE

Janet pays 3.5 per cent of her pay into her firm's pension scheme. In the 1995-6 tax year, she earns £13,000, which means that she pays 3.5% × £13,000 = £455 into the scheme. However, the cost to her is less than £455 because the contributions are deducted from her pay before income tax is worked out. This means that she gets tax relief on the full amount at her highest tax rate of 25 per cent. This gives her tax relief of 25% × £455 = £113.75, making the true cost of the contributions to Janet just 75% × £455 = £341.25.

The Inland Revenue limits the amount which you can pay into an employer pension scheme in any one year to 15 per cent of your pensionable earnings. In addition, if you are covered by the post-1989 regime, there is also a cash limit which is related to earnings: for 1995-6, only pensionable earnings up to £78,600 can be taken into account. This gives an overall maximum level on contributions of 15% × £78,600 = £11,790. The limit is usually increased each year in line with changes in the Retail Prices Index.

When is an employer scheme pension paid?

The rules of your pension scheme will set a 'normal retirement age'. In the past, this was often the same as the state pension age – currently 60 for women and 65 for men. But, since the early 1990s, many schemes have moved to an equal pension age – most commonly 65 – which applies to both men and women.

Inland Revenue rules prevent the maximum pension and other benefits being paid at very early ages. For schemes covered by the pre-1987 regime or 1987-9 regime, the earliest age at which the maximum pension can be paid is usually 60 for men and 55 for women. For post-1989 regime schemes, the lowest age for the maximum pension is 50 for both men and women. The Inland Revenue allows earlier ages than these for people working in certain types of job – for example, divers or professional footballers.

Special rules also apply if you have to retire early because of ill health, which allow a scheme to pay out higher than normal pensions. These may be based on the number of years you would have worked if you could have carried on until normal retirement age.

Except in the case of ill health, you should expect a lower pension if you decide to retire early. In a final pay scheme this will reflect the fact that you have fewer years' membership of the scheme and, possibly, that your final pay may be lower than if you had stayed right up until retirement. In a money purchase pension scheme, the lower pension reflects the fact that you'll have paid in contributions for fewer years, the invested contributions will not have had as long to grow and your fund will have to buy a pension expected to last for longer.

If you carry on working after the normal retirement age for your scheme, what happens to your pension will depend on the rules of your scheme. You may be able to carry on making

PENSION FROM AN EMPLOYER SCHEME

contributions and building up further pension. Often, however, you'll simply get what are called 'actuarial increases'. This means that your pension is calculated at your normal retirement age and is then increased each year reflecting the expectation that, when it does start to be paid, the pension will be paid out over a shorter-than-normal period.

If you leave a scheme early

Once you have belonged to an employer pension scheme for two years, it is required to provide you with a pension which will be paid at retirement – this is called a 'preserved pension' or, sometimes, a 'deferred pension'. You can either leave these pension rights with the scheme or transfer them to another employer scheme, to a personal pension plan or to a special plan designed for this purpose, called a 'section 32 plan' or 'buy-out bond'.

If the only rights you've built up are those to a contracted-out pension, the scheme might 'buy you back' into the state (SERPS) scheme, in which case you'll have no more claim on the employer scheme but will get SERPS pension from the state instead.

If you have belonged to a pension scheme for less than two years, the scheme does not have to promise you a pension and, instead, you can be offered the return of the contributions you've paid to date together with reasonable interest less tax deducted at a special rate. You can't receive any contributions paid on your behalf by your employer.

Boosting your pension

If you are concerned that your retirement income may not be high enough to meet your needs, you may be able to increase it by building up extra pension in your employer scheme. Provided your total contributions towards the scheme remain within the 15 per cent limit set by the Inland Revenue (and the cash limit if the post-1989 regime applies to you), you can pay in extra amounts called 'additional voluntary contributions' (AVCs). These qualify for tax relief in just the same way as other pension contributions.

AVCs are used to buy extra pension, pension increases, or widow's pension, say, either direct from the employer scheme or to top up the benefits from the employer scheme. However, AVCs which you started to make on or after 17 March 1987 can't be used to provide or increase a tax-free lump sum.

The extra contributions can either be paid into an AVC scheme run by your employer or paid into your own 'free-standing AVC' (FSAVC) scheme. All employer schemes must offer some kind of AVC facility. How it works will vary from scheme to scheme. For example, in a final pay scheme, your AVCs might buy extra years of membership, thus boosting the pension and other benefits, which are calculated according to a formula using the number of years you've been in the scheme. But often the AVC scheme works on a straightforward money purchase basis – the AVCs are invested to provide a fund which, at retirement, is converted into pension and/or other benefits at the going rates which then apply.

FSAVC schemes always work on a money purchase basis. They are similar to personal pension plans (see **Chapter 8**) except that the fund which builds up must be used to buy benefits which, when added to your benefits from your employer scheme, do not come to more than the maximum amounts allowed under the Inland Revenue rules.

The main advantage of an FSAVC scheme over an AVC scheme run by your employer is that, with an FSAVC scheme, you have the freedom to choose how your contributions are invested. Traditionally, employer AVC schemes have tended to take a cautious approach to investment in order to keep down the risks but, with an FSAVC scheme, you can choose a much higher degree of risk and potential reward, if you want to.

EXAMPLE

Mrs Black took out an FSAVC scheme four years ago and has recently taken early retirement from her job as a college lecturer. She has built up a fund within her FSAVC scheme of around £6,500. In January 1992, the insurance company with which she invested had estimated that her FSAVC scheme could be used to provide extra pension of around £641 a year. However, by the

PENSION FROM AN EMPLOYER SCHEME

time she retired in June 1993, a pension of only £366 a year was offered. The insurance company explained that annuity rates had fallen. The reduced income also reflects the fact that the pension has to be paid starting earlier and thus is expected to be paid out for longer overall. (The annuity rate takes no account of Mrs Black's ill-health.) Although Mrs Black accepts that the small print for the AVC did warn that the pension would be subject to current annuity tables she felt that the warnings were not clear enough. She explains: 'I am now locked into a pension which is much lower than my expectations and makes a nonsense of retirement planning.'

An FSAVC scheme can also be used for contracting out of SERPS (see page 78) but quirks in the rules mean that you'll usually do better to contract out via a personal pension plan rather than an FSAVC scheme.

Since the Inland Revenue maximum limits on the benefits you can have from a pension scheme are set in terms of your final pay, while FSAVC and some AVC schemes work on a money purchase basis, it is not easy in advance to know whether or not using the proceeds of your AVC or FSAVC scheme will take you over the limits. In the past, going over the limits could mean that your AVCs were wasted but, for AVCs started since 27 July 1989, any 'excess' contributions can be repaid to you at retirement after deduction of tax at a special rate. However, for the vast majority of people, there is plenty of scope to add to the benefits from the employer scheme without going over the Inland Revenue limits.

How safe is your pension?

The Robert Maxwell affair, in which nearly £450 million was stolen from the pension funds of companies (such as Mirror Group Newspapers) in the Maxwell empire, shook the complacent view which most people had held about the safety of company pension schemes. Yet, although this affair captured the newspaper headlines, employer pension schemes in general have not been prone to the scandals which have been so prevalent in other areas of the financial services industry. It's impossible to guarantee absolute safety from fraud, but employer pension schemes generally have a very good record. The risk to you of retiring with an inadequate income if you don't make pension savings far outweighs the risk that you'll lose your money if you put it into an employer pension scheme.

Although there is no shortage of pension rules and regulations, they are piecemeal and complex, with several different bodies being responsible for different aspects of scheme regulation. Following a comprehensive review of pensions law, the Government has proposed a number of changes to improve the security of pension schemes. The main proposals are:

- setting up a pensions regulator who will be able to investigate schemes and to whom anyone can report their suspicions if they are worried about the running of a scheme they are involved with. But the regulator will not replace the array of other regulatory bodies – he/she will have to work with them, so his/her (and their) effectiveness will depend crucially on how well they liaise and co-ordinate their activities
- giving trustees much more responsibility for ensuring that their schemes are properly run. Unfortunately, training for trustees is not to be compulsory, so there's no guarantee that trustees will be equipped for the task
- making it obligatory for scheme professionals – actuaries, lawyers and so on – to 'blow the whistle' if they spot problems in a scheme
- setting a basic rule that one-third of trustees in each scheme should be nominated by the scheme members. However, employers can opt out of this rule provided members do not object
- requiring every scheme always to have enough assets to pay all the benefits due if the scheme were wound up today
- setting up a compensation scheme to replace most of members' pension rights if pension fund assets are lost because of theft or fraud.

At the time of writing, the measures were being debated by Parliament and had yet to be passed as law.

Pension rights and divorce

Even in these days of liberation, many women still rely largely on their husbands to save for retirement. This reflects the traditional role of men and women, where in the past it was often expected that on marriage women would give up any career and concentrate on family responsibilities. Women might return to work later but often this would be to lower paid, possibly part-time jobs, which offered little or no prospect of adequate pension saving. Meanwhile, men have been traditionally cast as the breadwinners and are more likely to have spent their working lives in steady employment, often building up pension rights through membership of an employer pension scheme.

This traditional arrangement can work very well for a couple who have a stable relationship, but a third of all marriages in the UK now end in divorce. Apart from the family home, pension rights are likely to be the most valuable asset a couple own. Although the rights may have been built up by the man, it will frequently be the case that they should be viewed as a joint asset. For over 20 years, pension and legal professionals have been trying to sort out how pension rights should be treated on divorce in order to be fair to both the husband and wife. There are two broad approaches:

- The first is concerned with avoiding hardship. The wife is identified as the potential loser when a marriage breaks up if she must care for children or other dependants, or if she doesn't have enough working life left in which to build up an adequate pension of her own.
- The second approach is concerned simply with splitting the assets fairly between the couple.

Whichever approach is taken, however, there is no straightforward solution. Pension rights – particularly from a final pay scheme – are not easy to divide. In some cases, a cash payment to compensate for lost rights might be appropriate but since pension rights themselves cannot be realised until retirement sufficient cash needs to be available from other sources.

At present, there are no hard and fast rules and the solution adopted in any one case is left to the discretion of the judge. Where the wife is aged 40 or more, a court will usually take into account pension rights along with other factors. But younger women lose out and many separation or divorce cases are settled without the intervention of a court, so whether or not pension rights are taken into account will depend on the couple and their advisers.

In May 1993, a working party made up of pensions and legal experts published an influential report calling for changes in the law so that the courts could order scheme trustees to allocate some pension rights to the wife (or husband) in the event of a divorce. At first, the Government seemed reluctant to take the experts' advice. But, at the time of writing, a pensions bill was being debated by Parliament and it looked as if the Government would at least make it compulsory for courts to take pension rights into account, regardless of the age of the wife, and might even support a change to the law to enable pension rights to be divided with part being transferred to a former wife (or husband).

If you are involved in a separation or divorce, you should get advice about any pension rights. A solicitor may not be able to help since valuing pension rights is a specialist job, so consider getting the help of an actuary. You can obtain a list of members who could help from the Association of Consulting Actuaries★ or the Society of Pension Consultants★.

When you reach retirement

No later than three months before you reach the normal retirement age for your job, or before the date on which you decide to retire, you should get in touch with the administrators of your pension scheme to find out how much pension you can expect and what options you have. See page 20 for how to do this.

★*The addresses and phone numbers of organisations marked with an asterisk can be found in the address section at the back of the guide.*

CHAPTER 8

PERSONAL PENSION PLANS

If you are self-employed or an employee whose employer does not offer a pension scheme, you'll need to make your own arrangements about saving for retirement and the best way of doing this is to take out a personal pension plan.

Even if your employer does run a pension scheme, personal pension plans are open to you if you've chosen not to join your employer scheme. Personal plans can also be used to contract out of SERPS (see pages 39, 78 and 94) if you belong to an employer scheme which is not itself contracted-out.

You can invest in a personal pension plan provided you are 16 or more and under the age of 75. Like employer pension schemes, personal pension plans benefit from tax advantages, which make them a better route for retirement saving than most other forms of investment. These tax advantages are:

- what you pay in qualifies for tax relief
- your invested money builds up tax-free
- you can take part of the proceeds as a tax-free lump sum (the rest is taken as pension, which is taxable).

Unlike employer schemes, personal plans don't automatically give you a package of benefits. If you want life insurance or a widow's or widower's pension to be payable in the event of your death, you'll have to pay extra for these. And, when you want to start taking your pension, you'll have to decide whether you want regular pension increases and, if so, your starting pension will be a lot lower than if you'd opted for a flat pension.

A further disadvantage of personal pension plans is that a

sizeable part of your personal pension fund – around one-fifth on average – may go in charges. With an employer scheme, charges tend to be lower and are often paid directly by the employer rather than from the pension fund.

How much pension will you get?

All personal pension plans work on a money purchase basis. This means that you cannot have any clear idea, in advance, of how much pension you'll get when you do retire. It depends on four factors:

- how much you pay into your plan
- how long you invest for
- how well the fund of invested money grows
- how much pension you can buy with your fund (in other words, future 'annuity rates').

The younger you are when you pay into your plan, the longer your contributions will be invested and thus the larger your fund is likely to be. Similarly, if you intend to retire early, your contributions will not have so long to be invested, so you'll either have to settle for a lower pension or be prepared to invest more in your plan. You can choose how your fund is invested (see page 103), which will be an important factor influencing how your fund grows.

Converting your pension fund into an annuity dictates your pension income for your whole retirement. Traditionally, you have had to buy an annuity at the time you want your pension to start. This means that if annuity rates are low, you either have to put up with a low lifetime pension or put off your retirement in the hope that annuity rates will rise.

However, in the November 1994 Budget, new rules were proposed. With personal pension plans approved or altered after the proposals become law (expected to be early May 1995), you will be able to put off drawing your pension as late as age 75, if you want to, but draw an income direct from your pension fund in the meantime. The amount of income you can withdraw will be based on what an annuity would have provided at the then going rate and there will be periodic checks to make sure that your pension fund is not being used up too fast. The advantages of doing this are, first, that you can avoid the low annuity trap and yet still retire when you want to and, secondly, your fund is left invested and can carry on growing. But there are drawbacks too. If you invest your fund primarily for growth, you also risk it falling in value – a risk most people cannot afford to take near retirement. If you invest more cautiously – e.g. in deposits and government stocks – your fund may grow too slowly to support the income withdrawals you'd like. So these flexible annuity plans may not be suitable for everyone.

Choices on retirement

You don't have to accept the annuity rate offered by the company with whom you have built up your pension plan. You usually have an 'open market option', which gives you the right to shop around for the best available annuity rates. It makes sense to use this option, since some companies specialise in annuities and offer very competitive rates whereas other companies don't.

How much pension you get will also depend on what choices you make at retirement:

- The earlier you retire, the lower will be your pension because it will have to be paid out for longer. (Women also get less pension than men of the same age for the same reason – i.e. that they are expected to live longer on average.)
- Your starting pension will be higher if it is paid at a flat rate which doesn't change over the years. But, if you choose a flat-rate pension, you must realise that inflation during your retirement will reduce the buying power of the pension (see **Chapter 4**), so that what seemed a generous amount at the start of retirement may be a scant income twenty years later.
- If you are married, you may want to have a pension which will continue to be paid to your wife or husband if you die first – choosing this option will also reduce your starting pension.

- Another common option is to have a guarantee that your pension will be paid for at least five years even if you die within that time – this ensures that there is a pension (or cash equivalent) available for a time for your husband or wife or heirs.

Table 1 shows, for a fund of £10,000, how much pension you could have got in December 1994 (when annuity rates were rather low) if you'd taken up various options. Although not

Table 1: How much pension?

Type of pension	Men £ a year	Women £ a year
Flat-rate pension taken out:		
At age 55	1,016	949
At age 60	1,116	1,020
At age 65	1,260	1,135
At age 70	1,468	1,293
Pension increasing by 5% a year taken out:		
At age 60	727	608
At age 70	1,050	851
Flat-rate pension guaranteed for 5 years taken out:		
At age 55	1,007	944
At age 60	1,098	1,010
At age 65	1,222	1,104
At age 70	1,388	1,235
Flat-rate joint life [2]		
Man aged 60, woman aged 55		910
Man aged 65, woman aged 60		952
Both aged 65		999
Both aged 70		1,134

Amount of pension each £10,000 could buy [1]

[1] At compulsory purchase annuity rates on 5 December 1994.

[2] In other words, pension continues to be paid until both husband and wife have died.

Source: *Pensions Management*, January 1995

shown in this Table, you can also combine options, choosing, for example, a pension paid for the life of both you and your spouse and increasing by 5 per cent a year.

There are no Inland Revenue limits on the amount of pension you can take out of a personal pension plan, only on what you can put in.

Tax-free lump sum at retirement

You can take part of the proceeds from your plan as a tax-free lump sum instead of as pension. This is worth doing because, even if your greatest need is for income, you can use the lump sum to buy an annuity. Annuities you choose to buy are taxed differently from the 'compulsory purchase' annuity that your pension fund buys to provide you with a pension. The pension you give up would have been taxable, but the income from an annuity you choose to buy is only partly taxable. The income from an annuity you buy is deemed to be made up of two elements: pure income, which is taxable, and return of part of your capital with each payment – this element is tax-free. So the after-tax income from an annuity you buy with your tax-free lump sum should be greater than the after-tax pension which you give up.

Inland Revenue rules limit the amount of tax-free cash you can take from your plan. The limits have changed from time to time but, broadly, if you first took out your plan before 1 July 1988 (called here an 'old-style plan'), the maximum lump sum is three times the remaining pension. If you took out your plan on or after 1 July 1988 (called here a 'new-style plan'), the maximum tax-free cash is one-quarter of your pension fund. If you have an old-style plan, you can switch to a new-style plan at any time, in which case the new-style plan limit will apply. If you exercise your 'open market option' (see above) when you come to take your pension, an old-style plan will automatically be converted to a new-style one because old-style plans can no longer be started.

Contracted-out pensions

Provided you are eligible for SERPS (see page 39), you can use a personal pension plan to contract out. You can do this even if you already belong to an employer pension scheme, as long as you're not already contracted out through the employer scheme.

If you are contracted out using a personal pension plan, you give up your right to build up SERPS pension during the period you are contracted out. However, you do not pay lower National Insurance contributions (as you would if you contracted out through an employer scheme – see page 78). Instead, you and your employer both pay contributions at the full rate but part of them, called the 'National Insurance rebate', is paid back in the form of contributions to your pension plan. Tax relief at the basic rate on your part of the National Insurance rebate is also paid into the plan. In addition, you'll also qualify for a bonus from the state if you are 30 or more. Table 2 shows

Table 2: What's paid into your contracted-out personal plan

Description of payment	Percentage of 'middle band earnings' [1]	Maximum that could be paid into your plan in 1995–6 [2] £ a year
National Insurance rebate		
Of your contributions	1.8%	357
Of contributions your employer pays on your behalf	3.0%	596
Basic rate tax relief	0.6%	119
Bonus	1.0%	199
TOTAL	6.4%	1,271

[1] 'Middle band earnings' (also called 'upper band earnings') are earnings above a lower earnings limit up to an upper earnings limit. In 1995–6, the lower earnings limit is £3,016 a year and the upper earnings limit is £22,880.

[2] Assuming you earn £22,880 a year (the upper earnings limit) or more.

the amounts paid into your plan in the 1995-6 tax year. Different rebates and bonus applied in earlier years and they are due to be revised again from April 1996.

The rebate, tax relief and bonus paid into your plan are left to grow and the resulting fund is used at retirement (on or after the state pension age) to provide you with a pension. How much pension you get depends on how well the investment grows and annuity rates at the time you retire (note that the same annuity rate applies to both men and women). In other words, you are contracted out on a money purchase basis (see pages 79 and 80), so you could end up with more or less pension from your personal plan than the SERPS pension which you gave up.

Should you contract out?

At present, the same National Insurance rebate is paid regardless of your age or sex. This means that the rebate is more valuable to you if you are young, since it can be invested for longer. It also means that the rebate is a worse deal for a woman than for a man of the same age because the woman gives up relatively more SERPS: this reflects the fact that on average a woman can expect to live longer than a man and that, for women born before 6 March 1955, the state pension age is earlier than for a man. Obviously, if you qualify for the extra one per cent bonus, contracting out will look better than it would if you couldn't get the bonus.

Your view about future investment performance will also influence whether or not contracting out looks to be a good deal. If you expect investment returns to be good, contracting out will tend to look more attractive than staying in SERPS. But, if you are less optimistic about the return you'll get on the invested rebates, staying in – or contracting back into – SERPS will tend to look the better option.

Combining these factors and taking a fairly modest view of investment performance, contracting out through a personal pension plan looks preferable to staying in SERPS for women up to the age of about 30 to 35 and perhaps even 40 for women who'll have a state pension age of 65. For men, contracting out may be worthwhile up to age 35 to 40, say. After that, you'd be better off contracting back into SERPS. These can only be very rough guides and, when the National Insurance rebates are next reviewed, these pivotal ages will change. It is expected that, from the 1996-7 tax year, age-related rebates will be introduced in order to encourage people to stay contracted out as they get older.

What you pay

You can take out a plan to which you make regular payments – for example, £20 a month or £200 a year might be the minimum regular contribution – or a plan which requires just a single lump sum – £500 or £1,000 might be the minimum in this case. Some plans are very flexible allowing you to make additional payments as and when you choose.

There are few Inland Revenue limits on the benefits which you can take from a personal pension plan. But, as you might expect, given the tax advantages of personal plans, the Inland Revenue does put bounds on the amount you can pay into a plan. The limits vary according to your age and whether you have an old- or new-style plan. They are set as a percentage of your 'net relevant earnings'. If you're self-employed, this means your profits for tax purposes; if you're an employee, this means your total before-tax pay including the value of most taxable fringe benefits (such as a company car). Table 3 shows the contribution limits which apply to new-style personal pension plans. With new-style plans, only net relevant earnings up to £78,600 a year can be taken into account in 1995-6, which puts an overall cash limit on the amount of contributions you can make. This 'earnings cap' was first introduced in 1989 and is generally increased each year in line with changes in the Retail Prices Index.

Table 4 shows the limits which apply to old-style plans. These are set only in terms of a percentage of earnings – there is no overall cash limit. If you have both an old-style and a new-style plan, the relevant limits apply to each plan respectively but, also, your total contributions to both plans must not exceed the new-style plan limits.

National Insurance rebates and associated payments (see

PERSONAL PENSION PLANS

Table 3: Yearly contribution limits for a new-style personal pension plan [1]

Your age at the start of the tax year (6 April)	Contribution limit as a percentage of net relevant earnings	Overall cash limit on contributions for 1995–6
Up to 35	17.5%	£13,755
36 to 45	20%	£15,720
46 to 50	25%	£19,650
51 to 55	30%	£23,580
56 to 60	35%	£27,510
61 to 74	40%	£31,440
75 and over	You can no longer contribute	

[1] Personal pension plans taken out on or after 1 July 1988.

Table 4: Yearly contribution limits for an old-style personal pension plan [1]

Your age at the start of the tax year (6 April)	Contribution limit as a percentage of net relevant earnings
Up to 50	17.5%
51 to 55	20%
56 to 60	22.5%
61 to 74	27.5%
75 and over	You can no longer contribute

[1] Personal pension plans taken out on or after 1 July 1988.

'Contracted-out pensions' on page 94) do not count towards your contribution limit. If you are an employee, your employer can pay contributions into your personal plan. This is a fairly rare practice with individual plans, but some employers have arranged so-called 'group personal plans' as an alternative to an employer pension scheme, and, in the latter case, the employer may well contribute too. Any employer's contributions will count towards the limit on overall contributions.

How you pay

If you are self-employed, you make 'gross' payments to your personal pension plan – in other words, before deducting any tax relief. You then claim tax relief at your highest rate by writing to your tax office or through your tax return.

If you are an employee and you have an old-style personal plan, you'll make gross payments and you'll have to claim tax relief at your highest rate in the same way as a self-employed person. The tax relief due may then be given through the Pay-As-You-Earn system. If you are an employee and you have a new-style plan, you make payments after deducting tax relief at the basic rate. You get this relief even if you are a non-taxpayer or a 20 per cent taxpayer. If you are a basic-rate taxpayer, you have had the full relief due. If you're a higher-rate taxpayer, tax relief at the higher rate is payable and you'll have to claim this either by writing to your tax office or via your tax return.

The carry back rule

You can ask for pension contributions which you make in this tax year to be treated as if they had been paid in the previous tax year (and, if you had no net relevant earnings last year, then you can carry back the contribution two years). You must have enough unused tax relief in the earlier year to cover the contribution, and you'll get tax relief on your contributions at the earlier year's tax rates.

The carry back rule can be a particularly useful device if you run your own business since you may not know until after the end of the tax year how much you want to contribute. Furthermore, by using the carry back rule, you can often get tax relief more quickly than you would for a contribution credited to the current tax year because carrying back leads to a revised assessment for an earlier tax year.

When is the pension paid?

You don't have to retire from work in order to start taking a pension from a personal plan. However, the Inland Revenue does restrict you taking your pension at too early an age.

With an old-style pension plan, the earliest age at which Inland revenue rules let you start to take your pension is normally 60. If you have to give up your normal work because of ill health, then it may be paid at an earlier age. Also, earlier pension ages apply to some types of job – see Table 5. However, in practice, you can always switch to a new-style pension plan, in which case lower minimum pension ages apply.

With new-style personal pension plans, the youngest age at which you can start to take the pension is 50, though, once again, you may be able to take the pension even earlier if you have to retire from your usual work because of ill health. Earlier pension ages as shown in Table 5 are allowed for people in certain jobs – though obviously, the 'special' pension ages of 50 and 55 are not relevant to new-style plans since anyone can choose these ages.

With both old- and new-style plans, you must start to take your pension by the time you reach age 75.

EXAMPLE

Janet, who is self-employed as a freelance journalist, sends in her tax return for 1994-5 at the end of April 1995. In May, she receives a tax assessment showing tax due to be paid in July and the following January. Janet decides to reduce the tax bill shown there by setting against it tax relief on a £2,000 contribution to a new-style personal pension plan. She asks for this to be treated as if it had been paid in the 1994-5 tax year. This is a gross payment and, as she was assessed for basic rate tax on at least £2,000 of her income, she can claim tax relief of 25% × £2,000 = £500. The Inland Revenue sends her a revised assessment showing a reduction of £500 in the amount of tax to be paid. This means that the actual cost of investing £2,000 in her pension plan is only £1,500.

Table 5: Jobs with early retirement ages

Age	Occupation	Age	Occupation
35	Athletes Badminton players Boxers Cyclists Dancers Footballers Models National Hunt jockeys Rugby League players Squash players Table tennis players Tennis players Wrestlers	50	Croupiers Martial arts instructors Money broker dealers Newscasters Offshore riggers Royal Navy Reservists Rugby League referees Territorial Army members
40	Cricketers Golfers Motor cycle riders Motor racing drivers Speedway riders Trapeze artists Divers	55	Air pilots Brass instrumentalists Distant water trawlermen Fishermen (part-time) In-shore fishermen Money broker dealer directors Nurses, midwives etc. National Health Service psychiatrists Part-time firemen Singers
45	Flat-racing jockeys Non-commissioned Royal Marine Reservists		

Within the Inland Revenue limits, plan providers will set their own rules about the pension ages applicable to their plans. With some plans, you'll be required to say at the outset when you expect to take your pension – though you may be able to change your mind subsequently without penalty. Many plans are completely flexible and leave you to decide on any pension age (within the limits) at the time you want to start taking the pension.

You can have more than one plan at a time, so it can be a good idea to have several plans from which you can start to take a pension at different ages. This can help you ease gently out of work – perhaps cutting down to part-time employment before eventually retiring altogether. It can also help you to plan for extra income required later in retirement (see **Chapter 5**).

If you stop a plan early

You should be wary of ceasing to pay into a regular premium plan soon after taking it out. Charges made by plan providers tend to be heaviest in the early years of a plan and you could find that, if you stop the plan then, it has a very low value or even no value at all, in which case your contributions will have been wasted. Even when your plan does have some value, you need to check what will happen if you stop making the regular payments – with some plans, charges carry on being deducted and erode the value of your plan.

If you stop a plan and it does have some value, you can leave it invested with the plan provider or, if you prefer, you can transfer it to another personal plan or to an employer scheme, provided the plan or scheme agrees to accept the transfer. There may be charges for making the transfer and you may lose bonuses payable only to people who keep the plan with the original plan provider, so check carefully before making any decision.

Boosting your pension

As you get older, you're likely to develop a clearer idea of whether your expected retirement income is likely to be sufficient. If it looks on the low side, one way to try to boost it is by investing more in your personal pension plan. As page 97 shows, the amount that you can save through these plans increases as you get older, so there is scope for boosting your contributions. However, there is another way in which you can increase the amount you save and still qualify for tax relief on your contributions: by using the carry forward rules.

The carry forward rules

If you have unused contribution relief from any of the previous six tax years, you can carry forward this relief to cover a contribution made in the current tax year. You must use up the current year's limit first and you must always carry forward the earliest year's unused relief first. You get tax relief at the *current* year's tax rates.

You can combine the carry forward and carry back rules (see pages 98 and 101), so if you are asking for a contribution paid in 1995-6 to be treated as if it had been paid in 1994-5, you can also (if necessary) set the contribution against unused contribution limits from as far back as 1988-9. Bear in mind that the overall cash limit applying to contributions to new-style plans applied only from the 1989-90 tax year onwards.

The carry forward rules are very useful if you have unused relief and you have the opportunity to make an extra large amount of pension saving – for example, you might inherit some money which would enable you to set aside more than

EXAMPLE

Richard, aged 35, is an architect. In 1994-5, he took out a new-style personal pension plan. In May 1995, he inherited £10,000 from his grandmother and he decided to pay a large part of this into his pension plan. The £8,000 he intends to invest exceeds his contribution limit for 1995-6, but he can carry forward unused contribution relief from as far back as the 1989-90 tax year. His contribution limits are used up as follows:

Tax year	Net relevant earnings £	Contribution limit for tax relief £	Amount contributed that year £	Unused relief £	Year relief used
1989-90	7,600	1,330	0	1,330	1995-6
1990-1	8,200	1,435	0	1,435	1995-6
1991-2	9,100	1,593	0	1,593	1995-6
1992-3	8,200	1,435	0	1,435	—
1993-4	16,000	2,800	0	2,800	—
1994-5	22,700	3,973	2,800	1,173	—
1995-6	25,300	4,428	8,000	0	—

PERSONAL PENSION PLANS

> The contribution of £8,000 in 1995-6 uses up all of the contribution limit for that year together with the whole unused contribution limit for 1989-90 and 1990-1. It also uses up £807 of the unused limit for 1991-2. Richard can continue to carry forward the remaining £786 of unused relief for 1991-2 and the unused relief for 1992-3, 1993-4 and 1994-5.
>
> As a basic rate taxpayer, Richard qualifies for tax relief of 25% × £8,000 = £2,000 on the contribution made in 1995-6, so he actually pays in a net contribution of £6,000. The pension company claims the £2,000 tax relief from the Inland Revenue and this is added to the plan.

usual. Note that, while your contribution limits are worked out in relation to your earnings, you do not actually have to make pension savings out of your earnings in order to qualify for tax relief. Provided you have the necessary unused contribution limit and the total you contribute does not exceed the whole of your relevant earnings for the year in which the contributions are paid (or being treated as paid), the actual money invested can be from some other source such as your capital, an inheritance or a redundancy payment.

How your money is invested

When you take out a personal pension plan, you choose how you want your money to be invested. There are two main types of investment – on a with-profits basis or on a unit-linked basis.

With-profits basis

Traditionally, with a with-profits plan, the amount of your investment would never fall but would grow at a steady pace as bonuses (called 'reversionary bonuses') were regularly added. Once added, a bonus could not be taken away and, although the bonus rate could change, plan providers would try to maintain a stable bonus rate – though recent years have seen many companies cutting their bonus rates. In addition, when you came to take your pension, an extra bonus (called a 'terminal bonus') would be added to the plan. The size of the bonuses reflected the general profitability of the plan provider, which in turn would reflect the performance of the company's investments, expenses faced by the company, the proportion of profits paid out to any shareholders, and so on.

These days, it's very hard to find a personal pension plan which works on a traditional with-profits basis. Instead, most plan providers offer 'unitised with-profits policies'. With these, your contributions buy units in a with-profits fund. At regular intervals, either the value of the units is increased or bonus units are added (the equivalent of the traditional reversionary bonuses) and, when you come to take a pension, a terminal bonus is added to your units. The bonuses largely reflect the investment experience of the plan provider; instead of expenses entering into the bonus calculation, distinct charges are set against the plan. In many ways, unitised with-profits plans are similar to the traditional policies, but a major difference is that plan providers retain the right to revalue the cash-in value of units – downwards as well as upwards – if investment experience suggests that this is warranted. Thus, unitised with-profits plans are not as secure for investors as the traditional plans were.

Plan providers have switched to unitised with-profits policies for two main reasons. Firstly, some companies had in the past paid out too much in bonuses on traditional policies. The situation could not continue indefinitely and, rather than cut bonuses on existing policies, the companies preferred to start from scratch with a new type of policy. The second reason is that unitised policies do have some advantages for investors: an investment can be easily switched from a unit-linked fund (see below) to a unitised with-profits fund, and charges made on a unitised plan can be expressed much more clearly than expenses influencing a traditional plan.

Despite the departure from the traditional with-profits basis, unitised with-profits plans still offer a reasonably steady, medium risk investment which is likely to be appropriate if you are reasonably close (within ten years, say) to retirement, or if you are a person who feels happiest avoiding higher risk investments.

Unit-linked basis

If your retirement is ten or more years' distant, say, you should consider investing on a unit-linked basis. This means that your contributions buy units in a notional investment fund. The price of your units rises and falls with the value of the underlying investments. Because the price of the units can fall, unit-linked plans are generally more risky than with-profits plans. On the other hand, since the price is linked directly to stock market investments, you expect the value of your investment to beat inflation over the long term.

You can choose to link into different types of investment fund. 'General' and 'balanced' funds tend to be the lowest risk, being spread across a range of different investments or concentrating on very stable, solid, 'blue chip' shares. For the prospect of higher returns – but inevitably linked to higher risk of loss – you can choose more specialist funds, such as those investing in, say, Japanese stocks, small companies or special situations. You can usually invest in more than one fund at a time (subject to any minimum investment limits) and switch either your investment so far and/or your future contributions between different funds.

Cash or deposit funds

As you near retirement, you may want to lock into gains which you've made with a unit-linked or unitised with-profits plan. You can do this by switching to a cash or deposit fund. This works rather like a bank deposit account in that the amount of your investment can't fall and interest payments are added to it at intervals. The interest rate is usually linked to money market rates available on very large deposits (so it's higher than rates paid by high street banks or building societies) and it can vary.

The return on cash or deposit funds is unlikely to keep pace with inflation over the long-term, so this form of investment is not suitable if you are a long way off retirement.

Finding out about personal plans

Personal pension plans are run mainly by insurance companies. They can also be operated by friendly societies, banks, building societies and unit trust companies. Many banks and building societies offer pension plans but usually these will be operated either by a subsidiary which is an insurance company or by a separate insurance company with whom the bank or building society has a commercial arrangement.

Choosing a plan is a complex task. There are several hundred plans available and you need to decide which seems to offer you the best deal in terms of how you invest, the charges it levies – see Table 6 for a summary of charges you may come across – the options available, and so on. In the end, the most important factor determining the size of your pension will be how well the plan provider invests your money. Unfortunately, there is no way of picking the winners in advance. It may be a good idea to stick to companies which have performed *consistently* in the past; equally, you would be wise to avoid companies which have buoyed up past returns by dipping into their capital reserves.

You can also get information about plans direct from the plan providers and *Which?* magazine, and specialist magazines, such as *Money Management** (available in larger newsagents), also run surveys of pension plans summarising their main features. But the best course is to seek advice from an independent financial adviser – see **Chapter 11**.

How safe is your pension?

The majority of personal pension plans are covered by the Financial Services Act – see **Chapter 11**. It is illegal for an investment business – which covers most pension activities – to carry on without being authorised under the Financial Services Act. Authorisation is generally obtained by being a member of a Self Regulating Organisation (SRO). Most plan providers will be members of the Investment Management Regulatory Organisation (IMRO)* and the marketing side of their business will fall within the responsibility of the Personal Investment Authority (PIA)*. Financial advisers will usually also be members of the

Table 6: Charges often levied from unitised or unit-linked pension plan

Name of charge	Description
Administration charge/policy fee	Either a one-off or yearly charge deducted from your contributions before the remainder is used to buy units.
Bid-offer spread	The difference between the higher offer price at which you buy units and the lower bid price at which you can sell. Typically 5 per cent plus up to 1 per cent rounding.
Management charge	Yearly charge set against the investment fund to cover cost of managing the underlying investments. Typically 1 per cent or 1.5 per cent of the value of the fund.
Unit allocation	A given percentage of each contribution which is used to buy units. The percentage may be lower in the earlier years of the plan, and may be lower if you pay regular premiums monthly rather than yearly. Don't be misled by allocations over 100 per cent – it sounds as if you're being credited with more money than you paid in but this isn't the case. It may mean 100 per cent of the contribution less administration charge or you may be getting a refund of part of the management charge.
Capital units	You may be allocated 'special units' especially in the first year or two of the plan. They usually suffer a much higher management charge (for example 3 per cent or 5 per cent of the fund). This higher charge usually continues throughout the life of the plan.
Surrender charges	You're likely to be credited with only part of the value of your plan if you stop paying into it, or transfer it, in the early years. In the first few years, your plan may not have any value at all.
Switching charge	If you switch your investment from one unit-linked fund to another, the first one or two switches a year may be free. Thereafter, you're likely to face a charge.

PIA – some larger advisers belong to IMRO. SROs are charged with ensuring that their members are fit and proper persons to conduct their investment business, that they are solvent and that they conduct their business in a proper manner.

If you lose money through the fraud or negligence of an investment business, and you cannot recover it from the business because it has gone bust, you can claim compensation from the Investors Compensation Scheme* (ICS). The maximum payout per claim from the ICS is £48,000, which may be a good deal less than the pension fund you have built up. For more details about the protection given by the Financial Services Act, see **Chapter 11**.

Pension rights and divorce

As discussed in **Chapter 7**, a court considering a divorce settlement may be required to take into account any pension rights built up by the husband or wife. This includes pension rights within a personal pension plan. If your divorce is to be settled without the judgement of a court, you should consider getting advice about the value of pension rights and how they should be apportioned between you and your husband or wife.

When you reach retirement

About three months before you intend to start taking a pension from a personal pension plan, you should contact the plan provider for information about the options you have and an estimate of the pension and other benefits you can expect. See page 20 for what to do if you have problems tracing a plan provider. Bear in mind that, with all new-style plans and many old-style plans, you have an open market option, so get quotes from other companies as well to see who offers the best deal. If annuity rates are particularly low, consider whether you could put off taking your pension for a while until rates recover.

CHAPTER 9

FINANCIAL SUPPORT FOR THE FAMILY

As well as providing you with a retirement pension, the various types of pension scheme and plan can also provide financial support for your family in the event of your death.

What the state provides

The state offers support for widows – summarised in the flowchart overleaf – but no special support for widowers. If, despite this, your widow or widower is left with an inadequate income (from all sources), she or he might qualify for income support from the state – some details are given in **Chapter 6**.

What help a widow can get from the state depends on the record of National Insurance contributions which her husband built up over his working life up to the time of death. She could be eligible for some or all of the following benefits:

- **Widow's payment** A tax-free lump sum paid at a single rate of £1,000.
- **Widowed mother's allowance** A regular income available to widows caring for dependent children.
- **Widow's pension** A regular income available to widows aged 45 or more who have no dependent children.

Both widowed mother's allowance and widow's pension are taxable if all your income together is high enough for you to have to pay income tax. Both benefits are payable only as long as you don't remarry.

In the 1995-6 tax year, the full rate of widowed mother's

allowance is £58.85 a week. On top of this, a widow can receive any SERPS pension her husband built up. If her husband had an insufficient record of National Insurance contributions, the widowed mother's allowance will be reduced according to rules similar to those applying to the state basic retirement pension (see page 37).

If you are a widow with no dependent children and are under the age of 45 you are not eligible for any special help from the state. However, if you are 45 or over at the time you are widowed, or if you are 45 or more when your youngest child ceases to be dependent on you, you'll qualify for the widow's pension. This is paid at different rates according to your age at the time of your husband's death – see Table 1. Once the rate has been set, it does not increase with age. You qualify for the full rate shown in Table 1 provided your husband built up a sufficient record of National Insurance contributions during his working life. If he did not pay enough contributions, the amount of widow's pension will be reduced. You may also be entitled to some or all of any SERPS pension which your husband built up.

When you reach state pension age, you can switch from widow's pension (or widowed mother's allowance) to the state

Table 1: Amount of full-rate widow's pension in 1995–6

Age of widow at time of husband's death [1]	Amount of widow's pension £ per week
45	17.66
46	21.77
47	25.89
48	30.01
49	34.13
50	38.25
51	42.37
52	46.49
53	50.61
54	54.73
55 or over	58.85

[1] For women widowed before 6 April 1988, the relevant ages are five years younger, with the maximum widow's pension payable for new widows aged 50 or over.

retirement pension, which will be at least the amount you were receiving in widow's benefits. Alternatively, you can choose to carry on receiving widow's benefits for up to five years longer, but at the age of 65 you must switch to the state retirement pension. If you want to earn increased retirement pension by deferring it for up to five years (see page 160), you'll have to give up the widow's benefits as well.

What employer pension schemes provide

Death before retirement

Most employer schemes offer benefits for your dependants in the event of your death. These may take several forms:

- lump sum life insurance
- a pension for your widow or widower
- a pension for children or other dependants
- possibly a refund of your contributions (but not those paid on your behalf by your employer).

Your employer may run a life insurance scheme which provides cover for all employees – even those who are not members of the pension scheme – or just to pension scheme members. Provided the life cover meets Inland Revenue rules, tax relief is given on any amount paid to provide life cover (and the cover provided does not count as a taxable benefit for income tax purposes). To meet the tax rules, the maximum lump sum payable must not exceed four times your final pay (see page 75). For people covered by the post-1989 regime (see page 77), there is also an overall cash limit on the amount of life insurance, which is £314,400 for the 1995-6 tax year. Contributions returned can be paid out as a lump sum in addition to the life cover.

The pension scheme usually retains the right to decide who will receive the lump sum in the event of your death. This means that the lump sum does not become part of your estate, so it can be paid out rapidly without waiting for probate and does not count for inheritance tax purposes (see **Chapter 36**). You can nominate the person or people whom you would like

THE WHICH? GUIDE TO AN ACTIVE RETIREMENT

Help from the state for widows and widowers

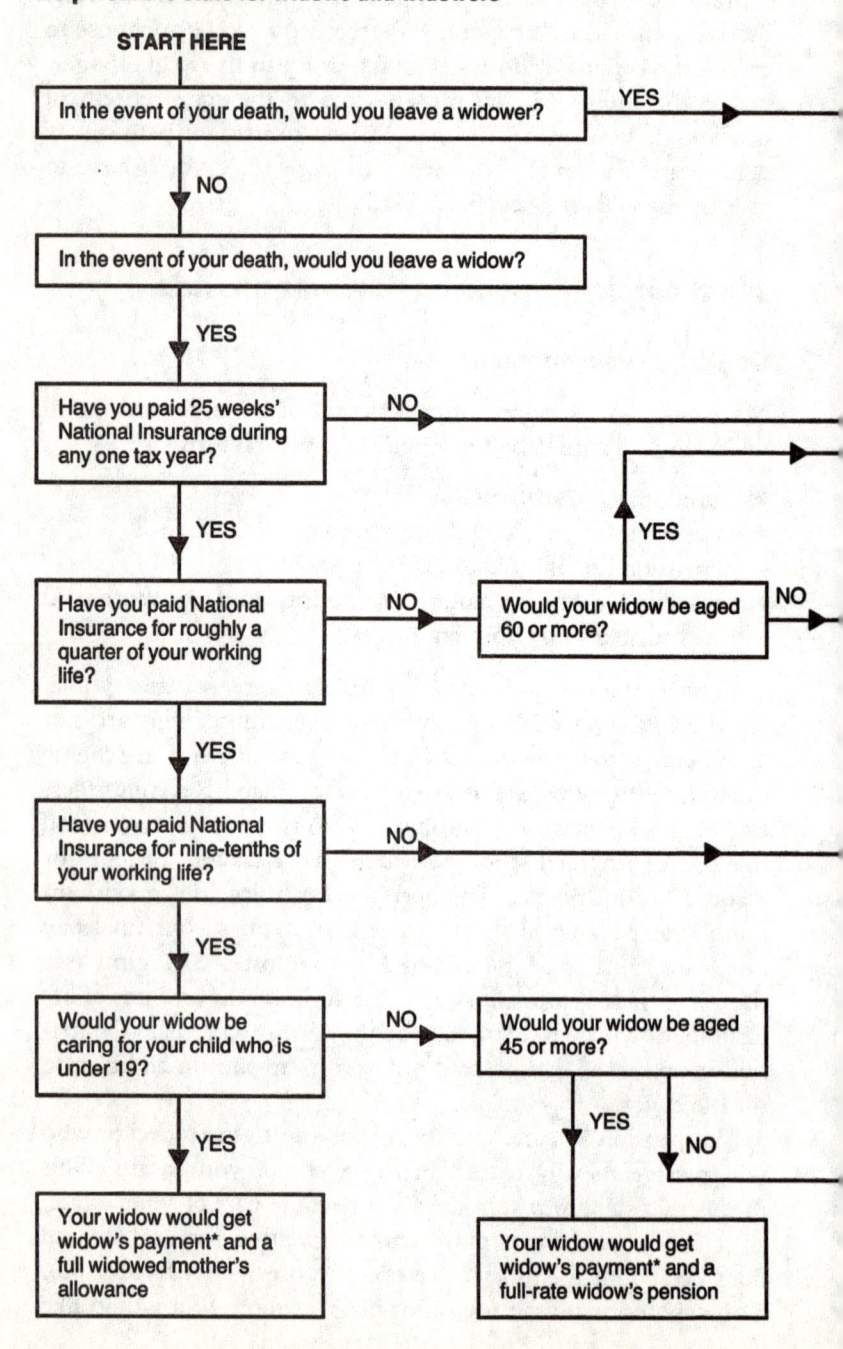

START HERE

In the event of your death, would you leave a widower? — **YES** →

↓ **NO**

In the event of your death, would you leave a widow?

↓ **YES**

Have you paid 25 weeks' National Insurance during any one tax year? — **NO** →

↓ **YES**

Have you paid National Insurance for roughly a quarter of your working life? — **NO** → Would your widow be aged 60 or more? — **YES** ↑ / **NO** →

↓ **YES**

Have you paid National Insurance for nine-tenths of your working life? — **NO** →

↓ **YES**

Would your widow be caring for your child who is under 19? — **NO** → Would your widow be aged 45 or more? — **YES** ↓ / **NO** →

↓ **YES**

Your widow would get widow's payment* and a full widowed mother's allowance

Your widow would get widow's payment* and a full-rate widow's pension

112

FINANCIAL SUPPORT FOR THE FAMILY

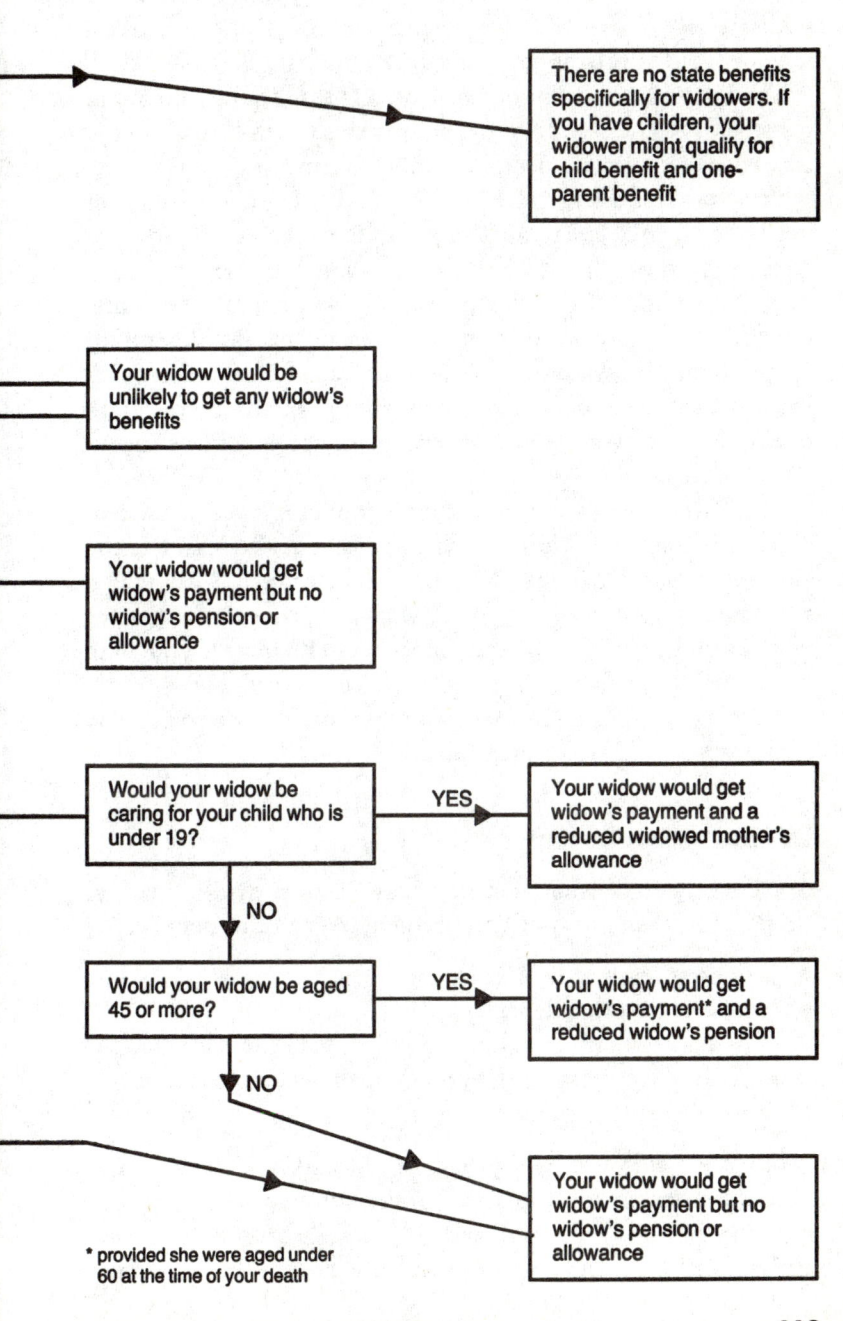

→ There are no state benefits specifically for widowers. If you have children, your widower might qualify for child benefit and one-parent benefit

→ Your widow would be unlikely to get any widow's benefits

→ Your widow would get widow's payment but no widow's pension or allowance

→ **Would your widow be caring for your child who is under 19?** —**YES**→ Your widow would get widow's payment and a reduced widowed mother's allowance

↓ **NO**

Would your widow be aged 45 or more? —**YES**→ Your widow would get widow's payment* and a reduced widow's pension

↓ **NO**

→ Your widow would get widow's payment but no widow's pension or allowance

* provided she were aged under 60 at the time of your death

113

to receive the lump sum and usually the scheme will respect your wishes. However, if you had failed to name someone – a young child, say – who was dependent on you, the pension scheme would probably override your nomination.

The Inland Revenue limits the amounts that can be paid out in pensions to your widow or widower to two-thirds of the *maximum* retirement pension, under Inland Revenue rules, which you could have received if you'd been able to stay on until the normal retirement age for the scheme. If you are covered by the post-1989 regime (see page 77), there is also an overall cash limit of £34,933 for the 1995-6 tax year. The same limit applies to any one pension for a dependant. But the sum of all pensions for widow, widower and any other dependants must not come to more than the maximum pension which you could have received at normal retirement age under the Inland Revenue rules.

If you were contracted out through your employer scheme on a final pay basis, the widow's pension must equal at least half the amount of the Guaranteed Minimum Pension (GMP) which you built up, provided your widow is 45 or over at the time of your death or has to look after dependent children. If you were contracted out on a money purchase basis, the whole contracted-out fund which has built up must be used to provide a widow's or widower's pension.

Death after retirement

An employer pension scheme may also provide financial support for your family after retirement. Again, this may be:

- a widow's or widower's pension
- pensions for other dependants
- a guarantee that your pension will be paid for a set number of years (five years, say), even if you die within that time
- possibly, a lump sum.

No one widow's, widower's or dependant's pension can exceed two-thirds of the maximum pension you could have had under Inland Revenue rules and all widow's or widower's and dependants' pensions together must not exceed the maximum amount of pension which you could have had under Inland Revenue limits. If you were contracted out on a final pay basis, any widow's or widower's pension must equal at least half the GMP you were getting. Similarly, if you were contracted out on a money purchase basis, your widow or widower must receive a contracted-out pension of at least half the amount you were getting.

If there is a guarantee that your pension will be paid for five years, say, and you die within that time, the scheme usually has discretion to decide who will receive the balance of the pension – you will be asked to nominate someone and usually your wish will be respected. The balance of the guaranteed pension may be 'rolled up' and paid out as a lump sum.

It is unusual for an employer scheme to provide you with life cover after you have retired. However, if you died so soon after retirement that you'd received less in pension than you'd paid in over the years in contributions, the scheme might pay out the balance of the contributions as a lump sum. Generally this lump sum would be tax-free.

What personal pension plans provide

Death before retirement

There is no automatic package of benefits when you take out a personal pension plan (except where the plan is a contracted-out one – see below), but you can choose to pay extra for:

- a pension for your widow or widower
- a pension for children or other dependants
- lump sum life cover from a related life insurance policy.

If you opt for your plan to include a pension for a widow or widower and/or other dependants, the only limit on the size of these pensions with an old-style plan (see page 93) is the fund you have built up. With a new-style plan, there is a restriction that the total of widow's, widower's and other dependants' pensions must not come to more than the retirement pension which you could have bought with your fund had you retired at the date of your death.

With a contracted-out personal pension plan, it must provide a pension for your widow or widower if they are aged 45 or more at the time of your death or have to care for dependent children. The pension would be whatever amount the contracted-out fund which had built up could buy.

If you haven't arranged for any widow's, widower's or other dependants' pensions to be paid from your plan, your plan will usually pay out a lump sum in the event of your death. With an old-style plan, this will usually be the value of your pension fund. With a new-style plan, the payout may be either the value of your fund or the sum of the contributions you paid in, plus reasonable interest or bonuses. You nominate whom this payment would be made to – it need not be someone who was dependent on you financially.

You can pay up to five per cent of your net relevant earnings (see page 96) as premiums to a special life insurance policy, which will pay out a lump sum in the event of your death. These policies are variously called 'section 621 policies' or 'section 226A policies'. You get tax relief on the premiums at your highest rate, but note that the premiums you pay count towards your overall limit on contributions to personal plans (see pages 96 to 97). If you are concerned to save the maximum possible for retirement, you might do better to take out ordinary life insurance instead. Provided you are eligible to take out a personal pension plan (see page 89), you can take out this special insurance even if you are not making any contributions towards a personal pension.

Death after retirement

You'll need to choose at the time you decide to start taking a pension what financial support for your family you are going to buy. The more cover you provide, the lower will be your own retirement pension. There are three options:

- a guarantee that your pension will be paid for a set period (five years, say) even if you die in the interim
- a pension for your widow or widower
- pensions for other dependants.

The maximum guarantee period allowed is ten years. You can nominate the person to receive the balance of your pension if you do die before the guarantee period is up – the recipient doesn't have to be someone who was financially dependent on you. The balance of the pension can be rolled up and paid out as a lump sum.

A pension for a widow, widower or other dependant may take the form of a joint annuity so that your pension would continue to be paid after your death during the lifetime of your dependant. The sum of pensions for your widow or widower and other dependants must not come to more than the pension you were receiving. If your pension plan was contracted out, it must allow for a widow's or widower's pension.

Life insurance

Employer schemes will set their own rates of pension and life cover which may be lower then the maximum allowed by the Inland Revenue, so you'll need to check the rules for your own particular scheme. With a personal plan, you must decide what benefits you can afford to include within the scope of the plan.

If the financial support for dependants under your pension arrangements is not enough, you should consider taking out life insurance. The main types of life insurance are described below.

Term insurance

You take this out for a fixed period (the 'term') and it pays out only if you die within that time – if you survive the period, it pays out nothing. Term insurance may pay out a set amount, or the amount to be paid out may increase – as a safeguard against inflation, say. There are also decreasing term insurance policies where the sum to be paid out reduces over the term: these are useful where you want cover for an expense which is reducing – a loan which you're paying off, say, or the possibility of inheritance tax on a gift (see **Chapter 36**). Another variant is family income benefit insurance which, if you die within the term, pays out a regular tax-free income starting from the date of death.

Life insurance savings plan

These pay out if you die within a fixed period but also if you survive to the end of the period. Since these policies pay out whether you die or not – i.e. there is an investment element – they are a lot more expensive than a term insurance policy. See **Chapter 10** for more about investment-type life insurance.

Whole life insurance

This pays out whenever you die. Since the policy must pay out at some time, it builds up a capital value, which means that you may get something back if you decide to cash in the policy – i.e. it also has an investment element. Whole life insurance can be particularly useful in inheritance tax planning (see **Chapter 36**).

Which type?

In general, if you need life cover at some stage during your life to provide for dependants, it's best to choose protection-only insurance – i.e. some form of term insurance – because you can usually get the cover you need relatively cheaply. However, as you get older you should look at both term and whole life insurance. If you take out a whole life policy now, you are guaranteed life cover for the rest of your life (provided you keep up the premiums), whatever your state of health. On the other hand, if you take out a term insurance policy now, you might not be able to renew it later if your health worsens.

CHAPTER 10

INVESTMENTS

New types of investment seem to be launched every week, to the despair of anybody trying to take a sensible view of investing money that will need to last them for the rest of their life, and probably a partner's too. But don't lose heart.

The 'newness' usually consists of combining two types of investment in an inventive way – so long as you look for what underlies the puff, and don't feel inhibited in asking what might seem basic questions, you should be able to find your way through the marketing literature to the reality. That's why the second half of this chapter describes the building blocks of investment, grouping the main types of investment into the following categories, depending on what they do:

- secure schemes, offering variable interest (page 126)
- secure schemes, offering fixed interest (page 129)
- investments offering the chance of capital gain or loss (page 130)
- British Government stocks (page 136)
- long-term savings plans (page 137)
- investments designed specially to produce income (page 139)
- index-linked investments (page 140).

In retirement, although it is important to review your investments regularly, jumping onto the latest investment bandwagon might not be for you. However the investments on offer may change, the sensible investment guidelines tend to prevail from year to year:

- Have you something put aside for emergencies in a place where you can get at it quickly?
- Do you know when you are likely to need lump sums, e.g. to replace your car, or extra income, e.g. if pension income will drop suddenly on the death of one partner?
- Have you thought about how much risk you can afford to take in search of higher growth? There are two main risks: the risk that you might lose your capital, or the risk that you might see its value steadily eroded by inflation. Unless you choose one of the few index-linked investments, you have to decide which type of risk you prefer.
- Have you spread your risk – in other words, do you have enough in different types of investments so that a downturn in one sector doesn't scupper your plans overall?
- Do you know the tax consequences of your investments, and have you minimised any adverse ones – without being obsessed by the desire to save tax?

EXAMPLE

Anthony retired at 56 and received an index-linked pension and a lump sum. He says: 'I found it important to be able to live comfortably with any investment I make. It is no use having one that makes you feel that you need to keep checking, although it is as well to check, say monthly, any investment subject to stock market fluctuation.'

This Chapter can give guidance on these general questions; what it can't do is tell you exactly how to put all the answers together to suit your individual needs. **Chapter 11** looks at getting advice.

Look for the real return

When comparing homes for your money, get into the habit of thinking of the return they give after both tax and inflation. Income from investments is taxed in one of four ways. It may be:

- tax-free, such as National Savings Certificates
- taxable, but received before tax, such as income from a National Savings Investment Account: you have to pay the tax separately
- taxed: you get the income after basic-rate tax has been deducted, for example most building society income. Non-taxpayers can reclaim the tax, or register to have the income paid before tax, while higher-rate taxpayers pay extra tax
- received with a tax credit, such as income from shares and unit trusts. Higher-rate taxpayers pay extra tax.

If you make a capital gain on an investment, such as shares, you may also be subject to capital gains tax. There's more detail, and a summary chart of how different investments are taxed, in **Chapter 17**.

Investing before retirement

Even before you get to retirement there are investment decisions to make. Most people probably regard their pension scheme as their main way of investing for retirement. But you may be prepared to sacrifice some of the tax advantages a pension offers in order to avoid tying up money you might need access to before retirement. For example, you may want to help a child through college, or foresee the need to tide yourself through the possibility of a few years between early retirement and getting your state pension.

In this case, you can either commit yourself to regular saving, or put something away when you can spare it, say in a building society, and then transfer it into a lump sum investment. However, there are some investments, described below, which offer tax advantages (though none are as generous as pensions).

If you can tie up savings for 5 years

Invest the maximum you can in a TESSA – tax-free savings accounts from banks and building societies; other tax-free schemes are National Savings Certificates (see page 129) and index-linked National Savings Certificates (see page 141).

If you can tie up savings for 5 to 10 years

An investment which gives the possibility of a capital gain, e.g. one based on shares, probably offers the best chance of beating inflation, and 5 to 10 years at least gives time for your investment to recover from periods when values fall. Either lump sum or regular savings are possible. Investing via a Personal Equity Plan gives returns free of income and capital gains tax, although high charges on some PEPs make them only clearly worthwhile for higher-rate taxpayers.

If you can tie up savings for at least 10 years

As well as investments where your capital can grow (or shrink), long-term savings plans (based on life insurance) are a disciplined way of saving. But steer clear of them unless you are sure you can keep the policy up, because there are steep penalties on early withdrawal. They offer tax advantages for higher-rate taxpayers (see page 138). Friendly society tax-exempt savings plans are completely tax-free (see page 138).

Investing after retirement

For income later

When you first retire, your pension income may be enough for you not to need much extra income from your investments, in which case you will be looking to make savings grow as much as you can against the day when you need the capital, either to turn it into an income or to replace expensive durables such as a car. If so, you need to balance up the risk of losing your capital against the risk of having it reduced by inflation. Assuming that you have enough money to spread over several types of investment, consider putting some in one of the index-linked investments (see page 140), some in one of the secure investments (see page 126 to 130), and some in one of the 'chance of a capital gain or loss' investments (see page 130). Don't forget that British Government stocks (page 136) are a very versatile investment. And don't assume that lump sum investments are

INVESTMENTS

the only ones to consider. If there is a particularly attractive savings scheme on offer you can always set up your own 'feeder' account in a bank or building society account, and transfer the money across by standing order. Alternatively, National Savings Certificates, say, bought regularly will produce a stream of income as they start to mature in five years' time.

For income now

The few investments whose main purpose is to produce income are covered on pages 139 to 140. However, do not confine yourself to them. For the advantage of regular income, you may have to accept other risks, such as tying up your capital. When interest rates are low you will have to be particularly inventive to get a decent income. Some ideas are:

- Unit trust and investment trust companies often market 'income' funds, which invest in companies which tend to pay high dividends.
- Unit trusts also offer income schemes which will pay out a set income, although to achieve this when prices are falling they may have to cash in some of your units.
- You can design your own income-producing portfolio by choosing types of investments which achieve a sensible balance between risk, security and growth, but then buying specific investments paying income at different times throughout the year. For example, shares pay their dividends at different times, as do British Government stocks, and the dates when building societies credit interest to accounts vary from society to society.
- Single-premium insurance bonds (see page 134) are useful for higher-rate taxpayers needing income.

Traps to avoid

Using up capital too fast

Nobody can tell for certain how long they (and their partner) are going to need an income. You have to take into account how

EXAMPLE
When planning his investments to give a mixture of income and growth, Bob first made his own judgement on future inflation, interest rates and the likely course of the stock market. He wrote his thoughts down, to avoid the temptation of changing his mind from day to day. He then allocated a proportion of his capital to different types of scheme – e.g. 'secure' ones, and those based on stocks and shares. At that stage he did not know enough to choose a best buy from the products in each type, so he obtained written recommendations from several financial advisers. He entered their recommendations under the appropriate categories on his plan – not always easy, he said, because you have to read the small print to determine the specific type – and compared their proportions with his own. Bob eventually followed the recommendations of the adviser whose proportions were nearest his own, and who also seemed to demonstrate the most competence.

much your investments will earn, how fast inflation will erode its purchasing power, and how long you are likely to live. For how inflation can affect your income, see **Chapter 4**.

Forgetting that things may change

If one partner dies, pension income may drop sharply, forcing the surviving partner to depend more upon investments (unless life insurance will fill the gap). For what happens to jointly held investments and savings accounts, see **Chapter 35** (they normally pass automatically to the survivor). The surviving partner's investment priorities are almost bound to change. They may be particularly at the mercy of inflation (for which see index-linked investments, page 140), and even though they will naturally want a secure investment, they should beware of putting too much in an investment which is secure in that its value can't go down, such as a building society account, but where inflation will erode its value over time. Also see 'For income now' (page 123) for ideas on maximising income.

Selling at the wrong time

When a long-term investment matures, for example a pension or unit-linked life insurance policy, you might lose out badly if the stock market happens to be low at the time. Clearly, you cannot foresee this when you invest. One way to avoid this is to ask the company if you can transfer your money to a safer (probably more pedestrian) fund, a little before maturity. You can, of course, sell things like shares or unit trusts at any time. But if at all possible, avoid being forced to sell them when their value is very low, by making sure that you always have a safer investment to fall back on until prices improve. A change to the rules on when you can draw a personal pension should also help – see page 90.

Losing age-related allowance

If you or your husband or wife is aged 65 or over at any point in the tax year, you get a higher tax-free allowance. But this extra allowance is reduced once your 'total income' (see page 210) rises above £14,600 (in the 1995-6 tax year). If you are in this position, consider tax-free or favourably taxed investments which won't swell your income, or investments where the return comes mainly in the form of capital gain. In particular, beware of making a taxable gain on a life insurance policy (e.g. by cashing more than 5 per cent a year of the amount you invested in a single premium bond). Although you will not have to pay basic-rate tax on it, it will be added to your 'total income' for the purpose of reducing your age allowance.

If you have problems

There is nothing you can do if you lose money by choosing, say, the wrong share. If a company goes bust, there may be a compensation scheme – details are given under each type of investment – though these have maximum limits. And for most types of investment there are Ombudsman schemes, or other independent adjudicators, such as the Personal Investment Authority Ombudsman* and the Banking Ombudsman*. For problems with a financial adviser, see **Chapter 11**.

The main types of investment

Secure schemes, variable interest

Building societies, banks and National Savings accounts are all 'secure' in the sense that the money you invest in pounds cannot fall – although the purchasing power of each pound will of course shrink as a result of inflation. The only way you can lose money is if the institution itself fails – virtually impossible with National Savings, highly unlikely with the major banks and building societies.

Smaller banks and building societies do get close to failure from time to time, but building societies in particular are usually taken over by their bigger brothers first. If they don't, there is a compensation scheme, which for building societies is 90 per cent of the first £20,000 deposited, i.e. up to a maximum of £18,000. For banks it is 75 per cent of the first £20,000, i.e. up to a maximum of £15,000, but due to rise to the level of the building societies scheme from July 1995. Since the maxima are fairly low, you might want to put smaller amounts in small institutions, or steer clear of them altogether.

Income from bank and building society accounts is usually received taxed – i.e. after deduction of basic-rate tax, currently 25 per cent. Higher-rate taxpayers have to pay extra tax, lower-rate taxpayers can claim tax back, and non-taxpayers can either reclaim tax or register to have their interest paid before tax (see page 236).

Below are the main types of variable interest schemes on offer. However, note that rates vary hugely from institution to institution: you may get higher interest from one society's instant access account than from another's notice account. 'Best buy' rates are given in *Which?* magazine from time to time and in some weekend papers.

Instant access

Nowadays these tend to have 'tiered' interest rates, so that the more you save, the higher your interest. But beware of schemes which give instant access only if you pay a penalty. Some also offer banking services, such as a cheque book and guarantee/debit card, so that you can use them as a current account.

INVESTMENTS

Notice accounts
If you are prepared to give, say, 30, 60 or 90 days' notice, a 'notice account' may give you higher interest than an instant access account. Most accounts allow you instant access if you pay a penalty, e.g. losing 30, 60 or 90 days' interest; others may waive the notice requirement if your savings exceed a certain amount. The minimum investment is anything from £500 upwards.

Term accounts
These tie up your money for a set term fixed at the outset, usually between six months and three years, in return for higher interest. Again, there will be a minimum investment.

Regular savings accounts
Although these are now few and far between, they give higher interest if you are prepared to save regularly. You may be able to miss, say, one payment a year. Check any restrictions on withdrawals.

High-interest cheque accounts
Hybrid schemes offered mainly by banks, these offer high interest and some limited banking services (e.g. a set number of cheques each year), usually in return for your commitment to keep a fairly high minimum balance in the account.

Postal-only accounts
Several building societies now offer these; some offer competitive interest rates, but apart from that they have no intrinsic differences from other building society accounts.

TESSAs
These 'Tax-Exempt Special Savings Accounts' offer a tax-free return, provided you stick to the following two rules:

- You must invest for five years. You can withdraw interest (but not capital) earlier, as long as it is no more than the amount already credited to your account, but if you do basic-rate tax will be deducted before you get it.

- The most you can save is £3,000 in the first year, and up to £1,800 in each of the following four years, with an overall maximum of £9,000 in total over the five years. But if you are reinvesting the capital from a maturing TESSA, the limit for first-year deposits in your second TESSA is the amount of capital (but not interest) saved in your first TESSA, i.e. up £9,000.

The other details are up to the bank or building society: some are for lump sums, some for regular savings, some allow you to invest as and when you like. However, beware of penalties on early withdrawal or closure – because of these, although you can in theory transfer your TESSA to another bank or building society, this is often impractical.

National Savings Ordinary and Investment Accounts

Both accounts offer variable interest, although the Ordinary Account interest rate tends to change infrequently. The Investment Account is taxable, but pays interest in full: the minimum investment is £20 and you have to give a month's notice to withdraw your money. The first £70 interest each year from an Ordinary Account (£140 in a joint account) is tax-free, while anything above that is taxable but paid out before tax. The minimum investment is £10, for which you get 2 per cent interest before tax (in January 1995), or, as long as the account is

---

HOW BANKS AND BUILDING SOCIETIES QUOTE INTEREST RATES

Gross rate – the annual flat rate before taking into account how often interest is paid and before deduction of any tax.

Net rate – the annual flat rate after deduction of basic-rate tax.

Gross CAR – or 'Compounded Annual Rate': a true rate of return taking into account how often interest is added to the account. The more often this is, the better: for example, an account paying 5 per cent will return £5 for every £100 if interest is added once a year, £5.06 if added twice.

Net CAR – the net rate compounded, and what basic rate taxpayers will earn over a full year.

open at least one calendar year, 3.25 per cent for each calendar month in which the balance is £500 or more. See the address section for National Savings addresses and the phone number to ring for the latest interest rates.

Secure schemes, fixed interest

Knowing exactly how much interest you will get is useful for budgeting. But you take on another risk: if interest rates generally rise after you've put your money in a fixed-interest scheme, you will lose out. You also usually have to commit yourself to saving for a fixed length of time. However, a fixed-interest scheme protects you against the risk of falling interest rates.

Building societies sometimes offer fixed-interest deals, usually on term accounts. However, National Savings is the main provider of fixed-interest schemes. For the phone number to ring for the latest National Savings interest rates, see the address section at the back of the guide. The Save As You Earn scheme which offered a tax-free return on five- or seven-year savings, closed to new business on 29 November 1994, and National Savings Yearly Plan on 1 February 1995. But see page 139 for National Savings Pensioners Bonds.

National Savings Certificates

These are sold in 'issues', each having a different interest rate, and only one being available at any time. They are tax-free: you buy them in units of £100 and the maximum you can invest is £10,000 (plus a further £20,000 if reinvesting money from previous issues). Interest is added to the value of your certificate over the period of its life (which is five years at outset). The amount of interest added increases as time goes by, giving you an added incentive to hang on to your certificates: you get no interest if you cash in during the first year. After five years the interest rate drops to a lower and variable rate of interest. Index-linked certificates are also available – see page 140.

National Savings Capital Bonds

The return on these five-year bonds is taxable: they are an

oddity in that you have to pay tax on the interest earned year by year, even though you won't receive the interest until the bond is repaid. You have to invest at least £100. You get no interest on withdrawals during the first year, but the interest rate then rises year by year.

National Savings FIRST Option Bond

Unlike other National Savings products, this bond pays interest after deduction of basic-rate tax. Non-taxpayers can reclaim this tax, higher-rate taxpayers must pay more. You must invest at least £1,000. The interest rate is fixed for a year at a time; at the end of the year, you can either cash in your investment, or leave it there for another year, in which case you will get the rate applying at that time. You get no interest on withdrawals during the first year. On withdrawals during the second year you get the value at the end of the first year plus half the fixed rate of interest for the period since then.

Chance of gain or loss

Investments based on United Kingdom or international stocks and shares or property are not 'safe'. Investment managers and unit trusts, and the marketing of investments, are regulated under the Financial Services Act, and there is a limited investors' compensation scheme – see page 153. But this won't compensate you against the normal risks of investing, i.e that the value of your investment could slump. On the other hand you could, if you're lucky, make a mint, outstripping inflation and the return available on more secure homes for your money. For this reason, once you have found a secure home for your emergency fund and money you really can't afford to lose, it is sensible to invest at least some of your money this way.

You can reduce the risk. One way is to invest money over several years, leaving time for the ups and downs in your investment's value to even out. You can then choose a time to cash in when values are high. The other way is to spread your money over several different companies in different fields. But stockbrokers' minimum commissions make this uneconomic unless you have at least £10,000, preferably much more. Unit

INVESTMENTS

trusts, investment trusts and single-premium insurance bonds are ways of pooling your money with other investors and getting professionals to manage your money for you, with minimum investments of a few hundred pounds upwards. Many unit and investment trusts also have regular savings schemes, with minimum investments of, say, £20 to £50 a month.

Unit trusts
Your money buys units in a fund, which then buys shares and other investments. The price of the units (and the value of your holding) fluctuates in line with the value of those investments.

Investment trusts
These are simply companies which specialise in investing in other companies' shares, as well as Government stocks, and property throughout the world. However, the value of their own shares is affected by supply and demand. For example, some trusts' shares sell at a price below the value of the assets held by the trust (or, as the jargon has it, at a discount to the 'net asset value'). But some trusts' shares, particularly popular ones such as 'split capital' trusts (see below for a translation) may sell for more – at a 'premium'. The value is also affected by the fact that an investment trust, unlike a unit trust, can borrow to buy things, which increases the tendency of a trust to rise and fall in value: this is known as 'gearing'.

Single-premium insurance bonds
These are lump-sum investments in life insurance funds, which work rather like unit trusts (but are taxed very differently – see page 134).

Different types of fund
Companies managing unit and investment trusts and single-premium bonds usually allow you to invest in a range of funds. These can be very specialist and therefore risky (e.g. 'recovery' or 'emerging markets') or pretty general and in theory, at least, less risky (e.g. 'UK General'). As well as funds investing in different areas of the world and different types of company, you can buy:

- **Unit trusts investing in other unit trusts ('funds of funds') or investment trusts** In theory, this rather incestuous arrangement should help you to spread your risk even further, though you may pay more in charges.
- **Property funds** These have not been very attractive over recent years, but are the only practical way for small investors to invest in commercial property.
- **International funds** These are a convenient and relatively cheap way to invest abroad, though changes in exchange rates can have a dramatic effect on your return.
- **Futures and options funds** Put very simply, futures and options give investors the right to buy or sell financial assets such as shares or 'commodities' such as coffee beans and gold at a fixed price in the future. The funds that invest in them are a way of spreading the considerable risks of doing so.
- **'Gilt' funds** These invest in British Government stocks (known as gilts). You can buy gilts direct easily and cheaply: gains are free of capital gains tax, while those bought through a unit trust are not. On the other hand basic-rate taxpayers now pay only 20 per cent tax on income from gilt unit trusts, but 25 per cent on income from gilts bought direct (see below). Which route is better for you therefore depends on your tax position.
- **Fixed-interest and cash funds** These invest in things like bank deposits (i.e. those for very large investors) and Government stocks.
- **'Managed' life insurance funds** These invest in a mixture of things such as shares, property and fixed-interest investments, the aim being greater security.
- **Split capital investment trusts** These offer different types of shares which give different types of return. For example, there are income shares and capital shares: people with income shares get all the income from a fund, those with capital shares all the capital. Both will receive more income or capital growth than they otherwise would, but at the cost of giving up any capital growth or income respectively.

INVESTMENTS

Tax, and how to save it
Some of the return from investing in shares, investment trusts and unit trusts comes in the form of income, and some as capital gains. Any capital gains are taxable, but only if your taxable capital gains come to more than an annual tax-free slice (£6,000 in the 1995-6 tax year).

The income is paid out after a 'tax credit' has been deducted. The tax credit is currently 20 per cent, but basic-rate taxpayers will have no further tax to pay. Higher-rate taxpayers will have to pay an extra 20 per cent tax to bring the total up to the 40 per cent they are liable to pay. Anybody who is a non-taxpayer, even after taking the income into account, can reclaim tax. Note that some unit trusts which invest in interest-producing assets, such as British Government stock, pay an income which is taxed like interest (i.e. 25 per cent tax is deducted).

However, there are three schemes which allow tax-free investment in shares. Personal Equity Plans should be considered by basic- and higher-rate taxpayers. In spite of the tax relief they offer, the Enterprise Investment Scheme and Venture Capital Trusts are intrinsically risky, because of the sort of company they invest in, so are probably only worth considering for higher-rate taxpayers.

Personal Equity Plans (PEPs)
The return from investing in shares, unit or investment trusts via a PEP is free of capital gains tax and income tax, within these limits:

- You can invest up to £6,000 a year, plus a further £3,000 in a 'single company' PEP (which holds the shares of only one company).
- Your money must be invested in United Kingdom or certain European Community shares. From 6 April 1995, you can also invest in some corporate bonds, convertibles and preference shares.
- You can invest all or part of your £6,000 either in unit or investment trusts with up to 50 per cent of their assets in United Kingdom or some European Community shares, or £1,500 in some other trusts.

- You must invest via a 'plan manager', who takes care of all the administration.

Other PEP conditions vary hugely, depending on the plan manager: some accept regular savings, others lump sums only, some allow you to choose your own shares, others choose them for you. But watch out for charges, which can cancel out any tax savings.

Enterprise investment scheme (EIS)
Since 1 January 1994, the EIS has been available for new investment in the shares of some types of unquoted companies. You get tax relief of up to 20 per cent on the amount you invest, and income tax or capital gains tax relief (you choose which) against losses made on the shares. Gains are tax-free, provided you hold the shares for at least five years, and if you are reinvesting money which arose from disposing of an asset on which capital gains tax would be due, you can defer the tax. The minimum investment in any one company is £500 and the maximum overall EIS investment is £100,000 each year.

Venture Capital Trusts (VCTs)
From the 1995-6 tax year, it has been possible to invest in a spread of unquoted companies through VCTs. VCTs are companies, rather like investment trusts, which are quoted on the Stock Exchange. You get tax relief at 20 per cent on up to £100,000 in any tax year, provided you hold the shares for at least five years. The proceeds are free of both income tax and capital gains tax, and if you are reinvesting money which arose from disposing of an asset on which capital gains tax would be due, you can defer that tax.

Single-premium insurance bonds
These are technically insurance policies, so you pay no capital gains tax or basic-rate income tax on them yourself – this is paid by the insurance fund. Higher-rate taxpayers may have to pay higher-rate income tax on any gain, but you can take an income of up to 5 per cent of your original investment and put off any tax until you finally cash in the bond – useful if, say, you are a

INVESTMENTS

higher-rate taxpayer now but will pay basic-rate tax when you retire.

How to buy

You can buy shares and investment trusts through stockbrokers or banks (the Association of Private Client Investment Managers and Stockbrokers* has a guide to private client stockbrokers). Commission rates vary widely, but usually range between 1 and 2 per cent for deals of up to, say, £7,000, with typical minimum commission of £15 to £25. You also pay stamp duty on purchases (not sales). Some brokers also charge a fixed fee for each transaction, others impose a 'compliance levy' of, say, £5, to offset their costs of complying with investment regulations. You can buy investment trust regular savings schemes direct from the company, commission-free: contact the Association of Investment Trust Companies* for companies offering such schemes.

You will find the unit trust and life insurance funds available, their prices, and fund managers' addresses, in the *Financial Times*; other papers also give some information. Instead of stockbrokers' commission, you will pay some or all of the following charges – your investment must grow to cover at least the charges before you will make any money:

- Initial charge when you first buy, typically 5 per cent but can be as low as 1 per cent (particularly if there is an exit charge) or as high as 6 per cent.
- Annual management charges, typically 1 or 1.5 per cent, but can be more, particularly if initial charges are low.
- The 'bid-offer spread': as with shares, you get a lower ('bid') price if you sell than if you buy ('offer' price).
- On some funds, exit charge when you sell.

'BROKER BONDS'

Many independent financial advisers pick and choose from the funds available to make up their own funds. They aim to choose investments which suit their own clientele and, by shopping around, to improve the return. However, some funds have high charges but mediocre or even poor performance.

British Government stocks

The Government puts issues of gilts up for sale as a way of financing the public sector. Often known as 'gilts', there are all sorts of different ones on the market, maturing from one to 40 years away. Depending on which one you choose, they can be useful for people who are happy to take a risk, or those who aren't, non-taxpayers and higher-rate taxpayers, income or growth. Also see page 141 for the index-linked variety.

Most have a set redemption date, when the Government promises to pay out a fixed amount, in multiples of £100 (the 'nominal value'). So if you keep them till then you'll know exactly what you'll get back, though, of course, their purchasing power will have been eroded by inflation. In the meantime, most gilts also pay out a fixed income – the 'coupon' – twice a year. Keeping gilts until maturity is the low-risk route.

Happy to take some risk? You can buy and sell gilts before maturity on the stock market, where their price will depend on supply and demand. Sometimes the price will be above the amount you'll get on maturity, sometimes less: it depends on things like how the fixed-interest rate compares with interest rates in general and how long it is until maturity.

Gilts are free of capital gains tax, so are worth considering for people who are liable to pay this tax. High-coupon gilts are good for people who need income, or for non- or lower-rate taxpayers: higher-rate taxpayers who don't need income can buy low-coupon gilts, which pay very little interest.

How to buy gilts

A useful leaflet, *Investing in gilts*, is available from some post offices or from the Bank of England*. New issues can be bought through advertisements in newspapers. Existing issues can be bought through stockbrokers or banks, in which case you'll have commission to pay (probably a bit less than for shares). Alternatively, you can buy gilts by post through the National Savings Stock Register (leaflets are available in post offices). This is cheap – it costs 0.6 per cent on the first £5,000, and 0.35 per cent on amounts over £5,000 with a minimum of £5 for purchases (no minimum for sales). Basic-rate tax will be deducted from the income before you get it, unless you buy through the National Savings Stock Register in which case although income is taxable, it is paid out before tax.

PERMANENT INTEREST-BEARING SHARES (PIBS)
These are a relatively new way of investing in building societies, but much the least secure. PIBS are bought and sold through stockbrokers and pay out a twice-yearly income. Gains are free of capital gains tax and income is paid after basic-rate tax. But there is no set repayment date. The other hitch is that although you are investing in a building society, PIBS-holders come last in the line of debtors if the society does fold, and they are not covered by any compensation scheme. There are now a few specialist investment funds which aim to reduce the risk by investing in a range of societies' PIBS.

Long-term savings plans

You can use many of the investments above for regular saving, provided you can meet the minimum investment. For saving over 10 years, investment-type life insurance and friendly society policies are good for discipline. But if you don't keep them up you can lose out badly: for example, if you cash in during the first couple of years you could get little or nothing back, and even after that, returns can be poor on early withdrawals.

The financial soundness of insurance companies is monitored by the Department of Trade and Industry*, and the marketing of their products is regulated under the Financial Services Act (see **Chapter 11**). If your company goes under, the Policyholders Protection Board protects at least 90 per cent of any (reasonable) sum guaranteed by your policy.

All types of policy must have some life insurance built in, in order to qualify for various tax advantages. How much depends on the policy – an endowment policy is mainly for investment and a maximum investment plan is a unit-linked saivngs plan;

*The addresses and phone numbers of organisations marked with an asterisk can be found in the address section at the back of the guide.

both have little insurance, while a 'flexible cover plan' allows you to vary how much of your money is invested and how much buys insurance. However, on the whole, keeping your investments separate from your insurance avoids tying up your money for 10 years.

With-profits policies
These add annual bonuses to the amount you are insured for: the amount depends on how well the company's investments perform. Once given, annual bonuses cannot be taken away, but there is usually an additional 'terminal' bonus on maturity or death. The annual bonus system tends to smooth out the peaks and troughs in your investment. When returns are high, the company may not pay them all out as bonuses, but use them to keep up bonuses in leaner periods. However, terminal bonuses have become more important over the years and can now make up as much as 50 per cent of your total payout – so if your policy matures in a bad year, you can lose out.

Unit-linked policies
These allocate your money to units in funds of things like shares or property. All gains (or losses), minus charges and tax, are paid out, so your policy can rise or fall in value. 'Unitised with-profits' policies, or 'with-profits' funds offered by unit-linked policies, are a mix: see page 105 for how they work.

Tax
There are tax advantages, but only for higher-rate taxpayers. The return from an insurance policy is free of tax in your hands (unless it is cashed in early, in which case some higher-rate tax may be payable), because the insurance fund pays any capital gains tax or basic-rate income tax due.

Friendly Society policies work like other life insurance policies, except for 'tax-exempt' schemes, which are completely free of tax. However, the maximum investment for tax-exempt schemes is low, at £25 a month or £270 a year; and the tax advantage could be outweighed by high charges.

INVESTMENTS

Income-producers

Many of the types of investment above can be used to give income – see pages 122 to 123 for some ideas. But there are some specialist investments. Note that minimum investments have to be fairly high (i.e. thousands, rather than hundreds, of pounds) in order to pay out a worthwhile monthly income.

Building Society Monthly Income Accounts
These normally have variable interest rates, so are affected when rates fall. Before buying, check how easy it is for you to get your money out.

National Savings Income Bonds
Income bonds also pay variable interest monthly, and you have to give three months' notice to get your money back: the rate of interest is halved on withdrawals during the first year. The minimum investment is £2,000. However, they are convenient for non-taxpayers since although the income is taxable it is paid out before tax. Buy them through post offices, or see under National Savings in the address section.

National Savings Pensioners Guaranteed Income Bonds
You have to be at least 65 to buy these. The minimum investment is £500, the maximum £20,000 and they pay monthly interest which is guaranteed for the first five years. You don't have to give notice to get your money back on any fifth anniversary of buying the bonds, but for withdrawals before then you have to give 60 days' notice, during which no interest is earned. Like most other National Savings schemes, the interest is taxable but paid out before tax. Leaflets are available in post offices, or see the address section for the National Savings phone number.

Guaranteed income bonds
Insurance companies sell lump sum investments which give fixed interest, providing you invest for a fixed period (usually four or five years, but it can vary between one and 10 years). As with all fixed-interest investments, the risk here is that you buy

at a time when interest rates are low. They are usually variants of single-premium insurance bonds (see page 134) and so are paid out free of basic-rate income tax; exactly how they work can vary so check before you buy, and see 'Losing age-related allowance' on page 125. The Saturday edition of the *Financial Times* lists companies currently offering highest rates.

Annuities

Also sold by insurance companies, annuities give an income, usually for the rest of your life. The amount depends on your age, sex, whether it is a joint annuity (you can arrange for it to continue either till the first death, or until both partners have died) and whether the income is fixed or increasing. However, you cannot get your money back again. This makes them a gamble: if you live longer than the company expects, you will do well, but the converse is equally true. You can, however, pay extra for 'capital protection', in which case a proportion of your capital will be returned if you die within a set number of years. Because the rate you get depends on interest rates generally at the time you buy, you could end up stuck with a very poor income if rates later rise.

The income is usually paid out after basic-rate tax (though non-taxpayers can arrange with the company to have it paid gross) but only part of your monthly income is taxable – the rest counts as a return of your capital. Annuity rates vary considerably between companies, so shop around. An independent financial adviser (see **Chapter 11**) may help, or see *Money Management* magazine*. And for schemes where you mortgage your house to buy an annuity (home income plans) see page 59.

Index-linked investments

There are only two types really worth considering at the moment, variants of National Savings Certificates and British Government stocks (gilts). But all sorts of schemes are marketed which guarantee to increase your investment in line with a stock market index – for example, guaranteed equity bonds. Approach these with care. Some guarantee that your capital is index-linked, but ignore the income which most stock market investments also pay out.

INVESTMENTS

Index-linked National Savings Certificates
Like other National Savings Certificates (see page 129), these are five-year tax-free investments for a minimum of £100 and maximum of £10,000 (plus a further £20,000 if reinvesting matured certificates). If you cash one in within a year, you get back only the money you invested. But after a year its value is increased in line with the change in the Retail Prices Index (RPI) since you bought it. If you hold your certificate for the full five years, you get interest on top of inflation. After five years, you can keep your money where it is and your investment will continue to be index-linked, and may also get a tax-free bonus, depending on what issue of Certificates you hold. If the RPI falls, the value of your certificate falls too, though you still get the interest, and it is guaranteed that when you cash in you'll get back at least what you invested (plus the interest).

Index-linked British Government stock
These work like other gilts (see page 136) but when the life of the gilt comes to an end the person then owning it will be paid the nominal value of the gilt increased in line with inflation over its lifetime. All the stocks pay out a small income, also guaranteed to increase each year in line with inflation. However, whether or not your investment keeps pace with inflation depends entirely on the price at which you buy (or sell) the gilt and whether or not you hold it until redemption.

CHAPTER 11

GETTING FINANCIAL ADVICE

At best, a financial adviser can steer your money into investments which are exactly right for your needs – in the process lifting a lot of work and worry from your shoulders. But at worst, an adviser can (and a few do) disappear with your money. Other pitfalls are less drastic, but also damaging to your pocket, for example ending up with an investment which suits the adviser – because it pays a high commission, say – but doesn't suit you.

So do you really need an adviser?

With such concerns in mind, you may think it's better to do it yourself. In any case it's worth finding out something about the different ways of saving and investing, whether or not you end up using an adviser. But there will be times when you feel you need help, or at least the chance to talk over your ideas with someone else.

Fortunately, the past few years have seen an improvement in the protection available to investors, with the implementation of the Financial Services Act 1986. But not all financial products are covered by this Act. Excluded are savings schemes where the value of your capital stays the same, for example bank and building society accounts, National Savings products and a rare type of personal pension plan, general insurance (for your home or your car, say), and investment in physical objects or mortgages. This doesn't necessarily mean that these are completely unregulated – see **Chapters 10, 21 and 23**.

Where to get advice

Accountants

All qualified accountants cover personal tax, and often some aspects of investment, during their training, and many will be able to introduce you to specialists, but some firms employ specialist financial advisers (not necessarily trained accountants themselves) or have subsidiary companies which are authorised under the Financial Services Act. So, while accountants can be a good source of advice on general financial strategy, tax planning and may sometimes manage portfolios of investments, it is important to check exactly what they are authorised to offer and what expertise they have.

Accountants usually charge a fee for their advice, which varies greatly depending on the firm. If they introduce you to an independent financial adviser they may get a cut of the adviser's commission. They may also get commission if you buy life insurance or unit trusts through them, but if they are qualified as either 'Chartered' or 'Certified' accountants, they must tell you how much the commission is. In practice, many will set the commission against their fees.

Actuaries

Actuaries are expert at calculating probabilities and future values from statistical and other data – for example, how much an insurance company will have to charge in order to cover what it expects to have to pay out in many years' time. They are often employed by pension and insurance companies, but there are also firms of 'consulting' actuaries who can give independent financial advice. Their specialisation and independence makes them probably the best source of help with a complex pension problem, but they do not come cheap. Expect to pay several hundred pounds for their advice (see page 145 for a source of free pensions advice through your Citizens Advice Bureau).

Banks

Most high-street banks can sell you their 'own-brand' insurance, savings schemes, investments and mortgages, or (through subsidiary companies) give you independent investment advice. They may also manage your investments for you, write wills and act as executors, or offer tax-planning or share-dealing services. For this reason it is important to check whether staff are acting as independent advisers or just as representatives for their own-brand products, before going ahead; as a general rule, virtually all banks sell their own products through their branches and other products and services through centralised departments or subsidiaries. If bank staff are acting as independent financial advisers, they cannot recommend the bank's own products unless they can show that they are 'better than the best' available elsewhere.

A bank is only as good as its parts, and before using one you should also see what a specialist can offer. The charge for advice will generally be in line with what a specialist would charge – e.g. if selling insurance, they will get commission, but if dealing in shares for you, they will make charges similar to a stockbroker's.

PORTFOLIO MANAGEMENT

This just means managing a lump sum or 'portfolio' of investments for you, in order to meet your aims in investing. There will be a fee for the service. The two basic sorts of service are:

- **Discretionary management** – you give them discretion to make decisions on your behalf.
- **Advisory management** – they make recommendations but leave the final decision to you.

The minimum portfolio you can get professionally managed could be anything from £10,000 to £100,000, sometimes more. Fees for portfolio management vary: they can be a yearly ½ to one per cent of the value of your portfolio, a flat annual fee or a slice of the profits, or a mixture of methods.

Building societies

All building societies will offer advice on their own savings schemes and mortgages. They also earn large amounts of commission through selling insurance and some types of investment. However, most can sell life insurance from only one company, and general insurance from a restricted number. Of the larger building societies, only the Bradford & Bingley and the Yorkshire offered independent advice (in early 1995), although some others offer independent advice through subsidiary companies.

See page 126 for how to get information on building society rates. You could try asking financial advisers whether they subscribe to any of the services which publish building society rates, but there is little incentive for commission-based financial advisers to give advice on building society accounts, which pay little, if any, commission.

Citizens Advice Bureaux (CABx)

There is a CAB in most towns, and some areas have specialist money advice centres, but they are often very busy. They tend to concentrate on social security, debt and income tax problems, but are also a useful source of leaflets and can direct you to other organisations. If you have a pension query, your CAB can also direct you to a local pensions expert from the network of volunteers run by the Occupational Pensions Advisory Service*.

Independent Financial Advisers (IFAs)

This has become the catch-all name for anybody authorised under the Financial Services Act as an independent investment adviser, but they do vary in what they are authorised to offer. Some are not much more than life insurance and pension sales people, paid by commission, while others offer a wide range of investment services, including portfolio management and their own broker bonds (see page 135), and employ specialists in areas like tax. Increasingly, they may offer you the option of paying them a fee rather than working on commission (if a fee is charged, they should either pass on any commission to you or re-invest it in whatever you buy or set it against the fee). You should be told the amount of any commission.

The range of their services depends partly on what they are permitted to offer by their regulator – only some firms are allowed to hold and manage your money, for example, while others act as middlemen only. So while independent financial advisers can be a good source of general advice, they may be biased towards products such as insurance which pay high commission, neglecting building societies and National Savings products which don't.

To get a free list of three IFAs in your area, ring IFA (Promotions) on 01483 461461, or, if you would prefer to pay a fee in order to reduce the possibility of the advice being affected by commission, *Money Management* magazine* can produce a list of advisers who charge a fee. Note, though, that advisers have to apply to get on these lists, so the lists are not exhaustive and are no guide to the quality of the advice available from the advisers.

Insurance brokers and advisers

Anybody can sell general insurance, but to call yourself an insurance broker, you must meet set conditions and register with the Insurance Brokers Registration Council*. Insurance brokers specialise in general and life insurance, but are often authorised to sell and advise on investments as well. They will usually be paid by commission, so be aware of the risk that this might influence their advice. Their code of conduct says that you should be told the amount of commission, if you ask (and for some investments you should now be told automatically).

Insurance companies

As well as general or life insurance, these also sell pensions and often have subsidiaries offering other products, such as unit trusts, too. If you know what you want, and are happy to be offered just one company's products, then an insurance company ought to be the best source of information about its own

GETTING FINANCIAL ADVICE

products. Unfortunately, many life insurance companies sell through a salesforce of commission-only representatives, who vary hugely in quality and training. So make sure what they say is backed up in the 'key features' information they are now obliged to give you.

Investment managers

In their purest form, these manage institutional funds of investments, e.g. unit trusts or pension funds. However, they will sometimes offer services, such as investment advice or portfolio management, to private investors with substantial sums to invest.

Again, they may not charge a fee if just selling you insurance or a pension for which they get commission, but they will charge for portfolio management. Services such as tax help may cost extra.

Publications and telephone services

Consumers' Association* publishes several books on financial topics – see page 6 – and best buy rates for a range of financial products, including building societies, are given in *Which?* magazine every few months.

Some newspapers publish 'Best buy' rates in their Saturday money sections. Daily papers also list a range of share price and other information, though the *Financial Times* is the most comprehensive. For very keen private investors, *Money Management** is one monthly magazine which publishes detailed surveys of particular investments, like unit trusts and pension plans. Age Concern* has some useful financial publications.

Solicitors

Like accountants, most solicitors should be able to give general financial advice, or refer you to an independent financial adviser, but some firms may employ specialists or undertake portfolio management. They also give tax advice and write wills and act as executors (but see **Chapter 35**). They may get commission if you buy things like insurance or pensions through them, but they can keep this commission only with your consent: they will usually set the commission against their fees.

Stockbrokers

Although stockbrokers specialise in buying and selling things like shares and British Government stocks (gilts), they may also offer unit trusts, portfolio management and general investment advice. As well as 'discretionary' services (where they take the decisions on your behalf) and 'advisory' services (where they advise, but you make the final decisions), some also offer 'execution-only' share-dealing, where they just buy and sell on your instructions. Not all deal with private clients – write to the Association of Private Client Investment Managers and Stockbrokers (APCIMS)* for a free list of those who do. Proshare*, an organisation which exists to promote share ownership, costs £30 a year to join but can give general information on shares and discounts on related products and services.

Stockbrokers charge commission when buying and selling shares for you (see page 135), and a fee for portfolio management. Extra services such as tax help may be charged for separately.

Trade associations

Look at an adviser's letterhead to see which trade associations he or she belongs to. These associations exist to promote the relevant product or service, and so are definitely not independent. However, they usually offer free leaflets, information packs and sometimes lists of members. You can also ask them for a copy of any code of conduct – not a guarantee of good behaviour, but a useful thing to wave at your adviser if you think you are not getting the treatment you deserve. If there is no independent system for handling complaints, they will sometimes mediate – though with varying degrees of vigour.

Financial Services Act protection

Authorisation

Under the Financial Services Act, anyone who carries on an investment business without being 'authorised' to do so (and who isn't in an 'exempt' category) will be committing a criminal offence, and any contracts you have with them can be made void. Investment businesses may be authorised by a number of bodies, depending on what sort of business they are (and they have some choice).

The leader of the regulatory pack is the Securities and Investments Board* (SIB). This is an agency to which the Government has delegated its powers to regulate and supervise the industry under the Financial Services Act. SIB in turn delegates the regulation of most investment businesses to a number of other regulators, whom it recognises and oversees. However SIB also authorises some businesses directly.

SIB recognises three Self-Regulating Organisations (SROs), who authorise and supervise most investment businesses. These SROs are:

- **PIA*** – Personal Investment Authority – covers unit trusts, friendly societies, insurance companies and their salesforces, and independent financial advisers.
- **IMRO*** – Investment Management Regulatory Organisation – predominantly covers institutional investment managers, e.g. pension fund managers, unit trust managers and some banks. Some independent financial advisers have joined IMRO instead of PIA.
- **SFA*** – Securities and Futures Authority – is made up of members of the Stock Exchange* (e.g. stockbrokers), dealers in international stocks and bonds and money market investments, and advisers, managers and dealers in futures and options.

SIB also oversees nine Recognised Professional Bodies, who are allowed to authorise their members to carry out limited

*The addresses and phone numbers of organisations marked with an asterisk can be found in the address section at the back of the guide.

investment business. These are:

- Chartered Association of Certified Accountants*
- Institute of Actuaries*
- Institute of Chartered Accountants in England and Wales*
- Institute of Chartered Accountants in Ireland*
- Institute of Chartered Accountants in Scotland*
- Insurance Brokers Registration Council*
- The Law Society*
- Law Society of Northern Ireland*
- Law Society of Scotland*.

You can find out whether or not a firm is authorised by telephoning the Securities and Investments Board (SIB) Central Register on 0171-929 3652, or by consulting Prestel (available in many local libraries). SIB also publishes a number of free explanatory booklets.

Independence

Advisers selling life insurance and unit trusts are allowed to be in only one of two categories. One category must give completely independent advice on all the products of that type on the market. The other acts only as a representative, selling and advising on just one company's or group's products. Representatives can be individuals, who may be self-employed, or separate companies, often known as 'appointed representatives', which might themselves employ several representatives. Both categories now have to tell you how much commission they get, if any, before you buy.

Standards of conduct

Once authorised, investment firms which fail to abide by the rules of their regulating organisations can be disciplined or, at worst, have their authorisation removed. SIB has issued 10 principles outlining the standards expected of investment businesses – though beware, some of this protection doesn't apply if you agree to be classed as an experienced investor (i.e. one with plenty of recent experience in a particular field of investment). The main points of the rules governing the conduct of businesses dealing with private individuals are:

- Investment businesses have to take into account your best interests when giving you advice.
- In most cases an adviser has to know the customer, i.e. be fully aware of your personal and financial situation.
- Independent advisers must take into account the range of products on the market and your particular needs, and must not sell you a particular product if they're aware of another one which would meet your needs better. Company representatives have the same responsibilities in respect of the range of products and services provided by the company to which they are tied. In either case, if nothing they can offer suits your needs, they must tell you so.
- When they start to sell you products like life insurance and unit trusts, both independent advisers and representatives must give you a 'terms of business letter' making their status clear – i.e. whether they are independent or tied and whether they are paid commission or charge a fee.
- You should get all the information you need about what you are buying and what you are being charged. In the case of life insurance and pension policies the insurance company should give you this information in a 'key features' document before you buy. This should tell you how much will be deducted in charges, expressed as a 'reduction in yield' – in other words, if your investment grows by 9 per cent a year, a 1.5 per cent reduction in yield will mean you end up with 7.5 per cent – and what you will get if you cash in early. The key features should also include the cash amount of commission going to whoever is selling you the policy and a statement explaining why he or she recommended the product. Similar information should be given about unit trusts from the second half of 1995.
- Advertisements and illustrations of benefits have to comply with rules about comparisons, references to past performance and give risk warnings if necessary. Note that all companies must work out illustrations using standard growth rates set by regulators, but incorporating the company's own charges.

- In most cases (but not when just buying life insurance or unit trusts), written customer agreements are required, which give details of the services being provided and their cost, set out your investment objectives and the responsibilities of your adviser, warn of the risks of certain investments and state if you have chosen to be classed as an experienced investor.
- 'Best execution' rules apply for most transactions. This means that the firm must carry out the deal on the best terms available.
- Proper arrangements must be made for keeping your money (e.g. money awaiting investment) separate from the adviser's money.

'Cooling-off'

Financial sales representatives are allowed to cold-call, i.e. visit or telephone you without your previous invitation, unless selling some particular investments. But if you buy life insurance, a pension or unit trusts as a result of a cold-call, during which advice was given, you get a cooling-off period. This allows you to cancel within 14 days of getting a notice telling you of your rights (or before the first payment, if later). But this doesn't apply to unit trusts or single-premium life insurance bonds if you received no advice (i.e. bought on an 'execution-only' basis), or bought either through an advertisement or in line with your customer agreement.

How to complain

Each of the regulators is required to have some system for dealing with complaints about the businesses they authorise. However, if you have a complaint against any investment business you should first take it up with the business itself; if you are still dissatisfied with its response, the business is obliged to tell you what to do next. For example, the PIA Ombudsman★ is the final adjudicator for complaints against PIA members, the Investment Ombudsman★ handles complaints against IMRO members.

Even if your investment is not covered by the Financial Services Act, it may be covered by an Ombudsman scheme. See the address section at the back of the guide.

Compensation

If you find yourself in the unfortunate position of having lost money in a bankrupt or fraudulent investment company, or through the negligence of an authorised adviser, there is an Investors' Compensation Scheme* (see page 126 for protection for bank and building society accounts). The scheme is financed by a levy on all authorised investment businesses, and you should be covered if your investments were made after 28 August 1988, when the scheme started. If you invested before then you might still be covered in some circumstances.

The scheme can pay up to £48,000 – full protection for the first £30,000 invested, then protection for 90 per cent of the next £20,000. If you've invested through someone authorised by a Recognised Professional Body you should also get compensation, but from a different scheme.

Getting the best from your adviser

Decide what your aims are
If you've got a clear idea of what you want from your money, it will be easier to choose an adviser to help you achieve those aims. Think about when you are likely to want the money back, what degree of risk you are willing to take, and whether you want your savings to provide you with an income or lump sum.

Contact two or three advisers
Decide what type of adviser you want, then draw up a shortlist of, say, three advisers. See page 146 for how to find independent financial advisers: otherwise try the British Insurance and Investment Brokers Association* (a trade association), *Yellow Pages*, or personal recommendations from friends in similar situations to you. Talk to all your shortlisted advisers before choosing.

Avoid advisers who don't ask questions

Under the Financial Services Act, advisers have a duty to 'know the customer' – in other words, know enough about them to make sensible recommendations. Exactly what questions they should ask is not specificied by law (and you are under no obligation to answer), but should include things like:

- your age, health and marital status
- number and ages of children and other dependants
- size and make-up of family income
- your regular financial commitments
- your tax position
- your existing savings and investments
- your home and mortgage
- your existing pension and insurance policies
- how long you want to invest for
- your reasons for investing, e.g. how important it is to you to get a high income or make a capital gain
- whether you want to be able to get your money back quickly
- what degree of risk you're prepared to take with your money.

Ask exactly what sort of advisers they are

Double-check what they tell you by looking on their business card or the Buyer's Guide if they gave you one. The stationery of anyone authorised under the Financial Services Act should say who the regulator is and, if the adviser is not independent, which company he or she represents. Also find out what qualifications and experience the adviser you will be dealing with has: these might be accountancy or legal qualifications, or specialist exams including those run by the Chartered Insurance Institute* (CII) or Life Insurance Association* (LIA). Check what compensation schemes they are covered by, and whether they have professional indemnity insurance. This insurance protects them, not you – it pays out if the adviser has to pay damages because of their negligence or, in some cases, fraud – but at least means that the money should be there if you make a successful claim against the adviser.

Be clear about what you want your adviser to do
Do you want advice on just one type of investment, or a range? Some advisers specialise in just one area. Do you expect your adviser to plan your investments and then leave day-to-day management up to you, or do you want them to take care of all this too?

Check the cost of advice
Ask whether the adviser will charge a fee or is paid commission. Even if you do not have to hand over any money yourself to get advice, this does not mean that the advice is 'free'. Commission is deducted from investors' funds (usually even if you buy direct from the company), so in the long run the return from your investment will be less than it might otherwise have been. An adviser may agree to 'rebate' some of the commission, either by giving you cash back or by arranging for more of your money to be invested for you. However, it goes without saying that you should not choose an adviser purely on the grounds of what rebate he or she will give you.

If the adviser charges a fee, make sure you know how much it will be, and what you will get for your money. For example, if the adviser is going to be managing your money, how often will you receive a progress report? What extras are available, and at what price – portfolio valuations, tax advice, share-dealing?

Get everything in writing
Note the time, date, person you spoke to, and content of any telephone conversations and meetings. Confirm them in writing if possible (with a copy for yourself). These notes could be vital if you have a dispute.

Avoid making cheques payable to a go-between
If you invest in something, make your cheque payable to the company providing the investment, not the adviser's firm. That way there's no temptation for fraudulent or hard-up intermediaries to divert the money to their own pockets. If a firm has got to handle your money (e.g. it is managing it for you) it should be held in a separate client account.

Keep an eye on your adviser
If an adviser is going to be looking after your money in the long term, ask how often the adviser will keep in touch, who will be dealing with you and what happens if they leave (the turnover of company representatives can be high), and expect regular reports on your investments.

Don't be afraid to ask questions
Beware of claims that seem too good to be true – they probably are. If an adviser does not take the time to explain, or cannot answer your questions, steer clear. Personal finance may be complicated, but need not be incomprehensible.

PART 3

WORKING IN RETIREMENT

CHAPTER 12

DECIDING TO CARRY ON WORKING

You may not feel ready to leave the world of work even when you've left your main job. Yet how realistic is it to think about carrying on working at a time when unemployment is high and research suggests that around one-quarter to one-third of press advertisements may carry age restrictions?

In practice, there are some trends which could favour older workers. First, while further job losses are anticipated in production industries, relatively high growth is forecast in service and information-based industries. Second, there is an increasing shift towards different patterns of work, such as part-time work, casual work and self-employment. For example, part-time work grew by 25 per cent between 1984 and 1994. Both these trends might be expected to suit older workers.

Nor are employers' preconceptions of the suitability of older workers necessarily borne out by reality. According to the health study undertaken by the Carnegie Inquiry into the Third Age, a person's performance is governed as much by their experience and skill as by their age. Indeed, as you get older, the difference between individuals can be more pronounced than variations between age groups – so what is 'average' becomes less meaningful.

Should you carry on?

Irrespective of what other people choose to do, you have to make your own decisions about whether to carry on with your current employer, if you have the option to do so, or to look for other work. There are a number of financial factors to take into account, as well as your feelings about carrying on work.

National Insurance

If you carry on working, you will have to carry on paying National Insurance contributions, unless you are over state retirement age (currently 60 for women, 65 for men) or your earnings are small. This applies whether you are self-employed or an employee: for more on types and amounts of National Insurance see page 38 and the leaflets on National Insurance available from any social security office (also called the Benefits Agency). If you are still working for an employer at state pension age, you should receive a certificate of exemption from the Department of Social Security to give to your employer, who will still have to pay contributions for you.

Effect on your tax bill

Once you reach 65, there is an unpleasant tax trap to watch out for, which may reduce the financial attractions of carrying on working. As explained in **Chapter 15**, this concerns the higher age-related allowances you qualify for at that age. These higher allowances are reduced once your taxable income is above a certain level (£14,600 in the year from 6 April 1995), making the effective rate of tax on income above this level 37.5 per cent. If this applies to you, you will need to set this tax penalty against your desire to carry on working for other reasons.

Effect on your state pensions

Carrying on working will nowadays either benefit your state pension or have no effect on it, depending on what you decide to do. The 'earnings rule', under which your state retirement pension was reduced by earnings above a certain amount, was abolished in 1989.

Once you reach state retirement age, you can choose to defer drawing your state pension for up to five years. Your pension is increased by 7.5 per cent for each year you put off the pension (and proportionately for shorter periods). The maximum increase you can earn is 37.5 per cent (i.e. 5 × 7.5 per cent). The extra pension is increased in line with the Retail Prices Index once it starts to be paid.

If you decide to defer your state pension, you have to give up all your pensions from the state for that time – in other words, you can't just give up your basic pension, you must also give up any SERPS and graduated pensions and, if you are a married man who would have received extra for your wife, or a wife who would have received a pension based on your husband's contributions, that pension has to be given up too. But once you start to take the pension, any increase will apply to all your state pensions – i.e. SERPS, graduated and extra for your wife as well as the basic pension.

Should you defer?
If you're a single man, it may not be such a good idea to defer your pension. At the age of 70, the average man can expect to live for another 10 years. But, if he gave up a full-rate basic pension for five years, he'd be giving up £15,301 in total in today's prices. Once his pension started to be paid, it would be 37.5 per cent higher but it would take 13 1/3 years before he had received as much in extra pension as he had originally given up. Women, who at age 65 have an average life expectancy of 17 years, and married couples, are much more likely to get a good deal out of deferring their pension. Of course, anyone who is in poor health (and thus has below average life expectancy) should also think twice before deferring a state pension in this way.

Another factor to take into account is your tax position: if your state pension would cause you to lose your higher age-related allowances (see **Chapter 15**), it might tip the balance in favour of deferring.

Effect on employer pensions

If you continue working for your current employer after normal retirement age, you will need to check the rules of your scheme to see whether you can continue to improve your pension – see page 82–83 for the main options.

If you move to a different job or into self-employment, say, you will be faced, like any other job-mover, with the decision of whether to leave the pension you have already built up in the employer scheme or whether to move it to a personal pension plan or a special scheme (see page 83). However, if you have built up a reasonable pension in one employer scheme, you should be cautious about moving it.

The effect on personal pensions

This is more straightforward: the more you contribute, and the longer you put off drawing your pension, the greater the pension fund you should have available to you when you eventually retire. You can contribute to a personal pension plan as long as you are under the age of 75, and as long as you continue to have 'relevant earnings' – i.e. earnings from self-employment or earnings from a job where you have chosen not to join an employer pension scheme. Older people are also allowed to contribute more than the normal maximum allowed by the Inland Revenue: see **Chapter 8** for how to use these rules to your advantage.

Pensions from your new job

You may want to use your new job as a last-minute chance to boost your eventual income on retirement. You may find your options drawing in, as your new employer's pension scheme may not accept people above a certain age. However, as long as you are under the age of 75 you will still be able to take out a personal pension plan instead, and this may be more suitable if you expect your pattern of working to be more variable than in the past, because, say, you are working on a consultancy basis with fluctuating earnings.

Will you be better off?

This is not as strange a question as it may seem. As **Chapter 5** makes clear, working can bring with it certain costs, the most obvious of which is the cost of getting to work (and which could be a higher proportion of your income than before if, say, you are still working five days a week but for half-days only). Before you take the plunge, particularly if you are proposing to take a pay cut, you need to cost out your new job thoroughly. For example, you may be better off in financial terms by claiming means-tested state benefits than by taking a low-paid job with no prospects. **Chapter 6** gives more information on benefits if you have a low income.

Non-financial factors

Although money is usually the main motive for carrying on working, other factors such as companionship and job satisfaction are also important. However, you will probably have to stop work, or at least scale it down, at some point, so even if you have the chance to carry on your current work after your normal retirement date, you may want to consider changing the way you work in order to build up alternative networks of friends and activities outside work.

Old employer or new job?

Even if you are happy with your current employer, you may feel that the time has come to move to, say, different hours or a different role within the company. Although some employers have schemes for seconding older staff to other roles, such as to work for charities for a few months, and others may welcome proposals for part-time working if they are trying to reduce staff numbers or change working patterns within the organisation, your employer may not agree to your proposals. You could strengthen your case by looking at your proposal from the employer's point of view and finding solutions to the objections you anticipate. For example, your bid to move to a job-share arrangement may be strengthened if you can make the bid jointly with another willing sharer. For secondments and volunteer placements, the organisation called Action: Employees in the Community* offers a service matching up companies and charities.

Part-time or full-time?

Part-time work can be an undeniably attractive way of weaning yourself off full-time work, and some employers are reducing the number of full-time employees in favour of part-timers. The employment rights of part-timers have also recently been improved. However, some employment rights (such as the right to statutory redundancy pay) are lost altogether to people over state pension age. And check what benefits a prospective employer is offering; they may be less generous to part-timers than to full-time employees. See **Chapter 13** for more on employees' rights.

However, do be on your guard against some of the 'get rich quick' ads in newspapers and against those home-working schemes, often paid on a piece-work basis, where it is virtually impossible to make a reasonable income.

Employee or go it alone?

An employer may not be prepared to keep you on as a part-timer but still consider giving you some work as a freelance or consultant. This gives them greater flexibility but may also suit you, freeing you up to work for other people as well or giving you the chance to develop your abilities along different lines. Being self-employed also has some tax advantages, since you can set more expenses off against your tax bill. And you may see retirement or redundancy, with a lump sum in your hand, as a golden opportunity to set up on your own.

But there are potential problems. One reason that your employer may be more prepared to consider this arrangement is that you will no longer qualify for sick pay, holiday pay, and other such benefits: you will have to earn enough to pay for them and other overheads such as stationery yourself. So don't make the mistake, when working out how much to charge, of simply taking your current salary and charging it by the hour or day (unless you have some greater tactical aim in mind!). Another potential hitch is that if you do most of your work for one employer, the Inland Revenue may class you as employed after all – see **Chapter 16**.

Types of work to consider

The careers department of the library in your nearest town should have directories of job opportunities at all ages. Some employers now actively seek to employ older people: examples are some food and DIY retailers. As described above, you may be able to continue in your current occupation on a freelance or consultancy basis: for example, executives in their 50s may be able to find short-term contracts. In Table 1 are other ways of using your skills, knowledge or other assets – many are suitable for part-time work from home, others could be the way in to a new career.

Table 1: Work possibilities

Using your knowledge
Consultancy
Trainer
Lecturer
Teacher/coach
Medical receptionist
Temporary accountant
Book-keeper

Using your skills
Selling
Freelance typing
Secretarial work
Gardening
Painter/decorator
Dress-maker
Florist
Cook/caterer
Home help
Counselling
Security officer

Using your assets
Landlord/lady
Taxi-driver
Word-processing
Desk-top publishing
Market gardening

Using your time
Caretaker
Warden
Club steward
Housekeeper
House-sitter
National Trust administrator
Market research interviewer

Ways back in
Housing officer (for local housing department or housing association)
Clerical assistant
Social work assistant
Nursing auxiliary

Voluntary work

If your primary reason for carrying on working is not financial – or you can't get a paid job at the moment but want to keep your hand in – voluntary work may be the answer. Try your local library, Citizens Advice Bureau or Council for Voluntary Service for lists of voluntary agencies in your area: local newspapers sometimes also carry ads. REACH*, the Scottish Corps of Retired Executives (SCORE)* and the Retired and Senior Volunteer Programme* are just some of the agencies that can provide information to retired people wanting to take up voluntary work. The British Executive Service Overseas* is an agency finding voluntary work overseas, usually in developing countries. However, before taking the plunge, check on the commitment you will be making and how expenses will be paid.

Effect on benefits

If you are receiving unemployment benefit, you have to be 'available for work' – which normally means looking for work and being able to start immediately. However, if you are doing voluntary work and can show that it would be unreasonable to give it up immediately if necessary, you may in some situations be classed as 'available for work'. See leaflet FB26 *Voluntary and part-time workers* from your local social security (also called Benefits Agency) office.

CHAPTER 13

Getting a new job

While discrimination on the grounds of age undeniably exists, older people may have a lot to offer employers and canny job-hunters can turn age to their advantage. This chapter looks at how you can improve your chances, as well as your rights once you are in work.

Turning age to your advantage

Research suggests that experience and skill has as much effect on your performance as your age. Bearing this in mind, first spend some time researching the fields of employment you're interested in, thinking about what you have to offer and how this corresponds to employers' interests. But be realistic: as well as your dream job, are you prepared to change direction if necessary?

When it comes to approaching potential employers, you may need (gently!) to challenge any stereotypes of older workers on the basis of solid fact: your own individual skills and qualities. Table 1 shows typical stereotypes of younger and older workers.

For example, in your application and at interview, you may need to go prepared to show, from your previous work, how flexible, computer-literate, or 'trainable' you could be. But, as for any job-hunter, of any age, it is essential to do this in the context of the job description: it's no good, and could even be counter-productive, concentrating on your 20 years of management experience, say, if the job description makes it clear that

Table 1: How employers perceive workers

Employers think that: younger workers have:	older workers have:
Ambition	Stability
Trainability	Reliability
Flexibility	Work commitment
Health	Responsibility
Skills in using information technology	Maturity
	Managerial skills
Qualifications	
Mobility	

Source: Institute of Manpower Studies

the job involves working largely on your own to produce your own work. Instead, in this example, you might find it more helpful to show how your management experience has helped you organise your own time efficiently.

Qualifications can be another false friend. With the continuous introduction of new types of educational system and training in different industries, you don't have to be very old for your qualifications to have been superseded by a new system. If so, the employer may appreciate being told what the current equivalent of your qualification is, or you might find it better to concentrate instead on relevant experience.

If you really aren't very computer-literate, or haven't got absolutely appropriate qualifications, and the field you are interested in requires them, you may need to consider getting some training yourself, in your own time, to demonstrate that you would be willing and able to acquire the necessary knowledge. Contact your local authority adult education service or local Training and Enterprise Council (your JobCentre can give you the address) to ask about courses available in your area.

The addresses and phone numbers of organisations marked with an asterisk can be found in the address section at the back of the guide.

Where to look

As well as the sources below, consider approaching employers 'on spec'. You can identify companies in your chosen field through directories like UK *Kompass Register*, specialist trade magazines, and local business directories. Main libraries should have these. Sources of vacancies include:

- JobCentres (in the phone book under 'Employment Service')
- newspapers
- specialist and trade magazines; the ads will also suggest which employment agencies specialise in your field
- local radio station 'job spots'
- professional and trade associations – some provide information on vacancies
- personal contacts – as well as being effective, this is one way of getting past employers' preconceptions
- employment agencies: check ads to see which advertise in your field of work; the Federation of Recruitment and Employment Services* publishes a handbook of its members and their specialist services; also check publications such as *The Executive Grapevine* (ask in your library).

Where to get help

Employment agencies

Employment agencies aren't allowed to charge you for placing you in a job, except for some jobs, for example actors and models. Instead, employers pay them – agencies may see this as an incentive to fill posts on their books, rather than only putting you forward for jobs that are exactly what you're looking for. Better agencies will interview you and give advice on the opportunities available, interviews, what salary you should expect, and how to prepare a CV. If you have any complaints about an agency, contact the Employment Agency Standards Office*.

If you are looking for paid work in the charity sector, try Charity Recruitment* and for ex-Service men and women there are, of course, the Forces Resettlement organisations. There are also a number of agencies which provide short-term work for business executives. These are the Board Appointments department of the Institute of Directors*, and members of the Association of Temporary and Interim Executive Services*.

Once you have booked up with an agency, keep in touch with them regularly. Make sure they check with you before circulating your CV; otherwise, it may be sent more than once to the same company, or to one where you don't want it to go. If you see ads they've placed for jobs you're interested in, ring up to make sure your details are put forward.

Self-marketing or career consultancies

These offer training and support in job-hunting, and may provide library facilities and secretarial services, too. Anyone can start up one of these consultancies (there are no controls), so be careful before committing yourself, especially since the fees can run into thousands. If you decide to use a consultancy, check:

- exactly what you'll get for your money
- how long the company has been in existence, how many of their clients found a job, and how long it took on average
- that there are staff with both experience of the market and counselling qualifications (the British Association for Counselling* can tell you which consultants are members)
- whether the company complies with the Institute of Personnel and Development* (IPD) voluntary code of conduct for career consultants (the IPD can tell you about members who follow this code).

Employment Service

This is the name of the government agency which runs local JobCentres and unemployment benefit offices: you will find your local offices in the phone book under 'Employment Service'. The leaflet *Just the Job*, from your JobCentre, gives information about the help available to job-seekers; to summarise, after you've been registered as unemployed for three months, you can go to a free Job Search seminar or a Job

Review Workshop. After six months, you may be directed to a Jobclub or Restart course, and after 12 months to a Jobplan workshop.

If you have special needs or difficulties in finding work because of a disability or health problem, your local JobCentre can put you in touch with a Disability Employment Adviser: and most local authorities have Careers Officers who specialise in helping people with disabilities. The Disability Alliance ERA* and the Royal Association for Disability and Rehabilitation* (RADAR) also publish useful directories.

Special help for older people

There are a number of groups and agencies, often set up on a voluntary basis by members, which help older people to find both paid and voluntary work. These groups, such as the Third Age Network* in the South-East, are often organised on a local basis: the Reaction Trust* is a network organisation that should be able to put you in touch with any local groups. Your local authority Careers Officer may also be able to help.

Sorting out a CV

Your CV should include your name, address and day and evening phone numbers: education, training and qualifications; achievements; career history and work experiences (most recent job first); and any skills you have, such as foreign languages. Stress the skills you have that are relevant to your potential employer, perhaps in a short introductory summary to your CV or in your covering letter.

Aim for two or three pages at most, typed or word-processed on one side of the paper only. Tailoring the CV to each job you apply for is an investment that will bear dividends, so it will help greatly if you can get it typed on a word processor. Jobclubs and Job Search seminars (run by JobCentres) provide access to word processors, stamps and stationery. Use good quality A4 paper: reserved shades of cream, grey or blue are acceptable, but won't get you any further than white. Binders, folders, title pages etc. are unnecessary and may be off-putting.

Shun the phrases that employers will see with monotonous regularity, such as 'good communication skills'. Instead, be specific and positive about what you've achieved. There's no need to mention salary details, referees, dependent children, marital status or religion, though you could give salary expectations in the covering letter. Don't leave unexplained career gaps – if you are not working at the moment, be honest about it but mention anything you're doing that may be relevant to the job you've applied for, such as voluntary work. Presentation, grammar and spelling are important, so get someone objective to check the CV.

If you're unsure about presentation, or don't have access to a word processor, you might benefit from getting a CV bureau to produce your CV for you: prices range up to around £60. If you decide to use an agency, don't expect miracles – you'll probably just end up with the information you give them repeated in a reasonably respectable format. And there is the risk that prospective employers might recognise a bureau CV, which might go against you. However, you might get a more imaginative result if your CV is produced after a face-to-face interview, rather than by post or over the phone. Bureaux are also quick: they take only a few days and some offer a same- or next-day service. Some will help with covering letters too. Always ask for a first draft and check it carefully.

Tips for job applications

You must show how your skills and experience match the requirements of the job. So, before you put pen to paper, analyse the ad carefully. Follow any instructions exactly – for instance, if it says phone for an application form, don't send your CV instead. Underline the key job requirements and write down how you fulfil them, backing up what you say with proof. But don't be put off if you don't exactly match the requirements. Application forms usually have a section for you to add extra supporting information, which is your chance to reiterate how you meet the requirements.

Covering letters should be short and to the point. Say why you are applying and why you should be considered for the job.

Views differ about whether application forms should be typed or handwritten. If you do use handwriting – and do so if you're asked to – it should be in black or dark blue ink. In your application, be positive about your achievements and don't mention failures or ways in which you don't meet the job criteria (though, as with CVs, you should be honest about any career gaps).

Coping with interviews

Find out as much as possible beforehand about the company (e.g. from its annual report) and the people who will interview you. Work out what they will look for, and list key points about yourself to mention. Write down answers to common questions such as 'Why do you want this job?'. Practise answers to tricky ones, too, and work out your own questions to ask.

Plan your route to the interview, and set off early. Don't smoke, even if invited to do so, and do remember that cups of tea or coffee can be difficult to handle.

Listen carefully to questions and answer them fully, but stick to the point. Watch how the interviewer responds. Find opportunities to mention the key points about yourself, and be positive about your achievements. Be wary about raising matters like holiday and 'perks' in a first interview, though you can ask about salary range.

Your rights as an employee

You needn't be so grateful to have a job that you put up with poor treatment from your employer. The first thing to check is that you are actually an employee, rather than an independent contractor. There are advantages to being an independent contractor, particularly for tax. But these are counter-balanced by the obligations and liabilities that bind your employer if you are an employee. In any case, even if you and your employer treat you as self-employed, the Inland Revenue may not agree. This can have some unwelcome consequences – see **Chapter 16**.

The main rights of employees are described below: leaflets on your rights as an employee are available from Citizens Advice

Bureaux, JobCentres or other Employment Service offices. However, in many cases, you acquire these rights only after working for the employer for two years. Table 2 summarises which of the main rights are available to which employees.

Written terms and conditions of employment
All but short-term employees have a right to get written details of their terms and conditions of employment within two months of starting. But, in practice, many employers confirm a job offer by letter, with which they include the terms and conditions. This should cover such things as who the employer actually is, your starting date, job title, place of work, rate and method of payment, hours, holiday pay, the pension scheme, notice period, length of employment (if not permanent) and (if there are at least 20 employees) disciplinary and grievance

---

Table 2: When you acquire employment rights

No minimum service
Statutory sick pay
Anti-discrimination rights
Right not to be dismissed for taking certain actions on health and safety grounds
Itemised pay statement
Time off in certain circumstances (see opposite)
Rights in insolvency (but 4 weeks' service to get pay in lieu of notice)

One month's minimum service
Payment on medical suspension
Written terms and conditions of employment

2 years' minimum service
Redundancy rights (not if aged 65 or over)
Unfair dismissal (not if aged 65 or over)
Written reasons for dismissal

procedures. You don't have to sign any contract you're given, although if you continue to work for the employer once you've received it, you're still likely to be bound by its conditions. The terms set out in the statement cannot be altered without the consent of both parties. Note that if a business is being transferred to a new owner the employees must go with it on the same terms and conditions (although it is not clearly established which pension rights need to be transferred).

Itemised pay statements
All employees are entitled to a pay slip, showing the gross pay, deductions (and the reasons for them) and the net pay.

Holidays
You don't have an automatic right to holidays, even bank holidays – it's all down to the contract you agree with your employer. So check that your holiday rights are specified in your terms and conditions of employment.

Time off
However, you are entitled to reasonable time off:

- to carry out trade union duties or relevant training, if you are an official of a recognised train union – with pay
- for some trade union activities, if you are a member of a recognised trade union – without pay
- to carry out your duties as a safety representative – with pay
- to carry out public duties such as being a Justice of the Peace or prison visitor – without pay.

Sick pay
However short a time you've worked for a company, and whether you are part-time or full-time, employers are responsible for giving you statutory sick pay when you are off sick for four or more days in a row. You get this for the first 28 weeks of any illness (after which you will move on to other types of state benefit – see page 25). But an employer does not have to keep your job open indefinitely, although they should treat you sympathetically.

Anti-discrimination

However recently you started work, it is illegal for an employer to discriminate against you:

- on the grounds of sex, race or marital status
- by failing to give equal treatment (in terms of both pay and conditions) to people of either sex carrying out 'like work'
- because you are (or are not) a union member.

There is no law against discrimination on the grounds of age – unlike in the USA, Canada and the Netherlands.

Rights on redundancy

For more on redundancy, see **Chapter 3**; but you have a right to redundancy pay, and paid time off to look for work only if you have two year's service (see Table 2) and not at all if you are over 65.

Rights on insolvency

If your employer is formally insolvent and owes you money, you may be entitled to some payments from the government's redundancy fund. These include up to eight weeks' arrears of pay, up to six weeks' holiday pay and pay in lieu of notice, subject to maximum weekly amounts (the maximum week's pay is currently £205). If you think you qualify, apply for these payments first to the liquidator or receiver, who will have the necessary application forms.

Unfair dismissal

Dismissing you will normally only be 'fair' if the employer can show that it was due to:

- a reason related to your conduct
- a reason related to your capability or qualifications for the job
- redundancy
- a legal duty or restriction which prevents the employment being continued (e.g. you are a lorry driver, but have been banned from driving, and your employer has no other suitable job for you)

- 'some other substantial reason' – (e.g. a close relative sets up a business competing with your employer, taking advantage of your connections).

You should be given written reasons for dismissal, if you request them, within 14 days. If you feel that you were unfairly dismissed (and are under 65 – if not, you don't get this protection at all), you can take your claim to an Industrial Tribunal. You may also have a claim for 'constructive dismissal' if you were placed in an untenable position and forced to resign. You must have two years' service with the employer to qualify for unfair dismissal, although there is no minimum service if you have been dismissed for seeking to enforce, in good faith, statutory employment protection such as anti-discrimination rights.

If you have worked for four weeks or more, you are entitled to a week's notice or pay in lieu, unless the contract of employment specified a longer period of notice. After two years, one week's notice is required for each year of work, up to a maximum of 12 weeks.

If you work part-time

The rights of part-time employees have recently improved. In December 1994 the House of Lords ruled that it discriminated against women, who are more likely to work part-time, to set different minimum lengths of service for full-time and part-time employees to qualify for various legal employment rights. As a result, the Government has removed all the previous qualifying conditions based on the number of hours worked per week – although the minimum lengths of service still apply.

Another 1994 ruling, this time in the European Court, ruled that part-timers barred from their employer's pension scheme who could prove sex discrimination would have the right to join the scheme, with some retrospective claims allowed. But the full implications for part-timers in the United Kingdom will not be clear until the Pensions Bill which was before Parliament at the time of writing passes into law.

Part-timers may still find that individual employers are less generous to them than to full-time employees, for example in the fringe benefits offered. However, since most part-timers are women the different treatment could be challenged if it is shown to be due to sex discrimination.

The European Community has put forward a draft 'directive' which will force companies to treat part-timers in all respects as full-time workers, in proportion to the hours worked. However, the United Kingdom has opted out of this directive.

If your rights are breached
If you have any concerns about your treatment at work, contact your local Citizens Advice Bureau. You may have the right to take your case to an Industrial Tribunal: your JobCentre can give you the necessary information. You may also be able to get help from ACAS* – the Advisory, Conciliation and Arbitration Service. And for worries about sexual or racial discrimination, contact the Equal Opportunities Commission* or Commission for Racial Equality* respectively.

CHAPTER 14

STARTING YOUR OWN BUSINESS

If you decide to set up on your own, you will immediately be beset by choices. Should you set up as a 'sole trader' or start your own limited company? Should you register for Value Added Tax (VAT)? Once you think about all the decisions to be taken, you may wonder whether it is worthwhile! Your attitude towards this sort of question is probably quite a sound indicator of whether you are really suited to self-employment, the sort of business to which you may be most suited, and to the help you are likely to need. For example, if your primary interest is in producing something and you find the organisation tiresome, you may need either to set up in the simplest way possible, or make your first task looking for someone to help with the administrative side of the business.

Which method of trading?

'Sole trader'

This does not mean that you have to work alone, but that you are totally and solely responsible for the business. You take all the profits, but you are also personally liable for all debts incurred to the full extent of your means – including personal possessions outside the business, such as your home. Many small businesses start as sole traders and are later turned into limited companies.

Partnership

This is an association of 2 to 20 people, trading together as one firm and sharing the profits. One or more of the partners may be a 'sleeping partner' who just puts in money. The partnership gets one tax return (each partner also gets a personal tax return), so what is shared out represents post-tax profits. If one partner absconded, the others would have to pay all the outstanding tax, including the absconder's share. All the partners can be held liable for the whole of the firm's debts, to the full extent of their personal means, in the same way as for sole traders. Partners pay the same National Insurance contributions as sole traders.

Limited company

A limited company is a legal entity, just as though it were a person, and must be conducted according to rules laid down by company law. These include producing audited accounts which must be filed at Companies House*, and the disclosure of the company's activities to the general public. However, statutory audits are no longer required for companies with annual turnovers of less than £350,000 (although an independent accountant's report is required for companies with turnovers between £90,000 and £350,000).

The shareholders are the owners of the company, but are liable for its debts only to the extent of the face value of their shares. (Under new EC legislation it is possible for one person to set up a company on his or her own but there must also be a separate company secretary.) If the shares are available to the general public and quoted on the Stock Exchange, then it is a public limited company ('plc'). Private companies – the majority – do not offer shares to the public and style themselves 'Limited' or 'Ltd'.

Franchises

The purchase of a franchise is the purchase of the right to use a particular method to run a particular kind of business. You – the 'franchisee' – are buying expertise and an image, sometimes the right to use and trade under a household name, from the 'franchisor'. You are at liberty to decide the most appropriate method of trading, whether as sole trader, in a partnership or through a limited company.

The entry price can be considerable, and will allow you to trade for a limited period only (typically five years) – it is for you to assess whether the potential rewards are worth it. Becoming a franchisee usually means that you will own the business assets (premises, equipment and so on) – although some franchisors prefer to own them and lease them to franchisees. But you will certainly not own the business method, and are likely to find that the franchisor lays down the essential business techniques you must use.

Which method for you?

The choice may not be clear-cut (and there are other less common options, such as setting up a co-operative). But key considerations will be the question of limited liability, the ease of raising finance, tax, and the administrative burden.

A limited company is clearly preferable if it is important to you to limit your liability (remember, though, that a director's liability is often extended by personal guarantees to a bank or other lender as security for a loan). Banks may prefer to lend to limited companies, and you may prefer to keep your business finances separate from your personal ones.

But these factors may be less important if yours is a very small business with low overheads, which is unlikely to run up debts. In this case, you may be swayed by the consideration that a limited company has to comply with the detailed rules of company law, is likely to cost more to set up, and will probably involve more paperwork. In any case, it is often better to start off as a sole trader, the most flexible form of business organisation with little red tape involved in setting it up.

Partnerships are a slightly different consideration, since they are the standard way of operating in some professions, such as medicine. However, you do have to consider the difficulties of working closely with a number of other people.

You need to be particularly careful if considering buying a franchise. For a franchise to be successful, it needs to combine a successful business idea with a proper level of support and promotion from the franchisor. If a capital sum is payable for an exclusive right to distribute goods or offer a certain service within a given area and no back-up is offered, consider whether you could set up a similar operation yourself and perhaps save a great deal of money.

Cowboy franchisors also exist. They charge a relatively high buy-in fee but offer little or no training or equipment. Or the sum involved may be low – about £5,000 say – but you get very little for it. To reduce the risks, get any potential agreement vetted by a solicitor and check the following points.

- Is the franchisor a member of the British Franchise Association*? Members are bound by a code of conduct.
- What experiences have the other franchisees had? A reputable franchisor should have no grounds to refuse a list of franchisees.

The formalities

If you don't do anything – in other words, simply set up as a freelance – you will technically be a sole trader. If setting up in a partnership, it is wise to have an agreement drawn up by a solicitor covering such things as each partner's share of the profits, how each share is to be valued if he or she wants to withdraw, and what happens on death. Other aspects are arrangements for holidays, how much each partner can draw, voting rights and what should happen in case of a dispute.

Limited companies must be registered with Companies House*, for which there is a fee. It is important to have professional help in registering a company: check whether your solicitor or accountant has expertise in this. You can also buy companies 'off the peg' through company registration agents: if you don't like the name you can change it through Companies House.

When you register your company, you must submit a 'memorandum of association' which must include details of the name of the company, the objects of the company, the amount of share capital and how it is divided into shares. There are other necessary forms on registration, including details of first directors and secretary and the address of the registered office.

Running the business

Your business name

You can trade under your own name or names. But you may prefer to use a name which attracts attention or says something about the business, and within certain limits you are free to do this. Useful booklets setting out the rules are available from Companies House*.

However, it is illegal to pass yourself or your business off as something which it is not, and if the name you have chosen to trade under is not your own surname, you must indicate the name of the owner(s) on all stationery and display it in your shop, office or place of work.

National Insurance

If you are a sole trader or partner, you must pay Class 2 National Insurance contributions: these protect your right to some state benefits, including state retirement pension and sickness benefit, but not to others. Class 2 contributions are £5.75 a week for the year from 6 April 1995, but you can claim exemption if your net yearly earnings from self-employment are below £3,260 (for 1995-6). You can pay them either by monthly direct debit or by quarterly bills. Details are available in leaflet NI 41 *National Insurance for Self-employed People*, from any social security (also called Benefits Agency) office.

People who pay Class 2 contributions must also pay Class 4 contributions, on any earnings between £6,640 and £22,800 (in the 1995-6 tax year), at a rate of 7.3 per cent. However, these contributions are assessed and collected by the Inland Revenue along with the income tax on your profits. Half the amount of Class 4 contributions can be deducted from your taxable profits before working out your income tax bill.

If you employ anyone you must pay Class 1 National Insurance contributions on any earnings between a 'lower' and 'upper' earnings limit – i.e. between £58 and £440 a week in the 1995-6 tax year. The rate for employers varies depending on earnings, but can be up to 10.2 per cent.

National Insurance contributions, of whatever class, no

longer have to be paid once you are over state retirement age. The only exception is the Class 1 contributions payable by employers.

If yours is a limited company, you as an individual pay the employee's share of your Class 1 contributions, and the company pays the employer's contribution.

Value Added Tax (VAT)

VAT is a tax on sales of goods and services, collected for the government by HM Customs and Excise. You may not have to register for VAT if your turnover is (or is expected to be) below a certain threshold, but it may save you money to register voluntarily.

The tax you pay on goods and services that you buy for your business is called 'input tax', and the tax you charge your customers is called 'output tax'. This is how it works: Bill buys raw materials for £235, inclusive of 17.5 per cent VAT: £35 is his input tax. He uses the materials to make goods selling for £450 before VAT, on which he has to charge output tax of £78.75. He deducts his input tax from his output tax and remits the balance (£78.75 − £35 = £43.75) to Customs and Excise, normally once a quarter. If his input tax had been greater than his output tax, he would have been refunded the difference.

The rate of VAT is 17.5 per cent (8 per cent on fuel), but some goods and services such as food are 'zero-rated' – i.e. taxed at 0 per cent – and others, such as insurance, are 'exempt' – i.e. outside the VAT system altogether. The difference is important. If you produce exempt goods or services, you don't charge VAT on them, but you can't claim the input tax on them either. If your product or service is zero-rated you can reclaim input tax without putting up your charges. And while trade in zero-rated supplies counts towards your turnover for the registration limit, trade in exempt supplies does not.

Do you need to register?

You must register if your 'taxable turnover' for the previous 12 months reaches £46,000 (in the 1995-6 tax year), or if you expect turnover for the next 30 days to exceed it, or if you buy a business which is already registered. To register, contact your local VAT office (under 'Customs and Excise' in the phone book), which can also supply a range of leaflets.

Once you have registered, you need to keep scrupulous records of all transactions: there are stiff penalties for failing to make VAT returns and payments on time. But there are some schemes which can simplify VAT for small businesses. For example, if your taxable turnover excluding VAT is less than £350,000 a year, you can opt to make annual rather than quarterly returns to the Customs and Excise.

If your turnover is below £350,000 a year, you can also opt for a 'cash accounting' basis. This means that the VAT you pay depends on the money you actually receive and pay out in each quarter, not what is invoiced. So you don't have to hand over VAT until you receive it from your customers – a great help, if payment normally takes some time to come through, or if you have bad debts.

Tax

From the tax point of view, there are advantages to being self-employed. For example, you can set more expenses against your income than if you are an employee. However, even if you class yourself as self-employed, the Inland Revenue may not agree. See **Chapter 16** for more on tax if you are self-employed.

Keeping records

The accounts you need to keep will depend on the business. If you have a limited company, you will have to pay for annual accounts to be produced and audited (unless your turnover is below a set limit – see page 180): if you are registered for VAT you will have to account for sales and purchases, and if you employ anybody, you will probably need to pay them under the PAYE system. All businesses need to keep some sort of accounts for the Inland Revenue (even if they need not necessarily always send them in – see page 230) in order to prove what their income and expenses are.

You can buy printed account books for small businesses

which may be suitable, or you can buy blank ledgers and mug up on simple accounting methods for yourself. If you are at all unsure about accounts, ask your accountant to set up a system and teach you how to use it. Some basic points to remember are:

- Always try to collect a written record of any transaction, even if it is only a till note or note on the back of an envelope.
- Never throw any paperwork away unless convinced it is unnecessary – keep copies of invoices sent, received, receipts, cheque-book stubs, bank statements etc.
- Keep a petty cash book to record out-of-pocket expenses.
- If you employ people, keep a separate wages book to record pay, income tax, NI contributions etc.
- Keep paid invoices separate from unpaid.
- If you are registered for VAT, there must be a special VAT column in all your records.

Bank accounts

Even if you are working as a sole trader and on your own, it is still worth opening a special bank account for the business. This makes it easier to draw up your accounts and easier to borrow money from the bank, and bank charges on a bank account can be claimed as an allowable expense against tax.

Banks offer a variety of services to small businesses, but their charges for small businesses can be steep. So it is worth shopping around and negotiating before setting up, since it may not be easy to transfer a business account if you have an overdraft or other loan.

Licences

Many trades and businesses need to be licensed, for example credit businesses. You can find out which businesses need licences by contacting your local authority planning office. The Office of Fair Trading★ also has leaflets describing trading regulations such as the Trade Descriptions Act.

Contact any local Employment Service office for the address of your local TEC.
- Grants from local authorities, the government or the European Community – not easily available, but always worth exploring, particularly if you are starting up in an area of high unemployment. Contact the Department of Trade and Industry* or your local Training and Enterprise Council (or Local Enterprise Company in Scotland).

If you are seeking large amounts of finance, it is essential to discuss the possible sources with an accountant, who can also advise on the most tax-effective ways to borrow and the right mixture of finance for your business. You may be able to reduce the amount you need to borrow by leasing equipment.

For certain types of business, factoring can help with finance: you hand over your sales invoices to a factoring company which pays you 80 per cent (say) of the amount you are owed straight away and chases the customer for the rest, generally keeping five per cent for the service.

Guarantees and security

Interest rates charged to small companies are often higher than those charged to the big blue-chip companies, to reflect the extra risks involved. And the lender will want as much reassurance as possible about repayment, often including personal guarantees from you as owner and perhaps insisting that you put up your home as security (so, if the business fails, you can lose your home). If your husband, wife or other relative approaches you to give a guarantee for their business, be particularly careful and consult your solicitor. Guarantees may be framed so that they last virtually indefinitely, so even after the original loan has been paid off you could find yourself being held responsible for your relative's financial position, or even losing your own home.

Finding sufficient guarantees can be difficult, and the government Small Business Loan Guarantee Scheme can help if you have already committed all your personal assets as security. The Scheme then guarantees 85 per cent of loans up to £250,000. The charge is 0.5 per cent a year of the whole loan on fixed interest rate lending and 1.5 per cent of the whole loan for variable rate lending. A booklet on the Scheme is available from Training and Enterprise Councils.

Sources of advice

A key one will clearly be your accountant, and, unless you have a cast-iron personal recommendation from someone in a similar line of business, it is worth interviewing several, asking about their areas of expertise and charges. You should find directories of accountants in your local reference library: some directories list accountants' specialisations.

Your local Training and Enterprise Council (called Local Enterprise Company in Scotland) is a good first point of contact if you're starting up a business. Each TEC is an independent company, with a contract with the government. They work with other business support agencies in the area to provide counselling, information, advice and business skills training for small and new businesses. For the address of your local TEC contact any local branch of the Employment Service, such as a Jobcentre or Unemployment Benefit Office.

A network of what are called 'Business Link' centres throughout the country is also being set up to provide advice and information on all aspects of business (in the phone book under 'Business Link'). And the DTI Small Firms Division publishes a variety of free leaflets, available from TECs. A useful source of information is the report 'Small Firms in Britain 1994' – published by HMSO for £5, or try your local library.

A large number of local enterprise agencies can also offer help to new businesses. Some run bureaux which exist to put entrepreneurs in touch with potential investors: the Local Investment Networking Company Ltd* is an umbrella organisation for these. The British Venture Capital Association* is the trade association for the UK venture capital industry and publishes an annual directory of members.

The Rural Development Commission* offers advice and loans to applicants from rural development areas who employ not more than 20 skilled people. There are around 20 local offices which can help with technical or business problems.

Who should be told?

Limited companies need to be properly registered, but all businesses also need to contact:

- The Inland Revenue – if you have left a job as an employee, send your P45 to your tax office as soon as possible, as you may qualify for a tax rebate.
- The Inland Revenue – for PAYE purposes, if you intend to employ someone.
- The DSS Contributions Agency★ (for National Insurance contributions).
- HM Customs and Excise, if you intend or need to register for VAT.
- Your bank.
- Your insurers (you may need a special policy – see page 187).
- Your mortgage lender.
- Any regulator from whom you will need a licence, e.g. the Office of Fair Trading★ if you intend to run a credit business and need a consumer credit licence.

Working from home

Planning permission

Your local authority planning department should have information, but you're unlikely to need permission if:

- the main use continues to be as a family home
- there are no employees
- there are no outward signs of the business, e.g. trade vehicles, business plate.

Above all there must be no 'nuisance' caused – i.e. no cause for your neighbours to complain.

Household bills may rise

If you're at home more, electricity and gas bills will go up, and probably your phone bill too. If you count as self-employed, you can get tax relief on any part of these expenses which was due to business use, and on insurance and cleaning costs.

Insurance

At the very least, you should tell your insurers that you are working from home – if you don't, and later make a claim, they could refuse to pay. You may be charged a higher premium if the risk of insuring you is higher – e.g. you are a decorator storing flammable materials at home. If you're not using anything more than a computer, say, your existing household policy may be adequate but check that your computer isn't worth more than the policy's 'single item limit'. If you use special or expensive equipment, employ people, or could be liable for loss or damage you cause, you will need a commercial policy – see page 187.

Will you pay business rates?

Business rates should not apply unless any part of your house has been altered or fitted with special equipment so that you couldn't immediately use it as an ordinary family home. If it has, you pay business rates on that part and council tax (domestic rates in Northern Ireland) on the rest.

Your home

If you own your home, it's sensible to tell your mortgage lender – especially if you're insured through them – but as long as it remains a home first and foremost you shouldn't have to pay extra interest. Beware of using part of your home just for work: you may have to pay capital gains tax on it if you make a gain when you move – see **Chapter 18**. If you're a tenant, check the tenancy agreement to make sure you're not breaking its terms. If you're self-employed, you can claim tax relief on the rent for any part of the home used exclusively for work.

PART 4

TAX AND RETIREMENT

CHAPTER 15

THE BASICS OF TAX

You may have waved goodbye to the work place but unfortunately this doesn't mean that you can wave goodbye to tax. Retired people are liable to tax on their income in the same way as anyone else, with one major exception: the benefits of advancing years can mean a lower tax bill because of higher personal allowances given to people of 65 and over.

If you've worked for an employer most of your life and paid tax through the Pay-As-You-Earn (PAYE) scheme, you may not have needed to give much thought to the thorny subject of tax. However, a basic grasp of the subject will help you to:

- make the most of the change that retirement brings to your financial circumstances
- identify ways you can rearrange your finances to make the most of the tax system
- prepare yourself for more direct contact with your tax office (you'll find a detailed look at dealing with the tax authorities in **Chapter 19**).

Most of this Chapter is devoted to income tax: the main tax that you'll have to pay on your income from pensions and investments. First you'll find an explanation of the basics of income tax to give you an idea of how income tax is worked out. Then there's a detailed look at tax on pensions: what's taxed and how you pay the tax. If you have income from savings and investments, you'll find an introduction to how it is taxed (**Chapter 17** gives a fuller guide to tax on investments).

Once you've got a clear idea of how your income is liable to be taxed, you'll find ways of keeping your tax bill to a minimum, which looks at the tax-reducing outgoings and allowances you can claim, with practical steps you can take to protect your entitlement to the higher age-related allowances. Finally, there's a look at how tax can affect your changing circumstances in retirement.

The basics of income tax

You don't have to pay income tax on all the money you have coming in (from your pensions, your investments and any sparetime earnings, for example). In any tax year – which runs from 6 April in one year to 5 April in the following year – you pay tax only on what the Revenue calls your taxable income. You can get a rough idea of this by taking these three steps:

- **Your income for tax purposes** Take all the money you have coming in and subtract any tax-free income and any other money you've received which isn't liable to income tax – e.g. the proceeds from selling unit trusts or a lump sum you took from your pension.
- **Your total income** Subtract payments you make on which you get full *tax relief* which are called your *outgoings*. But see below for what to do with outgoings on which tax relief is restricted. Examples of some outgoings you can deduct are Gift Aid donations to charity, allowable expenses in employment or, if you're self-employed, half your Class 4 National Insurance contributions. See page 204 for more outgoings.
- **Your taxable income** Deduct your full personal allowances (see Table 1) from your total income to arrive at your taxable income – i.e. the income on which you will pay income tax. But see below for where to include fixed-relief allowances.

How much income tax?

Once you know what your taxable income is, you can work out the amount of tax you owe in each tax year. For the 1995-6 tax year, there are three rates of income tax, each charged on different slices of your income (continues on page 198):

THE BASICS OF TAX

EXAMPLE 1

Wilf Smith is 60 and married: he retired early from his job as a university lecturer. By the end of the 1995-6 tax year the money he had coming in will have amounted to £22,600. But he won't pay income tax on all of this. First he takes away sums which aren't income: £50 tax-free income from his National Savings Ordinary account, £300 he inherited and the £1,000 proceeds from cashing in some unit trusts.

The next things to think about are his outgoings: £2,400 interest he pays on his mortgage, and the £600 he paid to Oxfam under the Gift Aid scheme. He ignores his mortgage payments, on which he has already received tax relief by making lower payments to his lender, but deducts his Gift Aid donation. Lastly, he takes away his personal allowance of £3,525 which leaves a taxable income of £17,125. He can also deduct the married couple's allowance, but because this is a fixed-relief allowance, he deducts its value once he's worked out how much tax he pays (see **Example 2**).

1	**Wilf's income for tax purposes**	
	Money coming in	£22,600
	Deduct tax-free income	
	Interest from National Savings Ordinary Account	£50
	Deduct money not liable to income tax	
	Inheritance	£300
	Unit trust proceeds	£1,000
	Income for tax purposes	£21,250
2	**Wilf's total income**	
	Deduct outgoings	
	Gift Aid donation	£600
	Total income	£20,650
3	**Wilf's taxable income**	
	Deduct allowances	
	Personal allowance	£3,525
	Taxable income	£17,125

- On the first £3,200 of taxable income, you pay tax at the lower rate of 20 per cent.
- On the next £21,100 (i.e. on taxable income between £3,201 and £24,300), you pay tax at the basic rate of 25 per cent.
- On any taxable income over £24,300, you pay higher-rate tax at 40 per cent.

To get your final tax bill, add up the amounts of tax due on each slice of your taxable income (see Example 2). This will give you your final tax bill unless:

- you are entitled to one of the fixed-relief allowances (see page 209)
- you can deduct an outgoing on which tax relief is restricted and you have not already received tax relief at source.

Doing the sums is simply a matter of multiplying the amount of the allowance and/or outgoing by the rate of tax relief – e.g. 15 per cent – and then deducting the result from the tax bill you've already worked out.

EXAMPLE 2

Wilf Smith's taxable income is £17,125. The first £3,200 of his taxable income is taxed at 20 per cent – a bill of £640 – and the remainder at 25 per cent – a bill of £3,481.25. So Wilf's tax bill before deducting his married couple's allowance is £4,121.25. The married couple's allowance is £1,720 but relief is restricted to 15 per cent so Wilf can deduct £258 from his tax bill so far to give a total tax bill for the year of £3,863.25.

Wilf's taxable income		£17,125.00
Tax: 20% of £3,200		£640.00
25% of £13,925		£3,481.25
Total tax on £17,125		£4,121.25
less:	£258	£3,863.25

Paying income tax

In practice, most tax is deducted on your behalf at source (i.e. before you get your income) and most tax relief is also given at source (i.e. by making lower payments). If you owe more tax than has been collected at source – for example, you're a higher-rate taxpayer, or you do the odd bit of self-employed work – you will be sent a bill for the tax you owe. If you owe less tax than has been deducted, you can usually reclaim the overpaid tax.

Pay-As-You-Earn (PAYE)

If you will be receiving a pension from a former employer, it's likely that you will pay your tax through the PAYE system as you did when you were still an employee and received your weekly or monthly payslip. The tax office will therefore continue to send your ex-employer or the pension fund a tax code and you a *Notice of Your Income Tax Code* which will enable you to check that what's included in the code is correct. If you have lots of different sources of income, it's likely that you'll be sent a tax return to fill in which gives the tax office the information it needs to get your tax code right.

Tax on your income

Once you've retired, your main source of income is likely to be the pension you receive, whether it's from the state, an employer pension scheme or a personal pension plan. You may also have income from savings and investments on which you may have to pay tax. Most state benefits are tax-free; the main exceptions are unemployment benefit, widowed mother's allowance, widow's pension, and a few benefits if you're disabled or sick.

Income from pensions

Some pensions are tax-free, but most are taxable.
State retirement pensions
You will be liable to tax on any of the following:

- **Basic state retirement pension** This is a flat-rate pension paid to anyone who has paid enough National Insurance contributions.
- **State Earnings Related Pension (SERPS)** The pension you get is linked to your earnings since 6 April 1978.
- **Graduated pension** This is paid if you were employed between 1961 and 1975.
- **Non-contributory retirement pension** This is paid to people of 80 or over who are getting less than the normal state retirement pension.
- **Adult dependency allowance** This is paid to a married man drawing state pension whose wife is not yet old enough to qualify for her own state pension.

Note that any state pension a married woman gets counts as her income, even if it is based on her husband's National Insurance contributions. The exception is any adult dependency addition her husband gets, which counts as his income for tax purposes. See **Chapter 4** for more on state pensions.

Although state retirement pensions are taxable, tax isn't deducted from them before they are paid. There will be tax to pay only if your state pension, when added to income from other sources (e.g. an employer pension or investment income), comes to more than your outgoings and allowances. If your only income is from the basic state pension, you'll have no tax to pay since your income (in the 1995-6 tax year) will be below the amount of your personal allowances.

The amount of pension which will be included in your income is the total of the weekly amounts payable over the tax year. This applies even if you have chosen to have your pension paid four-weekly or quarterly.

Employer pensions

If you receive a pension from a former employer, the full amount is taxable. Note that if you chose to take a lump sum from your pension when you retired, this is tax-free. Tax on the pension part will normally be collected under PAYE.

When you first receive your employer pension, it might appear that it is being taxed at a higher rate than your earnings were before you retired. This is because the tax deducted will also take into account other taxable income which your tax office expects you to receive before tax over the coming tax year, such as the state retirement pension or investment income. If, by the end of the tax year, you have overpaid tax, the overpaid amount will be refunded.

Personal pensions
The full amount of the pension you get from an annuity bought with the proceeds of a personal pension plan is taxable (unlike annuities you buy of your own accord – see page 93). Many insurance companies deduct tax from each payment under PAYE so the correct amount of tax should be deducted. Other companies simply deduct tax at the basic rate. If your income is too low for you to pay tax, ask the company for a form to send to your tax office so that your pension can be paid in full without deduction of tax.

Pensions from abroad
You are normally liable for tax on nine-tenths of any pension from abroad, whether or not you have it paid in the UK. Pensions from abroad are generally taxed on a preceding year basis, which means that your tax bill for the 1995-6 tax year will be based on nine-tenths of the pension you received from abroad in the 1994-5 tax year. Pensions paid to the victims of Nazi persecution by the governments of Germany and Austria are tax-free.

Tax on redundancy payments

If you're made redundant, earnings your employer owes you when you leave your job – e.g. normal wages, pay in lieu of holiday, pay for working your notice period, commission – are taxed in the normal way under PAYE, but the following are tax-free:

- Any lump sum for any injury or disability which meant you couldn't carry on your job.
- Compensation for loss of a job done entirely or substantially outside the UK.

- Gratuities from the armed forces paid under Royal Warrant or by Order of Council.
- Certain lump sum benefits from employer pension schemes.
- Money your employer pays into a retirement benefit scheme or uses to buy you an annuity (if certain conditions are met).

Other payments are also tax-free if, added together, they come to less than £30,000. These are:

- Statutory redundancy payments under the government's redundancy payments scheme or a scheme 'approved' by the Inland Revenue.
- Pay in lieu of notice, in most circumstances, provided your conditions of service don't say you're entitled to it.
- Other payments made to you, as long as they are not payments for work done, not part of your conditions of service, and technically, at least, unexpected. This would normally cover redundancy payments over and above the government minimum.

Note that ex gratia payments on retirement are taxable, unless it is premature retirement due to redundancy or disability.

WHEN YOU RETIRE

Give your tax office advance warning (at least a month if not longer) of your retirement date, and tell them how much and what type of income you expect to get after you retire. This should help the tax office to give you the right PAYE code if you pay tax through PAYE.

You should also check that the DSS knows the date of your retirement. You will then be sent a pension claim form which allows you to choose how you get your state pension paid: either four-weekly into your bank account, or weekly in cash from a post office. You'll also be asked to give details of your retirement date and the day on which you would like your pension to be paid.

Income from savings and investments

The pension you get is unlikely to be your only source of income in retirement, especially if you have invested any lump sums you got when you retired. Depending on the investments you have chosen, you'll have to pay tax on the income you get from them, and if you have gone for capital growth, possibly tax on any capital gain you make. There's also the question of the inheritance tax your heirs may have to pay on the accumulated wealth that you leave them. Below is a brief look at the way income from your savings and investments is taxed. **Chapter 17** looks at this in more detail, together with capital gains tax: inheritance tax is covered in **Chapter 36**.

This and **Chapter 17** won't tell you how to pick the best investments for your retirement planning – see **Chapter 10** for that – but they will give you the information you need to compare returns after tax has been taken into account. Later on in this Chapter you'll see how the investments you choose and how they're taxed can influence the amount of age-related allowances you get if you are 65 or over.

How investment income is taxed

Income from investments is taxed in one of four ways:

- **Tax-free** There's no tax to pay on the income from these investments, though there can be specific conditions that you have to meet to keep the tax-free status. Personal Equity Plans (PEPs), TESSAs and National Savings Certificates are all examples of investments which produce tax-free income.
- **Taxable** You'll be paid the income without having tax deducted but unless you are a non-taxpayer, tax will be due. National Savings Income Bonds and National Savings Capital Bonds are taxed in this way.
- **Taxed** This income, which includes interest on bank and building society accounts, will normally be paid with basic-rate tax already deducted, but if you're a non-taxpayer you can either reclaim the tax or register to have the income paid without tax deducted. Higher-rate taxpayers have to pay extra tax.

- **Taxed with a tax credit** This applies mostly to income from shares, unit trusts and investment trusts. The income is paid to you after tax at 20 per cent has been deducted and you get a tax credit to show that this tax has been paid. If your highest tax rate is 20 or 25 per cent, there's no more tax to pay. If you're a non-taxpayer, you can usually reclaim the 20 per cent deducted, and if you're a higher-rate taxpayer, you'll have to pay an extra 20 per cent.

Reducing your tax bill

As explained in 'The basics of income tax' at the beginning of the chapter, you don't have to pay tax on all of the money you have coming in. Apart from the unrealistic goal of choosing only tax-free income, the main way in which you can keep your tax bill down is by making the most of outgoings and allowances.

Making the most of outgoings

From a tax point of view, your outgoings are the amounts of money that you spend on which you get tax relief – i.e. which you can deduct from your income for tax purposes to arrive at your total income. There are three main types of outgoing:

- **Outgoings on which you receive full tax relief** where tax relief is given at your highest rate of tax and which can be deducted from your income for tax purposes to arrive at your total income.
- **Outgoings on which tax relief is restricted** where tax relief is fixed at the same rate – e.g. 15 per cent – for all taxpayers.
- **Expenses** which are outgoings which can be deducted only from the income to which they relate – e.g. the cost of advertising the home you let can be deducted only from the rent you get from letting the home.

The mechanics of getting tax relief vary depending on the outgoings. You may have to claim money back from the Revenue (or you'll get a lower tax bill), get it back through the

PAYE system by having the outgoings taken into account when working out your income tax code, or hand over less money in the first place. In practice, you will get tax relief on most fixed-relief outgoings at source. This means that whoever you are paying asks you to pay what you owe less 15 per cent, for example.

So, if you pay an insurance company £100 for a medical insurance policy for someone aged over 60, for example, you get your tax relief at source by handing over only £75 – i.e. £100 less £25 which is 25 per cent (tax at the basic rate) of £100.

Many of the outgoings you can use to reduce your tax bill, such as pension contributions and the payroll giving scheme, are linked to work – whether you're an employee or self-employed. See **Chapter 16** for more on these. But if you are no longer working there are still some useful outgoings that you can claim.

Interest on loans for your home
You get tax relief on the interest you pay on the first £30,000 of loans to buy your only or main home. Since 6 April 1995, you have been able to get relief at 15 per cent only. You'll get relief at this rate even if you pay no tax. Loans taken out before 6 April 1988 to improve a main home, or to buy homes for dependent relatives or a former wife or husband, also qualify for tax relief at 15 per cent.

In most cases, you get the tax relief at source by paying less to your lender through the 'Mortgage Interest Relief At Source' (MIRAS) system. If your mortgage is not in MIRAS, you have to claim the relief, usually by entering the amount of mortgage interest you pay on your annual tax return, and enclosing a certificate of mortgage interest paid.

Interest on loans for property you let
Interest on any amount of loans to buy or improve a property you let count as an expense which can be deducted from the rental income.

Interest on a loan to buy an annuity
You can get tax relief on the interest you pay on up to £30,000

of loans to buy an annuity if you are 65 or over and the loan is secured against your only or main home. Although you get tax relief in the same way as on a normal mortgage, it is in addition to any tax relief you get on mortgage interest to buy the home. Relief has been restricted to 25 per cent since 6 April 1991, but you get the relief even if you're a non-taxpayer.

Interest on loans to pay inheritance tax
If you are sorting out someone's estate after their death, you can get tax relief for up to 12 months on the interest you pay on a loan taken out to pay the inheritance tax you owe on the estate, provided you actually pay the tax before probate is granted or letters of administration are received.

Gifts to charity
You can get tax relief on gifts you make to charity in the following ways (plus payroll giving, explained on page 224):

- By making covenanted payments under a covenant which is capable of lasting more than three years.
- By making single donations of at least £250 (net of basic-rate tax) under the Gift Aid scheme.

You give yourself basic-rate tax relief by subtracting an amount equivalent to the basic-rate tax on the payments before making them. The charity can then reclaim the basic-rate tax from the Revenue. For example, if you want a charity to be £100 better off under a deed of covenant, you need to give only £75 – i.e. £100 less the £25 basic-rate tax. If you are a higher-rate taxpayer, you also get higher-rate relief through the PAYE system or by getting a tax rebate or lower tax bill.

Covenants to individuals
These now qualify for tax relief only if they were taken out on or before 15 March 1988, and provided they are not changed in any way. You give yourself tax relief by deducting an amount equivalent to basic-rate tax from the payments, but no higher-rate tax relief is available.

THE BASICS OF TAX

Private medical insurance
If you are aged 60 or over, you can get basic-rate tax relief on private medical insurance policies. There are restrictions on the kind of policies which attract tax relief – e.g. only policies for conventional medicine are covered and any cash benefit for policyholders while they are in hospital must be limited to £5 a day.

You can also get tax relief on these policies if, whatever your own age, you pay the premium on behalf of another person who is 60 or over.

Maintenance payments
You can get tax relief on maintenance payments that you're legally obliged to make to an ex-wife or ex-husband. You don't get tax relief on voluntary payments.

For payments under an order applied for before 15 March 1988 (and in place by 30 June 1988), relief is limited to the amount you actually paid (and which qualified for relief) in the 1988-9 tax year. The only exception is where the court order provided for automatic increases in payments. The same rules apply to maintenance paid to children.

For orders applied for on or after 15 March 1988 (or applied for before that date but not in place until after 30 June 1988), relief is restricted to 15 per cent of £1,720 – which is the same as the married couple's allowance. This is known as the 'maintenance deduction'. You get no tax relief on payments direct to a child. In some circumstances you can save money by switching from the old to the new rules, e.g. if you have increased payments to a wife or husband since April 1989 and they are still below £1,720, and you make no payments to children.

Making the most of allowances

Subtracting allowances from your income is the last step in arriving at your taxable income. You subtract them either from your income to reduce the amount of income before your tax bill is worked out, or from your tax bill. Unlike outgoings which depend on you actually spending money on specific things, allowances depend on your personal situation.

There are three types of allowances:

- Full allowances, these will give you tax relief at your highest rate of tax. You will get these in full provided you qualify for them.
- Fixed-relief allowances where relief is restricted to 15 per cent of the allowance (including age-related married couple's allowances).
- Age-related allowances, which are, in effect, means-tested allowances for people aged 65 and over. There's more detail on these allowances later in the chapter.

Table 1: Full allowances for the 1995–6 tax year

Personal allowance	£3,525
Blind person's allowance	£1,200

Table 2: Fixed-relief allowances for the 1995–6 tax year

Married couple's allowance	15% of £1,720
Additional personal allowance	15% of £1,720
Widow's bereavement allowance	15% of £1,720

Full allowances
Everyone automatically gets the personal allowance of £3,525 in the 1995–6 tax year. You may also qualify for one of the other allowances, depending on your personal circumstances.

Blind person's allowance
You can claim this allowance if you are registered blind. In Scotland or Northern Ireland, where there is no register, the equivalent requirement is that you must be unable to perform any work for which eyesight is essential. If your income is too low for you to use the allowance in full, you can transfer any unused allowance to your husband or wife, whether or not he or she is blind.

Fixed-relief allowances
Married couple's allowance
If you are a married couple, you are eligible to deduct 15 per cent of the married couple's allowance of £1,720 from your tax bill in the 1995-6 tax year. This is usually deducted from the husband's income, unless his income is too low to use it all. However, you can elect to split the allowance between you or for the wife to have it all. Use the boxes provided on your annual tax return, or, if you don't get a tax return, ask your tax office for form 18. You have to do this before the start of the relevant tax year. You cannot transfer any extra allowance you get because of your age.

Additional personal allowance
You will qualify for this allowance if you are supporting a child who is 16 or under and you are single, separated, divorced or widowed or if you are a married man whose wife is totally incapacitated. If the child you are supporting is aged over 16 at the start of the tax year, you can continue claiming the allowance only if he or she is receiving full-time education or training full-time for a trade or profession for at least two years.

You may have to share this allowance if the child lives part of the time with you, and part of the time with another person who would also qualify for the allowance.

Widow's bereavement allowance
You can claim this allowance for the tax year of your husband's death and the following tax year (unless you remarry).

Claiming allowances
Although allowances aren't actually sums of money that you can claim, you do need to let your tax office know which allowances you qualify for so that they can be taken into account when working out your tax bill. If you get a tax return each year, use that to claim your allowances. Otherwise, write to your tax office telling them which allowance you think you can claim and why.

Age-related allowances
Many people who are 65 or over pay less tax than a younger

person receiving the same income. This is because, provided they meet the 'total income' means test, older people can deduct higher age-related allowances in place of the basic personal and married couple's allowances. The other full allowances are not affected and you continue to deduct them from your income as before. Inland Revenue leaflet IR121 *Income Tax and Pensioners* is helpful.

In the tax year that you reach 65, your personal allowance and married couple's allowance (if you qualify for it) are increased, provided your total income is below £14,600. If your income is above this level, the amount of the allowance that you can deduct from your income is reduced by £1 for every £2 you are over the £14,600 limit. The allowance is never reduced below the level of the relevant full allowance. Table 3 gives the maximum age-related allowances you can claim.

EXAMPLE 3
After deducting her outgoings from the income she gets from her state and employer pensions, 68-year-old Maureen Turner (who is single) has a total income of £15,500. She won't qualify for the full higher personal allowance of £4,630 for a person over 65 because her total income is over the £14,600 limit. Instead, she will get her higher personal allowance reduced.

She is over the limit by £900 – i.e. £15,500 minus £14,600. The allowance will be reduced by £1 for every £2 she is over the limit so she divides the £900 excess by 2 which gives £450. She will therefore get a higher allowance of £4,180 – i.e. the full allowance of £4,630 minus £450. However, that's still more than the basic personal allowance of £3,525.

Married couples
If you are married, you each qualify for the higher personal allowance based on your own age and you each have a total income limit of £14,600.

You will get a higher married couple's allowance if either of you reaches 65 in the 1995-6 tax year, and a higher allowance still if either of you reaches 75. However, the amount of the

THE BASICS OF TAX

Table 3: Age-related allowances for the 1995-6 tax year

Personal allowance
Aged 65 to 74 at any time in the tax year: up to £4,630
Aged 75-plus at any time in the tax year: up to £4,800

Married couple's allowance (relief restricted to 15 per cent)
Either partner aged 65 to 74 in tax year: up to £2,995
Either partner aged 75-plus in tax year: up to £3,035

allowance you can deduct from your income is always calculated using the husband's total income, even though he may qualify only because of his wife's age and even if they have elected for the wife to have some or all of the allowance. In addition, if a husband's total income is over the £14,600 limit, it is his higher personal allowance which will be reduced first, so a married man could have the full higher married couple's allowance but a reduced personal allowance.

EXAMPLE 4

Bert and Molly Jones are 77 and 76 respectively so qualify for the higher personal and married couple's allowances for people over 75. Bert has a total income of £15,100 and Molly a total income of £5,800.

Molly will be able to deduct the full personal allowance of £4,800 for people her age. Bert, however, is £500 over the £14,600 limit, which means a reduction of £250 (i.e. £500 divided by 2) in his higher personal allowance from £4,800 to £4,550. He will get the higher married couple's allowance for people over 75 of £3,035. However, the deduction from his tax bill will be 15 per cent of the married allowance since it is a fixed-relief allowance.

Special personal allowance
If you are a man who qualified for the married couple's allowance in the 1989-90 tax year because your wife is older than you, under the system of independent taxation for married couples which started on 6 April 1990 you could be worse off.

So you can claim a special allowance instead of your personal allowance. This is now worth claiming only if your wife was born before 6 April 1915 and you were born after 5 April 1930.

How not to lose your higher allowances
If your total income for the purposes of working out your age-related allowances looks as though it will exceed the total income limit of £14,600, there are steps you can take to protect those allowances.

First check the outgoings that you can deduct from your income for tax purposes to make sure that you can't reduce your total income in this way. Then examine your investments.

If you have investments which produce taxable income (whether paid taxed or before tax is deducted) you would almost certainly benefit from exchanging them for investments which are tax-free – provided you don't sacrifice more in return than you would gain in tax savings.

Beware of making a taxable gain on a life insurance policy (e.g. by cashing more than five per cent a year of the amount you invested in a single premium bond). This gain will swell your total income for the purposes of calculating your age allowance.

If you are married and one of you is over and the other under the total income limit of £14,600, consider putting joint investments, such as building society accounts, into the sole name of the partner who is under the limit. In the example of Molly and Bert (Example 4), Bert could qualify for the full amount of his higher personal allowance if he agreed to transfer

---

GROSSING UP

When working out whether your total income will be over the £14,600 limit, your calculations should use gross, or before-tax, figures for both income and outgoings. If, for example, you get taxed income from a building society account, you will need to divide the amount you receive by 0.75 to get the gross amount. Using the same sum – i.e. dividing by 0.75 – you should gross-up any outgoings you make after deduction of basic-rate relief such as covenants to charity.

joint investments producing £1,000 (or more) of income into Molly's name only.

Tax and changing circumstances

If your personal circumstances change, it's likely that your tax position will too. Most of the changes concern the allowances and outgoings that you can deduct from your income.

Separation and divorce

In the tax year in which you part, a husband will continue to get the married couple's allowance – whether basic or higher age-related – plus his personal allowance. However, he will lose the married couple's allowance in the tax year following the tax year of separation.

The wife will get her personal allowance plus the additional personal allowance if she has a dependent child living with her – see page 209.

If either of you pays maintenance payments to the other under a legally enforceable agreement, you will be able to claim tax relief on some or all of the payments – see page 207.

If either of you receives maintenance it is treated as tax-free income, unless the payments are made under a legally enforceable agreement made before 15 March 1988 and in place by 30 June 1988, in which case only the first £1,720 is normally tax-free. Payments to children set up before that date are all taxable in the name of the child, except increases since 5 April 1989.

From the date you separate, you will each be able to claim tax relief on the interest you pay on a mortgage of up to £30,000 for each of your new homes.

If one of you dies

A widower gets the married couple's allowance for the tax year in which his wife dies. A widow can claim the married couple's allowance in the tax year her husband dies if he had insufficient income in that tax year to make full use of the allowance.

A widow can also claim the widow's bereavement allowance

for the tax year in which her husband dies and the following tax year, provided she does not remarry before the start of the following tax year. Inland Revenue leaflet IR91 *A Guide for Widows and Widowers* gives full information.

If you have children who are still in full-time education when your spouse dies, you can also claim additional personal allowance – see page 209.

If you marry or remarry

In the first year of marriage you get a reduced married couple's allowance if you marry after 5 May. The amount you get is one-twelfth of £1,720, multiplied by the number of months you were married in the tax year.

Widows who remarry will lose their widow's bereavement allowance because their new husband will be able to claim the married couple's allowance instead. Divorced women will continue to get the allowances they were claiming before remarriage except for the additional personal allowance – see below.

Widowers or divorced men who remarry continue to get the full basic or higher married couple's allowance if they remarry in the same tax year in which they were widowed or divorced. If they remarry in a subsequent tax year, they will qualify for the married couple's allowance from the date on the marriage certificate.

If you are claiming additional personal allowance in the tax year that you marry, you can choose to get it until the following tax year, when it is replaced by the married couple's allowance. This is worth doing because the married couple's allowance is reduced in the year of marriage.

CHAPTER 16

TAX IF YOU CARRY ON WORKING

To some extent, keeping your tax affairs in order is fairly straightforward if you work for an employer, because under the Pay-As-You-Earn system the right amount of tax should be deducted from your pay before you get it. But in tax terms there are advantages to being self-employed. Self-employed people can deduct many more outgoings to reduce their taxable income: their income does not have tax deducted before they get it, and there is a time lag between getting the income and paying the tax. Later in the chapter you will find an explanation of how to deal with tax in self-employment, but the first section deals with tax if you are an employee.

Employed or self-employed?

The Inland Revenue is fairly strict about whom it will class as self-employed. In general, you are on dangerous ground if all (or nearly all) your income comes from just one source, and you are paid on a regular basis without having to send in an invoice. But you will usually count as self-employed if you can answer 'yes' to all the following questions:

- Do you have final say about how your business is run (for example, where you work and the hours that you work)?
- Do you put your own money at risk?
- Do you bear any losses, as well as keep the profits?
- Do you provide the major equipment which you need for your work (e.g. a car, van, computer)?

- If you employ others, do you set their terms of employment and pay them out of your own pocket?
- Do you have to correct unsatisfactory work in your own time and at your own expense?

If you answered 'no' to some of these questions, but you still think you are self-employed, see Inland Revenue leaflet IR56 *Employed or Self-Employed?* and contact your local tax office. You can ask for a decision in writing on whether you count as self-employed.

Tax if you are an employee

Pay-As-You-Earn (PAYE)

PAYE is a way of collecting tax bit by bit over the tax year. The Revenue works out for you a PAYE code which indicates an estimate of the amount of free-of-tax pay you're entitled to over the tax year. Any excess over this free-of-tax pay is taxed.

You are sent a Notice of Coding which tells you how your PAYE code is calculated: your employer is told what your code is, and uses it, together with various tables supplied by the Revenue, to deduct the right amount of tax from your pay. Each pay-day, your employer gives you one fifty-second or one-twelfth (depending on whether you are paid weekly or monthly) of the free-of-tax pay, deducts some tax-free payments you make, such as pension contributions, and then pays out the rest after tax.

A PAYE code usually consists of a number and a letter: the number shows how much free-of-tax pay you're allowed in the whole tax year, and the letter shows what allowances you are getting. Example 1 shows how the letter and number are arrived at.

Changes to your PAYE code

The *Notice of Your Income Tax Code* (if you get one) will normally be sent out in January or February each year, and applies to the next year starting on 6 April. Any changes to

TAX IF YOU CARRY ON WORKING

EXAMPLE 1
Susan Jones is aged 66, single, and has carried on working part-time for her previous employer, earning £8,000 in 1995-6. She has deferred her pension, but has an income from her investments in British Government Stocks – because she bought these on the National Savings Stock Register, the income is paid out before tax. Her *Notice of Your Income Tax Code* shows first her allowances: since she qualifies just for the full amount of age-related allowance for someone of her age, the total is £4,630.

Then the Notice shows her deductions, e.g. any taxable perks from a job, any untaxed income such as state retirement pension or untaxed investment income, any higher-rate tax due on investment income, and any underpaid tax from previous years. In Susan's case, the only deduction is the £700 of untaxed income from her British Government Stocks.

Finally, to get to Susan's code, her *Notice of Your Income Tax Code* shows how her deductions are taken away from her allowances, i.e. £4,630 – £700 = £3,930. The final digit is knocked off and replaced by the letter P, which indicates that (before deductions) she gets the full age-related allowance for someone of her age, giving her a PAYE code of 393P. This tells her employer to give her £3,939 (since the last figure is always assumed to be 9) free of tax each year, so about £3,939 ÷ 12 = £328 of her pay each month won't be taxed.

---

allowances announced in the annual Budget should be taken into account in your PAYE code.

However, there are other changes which might mean you need a new PAYE code during the tax year. For example, you might start to draw your state pension, which is paid out before tax, or you might get married and qualify for married couple's allowance. If so, tell your tax office immediately: if you don't get a new PAYE code, you'll have paid the wrong amount of tax at the end of the tax year. If you've paid too much, your PAYE code will be adjusted so that less tax is deducted on future pay-days. If you've paid too little, and the underpayment is large, in order to avoid a large drop in your income, your code may be adjusted to what it should have been had you paid the right amount of the tax from the beginning of the tax year, and any underpayment will be collected through the next year's PAYE code or through a tax bill at the end of the year.

Income from several sources

If you have more than one source of income taxed under PAYE, you will normally get a PAYE code for each source, although your allowances and deductions will if possible be included in the code for the main source. So if, say, you have an employer pension from one job, untaxed income from investments and are also working for an employer, you will probably get a code for both your job and the pension, and tax on your untaxed investment income will be collected through one of your PAYE codes.

In some cases you may get no free-of-tax pay, for example because you have lots of untaxed income. If so, your tax office may give your employer (or pension provider) an amount to be added to your income, with the effect that all the tax you are liable to pay is collected from this source. In this case, you get the letter K in your code.

Changing jobs

When you change jobs, your old employer should give you a form P45. This shows your PAYE code and details of the tax deducted from your total pay for the year to date. Give this to your new employer on your first day so that the correct amount of tax can be deducted from your pay.

If you don't do this, and your earnings are above the PAYE limit (about £67 a week, £293 a month in 1995-6) your employer will give you only the 'emergency code', operated on a 'week 1' or 'month 1' basis. The emergency code assumes that you are entitled only to the basic personal allowance, and the 'week 1' or 'month 1' basis means that your employer takes no account of any free-of-tax pay due from the beginning of the tax year to the time you start work. Your employer will then send a form P46 to your tax office, which will contact you to sort out the correct code. Once you have been allocated a proper code any tax you've overpaid will be refunded to you.

TAX IF YOU CARRY ON WORKING

Temporary work through an agency
If you work through an agency, say as a temporary accountant, you will be treated as an employee (normally of the agency) and taxed under PAYE. But there are exceptions to this rule: you may be able to work through an agency and still be treated as self-employed if you're an entertainer, model, subcontractor in the building industry, or if all your work is done at or from your own home.

Other temporary or casual jobs
Tax won't be deducted unless your earnings are more than about £67 a week (£293 a month). If you are paid more than this, you are taxed as described under 'Changing jobs' above.

If you're off sick
Statutory sick pay paid by your employer and any sick pay from your employer's own sick pay scheme are taxable under PAYE. But if the amount you get is lower than the amount of free-of-tax pay you are entitled to, your employer will refund some of the tax you've already paid in each pay packet.

If you've been unemployed
If you are unemployed and living on benefits with no other taxable income for a full year, your total taxable benefit will be below your allowances, so there will be no tax to pay. But if you have been unemployed for only part of the tax year, when you return to work your benefit office will give you a new form P45. This will allow your employer to deduct the right amount of tax straight away.

Increases to your income

As well as your pay, any other 'remuneration' your employer gives you, such as taxable fringe benefits and expenses, will increase your income for tax purposes. However, some fringe benefits and expenses are tax-free.

Taxable fringe benefits

Whether or not you actually pay tax sometimes depends on your income, but the following perks are taxable whatever your income:

- rent-free or low-rent accommodation (unless you either have to live there to do your job properly – e.g. as a publican – or you need to live there to do your job better, and it is customary for the job)
- debts, credit and charge card bills settled by your employer (unless they are regular business expenses)
- travel and other vouchers.

However, other benefits are taxable only if you are paid at a rate of £8,500 or more a year, including taxable fringe benefits and expenses (or, if you worked for part of the year only, if your earnings would have come to this amount over a full year). These benefits are:

- company cars, free petrol and diesel
- mobile phones
- loans of money, if you pay less than the 'official' rate of interest prescribed by the Treasury – though not if the total maximum balance outstanding on all your cheap or interest-free loans does not exceed £5,000 at any time in the tax year
- loans of things
- private medical insurance.

Tax-free fringe benefits

These perks are tax-free whatever your income:

- your employer's contributions to an 'approved' or 'statutory' pension scheme
- the cost of providing life insurance and sick pay, provided the scheme meets certain conditions
- fees and subscriptions paid by your employer to various 'approved' professional bodies
- the first 15p-worth of luncheon vouchers each working day
- free or subsidised canteen meals if they're provided for all employees

TAX IF YOU CARRY ON WORKING

- in-house sports facilities, if open to staff generally and used mainly or wholly by employees
- essential travel, accommodation and subsistence payments if you are temporarily absent from your normal workplace (i.e. expected to return before 12 months are up)
- routine health checks or medical screening
- clothes needed specially for your work and paid for by your employer
- relocation expenses of up to £8,000 when you have to move to a new job or are transferred, whether or not you sell your old home
- genuinely personal gifts, such as retirement gifts, and awards for long service of 20-years plus – but not gifts or awards of money
- gifts from business contacts, providing you get no more than £100 from each source
- Christmas party or a similar annual function that is open to all staff and costs £50 a head or less
- the value of entertainment (e.g. business lunches) provided by someone other than your employer
- shares you get through an approved profit-sharing or SAYE scheme or executive share option scheme
- new shares bought under a preferential scheme through your job: any benefit you get from receiving more shares than members of the public will not be taxed as income, provided certain conditions are met
- awards from staff suggestion schemes – up to a £5,000 maximum
- books and fees paid for by your employer for some external training courses, and some extra travel and living costs
- retraining courses for employees who are leaving (if certain conditions are met)
- counselling services provided to redundant employees
- taxis paid for by your employer to take you home if you work until 9pm or later (within limits)
- free car parking at or near your workplace
- travel and subsistence payments when public transport is disrupted or for severely disabled employees incapable of using public transport.

221

Tax-free expenses paid by your employer

In order to qualify for tax relief, expenses have to be incurred 'wholly, exclusively and necessarily in the performance of the duties of your employment'. This rules out things like the cost of formal clothes which you could wear outside work, even if you'd never choose to, and travel to and from work. The expenses which do count as tax-free ('allowable' expenses in tax jargon) are:

- liability insurance, or legal costs paid by your employer if you are taken to court in a work-related case
- the cost of fees and books (and sometimes extra living and travel costs) for a full-time training course in the UK lasting between four weeks and a year. Your employer must encourage or require you to go, and carry on paying you in your absence
- the cost of cleaning and repairing protective clothing and uniform necessary for your job
- the cost of maintaining and repairing factory or workshop tools and instruments; also the cost of replacing them, less the proceeds of selling the old ones, providing the new ones are not inherently better than the old
- the cost of necessary reference books and stationery used strictly for your job
- a proportion of your home's heating and lighting and possibly telephone, cleaning and insurance costs, if it is a condition of your work that you work at home
- interest on loans (not overdrafts or credit card bills) to buy 'equipment' necessary for your job
- fees and subscriptions to professional bodies 'approved' by the Revenue
- travelling expenses that are incurred strictly in the course of your work, including any running costs of your own or a company car which are attributable purely to your work
- occasional late-night journeys home or extra travel costs if public transport is disrupted by industrial action
- travel costs (sometimes a proportion only) of your wife or husband travelling with you on a business trip (but this is

allowed only if she or he has and uses practical qualifications directly associated with the trip, or if his or her presence is necessary for the essential business entertaining of overseas trade customers, or if your health is so poor that it is unreasonable to travel alone)
- reasonable hotel expenses
- expenses of entertaining customers
- personal expenses, such as papers and phone calls home, if you stay away from home overnight on business – providing that the payment does not exceed £5 a night (£10 a night outside the United Kingdom)
- agents' fees (within limits) if you are an actor or theatrical performer taxed under PAYE.

Any other expenses are added to your earnings from the job, for tax purposes. If you get a fixed expense allowance, and don't spend all of it on tax-free expenses, you are taxed on the difference.

Deductions from income

There are some payments you make which you can deduct from your income before working out your tax bill. These 'outgoings' therefore save you tax. **Chapter 15** explained the main outgoings, but there are also some linked to your work.

'Allowable' expenses

In trades where it's customary to provide your own tools or clothing (e.g. plumbing) many trade unions have agreed a fixed deduction with the Revenue for upkeep and replacement – e.g. £70 a year. You can claim the whole amount even if you don't spend that much, and if you spend more, you can claim more.

If you have to pay expenses to do with your work, and you are not reimbursed by your employer, you can also deduct these from your income from that job, provided the expenses are 'allowable'. If your employer pays you part of the cost, you need to deduct that amount from what you claim. The expenses you can deduct are the same as those listed as 'Tax-free expenses paid by your employer' above, except for the travel costs of a wife or husband travelling with you, and the costs of business entertaining, both of which must be paid by your employer in order to be tax-free.

Pension payments
Within limits, you can get tax relief on contributions to employer pension schemes or personal pension plans, and on additional voluntary contributions either to an employer scheme or a separate free-standing scheme.

Payroll giving schemes
These are schemes run by employers allowing you to give money to charity free of tax. The maximum you can give this way is £900 a year.

Vocational training costs
You can claim tax relief if you pay for your own training. To qualify, the training must lead to National Vocational Qualifications or Scottish Vocational Qualifications up to level 4.

How you get the relief
Payments to employer schemes and payroll giving schemes are normally taken direct from your salary before the tax is deducted, so you get the tax relief automatically. You get basic-rate relief on vocational training and some personal pension plan contributions by paying smaller amounts; higher-rate tax relief on these, and tax relief on other outgoings, is given to you through your PAYE code or tax bill.

Tax if you're self-employed

Chapter 14 looks at the different ways in which you can be self-employed. This section gives an introduction to how you will be taxed if you're a 'sole trader' or member of a partnership; if you have set up a limited company, see page 232.

Sole traders and partners pay tax at the same rate as individuals, but what your tax bill is based on differs considerably. Broadly speaking, for businesses started up before 6 April 1994, you are taxed on your 'taxable profits' for your accounting year ending in the preceding tax year. So, if you make up your accounts to 30 April each year, your tax bill for 1995-6 will be based on your accounts to 30 April 1994. This is called the 'preceding year basis'. From 1997-8, under the new system of 'self-assessment' (see page 261), all businesses will be taxed on a current-year basis, i.e. on your profits in the accounting period ending in the current tax year. If you start in business after 5 April 1994 you will be taxed on this basis from the start. To make the switch to the current-year basis if you started up on or before 5 April 1994, your tax bill for 1996-7 will be based on half your profits made in 1995-6, and half those made in 1996-7. However, special rules apply if your business is in its first or last years, and, sometimes, if a partner leaves or joins a partnership: see page 228 for the rules on starting up.

Working out taxable profits

Your taxable profits are broadly your takings for the year less your allowable business expenses; you also need to take into account changes in the value of your stock, any money owed by you and to you, money spent on capital equipment, and any losses you make.

Business expenses
An expense is allowable only if it is incurred 'wholly and exclusively' for the business – a less stringent definition than for employees. The main allowable expenses are:
- the cost of goods bought for resale
- the cost of raw materials
- running costs such as advertising, delivery charges, heating, lighting, postage and phone bills, renting and cleaning your place of business, business rates, the cost of small tools and special clothing, stationery, relevant books and magazines
- accountant's fees and bank charges on business accounts
- VAT on allowable business expenses if you're not VAT-registered
- wages, salaries and employers' National Insurance contributions for employees

- if you work from home, a proportion of your telephone, heating, lighting, cleaning and insurance bills, plus a proportion of your rent if part of a rented home is used exclusively for business
- interest and arrangement fees on overdrafts and business loans
- contributions to Training and Enterprise Councils and some professional bodies
- cost of travel and accommodation, and some meals, on business trips
- travel between different places of work
- running costs of your own car (or a proportion if you use the car for private purposes too)
- legal costs of recovering debts, some bad and doubtful debts
- some legal costs
- business insurance premiums
- reasonable charge for hire of capital goods, including cars (though this may be restricted).

Stock values

You can claim as a business expense only the cost of raw materials and goods for resale which you actually sell during your accounting year. To work out stock values, you should usually use the cost to you – you can only use the price you charge your customers if you expect to sell the stock for less than it cost you. The cost of your supplies is measured by:

- taking the value of your stocks and items to be resold at the start of the year
- adding anything you spend during the year on buying more stock
- deducting the value of your stocks at the end of the year.

Money owed

The Revenue may (rarely) allow you to keep your accounts on a 'cash' basis, in which case they'll be based on amounts you actually receive and pay out during the year. Otherwise, you'll keep your accounts on an 'accruals' basis. This means that your turnover and expenses figures must be adjusted to take account of money owed both to you and by you.

Capital allowances

You're not allowed to treat the cost of buying capital assets as a business expense for the year in which you buy it, nor can you claim depreciation, but you may be able to claim capital allowances instead. These have the effect of spreading tax relief for the cost of capital equipment over a number of years. Broadly, capital equipment is anything that can't be used up within a year of purchase – this includes vans, cars, computers and machinery, and some types of property.

The cost of capital equipment you buy goes into a 'pool' of expenditure. Each accounting year, you can claim up to 25 per cent of the value of the pool at the end of the year as a 'writing down allowance' and deduct that amount from your profits for tax purposes. The pool is reduced by what you claim. If you sell something in the pool, its value (usually the sale proceeds) must be deducted from the pool before working out your writing down allowance for the accounting year in which the items were sold. If the proceeds come to more than the amount of the pool, the excess – called a 'balancing charge' – is added to your profits for the year.

You can claim less than 25 per cent of your pool as an allowance. Don't claim more of your capital allowance than you need to reduce your tax to nil (and remember to use up your personal allowances first – see page 207). Any capital allowances left unclaimed are carried forward to next year's pool of expenditure and can reduce tax in later years.

Separate pools

Things bought partly for business and partly for private use have their own pools (you get a proportion of the capital allowance in line with the business use). So do cars (but not lorries or vans), and any car costing over £12,000 must have its own pool. There is a maximum writing down allowance of £3,000 for each individual car pool in any year.

You can opt to have a separate pool for items of capital equipment which you expect to sell or scrap within five years –

a computer, for example. The advantage of doing this is that, if you sell the item during that time for less than what's left in the pool, you can deduct the difference – the 'balancing allowance' – from that year's profits.

Using your losses
It may not be all doom and gloom if you make a loss – you can use the loss to reduce other tax, due either now or in the future. Watch out, though, for strict time limits on doing so – Inland Revenue leaflet IR28 gives more details. You can normally do one of three things:

- **Set the loss against future profits** You set the loss against profits from the same business in the following accounting year. Any losses left over can be carried forward to the year after, and so on.
- **If you started up before 6 April 1994, set the loss against other income taxable in the following tax year** For example, you could choose to set your losses against next year's investment income – but only if your business is still carried on in the relevant tax year.
- **If you started up after 5 April 1994, set the loss against income and capital gains for the previous tax year.**
- **Claim immediate income tax relief** You can ask for the loss to be set against any other income (or capital gains once your income has been reduced to nil) you have for the tax year in which your accounting year ends (provided your business continues in the next year). Any losses left over can be carried forward, but only against income from the same business.

In addition, any loss incurred in the first four years of trading can be set against income from any source arising in the previous three years. If you make a loss in the last 12 months of trading it can be set against profits from the same trade arising in the previous three years.

Starting up

Your accounting year need not run from 1 January to 31 December, nor need it coincide with the tax year. Your first accounting year doesn't have to cover exactly 12 months, but once you've chosen a year end, changing it can be tricky – check with your tax office. If yours is a seasonal business, you may want to arrange a year end in a slack period.

Table 1 shows what your tax bill is based on when you first start up (different rules apply to businesses started up before

Table 1

What your tax bill is based on in the opening years of a business (for businesses started up after 5 April 1994)

	Tax is initially based on
First tax year of business	Actual profit[1] in that tax year
Second tax year	Profit in the 12 months ending with the accounting date in the year, *or* if there is under 12 months before the accounting date, the profit in the first 12 months, *or* if there is no accounting date in the year, your actual profit[1]
Third tax year	Profit in your accounting year ending in the current tax year (or, if your first accounting period doesn't end until this year, profits in the 12 months ending with the accounting date)
Fourth and following tax years	Profit in your accounting year ending in the current tax year

[1] Your actual profit for any tax year is the proportion of your profits (worked out on a time basis) which will be attributed to that tax year.

6 April 1994). If these rules mean that you are taxed on the same profits in two successive tax years, you may qualify for some 'overlap relief' which can be deducted from your profits in the last year of the business (or possibly earlier if you change your accounting date).

Paying the tax

When you tell your tax office that you've started up, you will be asked to fill in form 41G. After you've been in business for nearly a year, you will be sent an estimated assessment for your first trading period; after that you are likely to receive assessments covering the tax years up to and including the current year. The tax for the first and sometimes the second year will be payable in one go, depending on when the assessments are actually made. In the following year you will start to pay tax in two annual instalments, on 1 January and 1 July, so that the tax due for 1995-6 will be payable on 1 January 1996 and 1 July 1996. Note that these payment dates will change once self-assessment is introduced (see page 261).

You don't always need to send full accounts, and you don't need to get them audited. If your total turnover is less than £15,000 a year, you only have to submit 'three line accounts' giving your total turnover, allowable business expenses and your net profit. But you must be able to back up your accounts with proper records, if your Tax Inspector should challenge them. .

Partnerships

Profits from a partnership are worked out in the same way as profits for a trade or business and taxed like other businesses.

The same rules for opening and closing years apply (and may also apply when a partner joins or leaves). For partnerships started up after 5 April 1994, the taxable profits of the partnership for each accounting period are shared out between the partners in line with their shares under the partnership agreement for that period. So if, for example, the profits are £40,000 and there are two partners sharing the profits equally, each partner will pay tax on £20,000. Any capital gains made by the partnership are also shared out by the partnership.

If you are in a partnership started up after 5 April 1994, your share of the profits or gains (or losses) is taxed as if it arose from a business carried on by you alone, started at the time you became a partner (or started in business if you traded alone to begin with).

The rules for partnerships started up before 6 April 1994 are different, but will be aligned with the rules described above from the 1997-8 tax year.

Changes in a partnership
Each time a partner joins or leaves the partnership, the partnership can come to an end. In fact, for partnerships started up before 6 April 1994 it will come to an end, unless the partnership opts for what is known as a 'continuation election' – i.e. all the partners both before and after the change agree that it should continue and at least one of the partners before the change is still a partner after the change. If a continuation election is not made, special rules for the opening years of a business apply. However, for partnerships started up after 5 April 1994, and for all partnerships from 1997-8, the partnership will be treated as continuing, provided that at least one partner remains the same.

If you employ someone

When you take on staff, as well as taking on all an employer's obligations to comply with health and safety requirements, and other legislation for protecting employees' rights, you take on responsibility for:

- deducting income tax from your employee's pay under PAYE (assuming that your employee earns more than the basic personal allowance – about £67 a week, £293 a month, in the 1995-6 tax year)
- deducting Class 1 National Insurance contributions from your employee's pay and paying Class 1 contributions as an employer. Again, these payments apply only if your employee earns more than a set limit – £58 a week in the 1995-6 tax year.

When an employee starts
You need to tell the relevant tax office – this will be a PAYE office, and may be different from the office dealing with your business; your own tax office should tell you where it is. You will be sent a *New Employer's Starter Pack* telling you what to do, which encloses all the forms you will need. The first step is to ask your employee for his or her National Insurance number and form P45: you can use the PAYE code shown on the P45 to work out how much free-of-tax pay to deduct. Your PAYE office will let you know if the code needs to be changed. If the person hasn't got a P45, you need to send form P46 to the PAYE office, and in the meantime use the 'emergency code' to deduct the tax.

Month by month
You will also be sent tax and National Insurance tables. By using these with the employee's PAYE code, you will know how much tax and National Insurance to deduct. You then need to send these deductions off to the relevant Accounts office – quarterly, if the payments average less than £600 a month, otherwise monthly.

At the end of the tax year
You need to complete a form telling your PAYE office how much you have paid each employee during the year and what deductions you have made: a copy also goes to the employee.

Companies

Much of what has been said about how businesses are taxed applies to limited companies too. However, there are some important differences: the main ones are listed below.

Corporation tax
Companies don't get personal allowances, of course, and instead of paying income tax, they pay corporation tax. This is charged (in the 1995-6 tax year) at two rates:

- a full rate – 33 per cent
- a small-company rate – 25 per cent. This is payable on all

profits up to £300,000. Above this, the rate of tax gradually increases, according to a complex formula. The full rate applies on all profits over £1,500 million.

Business expenses
The salaries paid to company directors are an allowable business expense, like other salaries, and so are deducted in calculating profits. Any surplus profits can be voted to directors as bonuses, on which they pay individual income tax – but this is a complex area for which you will need help from an accountant. Any part of the surplus that is not paid out is called 'retained profit' and subject to corporation tax.

Capital allowances and losses
These are the same for companies as for sole traders and partners, but cannot be set against the directors' or shareholders' income from other sources: they apply only to the company's income.

Accounting periods
A company may choose any date it likes for its accounting period. However, profits are taxed by reference to the year which runs from 1 April to 31 March. If the accounting period is different, the trading profits of the two periods will be split on a time basis. Other income and any capital gains are not split in this way: the actual date received determines which year they are taxed in.

Tax if you are a director

If you are a company director, you are technically an employee, even if you own shares in the company. So you will be paid under PAYE, pay Class 1 National Insurance contributions and your company will have to pay employer's Class 1 contributions. However, for the purposes of working out whether you pay tax on fringe benefits you will almost always be classed as earning at a rate of £8,500 a year or more (see page 220), whatever your actual salary.

Capital gains

Businesses and companies, like individuals, may make capital gains, e.g. on the sale of a business property. These are taxed as described in **Chapter 17**, with some exceptions.

For example, if you sell shares in your own company and reinvest the money in some other 'qualifying' unquoted trading companies, any capital gains tax can be put off until you finally dispose of the new shares.

Retirement relief may also be available if you own at least a 5 per cent stake in a company and are over 55 or retire through ill-health. The first £250,000 of your gains on selling up will be tax-free, and half of the next £750,000. The relief is reduced if you have been running the business for less than 10 years.

Finally, while sole traders and partners pay capital gains tax, companies pay corporation tax on any capital gains (although this is calculated in the same way as capital gains tax).

When you need an accountant

If you have set up as a company, you will need an accountant in order to comply with the accounts and auditing rules for limited companies. If you have set up in any other way, it may not be essential (particularly if you need submit only 'three-line accounts' because your turnover is less than £15,000 – in this case, see Inland Revenue leaflet IR104). But it may be advisable, because accountants should be versed in all the latest rules and regulations and should be able to advise you on the various options open to you. In addition, they are likely to have a knowledge of how the Revenue will interpret the rules in practice. See page 190 for how to find an accountant.

CHAPTER 17

TAX AND INVESTMENTS

Tax has an important impact on the return you get from your investments and, as explained in **Chapter 15**, the investments you choose and how they're taxed can influence the amount of age-related allowances you get if you are 65 or over. However, tax isn't the only consideration when picking ways to save and invest. The other factors you should take into account in your retirement planning are dealt with in **Chapter 10**. Table 1 tells you how the investments discussed in that Chapter are taxed.

The most common tax you'll have to pay on your investments is income tax, which is charged on the income they produce. The other main tax to watch out for is capital gains tax, which you may have to pay on the profit you make from selling shares and unit trusts, for example. The rules for this tax are explained later in the Chapter. Then there's inheritance tax. Although this doesn't directly affect the return you get on your investments, it may affect the value of your accumulated wealth that you pass on to your heirs. You'll find an explanation of how this tax works in **Chapter 36**.

How investment income is taxed

Income you receive from investments is taxed in one of four ways:

- **Tax-free** There's no tax to pay on the income from these investments, though there can be specific conditions that you have to meet to keep the tax-free status.

- **Taxable** You'll be paid the income without having tax deducted but unless you are a non-taxpayer, tax will be due. If you've been getting interest of this type for a few years, it will normally be taxed on a 'preceding year basis' – i.e. your tax bill for the 1995-6 tax year will be based on the interest received in 1994-5. In the first, second and last years in which you got interest from the source, your tax bill will be based on interest received in the same tax year. In the third year, you can choose which basis is used. From 1997-8, you will pay tax on all income of this sort in the year you receive it (and if you first receive income from a particular source after 5 April 1994, it will be taxed this way from the start). To make the switch to this new system if you are already getting income on a preceding-year basis, for 1996-7 you will pay tax on half the income received in 1995-6, and half received in 1996-7.
- **Taxed** The income will normally be paid with basic-rate tax already deducted but you can either reclaim the tax or register to have the income paid without tax deducted if you're a non-taxpayer. To register, complete form R85 from the bank or building society or get leaflet IR110, *A Guide for People with Savings*, from your tax office. Higher-rate taxpayers have to pay extra tax.

Table 1: How investments are treated

	for income tax	for capital gains tax
Annuities you buy yourself	taxed[1][2]	no capital gain
Bank deposit or savings account	taxed[2]	no capital gain
British Government Stocks (gilts) bought on the National Savings Stock Register	taxable	tax-free
British Government Stocks bought any other way	taxed	tax-free
Building Society account	taxed[2]	no capital gain
Enterprise Investment Scheme shares	tax credit	tax-free
Friendly Society insurance policies	tax-free[3]	tax-free
Friendly Society tax-exempt savings plan	tax-free	tax-free
Gilts – see British Government Stocks		
Guaranteed income bonds	tax-free[4]	tax-free

TAX AND INVESTMENTS

Index-linked gilts – see British Government Stocks		
National Savings Certificates (fixed-interest or index-linked)	tax-free	no capital gain
Investment trusts	tax credit[5]	taxable[5]
Life insurance savings policy	tax-free[3]	tax-free
National Savings Capital Bonds	taxable	no capital gain
National Savings FIRST Option Bond	taxed	no capital gain
National Savings Income Bond	taxable	no capital gain
National Savings Investment Account	taxable	no capital gain
National Savings Ordinary Account	tax-free/taxable[6]	no capital gain
National Savings Pensioners Guaranteed Income Bonds	taxable	no capital gain
National Savings Yearly Plan[7]	tax-free	no capital gain
PEP (Personal Equity Plan)	tax-free	tax-free
PIBS (Permanent Interest Bearing Shares)	taxed	tax-free
SAYE scheme[8]	tax-free	no capital gain
Shares	tax credit[5]	taxable[5]
Single premium insurance bond	tax-free[4]	tax-free
TESSA (Tax Exempt Special Savings Account)	tax-free	no capital gain
Unit trusts	tax credit[5][9]	taxable[5]
Venture Capital Trusts	tax-free	tax-free

[1] Only part of the monthly income is taxable – see page 93.
[2] Non-taxpayers can register to have income paid without tax deducted.
[3] Tax-free unless you cash in early and are a higher-rate taxpayer – see page 138.
[4] Usually tax-free to basic-rate taxpayers but proceeds may push you into the higher-rate band or mean you lose age allowance – see page 139.
[5] Income comes with tax credit, any capital gains on disposal chargeable to capital gains tax.
[6] The first £70 of interest (or £140 if it is a joint account) is tax-free.
[7] Applies to existing plans only. Yearly plans were due to be withdrawn from 1 February 1995.
[8] Existing schemes only – i.e. those taken out before 30 November 1994.
[9] Unit trusts which invest in interest-producing assets e.g. British Government stocks may pay out income which is treated like interest and has 25 per cent tax deducted.

- **Taxed with a tax credit** This applies mostly to income from shares, unit trusts and investment trusts. These all have a 'tax credit' of 20 per cent deducted from the income before you get it. Basic-rate taxpayers will not have to pay any further tax, but higher-rate taxpayers will have to pay an extra 20 per cent in tax to bring the tax up to the 40 per cent they pay. If you're a non-taxpayer, you can usually reclaim the 20 per cent deducted.

Married couples

If you are married and own investments in joint names – a building society account, for example – the income will automatically be treated as if it is paid to you in equal shares, with each of you paying tax on half the income. However, if you own the investment in unequal shares, the income can be taxed accordingly. You both have to make a joint declaration to one of your tax offices setting out how the capital and income are shared between you using form 17. The different tax treatment applies from the date that you make the declaration. You cannot choose the proportions in which the income from joint investments will be taxed. You can make a declaration only to be taxed according to your real shares in the capital and income.

WARNING
Although the proceeds of life insurance policies are usually tax-free in your hands, this is only because the life insurance fund has already paid some tax.

Special rules for tax-free investments

With most tax-free investments, the rules are straightforward: when you receive the income, you don't pay tax on it. However, some investments are tax-free only if you meet certain conditions, which are usually linked to the amounts you can invest and the amount of time for which you have to invest. These are TESSAs and PEPs, the rules for which are explained on pages 127 and 133 respectively.

The Enterprise Investment Scheme (EIS) which was introduced on 1 January 1994 to replace Business Expansion Schemes (BES) is another tax-free investment with strings. Under the scheme, designed to encourage investment in new companies, you can get tax relief at 20 per cent on up to £100,000 invested in EIS in one tax year. Shares are also free of capital gains tax provided you hang on to them for five years. If you eventually sell shares at a loss, you can use the loss to reduce your tax bill. see pages 134 and 237 for the tax advantages of Venture Capital

Trusts. Shares must be in some types of company only, and not quoted on the Stock Exchange.

Life insurance
The proceeds you get from life insurance policies (including friendly society policies which aren't tax-exempt) are free of basic-rate income tax in your hands. There are two types of policy for tax purposes:

- Qualifying policies, which include regular-premium policies such as most endowment policies. Provided you keep these policies going for at least 10 years (or three-quarters of the term of the policy if less), there will never be extra tax to pay: if you don't meet these conditions, the policy is taxed in the same way as a non-qualifying policy.
- Non-qualifying policies include single premium insurance bonds. You may end up paying extra tax, either directly if you are a higher-rate taxpayer (see page 133), or indirectly if the gain from your insurance policy swells your total income with the effect of reducing your higher age-related allowances. Any taxable proceeds from the policy are added to your income for tax purposes before your tax bill is worked out, though what's called 'top-slicing relief' may reduce the tax. Note, though, that the taxation of this type of policy is currently being reviewed.

Capital gains tax

As explained in **Chapter 10**, it's likely that you'll be investing for capital growth as part of your longer-term investment strategy. But capital growth means capital gain, which for some investments means the possibility of paying capital gains tax.

The main investments which attract capital gains tax are shares, unit trusts and investment trusts. You make a capital gain on these (and other 'assets') when you sell them or give them away for more than you paid for them (or for more than their value when you were given them). Some gains are tax-free and with others – e.g. shares you've sold at a profit – you don't have to pay tax on the whole of your gain because of the various deductions you can make.

Tax-free capital gains from investments are summarised in the Table on pages 236-7. Other tax-free gains include:
- your only or main home (see page 250)
- private motor cars
- prizes, betting and lottery winnings
- sterling cash or foreign currency for your own use – e.g. on holiday
- compensation for personal or professional wrong or injury.

Working out your gains for tax purposes

To work out the gain (or loss) you make on an asset which isn't tax-free – the profit you make from selling shares, for example – you need to do the following calculations:

1 Final value
Take the final value of the asset when you dispose of it – i.e. its sale price or, if you gave it away, its market value.

2 Initial value
From the final value, deduct the asset's initial value when you got it – i.e. the price you paid for it or its market value if you were given or inherited it. See also the Box.

> **TIP**
>
> If you acquired assets on or before 31 March 1982 you can choose to use the market value on 31 March 1982 as the initial value instead of the real initial value when you actually acquired the asset. However, if you do this, you can't deduct expenses you incurred before 31 March 1982 in your calculations. It's worth using this method if your expenses were minimal and the value of your assets was greater on 31 March 1982 than their value when you bought them. If the value of your asset at 31 March 1982 was less than its value when you acquired it, you'd be better off using the real initial value.

3 Allowable expenses
Once you've taken the initial value from the final value, deduct any allowable expenditure which you incurred when acquiring

or disposing of the asset – e.g. stamp duty and commission costs when buying or selling shares. You can also deduct any money you've spent on increasing the value of the asset (unlikely with most investments) but you can't deduct maintenance costs.

If these three steps give you a plus figure, you have made a gain for tax purposes. If they give you a minus figure, you have made a loss for tax purposes, which you can set against gains either in the same or future tax years. Carry on to see if you can reduce your gain.

Reducing your gains

You can make deductions from your gains for tax purposes before arriving at your net taxable gains – i.e. the amount on which you will pay capital gains tax.

Indexation allowance

The next deduction from the final value of your asset is indexation allowance. This is an allowance that makes sure that you don't pay tax on gains that are simply the result of inflation. A gain can be reduced or eliminated by your indexation allowance, but since 6 April 1995 you have not been able to use your indexation allowance to turn a gain into a loss, or increase a loss (and between 30 November 1993 and 5 April 1995 there were limits on the amount of allowance that could be used in this way). Indexation allowance is equal to the increase in price of the asset and any allowable expenses (except disposal costs) in line with increases in the general level of prices since March 1982 as measured by the Retail Prices Index (RPI).

To calculate the indexation allowance, you first need to calculate the indexation factor. To get this, take the RPI for the month of disposal (RPId), then subtract the RPI for the month you acquired the asset (RPIa). If you acquired the asset before 31 March 1982, you use the RPI for March 1982 as the RPIa. Divide the result by the RPI for the month you acquired the asset (RPIa).

$$\text{Indexation factor} = \frac{RPId - RPIa}{RPIa}$$

Round the result to three decimal places, then multiply this figure by the initial value to give you the indexation allowance.

If, when working out your gains for tax purposes you have deducted expenses incurred when acquiring or improving the asset, you will need to work out an indexation allowance for the expenses. Use the calculations above, but use the RPI for the month you incurred the expense as RPIa. If you incurred the expenses in the same month as the month in which you acquired the asset, you can work out the indexation allowance for both together by adding the expense to the initial value before starting the calculations.

> **TIP**
>
> You'll find RPI figures in the Employment Gazette published by the Department of Employment – try your local library – and in Which? magazine every few months. Or you can call 0171-217 4905, an information line for the current RPI.

Making up for losses
Gains after indexation are called chargeable gains, and any losses after indexation are called allowable losses. You can deduct losses from your gains, and any losses left over can be carried forward to reduce chargeable gains in future tax years.

Your tax-free slice
Once you've deducted any losses made in the same tax year, you can deduct your tax-free slice of £6,000 in the 1995–6 tax year (up from £5,800 which applied for the previous three tax years). If you are married, you will have a tax-free slice each to deduct from your own gains. If this doesn't reduce your chargeable gains to nil (or a minus figure), you can deduct any unused allowable losses from previous tax years. If, after all this, you still have net taxable gains, you will have to pay capital gains tax.

How much capital gains tax?
Capital gains tax is charged at the same rate that you'd pay if your gain was your top slice of income. So to work out the rate of capital gains tax you will pay, you need to add your net

taxable gains to your taxable income – i.e. your income after deducting outgoings and allowances (see page 196). However, when working out how much of the gains are taxed at 20 per cent the grossed-up amount of income which comes with a tax credit (e.g. share dividends) is ignored.

Paying capital gains tax

If you receive a tax return, you can give details about any gains on that (the notes accompanying the tax return also have spaces for doing the calculations), provided you send your tax return back to the tax office within six months of the end of the relevant tax year. Otherwise, you should send a letter with the details. Note that for 1995-6 you need give details only of chargeable gains of over £6,000 arising from total disposals of over £12,000 in the tax year.

You will be told how much tax you have to pay on a Notice of Assessment. You will have to pay the tax due on 1 December after the end of the tax year in which the gains were made, or 30 days after the date on the assessment, whichever is later. If you disagree with an assessment, take it up with your tax office in writing within 30 days of receiving the assessment.

Special rules for shares and unit trusts

If you own one lot of the same type of shares in the same company (or units in the same unit trust), and you acquired them all at the same time, there's no problem deciding which date you use for the initial value when you come to working out the gains when you sell them (or give them away). However, if you acquired shares (or unit trusts) in the same company at different times and then you sold at different times, the Revenue has special rules for deciding which shares you disposed of, how much they cost you, and what your indexation allowance is. If this affects you, ask your local tax office for the free Inland Revenue leaflet CGT13.

EXAMPLE

When she retired in May 1990, Charlotte Smart used £10,000 of the lump sum she received from her employer pension scheme to buy shares. In December 1994, her shares are worth £18,500, so she decides to get out while the going is good and sells them. To see how much capital gains tax she will have to pay, Charlotte first calculates her gain for tax purposes:

Charlotte's gain for tax purposes	
Final value of shares	£18,500
less	
Initial value of shares	£10,000
less	
Expenses on selling	£325
Gain for tax purposes	£8,175

To calculate the indexation allowance, Charlotte first needs to know the RPI for May 1990 when she acquired the shares and the RPI for December 1994 when she sold them. She gets the figures from *Which? Tax-Saving Guide*.

December 1994 (RPId) = 146.0
May 1990 (RPIa) = 126.2

$$\frac{146.0 - 126.2}{126.2} = 0.1568938$$

She rounds this to three decimal places to get 0.157.

To calculate the indexation allowance, she multiplies the initial value by the rounded figure, i.e. £10,000 × 0.157 = £1,570.

Charlotte then deducts this from her gains for tax purposes to arrive at her gains after indexation:

Gains for tax purposes	£8,175
less	
Indexation allowance	£1,570
Gains after indexation	£6,605

At this point, Charlotte should add up all her chargeable gains for that tax year – i.e. all her gains after indexation – and deduct any allowable losses she has made. However, the gain on her shares is the only gain she has made in this tax year and she has no losses either from this or previous tax years. The last thing to deduct is therefore her tax-free slice of £5,800 (for the 1994-5 tax year) to arrive at her net taxable gains on which she'll pay tax:

Gains after indexation	£6,605
less	
Tax-free slice	£5,800
Net taxable gains	£805

When she adds her gain of £805 to her taxable income for the same tax year of £14,600, she finds that she will pay capital gains tax at 25 per cent, giving her a capital gains tax bill of £201.25 (i.e. 25 per cent of £805). Note that if Charlotte had waited until after 5 April 1995 to sell her shares (i.e. until after the beginning of the 1995-6 tax year), she would have been able to deduct a tax-free slice of £6,000 rather than £5,800 which applied to the three tax years since 6 April 1992. However, she would have risked a fall in the share prices during the wait.

Capital gains tax on gifts

Odd though it may seem, you may have to pay capital gains tax when you give an asset to someone else. The calculations are the same as if you'd sold the asset for its full market value. However, the following gifts are free of capital gains tax:

- gifts to charities, 'national heritage bodies' (e.g. some museums), local authorities, Government and universities
- gifts of land to a registered housing association.

Gifts between a husband and wife are free of tax when made, but when the recipient finally parts with the gift, any capital gains tax will be worked out over the period *both* partners owned the asset.

CHAPTER 18

TAX AND YOUR HOME

If retirement has brought with it thoughts of moving to a smaller home, investing in a second home, or simply making the most of the one you've got, tax will be one of the factors that you will need to take into account. The other more personal factors are dealt with in **Part 5** of this book, where you'll find information on what to consider if you're on the move, a guide to buying and selling, the practical aspects of moving, plus a look at security, safety and insurance.

Buying a home is by far the biggest single transaction you're likely to make. In this chapter you'll see how you can make use of the tax relief on mortgage interest, even if you can now afford to buy your home outright. You'll find information on the tax position on the money you make from your home – whether it's by renting a room, letting a whole property or by getting your home to pay you an income with a home income scheme. There's also an explanation of how capital gains tax can affect your home – or other property – when you sell.

Making the most of a mortgage

If you have a mortgage on your only or main home, you can get tax relief on the interest you pay on the first £30,000 of the loan.

However, the amount of tax relief you get in the 1995-6 tax year is fixed at 15 per cent of the interest you pay on £30,000 of your mortgage (in the 1994-5 tax year, relief was fixed at 20 per cent). You will get tax relief even if you pay no tax on your income.

In most cases, you get tax relief at source by paying less to your lender through the Mortgage Interest Relief At Source (MIRAS) system. If your mortgage is not in MIRAS, you have to claim the relief, usually by entering the amount of mortgage interest you pay on your annual tax return, and enclosing a certificate of mortgage interest paid.

With a loan within the MIRAS system which takes you over the £30,000 limit, lenders calculate your payments so that you pay the correct net amount of interest on the first £30,000 of the loan and the gross amount of interest on the rest.

Do you need a mortgage?

If you've decided to move home on retirement, you may be thinking about dispensing with a mortgage altogether, but in certain circumstances this may not be the best course of action. This is because, apart from not being able to claim tax relief on mortgage interest (which makes a mortgage probably the cheapest available form of borrowing), buying a home without a mortgage may mean that all your capital will be tied up in your property.

If you have enough income to cover repayments on a mortgage up to the £30,000 limit (plus the insurance premiums), you may want to consider keeping some of the equity from the home you're selling as a cash lump sum to help keep your finances fluid. If you choose to invest the lump sum, the income from it will cover the costs of your mortgage interest if the after-tax return you get is the same or more than the interest you pay on your mortgage less the tax relief. So a basic-rate taxpayer paying interest at 8 per cent before tax relief on a mortgage needs to look for investments producing a return of at least 6.8 per cent after tax – i.e. 8 per cent less tax relief at 15 per cent.

MOVING HOME

If you're moving home, and you have to take out a loan on the new home before you've sold the old one, you can get tax relief on both loans for up to 12 months (longer in deserving cases).

Making money from your home

In general, you will have to pay income tax on money you make from your home whether it's income from letting, or income you get from a home income scheme. There may also be capital gains tax to pay when you come to sell your home – see pages 250-2. Below are the effects on your income tax bill.

Letting a room

If you've decided to supplement your retirement income by taking in a lodger, you can take advantage of the 'Rent-a-Room' scheme which began on 6 April 1992. The rent your lodger pays you will be tax-free up to a limit of £3,250 a year (including any money your lodger pays you for meals).

If your lodger pays you more than £3,250 a year, you have a choice of how the money is taxed:

- either you can choose to pay tax on the amount above £3,250 (but you won't be able to deduct expenses – see below)
- or you can agree to pay tax on the whole of the income you receive less expenses. If you do this, the first £3,250 won't be tax-free. It's worth choosing this method if the tax bill on the excess above £3,250 would be more than the tax bill on the money your lodger pays you after you've deducted all your expenses (including the cost of providing meals).

Letting your home

If you've decided to travel for a while, you may need to let your home while you're away or you may decide to let a holiday home to boost your income. Here are the tax rules for income you get from letting your main home or a second home whether furnished or unfurnished. (For the capital gains tax implications, see page 250.)

Reducing your income from letting
All the income from the letting is liable to income tax. However, before adding your income from letting to your

other income for tax purposes, you can deduct certain expenses, the most common of which are:

- water rates, ground rent, feu duty (in Scotland)
- normal repairs and decoration
- management expenses as a landlord (e.g. stationery, phone bills, the cost of rent collection)
- cost of insurance
- legal fees for renewing a tenancy agreement
- estate agent's fees, accommodation agency fees and advertising costs
- costs of services you provide (if the rent includes them)
- lighting and heating bills (if you, rather than your tenant, pay them)
- wear and tear – you can either claim the actual cost of what you've had to replace or a fixed amount, which is normally 10 per cent of the rent (less council tax).

Interest on property you let

If you're not already getting tax relief on the mortgage for the property you're letting, you can deduct the interest you pay on a loan to buy the property from your income from letting.

Your home, your business

If your letting falls into any of the following categories, the income will count as earnings from a business and will be taxed accordingly.

- You run a guest house.
- You let furnished holiday accommodation in the UK (i.e. it is available for at least 140 days during each 12-month period, actually let for 70 of those days, and during the 12-month period there must usually be at least seven months when no one tenant occupied the property for more than 31 days at a stretch).
- The services you provide, such as meals and cleaning, are not included in the rent – i.e. you charge extra for them on top of the rent.
- You pay someone to provide services in furnished accommodation.

Basically, you'll have to keep separate accounts and (except for furnished holiday accommodation, which has its own section) enter the income under 'Income from self-employment' on your tax return – see page 224.

Home income schemes

If you own your own home, and you don't fancy sharing it with a lodger, you can use the value of your home to help boost your income with a home income scheme. However, home income schemes are not really worth considering unless you are at least 70 years old (so they may be worth a look if you have an elderly parent in need of income). See **Chapter 6** for more on home income plans.

How they are taxed
Whoever is running the scheme – often a building society or insurance company – arranges a loan for you which is secured on the value of your home. You get basic-rate tax relief on the interest you pay on the loan up to a limit of £30,000, provided that at least 90 per cent of the loan is used to buy an annuity. The annuity pays you an income for the rest of your life. Only part of the annuity income is taxable (the rest is regarded as a return of your capital).

Basic-rate tax is deducted before you get the income: non-taxpayers can register to get the income paid before tax, higher-rate taxpayers will have to pay more tax through their PAYE code or tax bill.

Capital gains tax on your home

You need worry about capital gains tax only when you come to sell your home, and you won't have to pay it if the home is your main home and you've lived in it for most of the time that you've owned it. But there are steps you will need to take if you own a second home, or have let your home or part of it.

More than one home?

If you have two homes, only your main home is exempt from capital gains tax when you come to sell. You can choose which home you want to be regarded as your main one – it doesn't have to be the one in which you spend most time, though in most cases you must live in it at some stage.

Unless it's obvious to both you and the Inland Revenue which is your main home, you should write to the Revenue within two years of acquiring the second home to tell them which is your main home for capital gains tax purposes. If you miss the two-year deadline, your main home will be decided for you. If you don't like the decision, it's up to you to prove that the one that's been chosen isn't in fact your main home. However, if you have a home in London where you've been living and working for 20 years but also have a holiday cottage in Suffolk, for example, it's unlikely that the Revenue will choose the holiday cottage as your main home, and even if they did, it would be easy to prove that the London home was, in fact, your main home.

The home to nominate as your main home should be the one you're likely to sell first, especially if you're likely to move into the other home. If you don't know which you're going to sell first, nominate the home which will make the bigger gain after indexation (see page 241 for how to work this out). Once you make your mind up about which you're selling, you can change your nomination by writing to the Revenue, but this cannot affect the period more than two years before you changed your nomination.

A home you let

You won't lose any exemption if you have lodgers who share your living rooms and eat with you. And if the home you let has also been your main home for the whole time you've owned it, the whole of the gain you make when you sell will be exempt from capital gains tax, even if you let it out while you were away, provided all your absences count as qualifying absences. These include:

- any absence before 6 April 1982
- absence because you couldn't move into your home in the first year because of building work
- absences while you were living in a home which went with your job
- most absences because of your job
- absences in the three years before you sell the home
- any other absences of not more than three years in total provided you live in the home before and after the absences.

If you were absent from the main home you let for any other reason, the Revenue will work out the portion of the whole gain from selling your home, which relates to the time for which it was let. It's this portion (which, broadly speaking, is the fraction produced by dividing the time you let the home by the time you owned it) on which you will be liable to capital gains tax. The portion which relates to the time when you lived in the home yourself is still exempt from tax. However, there will be no capital gains tax to pay, even on the portion which relates to letting, if this is less than £40,000 *and* it's smaller than the portion of the gain relating to the time when you lived there.

If you let part of your home, the same rules apply, though the portion of the gain for the part you let will take into account the number of rooms or floor area as well as the time you let this part of the property.

If you work from home

If you are self-employed and use part of your home exclusively for business, the part you use will not be exempt from capital gains tax for the period you use it. However, most people will be able to show that they do not use it exclusively for business.

CHAPTER 19

DEALING WITH THE TAX AUTHORITIES

If the words 'Inland Revenue' conjure up images of pinstriped suits, black brief cases and incomprehensible forms, it's likely that you haven't had much contact with them recently. Retirement may change all that. However, in the last few years, the Inland Revenue has been making a concerted effort to improve the way they treat taxpayers. The initiatives they have taken range from making forms clearer and easier to use, to setting a time limit for replying to queries, to relaunching the taxpayer's charter, which sets out how you can expect to be treated in your dealings with the tax office.

Despite all these good intentions, however, you may meet the odd problem. This chapter starts with how to find your tax office, then looks at giving the Revenue information: which forms you have to fill in and then how to check the forms which tell you how much tax you have to pay. If you think you've paid too much (or too little) tax, you'll find advice on getting problems sorted out. Finally, if your relationship with your tax office breaks down, there's information on how to appeal.

Finding your tax office

The tax office which deals with your tax affairs isn't necessarily the one nearest to where you live. It largely depends on which tax office deals with your major source of income.

If your main income is from a pension from an employer which is taxed under the PAYE scheme, your employer will be able to give you the name and address of your tax office. This is likely to be the same one that dealt with your tax affairs while you were still an employee. However, if the pension fund which pays your pension is in a different office from your employer, your tax office may well be the one which deals with that area.

If you receive income from a personal pension, because you were self-employed, for example, or your main income is from your investments or the state pension, your tax office will be the one which deals with the area in which you live.

Collecting tax

Your tax office is concerned with assessing how much tax you should pay, not with the collection of it. Tax collection is the responsibility of the Collector of Taxes either through a local Collection Office, or one of the two Central Accounts Offices, depending on the address on your tax bill.

General enquiries

If you just want to make a general enquiry, or you want to get hold of one of the free Inland Revenue explanatory leaflets, you don't need to go to your own tax office. Instead, you can telephone any tax office or a Tax Enquiry Centre. Leaflet IR52 has a full list of Tax Enquiry Centres (or try the telephone book under Inland Revenue). If your enquiry is specific to your own tax affairs, it's always best to write to your own tax office.

The taxpayer's charter

This states clearly that taxpayers are entitled to expect the Inland Revenue:

- **To be fair** The Revenue should treat everyone with equal fairness and impartiality and you should be expected to pay only what is due under the law
- **To be helpful** The staff at your tax office (and any other Revenue official) should be courteous and assist you in getting your taxes right by providing clear information.
- **To help you understand** your rights and obligations.

- **To be efficient** The Revenue should be prompt, accurate and keep your tax affairs confidential. Information obtained from you should be used only as allowed by the law. It should also strive to keep both your expenses and those of your tax office down.
- **To be accountable** Standards, and how well the Revenue lives up to those standards, should be made public.
- **To be open to criticism** Taxpayers should be told how to complain, and be able to have their tax affairs re-examined. An appeal can be made either to an independent tribunal, or your MP can refer you to the Parliamentary Commissioner for Administration.

In return, you the taxpayer have an obligation to be honest, to give the Revenue accurate information, and to pay your tax on time.

Giving and getting information

One of your obligations as a taxpayer is to give the Revenue accurate information. To help you do this, the Revenue issues various forms. The main one you will have to deal with is likely to be the tax return. Once you've given the Revenue the information they need to calculate your tax bill, you're likely (though not bound) to receive a *Notice of your income tax code* if you pay tax through PAYE, and/or a Notice of Assessment.

Your tax return

Even if you never received a tax return while you were still working, you may get one once you've retired. There are two main reasons for this. First, if you're likely to have untaxed income coming in (from your state pension, for example), your tax office will need to work out how much tax is due on it, and then change your tax code if you pay tax under PAYE, or send you a bill. The other reason is to make sure that you get the correct amount of any age-related allowances that you're entitled to.

The tax returns have recently been rewritten and redesigned.

There are several different returns (though some are currently under review) but it doesn't really matter which one you get since your obligations as a taxpayer don't change. All tax returns have space for you to give details of your income, to deduct your outgoings and expenses, and to claim your personal allowances. And they all come with a set of explanatory notes which tell you what you need to fill in and when you may need to approach your tax office for more information before giving your details.

The tax return is designed to cover every eventuality, so don't be put off by its length. It's unlikely that you'll have to fill in all of it. If you are sent a tax return, you are required by law to fill it in and send it back within 30 days of receiving it – though in practice, you have until the end of October in the year you receive it before the Revenue will penalise you with interest on any tax you owe. Don't forget to take a copy before you send it back.

Of particular interest if you are receiving a pension is that you are asked to give your expected income for the next year. You don't have to give this information, but it helps your tax office to get your tax code right (if you pay tax under PAYE). This helps you to pay the right amount of tax and may mean that you don't then have to fill in a tax return every year.

Tax claims

If your only income is from investments, and you receive the income with tax deducted from it, you will probably be sent tax claim form R40 (though this form is under review). This is like a tax return but is sent to people who claim a repayment of tax each year – i.e. their income is less than their personal allowances. This form is usually sent at the same time as you receive a cheque for the previous year's repayment of tax, unlike tax returns which are sent out in April at the end of the tax year.

Your Notice of Coding

If you pay tax under PAYE – e.g. you get a pension from a former employer, or you do part-time work for an employer – you may receive a *Notice of Your Income Tax Code*. This is basically the Revenue's way of telling you which allowances you're getting and how much untaxed income they think you're receiving – i.e. what has gone into working out your tax code, which determines how much tax you pay under PAYE. See **Chapter 16** for how your PAYE code is worked out.

It's easy to see what allowances you're getting because they are shown by their names (see page 208 for a full list). If an allowance you can claim doesn't appear on your Notice of Coding, you're not getting it and you should write to your tax office pointing this out. Note that fixed-relief allowances have to be adjusted for the right amount of tax to be collected. Under the allowances column of the notice, you will see the full amount of the married couple's allowance, widow's bereavement allowance or additional personal allowance of £1,720 (or a higher amount if you're entitled to age-related married couple's allowance). In the other column you will see an entry called ALLCE RESTRICTION which is how the Revenue makes sure that you get relief at 15 per cent only. To check that the amount of the allowance restriction is correct, subtract the amount of the allowance restriction from the amount of your married couple's allowance and multipy the rest by your top rate of tax. The answer should be the same as 15 per cent of your allowance.

If you qualify for a reduced age-related allowance because your total income is above £14,600, you'll also see 'EST INCOME £', which is an estimate of your total income. If this isn't correct, you won't get the right amount of age-related allowance.

If you're receiving a state pension, this will be shown as 'STATE PENS'N/BENEFIT' or 'PENSION'.

If you owe tax from a previous year which hasn't already been collected, an amount will appear next to 'UNPAID TAX'. The figure will be four times the tax you owe if you are a basic-rate taxpayer, and two and a half times if you pay tax at the higher rate.

If you think any of these figures are wrong, you should write to your tax office telling them why. If you need more information on what appears on the notice you receive, ask your tax office to send you leaflet P3(T) *PAYE: Understanding Your Tax Code*, or consult the *Which? Tax-Saving Guide*.

Your Notice of Assessment

If you owe tax, or, sometimes, if you're due a repayment, you will receive a Notice of Assessment which explains how the tax you owe – or are owed – has been calculated. The entries which appear on the Notice of Assessment should match the figures you gave on your tax return. If they don't, tell your tax office which figures are wrong within 30 days of receiving the assessment.

If you get a Notice of Assessment, but you haven't yet filled in a tax return, there are likely to be a lot of estimated figures (marked 'E'). You should send the correct information back to your tax office within 30 days. At the same time you should apply for a postponement of the tax. You may then get a revised assessment showing the information you sent them. It's particularly important to get the assessment corrected if the estimated figures show that you owe tax.

Solving problems

If you think there's something wrong about your tax affairs, for example your tax code hasn't taken account of an allowance you can claim, or you think you've paid too much tax for another reason, it's always best to write to your tax office.

Letters to the tax office

If you are moved to write to your tax office, it will probably be for one of two reasons: to point out their mistake, or to confess to a mistake you have made.

Pointing out mistakes
When you write to your tax office, explain briefly what you think is wrong and why.

To help your tax office deal with your letter efficiently, always quote your tax reference number (shown on any correspondence or form that you've received from the Revenue) and your National Insurance number.

You should get a reply to your letter within 28 days, although if you have written to reclaim tax, it may take longer if they have to issue a cheque. If you don't get a reply within this period, it's worth telephoning your tax office to see what is happening. Again, it will help if you can quote your tax reference number and National Insurance number.

Tax rebates
If the Revenue owes you more than £25, you may be entitled to interest – called a repayment supplement – on the amount that you are owed. Your rebate starts to attract interest 12 months after the end of the tax year for which it is due, or after the end of the tax year in which you paid too much tax, whichever is later. If the rebate due is less than £50, it won't be paid until the end of the tax year. The Revenue aims to deal with repayment claims within 42 days at peak periods (April to September) and within 28 days at other times.

Confessing to mistakes
If you have made a mistake in the information you gave to the tax office, you must write and tell them as soon as possible.

If your mistake meant that you didn't pay enough tax, you'll have to pay all the tax you owe and you may be charged interest on it.

If your mistake meant that you paid too much tax – for example you forgot to deduct an outgoing or claim an allowance – you can make a claim for the tax you've overpaid. The time limit for this kind of claim is six years from the end of the tax year in which the assessment giving rise to the overpayment was made. But you can't claim if the assessment was determined by the Commissioners because you hadn't given the Revenue the information they needed to assess your tax correctly.

Letters from the tax office

If your tax inspector thinks there's something wrong with your tax affairs, or if your tax office needs more information in connection with your tax return, for example, they may write to you. If you think what they are requesting is reasonable (most requests should be), give the information requested if this is possible. If you haven't got the information, you need a certificate from your building society, for example, let the tax office know that the matter is in hand and give an estimate of when they can expect to receive the information.

Dealing with unhelpfulness

If you think that your tax office is being unreasonable – for instance you think that points you made in a previous letter have been disregarded, write a letter repeating your position. If this fails, write directly to the District Inspector, whose name should appear at the top of any correspondence from your tax office. The District Inspector should reply personally, and should either agree with you or set out fully the reasons why your argument is not accepted.

If you are still unable to get any satisfaction from your tax office, write to the Regional Controller who deals with your tax office (names and addresses of Regional Controllers are available from any tax office). Mark your letter for his or her personal attention, set out concisely and clearly your grounds for complaint against your tax office and ask for an investigation. If you still have no joy, you can refer your complaint to the Revenue Adjudicator's Office*. The adjudicator will be able to look at your case impartially while still having access to all the files. Alternatively, try your MP, who may refer your case to the Parliamentary Commissioner.

Dealing with mistakes

If your tax office gets something wrong and you find that you owe tax as a result of their mistake, you may not have to pay all (or any) of the tax you owe. This will apply only if you've taken reasonable care to keep your affairs in order – for example you've dutifully filled in all your tax returns – and it was reasonable for you to believe that you didn't owe any tax.

You may have to pay only a percentage of the tax owed, depending on your gross income in the tax year *that you receive the assessment which reveals that you owe tax* – i.e. the assessment which has been amended in the light of the Revenue discovering their earlier mistake. It is *not* based on your gross income when the assessment was originally issued. This works to your advantage if your gross income when you receive the amended assessment is less than it was when the assessment was issued – e.g. because you have retired.

Gross Income	Percentage of tax owed to pay
£15,500 or less	none
£15,501 – £18,000	25%
£18,001 – £22,000	50%
£22,001 – £26,000	75%
£26,001 – £40,000	90%
£40,001 or more	all

CHANGES ON THE WAY

A ten-year 'Change Programme' due to be completed in 2002 has been put in place to improve the workings of the Inland Revenue. The core of this programme is the changeover to self assessment, but the programme also covers streamlining and simplification of Revenue working methods and procedures, reorganisation of the office structure, and greater use of information technology. If you've dealt with the Revenue in the past, these should be welcome changes which make it easier to get mistakes and misunderstandings sorted out. However, it will be self-assessment which makes the biggest difference. This is because it will be up to you to tell the Revenue how much tax you think you owe rather than the Revenue telling you (although you can still ask your tax office to work out the tax).

If your tax affairs are straightforward and the tax you owe is collected at source – e.g. through PAYE – self-assessment won't have much impact. However, if you're self-employed, in a business partnership, a company director, a higher-rate taxpayer, or if you have several sources of income and/or capital gains you'll see a major difference in the way your tax affairs are dealt with. First, all your income and gains will be assessed on a current year basis (i.e. one tax year's tax bill is based on income received in that year), will be dealt with on the same form and all the tax will be due at the same time. There will be fixed dates by which you have to supply information and automatic penalties if you don't meet the Revenue's deadlines together with interest charges on tax paid late. There will be new rules about record-keeping and the length of time for which you have to keep records in support of your own tax calculation.

The first self-assessment tax returns will be sent out in April 1997 – i.e. at the end of the 1996-7 tax year and it will deal with all your income, gains, outgoings and allowances for that tax year. If you want your tax office to help you with working out the figures, you'll have to send your return back by 30 September 1997. However, if you want to work out your own tax bill, the return won't be due back until 31 January 1998 when the first payment of tax will also be due. The second payment will be due on 31 July of the same year. The final payment of tax – or refund if you're claiming tax back – will be due six months later, on the next 31 January.

Appeals

If you think you have paid too much tax, and you cannot reach agreement with your tax inspector, you can appeal. Your case will go to a hearing of the Commissioners of Tax. General Commissioners deal with most cases while Special Commissioners deal with cases which require tax expertise. You can request that your case be dealt with by the Special Commissioners instead. But whoever hears your case, you can be represented by a lawyer or accountant if you wish, though this can be expensive.

If you don't agree with the Commissioners' decision on a point of fact, you have no further appeal, but you can complain about maladministration – see 'Dealing with unhelpfulness' above.

If you don't agree with the Commissioners' decision on a point of law, you can take your case to the High Court in England and Wales, the Court of Session in Scotland or the Court of Appeal in Northern Ireland. Tell the Commissioners' Clerk in writing within 30 days of the decision, and enclose £25. Before you take this route, it's worth weighing up the possible costs of pursuing your case against the amount of tax in question – and the interest that you may have to pay if you lose.

PART 5

YOU AND YOUR HOME

CHAPTER 20

WHERE TO LIVE IN RETIREMENT

For many people, retirement is synonymous with moving to a long-dreamt-of cottage in the country with roses round the door and a garden to potter about in. However, unless you have been forced to live in an area you actively dislike for the sake of your job, you should put a lot of careful thought into the matter before you pack up and go. It's a good idea to make a list of the advantages and disadvantages of your present house or flat and its locale, bearing in mind the following points:

- Do you have family nearby? Do you lead an active life in the community, with long-term friends whom you see regularly?
- Are facilities such as the library, health centre, post office, church and so on within easy reach? Do you normally travel to them by car? Remember that there may come a time when you are no longer able to drive; are they on main routes that are likely to be well served by public transport?
- How quiet will you find the area when you are at home all day? Is there much traffic? Your current neighbours may be quiet, but how much would you suffer if they were to be replaced by noisier ones? Might it even be *too* quiet? You might find you like to see other people going about their business if you have been used to plenty of social contact in your working life.
- Is your home light enough, warm enough, small or large enough? (See also **Chapters 24 and 34**.)
- Is the garden sufficient for your needs now? Will it be hard for you to manage in later years?

Staying put

If you still live in the house in which you brought up a family, you may have been finding it too big for your needs. However, if there will now be two of you at home all the time, you are bound to need more room than when you were out at work all day. No matter how devoted you may be you will need space to follow your own interests; one of you may need a quiet room in which to study, while the other might be doing upholstery, keep fit, carpentry or any number of potentially noisy or untidy pursuits. A separate room each is a tactful solution.

You will also probably want sufficient space to have relatives and friends to stay in comfort. Ideally, you should be able to have people to stay for a week or two without it proving a strain for anyone.

If you have a large old house you may think it too expensive to keep. However, if you are particularly attached to it you could consider taking in lodgers. If you live near a university you might be able to find postgraduate students, perhaps from abroad, who will probably be more mature and responsible than younger undergraduates. Such students can bring a good deal of interest into your life, as well as extra income. Make careful enquiries first from the university as to your legal position when you want them to go.

Adapting your home

Unless your home is already perfectly suited to the needs of older people it is best to adapt it before you retire so that you do not have the worry of major alterations later when your income is reduced. If the house is old, consider having a survey done to identify potential troublespots so that you can carry out any necessary repairs that will cut down on future expense.

If you live in a two-storey house with only one bathroom, it is a good idea to install one on the other floor. Both bathrooms should be suitable for older people, with grab rails on the bath and perhaps a handrail by the lavatory. A shower is more economical than a bath and may be more accessible for people with mobility problems.

Check that the electrical wiring is in good order and consider having more fittings put in so that there is good lighting throughout the house, particularly on the stairs. If need be, reorganise the kitchen so that you do not have to bend or stretch too far to reach any of its components.

The crime prevention officer from your local police station will visit free of charge to give you advice on security; time the visit before that of the electrician as you may be recommended to install outside lighting. Most importantly, fit a smoke alarm on each floor – most cost around £18 and are simply fitted by means of two or three screws.

For more ideas and information on adapting your home see also **Chapters 24 and 34**.

Gifted housing plan
If you feel that your house will in due course become too much for you to cope with, you might wish to consider the gifted housing scheme run by Help the Aged*. You give the house to them but continue to live there, freed of all responsibility for upkeep of the house and garden and for payment of buildings insurance and Council Tax. Help the Aged will house you for life, but if you wish to move later they will find you a home within one of their housing developments. For more details obtain their booklet *Gifted Housing Plan*.

Moving elsewhere in the UK

If you do decide to move, most of the points outlined above are equally applicable to your choice of a new home. It may be that you are now liberated to move near to family members, in which case there is a focus for your choice of area. However, if you are thinking of moving to a part of the country where you have perhaps enjoyed several holidays, or which simply appears suitable for retired people, a good adage is to look before you leap. A fellside cottage in the Lake District may seem irresistible if you have seen the Lakes only in summer or in the blaze of autumn colours – but how would you manage struggling to open the gate in a high wind and lashing rain? If one of you has to spend time in hospital, will the other be able to cope with a journey of maybe 30 miles or more each way at visiting times?

Likewise, a huddle of whitewashed cottages in a coastal Cornish village loses its charm somewhat in the winter months. The best way of getting a realistic picture is to rent accommodation for several months at the most unappealing time of the year and, while there, to keep within the level of income you will have to live on rather than splurging out on holiday treats.

If after this experience at the coalface you still want to move to your dream home in the country, bear in mind one final but major point; public transport in country areas is constantly diminishing (and increasing in cost) and the village shop is fast disappearing as the majority of country-dwellers use their cars to reach the supermarket. In some areas, the traditional village community is also vanishing as holiday homes stand vacant for the greater part of the year or commuters make up the bulk of the population. Elderly people who have grown up and spent their lives in the area usually have a network of family and old friends who will help them get into town or to the doctor; will you, as newcomers, want to rely on the goodwill of relatively recent acquaintances if you are no longer able to drive? Or will you be able to afford taxis?

Moving to an area which has traditionally been popular with older people, such as one of the towns on the south coast, brings different problems. With a large older population, the town's welfare services may be severely strained; GPs may be reluctant to accept any more pensioners on to their lists, and waiting lists at, for example, hearing aid clinics may be very long. Consequently, careful research is vital before you actually begin to look for a new house or flat.

If you can afford to, you may wish to buy your next home a few years before you retire so that you can begin to take your place in the community while you are still employed. This does have its advantages in that you will not find unaccustomed leisure coinciding with new surroundings and a dearth of social life, but it will limit the time that you are able to spend househunting and making a careful choice of area.

Buying a flat

If you decide to scale down from a house to a flat in order to economise, there are some points you should check up on. The repair of the building as a whole can be a minefield: if the leasehold tenants share the ownership of the freehold there may be frequent meetings (and frequent disagreements) on the subject of what maintenance work needs to be done. On the other hand, if the freehold belongs to a separate landlord, there may be a different set of problems: sometimes a service charge is levied to cover maintenance, with the proviso that if the set charge is not sufficient the leaseholders will be jointly responsible for the extra cost. This sort of arrangement can be a licence for an unscrupulous landlord, who can pocket the service charge year after year while doing negligible maintenance, then carry out all the repairs at once and call on you to foot the bill. Sometimes the landlord may hand over maintenance to a management company, which may not be properly run.

Guard against falling foul of such situations by taking a thoughtful look at the condition of the property as a whole and asking a few of the current tenants about the way in which the flats are managed. Ask, too, for detailed accounts of the expenditure on the building over the last few years. Some service charges include central heating and hot water; if you are planning to spend your winters in the sun, you would be letting yourself in for unnecessary expenditure by taking on such a lease. Always make a very detailed examination of the charges that will be imposed and the legal obligations of the leaseholders and freeholders before buying.

A further point to bear in mind is the soundproofing of the flats; walls and ceilings may be thin and future neighbours noisy. Try to look round the flat in the evening and at a weekend when most of the other tenants will be at home.

Council tenants

If you wish to give up a large council house and move to smaller accommodation you may be able to effect an exchange. Some councils keep an exchange list for homes within their area, while most councils and housing associations participate in the National Mobility Scheme and will have a list of tenants in other areas who wish to exchange. This scheme is principally for those who have an urgent reason for moving, such as being near a relative who needs help, but there is a Tenants Exchange

Scheme with which you can register, whatever your reason for moving. Leaflets on these two schemes are available from housing authorities.

Sheltered housing

You may decide you want to opt for sheltered housing, which is now available in many areas of the UK. This usually consists of a development of living units, whether houses, flats or bungalows, which are sold to people only above a certain age, probably 55 or 60. There is a resident manager or warden, and each unit normally has an alarm system whereby a resident can call for help if needed. However, they are intended for residents who can look after themselves.

You should buy sheltered housing, whether new or second-hand, only if the builder is registered with the National House Building Council*; he will have had to comply with the NHBC's Sheltered Housing Code of Practice, which came into force in April 1990. All sheltered housing sold after this date will be handled under a management agreement that will protect residents' rights. As soon as you pay a reservation fee the builder must provide you with a Purchaser's Information Pack (PIP), which will confirm in details the type of lease, service charges, insurance, the warden's duties and reselling restrictions (for example, you can sell only to people over a certain age). You may have an option to buy only 70 per cent of the lease, with the remaining share funded by the Housing Corporation subsidy. Alternatively, the developer may offer a discounted purchase price. Both of these conditions will, of course, be mirrored in any future selling price.

Check how experienced the management organisation is; if the scheme is not a new one, find out what the increases in service charges have been in previous years. All schemes have a sinking fund to cover the cost of long-term repairs; contributions to this may be included in the service charge, or may be deferred until the property is sold. If they are to be deferred, ask how major repairs will be funded if they become necessary before there is sufficient money in the fund.

Apart from the legal obligations involved, find out how generous the communal facilities are. Some include laundry rooms and common rooms for functions. Make sure, too, that the units are well designed for the needs of older people.

Lists of sheltered housing developments are available from the New Homes Marketing Board*, the Elderly Accommodation Counsel* and Sheltered Housing Services Ltd*. The latter two organisations charge a small fee for their lists. *A Buyer's Guide to Sheltered Housing*, published by Age Concern* at £2.50, will give you more details.

For details of residential and nursing homes see **Chapter 34**.

Moving abroad

You may feel that you want to leave the British weather well behind you along with your job, but a move to sunnier climes can bring problems of its own. You need to weigh up the pros and cons even more carefully than when considering a move within Britain: while an ill-planned move at home can lead to the expense and stress of a second upheaval, a sojourn abroad can also leave you some rungs down the British property ladder.

The advice given above on having a trial period of residence holds good here too. Make sure you see the area at all times of year and, if there are British people already in residence, find out their opinions. Compare the prices of a wide range of goods and public transport, checking the availability and comfort of the latter. Most important of all, research the local health facilities. Are they of a reassuringly high standard, and are there special facilities for the older person? Are you eligible for free health care? If you have private health insurance in Britain, would it cover you in your chosen country?

If you don't already speak the language of the country you are planning to live in, how well will you be able to learn it before you move? If your grasp of it is only limited you will be restricted to the company of other expatriates for your social life. Bear in mind that in times of stress or ill-health you will probably find it harder to express yourself, so don't regard

---

*The addresses and phone numbers of organisations marked with an asterisk can be found in the address section at the back of the guide.

learning the language as one of the aspects of moving abroad that can wait until last.

Check what the pension arrangements are. You can receive your UK state pension in most countries, but you would not necessarily be entitled to subsequent increases. Contact the Department of Social Security (Overseas Branch)* for full details of the rules applying to the country in which you are planning to live. You should also find out how changes in exchange control regulations would affect pension payments, dividends and banking arrangements.

For advice on conditions of residence, local tax regulations, your legal position as a foreign resident and whether you will need a work permit if you plan to take on any sort of job, enquire first at the embassy or consulate of the relevant country.

You may want to keep property in the UK for an eventual return, in which case you will be regarded for tax purposes as being resident in the UK for any year during which you pay a visit. For details, consult the Inland Revenue booklet IR20, *Residents and Non-Residents – Liability to Tax in the United Kingdom*, available from tax enquiry centres and tax offices.

CHAPTER 21

BUYING AND SELLING

You've made the decision to move house, decided on the area you want to live in – now it's time to set the ball rolling. This chapter takes you step by step through the whole process of buying and selling, from choosing a property through to completion, and gives advice on estate agents, surveys and conveyancing. For buying and selling in Scotland see page 287; for information on renting see pages 287–9; for how to sort out a trouble-free move, see **Chapter 22**. Consumers' Association also produces *Which? Way to Buy, Sell and Move House*.

Getting a mortgage

If you have already paid off your mortgage, or you have enough cash from the sale of your home to buy a smaller property outright, then getting a mortgage is one less thing to worry about. If you do need a mortgage, you may have wondered whether your age could be a hindrance. Although some lenders do still require mortgages to be repaid by retirement age, many are now more flexible, looking instead at what people can afford to pay. Some lenders have special deals for older people.

Types of mortgage

The two most common types are repayment and endowment mortgages. With a repayment mortgage, your monthly repayment is split into two – part reduces the amount you owe, the rest is interest on the amount still owing. With a level repayment mortgage (by far the most common), your repayments after tax relief stay the same, unless the interest rate changes. With an increasing repayment mortgage, your monthly repayments start lower, but gradually increase.

With an endowment mortgage, you pay interest on the loan, together with premiums for an investment-type life insurance policy. The policy matures at the end of the mortgage term to pay off the loan (though there is no guarantee that it will produce enough to do so). You keep any money left over.

If you have a repayment mortgage, your lender may insist that you take out a mortgage protection policy to repay the mortgage if you die during the term of the loan. With endowment mortgages, you don't need any extra life insurance.

However, both these types are normally set up to last over a period of at least 20 years – otherwise the cost of repaying the loan, or building up a big enough investment to repay it, will make the monthly payments very high. Unless you need to borrow only a small amount, this could be a problem for you if you expect your income to fall once you retire. But there are alternatives to consider.

Using an existing endowment policy

If you already have an endowment policy in force, e.g. from an earlier mortgage, don't cash it in – you could get a very poor return. Instead, look for a lender who will let you use it to repay the new mortgage – lenders make a lot of money from the commission on selling new endowment policies (although from now on they will have to disclose a lot more information about the costs involved), but should be prepared to let you use an existing one.

Using an existing pension plan

Lenders may be prepared to give you a loan on the understanding that you will repay it on retirement using the tax-free lump sum from a personal pension plan (or occasionally, an additional voluntary contributions scheme – see page 83). However, this option will reduce your income in retirement – don't take it unless you are happy that you will have enough pension to live off.

Interest-only mortgages

An increasing number of lenders are prepared to offer these mortgages, which are both flexible and keep your monthly outgoings low. As the name suggests, you pay interest only on the loan – it's up to you to decide how and when to repay it, e.g. by selling shares or a second home, or by using the proceeds of a Personal Equity Plan. They are sometimes marketed specially for retired people, with no obligation to repay the capital until the house is sold or the borrower dies.

Fixed-rate or variable interest?

Fixed-rate mortgages, where the interest rate is fixed for, say, two years, are now common. After the fixed-rate period is over you pay the standard mortgage rate. There are potential problems – if interest rates generally fall after you've taken one out, you could lose out, and there are usually stiff penalties to discourage you from repaying the loan during the fixed-rate period. Lenders may also insist that you buy house insurance through them. But if you can find a deal without too many strings, and think that interest rates are more likely to rise than fall, then they offer certainty – useful if you're living on a fixed income.

> **TIP**
>
> Many lenders offer a mortgage certificate to potential borrowers, stating how much they are prepared to lend you. This certificate could be useful if you need to persuade a seller that you are a serious buyer who will have the finance to proceed.

Buying

If your family has left home you may well consider moving from a large house with its responsibilities into a small house, bungalow or flat. See **Chapter 20** for the practical considerations to think about.

Moving to a flat

If you sell your family house you could probably buy a flat for cash in the same area with something left over for investment.

Most flats in England and Wales are leasehold, which means that the ownership will revert to the lessor after a set period of time – usually 99 years. The resale value decreases towards the end of the leasehold period, and you may find it difficult to get a mortgage on anything with a lease of less than, say, 65 years.

The landlord or freeholder usually has control over the management of the property. This can be convenient, but more often is a source of dissatisfaction. It is now possible to buy the freehold of your flat as a group or as an individual. The new proposals mean that you have a right to buy at a fair price, regardless of the freeholder's wishes.

In most blocks of flats, there is a service charge to cover porterage, cleaning of communal areas, insurance and the maintenance of the building, drains, garden and driveway. This charge is bound to increase annually and in addition you'll have to pay your share of any major repair work to be done.

House hunting

Estate agents

To find names and addresses of estate agents, as well as using the *Yellow Pages*, look for agents advertising property in the local paper.

To give you an idea of the type of property and the price range handled by an agent, have a look at the advertisements in the windows. Don't restrict yourself to just one agent. Enquire of all the agents in the locality, and see if there are any, perhaps not so close, who specialise in the type of property you want.

Be prepared to spend time initially calling in or ringing up regularly in order to establish a good relationship with the agents. The better the contact you have with an agent, the more likely they are to remember you when a suitable property comes their way.

The estate agent will give you details of available properties which they think may be of interest. The facts given in the description of a property must be accurate. But you may find

WARNING
Estate agents are paid by the seller, not the buyer, so don't expect them to have your interests foremost in their minds. And be aware that estate agents are keen to sell financial services, or introduce clients to financial organisations (for which they get commission). You may get a good deal, but there is evidence to suggest that, particularly when buyers are easy to come by, some may discriminate against people who decline financial services.

that because a room is on an upper floor, it is counted and described as a bedroom when it may not be big enough to hold a bed, so check measurements if they are given. Photographs of properties serve as a rough guide, but they can be misleading and should be regarded with caution. For instance, a house may have been trimmed of its less attractive surroundings.

Following recent legislation, estate agents now face stricter controls. The Property Misdescription Act makes it illegal for estate agents and other property sellers to give inaccurate descriptions of properties. Regulations extending the scope of the Estate Agents Act 1979 also mean that estate agents must now be more open in their dealings with consumers. For example, individuals may be banned from estate agency work if they discriminate against potential buyers who don't buy financial services from them, or if they fail to pass on details of offers to the seller.

If you need to complain
If you have a complaint about an estate agent, write in the first instance to the head office. If this does not lead to a satisfactory conclusion and your agent is a member of Ombudsman for Corporate Estate Agents (OCEA)*, write to the Ombudsman – but you must do this within six months.

If your estate agent is not a member of OCEA, find out if they belong to a professional body: the National Association of Estate Agents (NAEA)*, the Royal Institution of Chartered Surveyors (RICS)* or the Incorporated Society of Valuers and Auctioneers (ISVA)*. If so, write to the appropriate one, explaining the problem: they may be able to help. Another option, if you suspect that any law has been broken, is to contact your local Trading Standards Department (address in the *Yellow Pages*), or to write to the Office of Fair Trading★.

Property shops
Some areas of the country have property shops, displaying details, including photographs, of houses and flats. The seller pays for this, usually around one to two per cent of the selling price. You can get particulars of any property you think looks suitable and arrange to see it.

Moving to a new area
It's not easy to house-hunt at a distance. If you are not able to go to the area, you can call on an agent in your home town and ask if they have contacts with fellow agents in another area. The *Estates Gazette* publishes a monthly regional directory of agents. If you are moving to another area, ask at the local library what papers cover the district, and on what day property adverts appear.

Some agents are linked to a regional or national computer. You register your requirements with one agent, and receive details of properties matching your specifications that are currently on the books of all the others. National Homelink Service is operated by members of NAEA★. They provide a referral service for anyone moving from one area to another. The Homelink member in your present locality will contact another Homelink member in the area to which you are moving, giving details of your requirements. The names and addresses of Homelink agents in any area can be obtained from the NAEA★.

Relocation agents act solely on behalf of buyers, and vary from individual consultants to fairly large organisations. They offer various services, ranging from finding a suitable property, through to overseeing the sale of your home and making removal arrangements. You can find them in the *Yellow Pages* under 'Relocation agents'; there is also an Association of Relocation Agents★. It's usual to be asked to pay a 'retainer' in the region of £200 for the initial work. A further fee, usually of one per cent of the price, is payable on exchange of contracts.

BUYING AND SELLING

Making an offer

When you decide that you want to buy a particular house or flat, put your offer in writing to the estate agent, with a copy to the seller. The offer does not commit you, provided it is made 'subject to contract or to survey', so you can still withdraw if, say, a survey decides you against continuing with the purchase. If there is any objection to the deal being on a 'subject to contract' basis, do not proceed; and don't sign any kind of contract at this stage without taking legal advice.

Stamp duty

A buyer has to pay stamp duty on the transfer of any house or flat where the purchase price is more than £60,000. The rate of duty is one per cent on the total purchase price paid, including the first £60,000 – so if your purchase price is just a little above £60,000 you could save £600 by agreeing to pay for items such as carpets separately, bringing the purchase price below the limit.

Paying a deposit

When you make a firm offer the estate agent may ask you to pay a deposit (£200, say). You are under no obligation to do this. If you do pay a deposit, you should get a receipt stating that the deposit was paid 'subject to contract and to survey'. If the sale should fall through before contracts are exchanged the deposit has to be returned in full.

Surveys

The valuation

If you are applying for a mortgage the lender will ask a local surveyor to carry out a mortgage valuation survey to help assess the amount they're willing to lend. The cost (which you pay) depends on the value of the property. It is not a structural survey and does not guarantee that the house is structurally sound and without defects, so it's important to pay for a proper survey too.

The offer of a loan may be altered or withdrawn after the

valuation. You would then need to start again with a different property or a different lender. The valuer can include a recommendation to the lender not to make a loan unless specified work is carried out, or he or she can advise the lender to withhold an amount (£5,000, say), which will be paid out when the work has been carried out satisfactorily.

A house- (or flat-) buyer's report
This should provide a good idea of the general condition of a property, but it won't include an inspection of areas that aren't easily accessible (because they're covered by carpets, for example). This is usually carried out by the surveyor when doing the mortgage valuation. It costs roughly twice as much as a valuation.

Full structural survey
This is the most detailed and expensive option and should be carried out by a qualified surveyor who specialises in this kind of work. Your solicitor or a friend may be able to recommend one to you or you may be able to use the surveyor who is doing the mortgage valuation if he or she is properly qualified. It is preferable to use a surveyor local to the property being inspected since he or she may know of any relevant conditions in the area which might affect it.

Discuss with the surveyor how comprehensive a survey you want carried out and ask how much you would need to spend to put the house into good order. Bring to the surveyor's attention anything about the property, the neighbourhood or the sellers that you think could create problems. The extent of the survey will depend on the age and condition of the property – and how much you can afford. You should obtain written confirmation from the surveyor, setting out the extent of the inspection. Expect to pay at least three times as much as for a valuation.

Survey for a flat
A survey for a flat, particularly if it is in a converted house, should cover an inspection of the whole building. This should include the roof, foundations, drains, gutters and so on; also any communal services such as electricity, water or gas supplies or

anything that you will be liable for under the terms of the lease. If you can, give the surveyor a copy of the lease, so that he or she can comment on your responsibilities for repairing and decorating the flat and for contributing towards the cost of maintaining communal parts of the buildings.

Before completion

During the period between making an offer and exchanging contracts, neither buyer nor seller has entered into a legally binding contract. If the seller accepts your offer straight away, the house is then 'under offer'.

Sometimes an offer may be accepted with the proviso that exchange of contracts should take place within, say, a month: otherwise the property may be put on the market again. If two or more people want to buy the same property, the seller will sometimes tell the solicitor or conveyancer to send out a second set of contracts to the would-be buyers' solicitors. The buyers then have to race each other – the first to send a deposit and signed contract gets the house. Solicitors and conveyancers are required to tell you when there is a contract race.

Gazumping
This is where the seller, tempted by a higher offer, goes back on the agreement with the potential buyer and accepts a later, higher bid. You are not protected against gazumping until you have entered into a binding contract.

Conveyancing

As soon as you start seriously house-hunting, you should organise someone to do the conveyancing – the legal and administrative work involved in buying or selling a home – so that whoever you choose can be ready when you decide to make an offer or advise on any legal snags. You have three options: appoint a solicitor or a licensed conveyancer, or do it yourself.

The choice between a solicitor and licensed conveyancer is very much a matter of personal preference. Both should be able to provide a full house-buying service and carry out the basic legal work for you: both are free to charge what they choose. It is worth getting estimates from more than one solicitor or conveyancer before choosing one. Many charge a flat fee for all the work involved. In addition to the basic fees, you'll have to pay for disbursements – bank charges for transferring money, telephone charges and other sundry costs – as well as Land Registry fees, local authority searches and stamp duty.

You could save money by doing the conveyancing yourself. It is worth considering if you've got the time and confidence.

As soon as an offer has been accepted, the seller's conveyancer draws up a draft contract. A set of 'preliminary enquiries' are sent to the seller's conveyancer. These are standard questions about boundaries, restrictions and so on.

Agreeing amendments to a draft contract can take time. It may take a while to obtain a mortgage offer or to get the results of local searches. At this stage a good solicitor or conveyancer will be happy to go through all the paperwork with you. Don't be afraid to ask questions on any points that are still unclear. It is important to make sure that everything is right now – it will be too late to change things after exchange of contracts.

Exchange of contracts

Once contracts are exchanged you and the seller are locked into a legal agreement from which neither side can withdraw. At this point a deposit has to be paid by the buyer to the seller – usually 10 per cent of the purchase price, but a lower figure can sometimes be negotiated. The deposit is non-refundable and is used as security for the performance of the contract. The amount will be deducted from what has to be paid at completion.

Insurance

Insurance remains the responsibility of the seller until you exchange contracts. If you are getting a mortgage, the lenders will make it a condition that the property is insured (the mortgage valuation will say how much it should be insured for). The lenders will probably be keen to arrange the cover – they get commission for doing so. Most lenders will allow you to arrange your own insurance, but they will want proof that the policy provides adequate cover for their security, and will often charge a fee for the administrative costs of doing so.

Completion day

The date for completion is agreed at the time contracts are exchanged and is specified in the contract. Don't agree to a completion date unless you can meet it – you will have to pay interest from the agreed date until completion actually takes place. For bridging loans, how to make moving as trouble-free as possible, and what to do if you are caught in a 'chain', see **Chapter 22**.

On the date of completion, the seller has to give you vacant possession – that is, to move out on or before the day with all furniture and belongings. And the buyer must be able to pay the remainder of the purchase price. This is usually done through the solicitor or other conveyancer, so you need to send the money to them in good time for any cheques to clear. When the final payments are made, the deeds will be handed over, including the conveyance or transfer to the buyer. If you have a mortgage, the title deeds of the property or the land certificate are kept by the mortgage lender as security for the money being lent.

Selling

You can either handle the sale yourself or commission an estate agent to do it for you. An estate agent will do most of the work for you, but this will probably be the largest single cost of moving home.

Selling through an estate agent

Although it's a costly business, there are advantages to selling through an estate agent. They take some of the work and worry from the seller, they have good facilities for publicising the sale and ready access to more would-be buyers. They also offer better security if you are living alone: for example, you can ask for the agent's representative to accompany all viewers.

It is a good idea to visit several agencies to get some idea of the costs involved. Choosing the cheapest estate agent is not necessarily the best option; it's also obviously important to find one who can sell your home quickly and efficiently. Recommendation and personal experience count for a lot. If you're buying and selling in the same area, you could sign up with a few agents as a buyer, before you try to sell, in order to get an idea of which one offers the best service.

How estate agents charge

There are various types of agreement, which affect how much you pay:

- **Sole agency** – in return for agreeing to sell through only one agent, you're charged a relatively low rate.
- **Multiple agency** – you instruct as many agents as you like, but pay only the one who comes up with the buyer. In return for the flexibility, charges are higher.
- **Joint sole agency** – you sign up with two agents only – both agree to the arrangement and to who gets the commission.

Some estate agents make a charge (which could be up to £200) for the marketing and administrative costs they've incurred, irrespective of whether they manage to sell your home. This is more common north of the Midlands. However, if they do sell the property, the commission is likely to be lower than with a 'no sale, no fee' agreement.

Commissions and the deals available vary widely across the UK. For example, a survey in *Which?* magazine in March 1992 found that sole agency deals, with commission of about one to two per cent, were more common north of the Midlands: multiple agency deals, with commission of two and a half to three and a half per cent, were more widely available in the south.

If you need to sell quickly, multiple agency may be best (if available). If you go for this, sign up with at least three agencies. Otherwise, the amount you save with a sole agency makes this the best option. If the agent you've signed up with doesn't manage to sell your property quickly, you have the option of leaving and instructing another agent on a sole agency basis. Telling each agent at the outset that you will reconsider after, say, six weeks, should encourage them to 'push' your property in that time. But remember, unless you've got a 'no sale, no fee' agreement, you'll probably have to pay each agent's marketing and administration costs – sale or no sale.

Once you've decided on the type of deal, negotiate the cost and terms (easiest when the housing market is stagnant): as well as bargaining for a reduction in the commission, you may be able to get add-on costs such as advertising waived. Whatever agreement you make with the agent, you should get it confirmed in writing.

WARNING

Beware of 'sole selling rights'. This means that if you sold your home other than through the agent – through a newspaper advert, for example – you might still have to pay the agent commission.

And never accept wording that says charges will be payable for introducing a buyer who is ready, willing and able to buy. If the sale does not go through, you'll still have to pay.

Selling without an agent

If you want to sell your house privately there are several steps you'll have to take:

- Decide on an asking price – you can ask a local estate agent to give you a valuation, though they may charge if you are not selling through them. If you are uncertain about whether there are structural problems, ask a surveyor to look over the house. Build into your asking price some allowance for this.
- Decide what items are to be included in the sale.
- Draft an advertisement – include information on location, number of rooms, type of heating system etc., as well as

any special features which would make good selling points. A photo could help.
- Choose the right newspapers or magazine to place the advertisement. Local newspapers are usually the best place to start, though it is unlikely that one entry will be sufficient. You could put a card in shop windows, or pay a 'property shop' to display details of the house, if there's one in your area.
- Make or buy a 'For Sale' board, if you're going to put one up. Remember that there are laws governing the maximum size of boards.
- Draw up the particulars to give to potential buyers. Get hold of a few sets of estate agents' particulars first so that you can see how they do it.
- Arrange the appointments to view the house and show the viewers round.
- Evaluate the merits of rival bids – don't necessarily accept the offer of the person who promises to pay most. It may be better to choose the one who seems the most likely to be able to pay when the time comes, or the one who is not dependent on selling a home.
- Negotiate a final price with the buyer you choose. A viewer may ask you for 'first refusal'. This would mean that you could not deal with other offers and could lose a sale. Instead, counter this approach by suggesting that the viewer makes a firm offer.

Once you accept an offer

Your estate agent may suggest that a buyer whose offer you have accepted should put down an initial deposit of say, £200, though this is not binding. The estate agent doesn't withdraw the property from the market until contracts have been exchanged, unless you request this. Inform your solicitor or conveyancer that you have a buyer and give him or her the relevant details.

Buying and selling in Scotland

The Scottish system differs from the English system in a number of important ways.

Estate agents sell only about 35 per cent of houses in Scotland: most business is done through solicitors. Properties are usually advertised at 'offers over £x', often with a closing date. Any offers received up to that date will be considered. You need to get a mortgage (and a structural survey, if you want one) before making an offer.

Offers in Scotland aren't 'subject to contract'. If you make an offer and it is unconditionally accepted, there is a binding deal – the seller has to sell, and you have to buy. Offers are submitted in writing and include things like the price offered, what's included in the price, and the date you want to move in. The offer may be conditionally accepted, with proposed changes in terms. This may lead to a series of letters between the solicitors, until agreement is reached and moving day fixed. You probably won't have to pay a deposit: you pay the full price when you move in.

This system has pluses and minuses. Valuations and surveys are done before the buyer makes an offer – so if you make a few unsuccessful bids, the costs could mount up before you've even found a place to buy. On the other hand the system does seem to speed things up and remove some of the uncertainty.

If you do have a disagreement with an estate agent, the Ombudsman for Corporate Estate Agents* may be able to help (see page 277). Members of the OCEA have to abide by a Code of Practice which has been drawn up specially for Scotland.

Renting

If you decide to rent a house or flat, start by looking in the local papers, but don't forget to ask friends and neighbours too. Some estate agents handle rented accommodation and there are letting agencies that specialise in rented accommodation. Be prepared to pay them a fee – two weeks' rent, say, in addition to the deposit (usually equivalent to one month's rent) and the first rent payment.

Tenancy agreement

It's advisable to rent property that has a proper tenancy agreement, so that both you and the landlord are covered by law. The tenancy agreement sets out the rights and duties of both landlord and tenant. Make sure that you are clear about your duties as a tenant before you sign the agreement. If you are in any doubt a Citizens Advice Bureau or solicitor may be able to help.

The main types of agreement are as follows.

Regulated tenancies
Most lettings by private landlords which began before 15 January 1989 are known as regulated tenancies under the Rent Act.

- The landlord cannot evict the tenant unless he or she gets a possession order.
- Either the landlord or the tenant can apply to the rent officer for a fair rent to be registered – this is the maximum the landlord can charge until it is reviewed.
- The tenancy will last for a fixed term of between one and five years.

Assured tenancies
These are tenancies created after the 15 January 1989.

- The landlord cannot evict the tenant unless he/she gets a possession order.
- The rent charged is a matter for agreement between the two parties involved. This is known as an 'open market' rent.
- The tenancy can be either a fixed term – it's fixed for a number of years or months – or for an indefinite period.

Rent
You must pay your rent on the due date whether or not you have a received a reminder. Try and get receipts for payment, or keep a record which could be used as proof of payment. The landlord may use a letting agency, in which case rent should be

paid directly to the agency. The rent will go up at agreed intervals, depending upon the type of tenancy you have.

Eviction

A landlord must give you written notice to quit – usually four weeks. Before a landlord can evict you he or she has to obtain a court order. If you want to go, you must give the landlord the minimum notice as specified in the tenancy agreement.

Where to go for help
If you have a problem with a landlord or with the tenancy agreement, go to a Citizens Advice Bureau, a solicitor, a law centre or a local housing advice centre.

The Department of the Environment publishes a series of housing booklets, explaining the law and your rights as a tenant in details. These are available from local libraries, housing advice centres and Citizens Advice Bureaux.

CHAPTER 22

Moving home

Moving home can be both stressful and expensive. Making good removal arrangements is one step on the road to a smooth move. This chapter covers the steps to take when choosing a removal firm and what to do if you are involved in a 'chain'. There's also a checklist of people to tell about your move.

Choosing a removal firm

Cost is one of the main considerations when choosing a removal firm, and it can vary by hundreds of pounds. How much you'll have to pay depends on how far you're moving, how many possessions you have and how much packing you want the firm to do. It's worth getting at least three quotes before deciding.

Find out the names of removers – both local firms as well as the larger national companies – by looking in the *Yellow Pages*, by asking the British Association of Removers (BAR)* for a list of local members, or by sounding out friends. Don't choose on cost alone; find out how many people would be allocated to the job, check the small print (for example, the remover's liability if something went wrong) and ascertain how they would deal with awkward and valuable items.

Getting quotes

As soon as you have some idea of the moving date, ask the removal firms to send someone round to give you a quote. They should look right round your property, including the loft, garage and garden, to see what quantity and type of furniture and belongings are involved. Tell them if you're planning a clear-out – this could reduce the quote.

Get each quote in writing. (If you accept a verbal quote the firm could alter it after the move.) A written quote is normally binding on the company if it is accepted within, say, 21 days and the work is done within, say, three months. Some firms provide estimates – these are only a guide to the final cost, not a binding price.

When getting quotes you should point out to the removers any belongings that may need special packing, or may present problems in handling or transporting – for example, pictures, audio equipment, records, books, antiques and fragile items, collections of valuable objects, plants, piano. Point out any built-in cupboards or shelves that will need dismantling and decide if you want to take the carpets with you. Lifting and laying fitted carpets may cost extra.

What does the quote include?

Some firms will quote a basic figure, then add on things like packing boxes, insurance and VAT. If you want to put your possessions into storage, most firms will give you a quote for the actual removal, plus the weekly cost of storage in a warehouse.

Most removers offer a variety of packing and unpacking alternatives. You may think it worth the cost of paying for all the packing, unpacking and moving to be done by experts, so that all you have to do is supervise the work. This is the most expensive option. It's cheaper to pack yourself, but you need plenty of time in advance and you're unlikely to be insured for damage to breakable items in transit. A way round this is to pay the removers to pack 'breakables' and for you to pack the rest.

> **TIP**
>
> It's important that you read the contract before you sign on the dotted line, so that you know what the firm is promising to do. If there's anything you're unhappy with take it up with the firm and consider altering the contract before you sign.

Generally, payment has to be made in advance or on the day of the move. When you accept the quote you are expected to give a firm date for the job: having booked a date, you would have to give reasonable notice if you wanted to change it; otherwise, the company might well charge a cancellation fee.

Moving abroad

You have the choice of sending your goods individually or as 'groupage' – meaning that your belongings make up a part-load in a container. Charges and packing costs are lower for groupage, but you don't have as much control over when the move is made, since the firm has to take account of the wishes of at least one other customer. However, shared loads may be easier to arrange for popular routes.

Insurance for the move

Removal contracts usually limit the removal firm's liability to, say, £20 per item, so you'll need extra, more comprehensive, insurance. While your belongings are in transit they may be covered by your existing house contents insurance policy. Check with the insurers beforehand – if it doesn't provide you with adequate cover you may be able to extend your policy. Alternatively, the removal firm may offer, or in many cases insist on, their own insurance. This usually costs around five to ten per cent of the removal costs.

What to do if things go wrong

If anything gets broken or damaged, try to make a written note of it at the time, and ask the removers to sign it. Complain in writing to the removal firm. If you get no satisfaction, write to the British Association of Removers (BAR)*, if your removal firm is a member. If you're still not happy you can go to court or arbitration. If the firm is a member of BAR they will subsidise the cost of arbitration, which is binding on both parties.

The house-buying chain

You will probably be trying to buy one property and sell another – and ideally, to keep the timing of the two closely linked. If your ability to buy your new home depends on someone purchasing your old one, you're involved in a 'chain' of sales and purchases.

If the 'link' is broken by a buyer pulling out, say, you have three possible courses of action:

- Drop the asking price to find another buyer quickly.
- Take out a bridging loan to finance short-term ownership of two properties.
- Use a 'chain-breaking' scheme.

Bridging loans

Bridging loans are offered by banks and building societies and cover the period between paying for your new home and getting the proceeds from your old one. Bridging loans are not normally secured on either property – so the lender has no rights over your home if you fail to pay up. However, this does put the price up. There are two types of loan:

- **Closed** – you borrow for a fixed time because the completion date for selling your home has been set; this is usually the cheapest option for most people.
- **Open-ended** – when you're unsure when it will be sold. Banks and building societies are less willing to offer these because of the uncertainties involved. Don't consider getting one unless you can afford to pay for both homes, for, say, six months.

Bridging loans can be expensive and there's usually an arrangement fee to pay on top. You can get tax relief (at 15 per cent from 6 April 1995) for up to one year on the interest on the first £30,000 borrowed – though you may have to claim this back from the Inland Revenue. This is in addition to mortgage interest relief (MIRAS) – see **Chapter 18**.

Chain-breaking schemes

Some estate agents and property developers offer these schemes as an alternative to bridging loans. They agree to buy your home, which is revalued to produce a quick sale (it may be lower than your asking price). The agent or developer then buys it at a price generally between 8 and 14 per cent below the revised valuation.

You are then free to buy your new home, while the estate agent sells your old one. Generally, if the agent sells it for more than the valuation they keep the extra; if they sell it for less, they suffer a loss.

These schemes are not cheap: it could cost up to £10,000 to sell a £100,000 property. A bridging loan might cost less.

Who to tell about your move

Services

Arrange to have service meters read before you move. If this is not possible, make a note of the readings yourself. This can help if there are disagreements when the bills arrive. Arrange for the disconnection of appliances such as cooker and washing machine and make arrangements for them to be connected in your new home.

Gas and electricity

Give seven working days' notice. Contact your gas region/local electricity board (addresses and phone numbers will be on the bills). They'll need to know the completion date and your account number and new address. If you're moving to a new area you'll need to contact the local gas region/electricity board there, too.

Water

As for gas and electricity. You are responsible for water rates until completion date. If you've paid in advance you can claim a portion back. If the water has been turned off in your new home, contact the new water authority and give at least two days' notice to have the water reconnected.

MOVING HOME

Telephone
As for gas and electricity. Contact your local sales office (address and phone number on bills, or dial 150 to be connected to your local office) and tell them the moving date and new address. Contact the sales office in the area you're moving to, in order to sort out a phone in your new home. If you simply take over the existing number the day the seller moves out there will be no charge. If there is a delay there will be a reconnection charge. If you're moving within the same exchange area you can usually take your existing number with you, though there will be a charge. If there's no existing line or if it has been relocated you can have a new one installed, though again there will be a charge.

Mail
For a charge, you can get your mail redirected. Contact any post office and fill out form P944 – give at least five working days' notice. Leave your new address at your old home in case any mail does slip through.

Finances

Let any of the following organisations with whom you have an arrangement know of your change of address.

Banks and building societies
If you're moving to another area you may want to transfer your account to a local branch. It may be a good idea to wait until after you've moved, in case payments in or out of your account go astray at this crucial time.

If you have standing orders and direct debits, write to the companies with which you have these arrangements and give them details of your address and your new account if you've moved it.

Credit cards
When you pay the last bill before you move remember to fill in the back of the payment slip. If you have given someone a 'continuous authority' to deduct money from your credit card

account (like a standing order), write to the company with which you have the arrangement and give details of your new address.

Loans and rental companies
Rented TVs and videos can usually be taken with you and your account transferred. But let them know first when you give them your new address.

Investments
Tell institutions of any change in the account to which direct payments, of dividends, say, should be made.

State pensions and benefits
Notify your local DSS office and if necessary nominate a new post office at which to cash your payments, using form P80MA.

Other pensions
If you're getting paid any other pensions make sure that the payers know when you're moving (and new bank account details if the pension is paid directly into your account). Don't forget to do this if you've got any pension built up with a previous employer.

Life insurance and pension policies
Send your new address along with the policy numbers to the company.

Tax inspector
Write to your tax office, quoting your National Insurance and tax reference numbers. You'll find the address on your notice of coding or tax return, or you can ask your employer or pension provider.

Council tax
Tell both your old and new Council Tax Offices. You have to pay Council Tax from the day you move into your new home. If you have paid in advance at your old one, you are entitled to a refund.

House insurance
Let your insurer know in writing before you move. The cost of insurance varies, depending upon where you live, so you may be charged a higher premium or get a refund; however, the move might provide a good opportunity to change insurer (you should get a refund for the unexpired portion of your existing policy).

Remember that once you've exchanged contracts the new property becomes your risk, so you'll need to arrange buildings insurance to start on the date of exchange. You should keep your buildings insurance cover on your existing home until completion, in case the buyer defaults.

Car insurance
You'll need to tell your insurer, intermediary or broker before you move – otherwise you could find that your insurance isn't valid. As with contents insurance the premium may change.

Other people to tell

Driving licence and vehicle registration
Complete the section on your current licence/registration document and send to DVLC, Swansea, using the postcode SA99 1AB for the licence and SA99 1AN for the registration document.

TV licence
Write to Barton House, Bristol BS98 1TL. You can also notify your change of address at a post office.

Professional advisers
Tell your accountant, solicitor, investment adviser or stockbroker, trade unions/professional bodies.

Other services

Tell your doctor, dentist, optician, magazines and other subscriptions, newsagent and dairy (remember to pay any outstanding bills). At your new address, register with a new doctor and find a dentist as soon as possible – see **Chapter 32**.

CHAPTER 23

HOUSE INSURANCE

Are you insured for too much, or too little? Insure for too much, and you are throwing money down the drain, for too little and your insurer could be entitled to scale down the payout if you make a claim. Many people insure through their mortgage lender, but you don't have to, and indeed it may not be the best option for you, particularly since people in their fifties or older can often can get discounts – see the box later in this chapter.

How much to insure for?

The amount you are insured for should be the maximum amount the insurance company stands to lose as a result of the total destruction of your home and possessions. If you are insured for too little, the insurance company can scale down your claims according to the extent of under-insurance. Say you have house contents insurance with £10,000 of cover, but in fact, your possessions are worth £20,000. If you claim £200 for a stolen television, the insurance company may pay you only £100.

With 'sum-insured' policies you have to calculate the sum you need to insure for, and the insurance company calculates the premium accordingly. With other policies the premium depends on the number of bedrooms in your house. These 'bedroom-rated' policies may provide unlimited cover, in which case you don't need to work out how much to insure for. However, most do have a maximum limit which, for contents cover for a three-bedroom house can be as little as £15,000 or as much as £30,000. Even so, you should still check that you don't exceed the limits.

Valuing your contents

You usually have to insure for the cost of replacing all your possessions. Rather than make a guess, add up the cost of replacing everything in your home – many insurance companies provide checklists to help you do this. Most house contents policies are index-linked so that the amount you are insured for keeps pace with inflation. However, this will not take account of new possessions or fluctuations in the value of antiques, so review the sum you are insured for periodically.

There are two types of cover you can buy – indemnity and new-for-old. **New-for-old** means that the insurance company will pay to replace damaged items with new ones. **Indemnity cover** means that the insurance company will pay you only the actual value of items damaged or lost. So, if you had a ten-year old cooker destroyed in a fire, with new-for-old cover you would get the price of a new cooker, whereas indemnity cover would pay only the value of a ten-year old cooker.

Most house contents insurance policies offer new-for-old cover, except for clothes, linen, pots and pans and, sometimes, bicycles. If you decide to cover some or all of your possessions on an indemnity basis you can calculate the value as follows. Take the current price of the item, and divide it by the number of years you would expect it to last for. Multiply this amount by however many years old it is, and deduct the result from the current shop price. This calculation gives you the value less a deduction for wear and tear.

Jewellery, antiques and valuables

Having a valuation is important when you need to make an insurance claim for any valuable, and to play safe you need to update valuations every three years or so. However, the insurance valuation for jewellery, 'collectables' or fine art could be as much as twice the amount you paid for it – or up to four times as much for rare or hard-to-replace items. The valuation reflects the amount you might have to pay, if you needed to buy a replacement or get a copy made. When getting valuations, always make clear you want a valuation for insurance purposes.

You can get valuations from auction houses, jewellers and antique dealers: look out for qualifications such as those from the Royal Institution of Chartered Surveyors*, the Incorporated Society of Valuers and Auctioneers* or the National Association of Goldsmiths*. Costs vary from one to four per cent of the valuation figure, plus VAT, though some valuers charge on an hourly basis and there is often a minimum charge, too. You may not get a valuation immediately – some valuers prefer to hold on to the goods for a week or so to research them. It is also helpful to have photos taken from more than one angle.

Buildings

You need to insure your buildings for how much they would cost to rebuild, including the cost of removing rubble, and architects', surveyors' and other fees. This is calculated from the floor space of your home and standard rebuilding cost tables, which tell you the cost of rebuilding houses of different ages in different areas. A version of these tables, and advice on how to calculate the rebuilding cost of your home, are available in a leaflet called *How to work out the rebuilding cost of your home* from the Association of British Insurers*. Remember that this is the approximate cost of rebuilding, not the likely resale value of your home, which could be much more or much less. Virtually all buildings insurance policies automatically adjust your cover each year to keep pace with rising (or falling) building costs. Even so, you may find that over the years the sum insured grows too much or too little and you become over- or under-insured. So recalculate the sum you are insured for every five years or so.

What does house insurance cover?

Most house insurance policies come in two parts – insurance for buildings and insurance for contents – but you don't usually have to buy both from the same insurer. What's normally covered is listed below, but check how your own policy compares.

Cover for buildings

This covers the building you live in plus any outbuildings and underground pipes and cables connected to your building. This includes any permanent and immovable fixtures to the building, such as fitted bathrooms and kitchens.

Fences and gates are covered under your buildings policy but there is no cover for damage to these by storms or floods. Swimming-pools and tennis courts may also be covered, but damage by subsidence or heave (see below) may be excluded.

Cover for contents

This covers all your possessions in your home which are portable, plus aerials and often, but not always, satellite dishes. Cover is available for the contents of your freezer but with some policies you have to pay extra for this. Items used for business purposes are not covered.

All-risks insurance
Outside the home, your possessions will be covered only if you have taken out optional all-risks insurance. This will cover you against most eventualities, for example, if you accidentally leave your briefcase on the bus. This cover extends throughout the UK, sometimes throughout Europe and worldwide, so it can often be useful if you lose something on holiday.

Cover in the garden
Cover for possessions in the garden will be limited with most policies – the overall maximum ranges from £100 to £1,000. Many policies only cover items 'temporarily removed' to the garden, not items which are permanently there, so if something is always in the garden, such as a swing or climbing frame, check to make sure it's covered. If it is permanently fixed to the ground, your buildings policy may cover it.

Matching items
If you have matching items, e.g. a three-piece suite or carpets that match throughout the house, your insurance will usually pay to replace only the damaged items. The insurers should pay

any reasonable cost towards making or finding a matching replacement, if possible. You can ask your insurance company to insure matching items as one item so that if any part is damaged all will be replaced, but this will cost extra.

Moving house
If you are moving house, some insurance companies will cover you for any damage to your property in transit, so long as it is being moved by professional removers. For insurance from the removal company see **Chapter 22**.

Valuable items
If you have valuable items worth over a set amount, these will be covered only if you have informed your insurers that you want them covered. Definitions of valuables vary – check your policy.

Other cover
Money, securities, documents, cheque books and credit cards are covered in the home, usually up to a limit of around £200. Cover outside the home is also available, but you will probably have to pay extra. If your keys are stolen (or, sometimes, lost), most contents policies will pay to have the locks on your house replaced. Bicycles, boats and caravans can all be covered under house contents insurance, usually for an extra charge. If you want cover for something unusual, such as a powered wheelchair, consult the *Insurance Buyer's Guide* (Kluwer Publishing – try your local library) or an insurance broker or adviser (see page 146).

What are you covered against?

Natural disasters and accidents
You are covered against damage by storms, floods, lightning, fire, earthquakes and explosions, and against damage by water or oil which escapes from your heating or plumbing system or from washing-machines and dishwashers. You are also covered against damage by falling trees, branches and aerials; aircraft and objects falling from them; and collision by vehicles and animals.

If your home is uninhabitable after a disaster, your insurance will pay some money towards alternative accommodation until you can move back. Damage by smoke, frost and freezing is covered by some policies but not by others.

Subsidence and heave
This happens when the land upon which your house is built falls or rises, which can cause cracks to appear in your walls and, ultimately, makes your house unsafe. But there are many exclusions and it can be difficult to prove that it is subsidence causing the problem. With most policies you will have to pay at least £500 towards the cost of any repairs.

Theft and vandalism
You are covered against any damage or loss caused by thieves or vandals. However, most policies do not cover you against theft by deception or fraud. Cover may be withdrawn or limited if you go away on holiday for a long time (usually defined as 30 days) or if you rent out all or part of your home.

Accidental damage
Your buildings policy will automatically cover you for accidental damage to underground pipes and cables, and to any fixed glass, ceramic hobs and washbasins, sinks, baths, toilets and so on. Your contents policy will cover you for accidental damage to mirrors and plate glass in furniture, and for accidental damage to hi-fi equipment, TVs and videos, and sometimes personal computers too.

If you want to get accidental damage cover for anything else, you have to ask for an accidental damage cover extension, which will cost extra. But watch out for the exclusions.

Insurance Premium Tax

From October 1994, Insurance Premium Tax has added 2.5 per cent to the cost of most types of insurance (except life insurance). Most insurance companies are passing on all the tax directly to consumers.

Legal liability

Your buildings insurance will cover you for any legal liability as owner of the home, your contents cover for liability as occupier or for personal liability claims. So, if a tile falls off the roof and hits someone on the head, or if your dog tears the postman's trousers, you may find that you can claim any costs you have to pay from your insurance.

Exclusions

Standard exclusions

All policies have a standard list of exclusions, which includes damage caused by war, sonic boom, radioactive contamination and riot. Some policies also have 'excesses', which means that you have to pay the first part of any claim (£25, say) yourself.

Wear and tear

If, say, a roof collapses in a storm, and you claim on your insurance, the insurers may argue that the roof collapsed partly because of the storm and partly because it was old and in poor condition and would have collapsed soon anyway. The insurance company will then make a deduction for wear and tear.

Some buildings policies guarantee not to make a deduction for wear and tear. However, with all policies you still have a duty to maintain your property in 'reasonable repair'. If you do not do this, your insurance company can refuse to pay your claim.

Disclosure

With any type of insurance, you are legally obliged to tell your insurers of anything which might affect the risk they are taking on, whether or not they ask you about it. In particular, you should tell your insurers if you have any lodgers, if you go away for more than 30 days, if you are carrying out building or decorating work, or if you have made claims in the past. Cover may be limited in these circumstances.

The addresses and phone numbers of organisations marked with an asterisk can be found in the address section at the back of the guide.

MONEY-SAVING TIPS

- Many companies offer discounts or special policies to people who are retired or over a certain age. These companies include Age Concern*, Landmark, Norwich Union, Saga and Sun Alliance.
- You could get a discount on the cost of a policy by agreeing to pay a certain amount (a 'voluntary excess') towards a claim, in addition to any compulsory excess.
- Many insurers offer discounts on house insurance if you fit extra security devices, such as locks or alarms, to your home. But you must be scrupulous about locking up every time you go out: otherwise you could find your claim refused.

Making a claim

Where the building has been damaged, get a couple of builders to estimate the cost of repairs, and ask what they think was the cause of the damage. Preferably get this in writing. If you disagree with one builder's verdict, get a second opinion. Make sure you have copies of any guarantees and receipts for new building work, or surveyors' reports on your buildings.

If there is any damage which requires immediate repairs, such as a leaking roof, call your insurers and get their agreement before making repairs, if possible, or you may damage the evidence. Take photos if you can't contact the insurers. Bear in mind that if the insurers agree to your making repairs, it does not automatically mean that they agree to pay the claim.

Inform the police of a burglary immediately, and check very carefully to discover what is missing. Often people notice that something is missing only some weeks after a burglary. When making a claim make clear that the list of items stolen is 'so far as we can see at present'. Find out the cost of replacing any lost items. Try to find the cheapest equivalent but do not accept anything of a lower quality than you had before.

If your claim is refused or reduced

- If your claim isn't accepted in full, first complain to the head of the company. Be cautious about accepting any

offers of less than the amount you are claiming. You are sometimes asked to complete a form agreeing to 'full and final' settlement. Don't do this if you think you may need to claim more.
- If the dispute is over the cause of the damage, get together evidence to support your case. For example, if there is a dispute over what caused something to break, find out how old the item was and its normal natural life. If necessary, get expert witnesses, such as electricians, builders and so on, to look at the damage and give an opinion.
- If the dispute is over the value of damaged items, and you don't have any receipts or valuations, get new estimated valuations by describing the items to experts – e.g. proprietors of antiques shops, electrical goods shops. Find photographs showing the items or try to get witness statements from people who have seen them.
- If the disputed loss is very large, you can hire a loss assessor to collect evidence on your side. Loss assessors usually work for a percentage of the final insurance payout. Contact the Institute of Public Loss Assessors*.
- If the insurance company sends a loss adjuster to examine the damage, ask for a copy of his or her report. Insurance companies are not required to show you this, but some will do so. (A loss assessor works for you; a loss adjuster works for the company.)

Complaints schemes

As well as the option of going to court, there are two main complaints schemes for house insurance disputes – the Insurance Ombudsman Bureau* and the Personal Insurance Arbitration Service* (PIAS). Both are free and most companies belong to one or the other (it will say which in your policy document), although the Ombudsman is much the most effective. But with both schemes you should have taken up your complaint within the company, at the highest level, first.

If you complain to PIAS you must agree to abide by the decision and surrender any right to take the dispute to court. With the Insurance Ombudsman Bureau, the decision is binding on the company up to £100,000, but if you are not happy you can reject the decision and go to court.

CHAPTER 24

SECURITY AND SAFETY IN THE HOME

Security

From reading the papers, it may seem that older people are frequent victims of crime. This is not so – it's just that these incidents often receive considerable, and sometimes dramatic, publicity, which tends to give a distorted impression of the facts. Statistically, your chances of being a victim are slim – crime against older people is, in fact, rare. However, fear of crime still can have a debilitating effect on the quality of life of many people.

Many crimes are preventable if you take the right precautions and don't take unnecessary risks.

A secure home

The basic principle of home security is to make your property as unattractive a target as possible to the opportunist thief. Burglars like to work unseen. Take a look at your house from their point of view. Can they easily get round the back of the house, or work hidden from view behind trees or fences, for example?

Many thieves manage to enter houses by finding doors or windows which aren't even shut properly. Even if you're leaving the house for only two minutes lock the doors and windows.

Spare keys
Be careful with your spare keys. Never keep a key on a string tied to the inside of the letterbox, or under an outside doormat or flowerpot, however convenient it may be. When you go out, don't leave any exterior keys in an obvious place; otherwise, if someone did break in they would be able to carry out goods through a door. If you lose your door keys, change the locks as soon as possible – keep the name of a locksmith handy.

If possible, find a local person whom you trust and give him or her a set of keys in case you lock yourself out or need help while you are indoors. Make sure that your friend doesn't label your keys with your name and address.

Free security advice
A crime prevention officer (CPO) is a police officer specially trained in crime prevention techniques. He or she will conduct a free security survey of your home and give you impartial advice. Also, tell the CPO if you have any ideas or comments on local crime-related issues – your feedback is important. Ring your local police station and ask to be put in touch with the CPO.

Locks and bolts

Door locks
There are two main types of door lock. The most secure locks are Kitemarked to British Standard (BS) 3621 and have to pass a number of stringent physical tests.

Cylinder rim locks fit on to the surface of the door and the frame, and are usually operated by a lever inside and a key outside. Buy one that has a 'deadlock' device – this means that

---

DISCOUNTS
Some of the large do-it-yourself superstores offer discounts for the over-60s on certain days. If you need to buy any locks, lights or other items for the house, you should be able to save some money by using one of their discount cards.

the bolt automatically locks each time the door is closed (though be careful about locking yourself out). A **cylinder rim nightlatch** is a basic type of lock and shouldn't be used as the only lock on any exit door.

A **mortice lock** fits into the width of the door – always use a 5-lever version on any exit door. They don't automatically deadlock so you have to remember to lock them each time you go out (you can also keep them locked when you're in but leave the key in the lock). A **mortice sashlock** is a mortice lock with a handle, commonly used on back doors but also appropriate to some front doors. Again, look for a 5-lever (as opposed to a 2- or 3-lever) lock.

For a high level of door security, fit two locks to the main exit doors, front and back – a Kitemarked mortice lock (or mortice sashlock) and a cylinder rim lock higher up. Two locks help to spread the load and look formidable from the outside. If there's room for only one lock, choose a Kitemarked cylinder rim lock. You'll need to be particularly careful if any door has glass panels: make sure that at least one lock is out of reach of the panes, and preferably fit laminated glass for extra security.

Other security measures for doors

As well as locks, there are several other pieces of door furniture to secure the door and to help you see who's calling. A **door chain** allows you to open the door slightly to check a caller's identification. Buy the sturdiest chain you can find and secure it with screws that are at least 30mm (1¼in) long. You can also buy metal **door limiters** that are, in effect, heavy-duty door chains. A **door viewer** is a small wide-angle lens fitted through the door, so that you can see the identity of callers before opening the door. Some are clearer to see through than others, so have a look through them in the shop first. **Security mortice bolts** or **surface-mounted sliding bolts** will help to strengthen the top and bottom of the door, and **hinge bolts** (sometimes called dog bolts) will protect the hinged side of the door from being forced.

Window locks

Fit locks to all downstairs windows and any upstairs windows where a burglar might be able to gain access via a flat roof, porch or balcony. The type of lock will depend on what your windows are made of, how they open and close, and whether you want the lock to show from the outside. Most are operated by a standard key. Window locks are fairly easy to fit, needing a screwdriver. You should also fit locks to the top and bottom of patio doors.

Locksmiths

If you need someone to fit locks for you, ask the crime prevention officer to recommend a master locksmith, or ring the Help the Aged Seniorline*. It may be possible to get someone to fit them at a discount or even for free.

Fire security

Remember that you may need to get out of the house quickly in case of fire, so don't barricade yourself in to the extent that you can't get out in a hurry and others can't get in to help you. If you're indoors, keep keys handy and make sure everyone in the house knows where they are.

Alarms

Burglar alarms

There are two types of standard burglar alarms: bell-only and monitored. A burglar alarm is a good deterrent and can give you peace of mind, but of course it cannot guarantee that you will not be burgled.

Bell-only alarms have a central control panel linked to a number of different types of sensor. If the alarm is on and any of these sensors detects an intrusion, the bell on the outside of the house (and the siren inside) will ring for 20 minutes or so, hopefully attracting attention and scaring off any burglar. Most alarms consist of a combination of sensors that guard the main doors and windows, plus a number of movement detectors (called passive infra-red or PIRs). Many control panels operate via your own four-digit code number, although it is possible to buy some that are key-operated. A bell-only alarm will cost from around £450 up to about £1000, depending on size.

A **monitored alarm** has similar components to a bell-only alarm, except that when the alarm is triggered, a signal is sent to a 24-hour monitoring centre, who will call out the emergency services if they believe there's an intrusion, fire or medical emergency. You will have to pay more for a monitored alarm – usually well over £600 plus an annual monitoring fee to the control centre.

Burglar alarms can be adapted to fit any property – the installers will generally come up with their own design of the components. But first you should think carefully about what you want the alarm to protect and exactly how you want to use it, and make this clear to the installers. For instance, you may want to have the alarm set when you're in the house. Always get at least three quotes for an alarm from installers – choose a selection of local and national firms.

Be wary of any maintenance contracts: some may tie you to a contract for several years, with rapidly increasing annual fees. You don't have to have a maintenance contract with a bell-only alarm, but you probably will with a monitored alarm. Look for a contract that lasts for only one or two years (this information may well be hidden in the small print).

Never buy an alarm from a door-to-door salesperson.

Social alarms
A social alarm which you wear round your neck or wrist or clipped to clothing lets you call for help at any time from anywhere in the house – see pages 473–4 for details.

Leaving the house

If you're going on holiday, remember to cancel the milk and the papers, move items such as the television and hi-fi out of view of the windows, set a timer switch (or two) for lights to come on in the evening, and lock away garden tools and ladders. Tell friends that you're going to be away and ask them to keep an eye on your home.

Storing valuables

If you have important documents, spare cash, jewellery or other small valuables that you don't need to keep at home, put them in a safety deposit box at a bank. Don't keep large amounts of cash at home – burglars like nothing better. Photographs of any other valuable items, such as antiques, will help the police to trace them if they are stolen. For televisions, videos and cameras, use an ultra-violet marker pen (available from stationers) to write your postcode and house number on each item.

Exterior lighting

Exterior lights can illuminate dark corners and alleyways. You can buy lights that stay on all night (often called dusk-to-dawn lamps) but they may work out quite costly to run unless you use a low-energy fluorescent light bulb. Other types switch on when they sense someone crossing their beam and stay on for a few minutes (they have a passive infra-red sensor that detects movement). Both will illuminate your entry and exit, and should help to deter an opportunist thief.

Fitting most exterior lights involves drilling holes in an exterior wall and wiring up the light to the internal electrical circuit. If you're not confident of your own skills, use a reliable electrician.

Letting people into your home

Always use the door viewer and chain when answering the door. Some officials may call on you unannounced, such as gas

---

VICTIM SUPPORT SCHEMES

Victim Support Schemes offer free support and advice to anyone who has suffered as a victim of a crime. They will visit you in your home and offer practical and emotional help. You can contact them through your local police station or via the National Association of Victim Support Schemes*.

or electricity meter readers. Always insist on seeing an identity card with a photograph first, even if the caller is in uniform. If in doubt, shut the door on them and ring their company to check identification. If you're still suspicious, ring the police.

In general, don't let salespeople in but deal with them on the doorstep. If you do let someone into your house, stay with them and don't let them wander around alone.

Anyone with a legitimate reason to call on you should carry an ID card, and will willingly display it. Don't let anyone you don't know – adult or child – into your house, even if they claim it's an emergency.

A watchful eye

Contrary to popular belief, most burglaries take place during the day when people are out at work. People at home during this time can be particularly valuable in keeping an eye out for anyone acting suspiciously in the locality. If you see anything out of the ordinary, make a note of the person's description and contact the police. Don't be tempted to get involved yourself in any situation.

Get to know your neighbours, and agree to keep an eye on each other's houses. Take the phone numbers of those people you trust, and give them yours.

A Neighbourhood Watch scheme is a voluntary group of local residents working in liaison with the police, and is designed to help prevent burglary and other crimes in the area. If you would like to help start up a local Watch, contact your local crime prevention officer at the police station.

Contacts

Keep a list of these phone numbers near to the phone:

- the local police station
- your doctor
- neighbours, particularly those with keys to your house
- a locksmith
- the gas and electricity authorities

- two plumbers (for quotes)
- two electricians (for quotes).

The best way to find a tradesperson is to go on personal recommendation. Ask friends and neighbours if they can give you the name of someone reliable. Otherwise, it's wise to choose a member of a trade association – at least you should have some comeback if something goes wrong.

Emergencies

Don't be inhibited about ringing the emergency services in urgent cases at any time of day or night. They will assess your situation over the phone and will respond immediately if necessary. If they don't think it warrants an emergency call-out, they may recommend that you contact your local police station or doctor for further advice.

Safety

By far the most common type of home accident involving older people is a fall, making up about two-thirds of all cases needing treatment. These figures increase for those aged 75 and older, in particular people who live alone and women who suffer from osteoporosis. Falls and injuries most commonly occur on stairs and outside steps.

Preventing falls

Illuminate your home well – good lighting can help prevent a fall, particularly on the stairs. Keep spare light bulbs handy, and use table lamps in poorly lit places. If the stairs are steep, add an extra handrail to the inner wall. Make sure that there are no rucked up carpets or loose corners that you could trip over, and run appliance cables as close to the wall as possible, not across the room and never under the carpet. For a rug on a slippery floor, fit small stickers to the corners to prevent it sliding across the floor. In the kitchen, mop up any spills immediately, and don't overstretch to reach high cupboards. In the bathroom, rubber mats and extra handrails in or near the bath are useful to prevent slipping. If you're using a ladder, place it at a safe angle to the wall and don't lean out from it at the top. Make sure that someone else is on hand in case you fall, preferably supporting the ladder at the bottom.

Electrical safety

Most electrical appliances are now sold complete with a fitted plug. If not, there are a number of 'easy-to-wire' plugs on the market that make the task slightly simpler. When fitting a plug, follow instructions carefully, use the correct fuse as recommended by the manufacturer and check that the cable is securely fixed. Some plugs have special handles or mouldings for easy grip. Replace any plug with signs of scorching or burning, or the flex if it is worn. Don't overload power points by using multiple adaptors – each socket should carry no more than 13 amps in total.

Don't use any electrical appliances in the bathroom that have an ordinary 3-pin plug. Any appliances for use there should be specifically designed for the bathroom and permanently wired into the mains.

If any electrical appliance shows signs of wear or a fault, have it checked by an electrician or dispose of it and buy a replacement.

If you are worried about the wiring circuit in your home, ring your regional electricity company and ask if they offer a free visual wiring check of the mains circuit – some may charge a small fee. Otherwise, use a reliable electrician, but get at least two estimates first.

Gas safety

If you are worried about gas leaks, there is now a British Standard for gas detectors for home use – look for those bearing the Kitemark BS 7348. They will detect gas leaks and sound an alarm, but need to be permanently wired into the mains rather than plugged into a socket. See also **Chapter 25** for more details on gas services.

Fire safety

Smoke alarms
Smoke alarms are cheap, easy to fit and will alert you if there is a build-up of smoke in your home – they have saved many lives in recent years. The best advice is to fit as many – bearing the Kitemark BS 5446 – as you can afford. If you are fitting only one or two, place them in common areas such as at the bottom of the staircase, in a hallway or an upstairs landing, preferably in the centre of the ceiling. Don't fit one in the kitchen or bathroom – they may go off accidentally. Closing internal doors helps to prevent a fire spreading quickly.

Heaters and fires
If you use any electric, gas, paraffin or solid-fuel fires or heaters, make sure that they all have secure fireguards and are placed well away from any bedding, clothes or curtains and cannot be knocked over. Never leave clothes drying in front of any fire or heater, and don't sit too close to one. If you use a fuel-burning fire, the room should be well ventilated, so make sure that airbricks and ventilators are not obstructed. Don't move any portable fire or heater when it's on or alight.

Smoking in the home
If there is a smoker in the house, ensure that there are plenty of ashtrays around where they cannot be knocked over easily. Never leave a burning cigarette in the ashtray – always stub it out properly. Be wary of falling asleep while holding a cigarette – this is how many fires begin. In particular, old foam-filled furniture may be highly flammable. Smoking in bed is particularly dangerous and should be avoided.

Fire extinguishers
Only attempt to tackle a fire if it is very small; otherwise, ring the fire brigade. Fire safety experts don't recommend small fire extinguishers for home use, as you may take time trying to tackle the fire rather than getting everyone out of the house. If you feel you must have one, contact your local fire brigade's fire prevention officer for a Home Office leaflet detailing the different types of extinguishers available.

Fire blankets are good for smothering flames such as those caused by a chip-pan fire – choose one that's Kitemarked to BS 6575. Never throw water on to burning oil or fat fires.

Electric blankets
Some electric blankets can be left on all night, while others must be switched off before you get into bed. Whatever type you have, follow the instructions carefully, and make sure that the blanket is kept in good condition, stored without creasing when not in use and serviced every few years. Never attempt to repair one yourself. If it shows signs of damage or wear, return it to the manufacturer.

PART 6

DAY-TO-DAY LIVING

CHAPTER 25

BASIC UTILITIES

Being able to keep warm, cook, have running water and use the phone are things that most of us take for granted. But if being at home all day means running up phone or fuel bills that you can't afford or if your hands become too stiff to turn on the tap, life at home can become very difficult.

The companies that provide gas, electricity, water and the telephone offer a wide range of services, some specifically designed for older people, that will help you budget, cope with bills and use your appliances safely.

Special services

Gas

British Gas offers special services to its retired customers. All older and disabled people are invited to join the British Gas GasCare Register. Your name and address are kept with details of any special requirements you might have. For example, if you let the Register know that you can't get around quickly, the British Gas engineer will wait a bit longer for you to answer the door. The GasCare Register is free, voluntary and confidential, and those on the mailing list receive a newsletter detailing all the extra services that older people are eligible for. Contact your local British Gas office for more information.

The leaflet *Our Commitment to Older or Disabled Customers* gives details of all the special services available to retired people.

Electricity

Each electricity company has to publish a special code of practice for elderly and disabled people – you should be able to pick up a copy at your local showroom. Some companies run schemes similar to the GasCare Register (see above). The codes of practice also set out the different ways you can pay your bill, the rules about disconnection, and the special facilities and services available for elderly or disabled customers.

Telephone

For more details of special services offered by BT, call 0800 800150 for two leaflets: *Special Help for People who are Older or Disabled* (available in Braille), and *The BT Guide for People Who are Older or Disabled*. For details of special Mercury services, call 0500 500194.

If you don't use the phone very much, you may be able to take advantage of special rates – such as BT's Light Users Scheme, offering a rebate of up to 60 per cent on your line rental if you make no outgoing calls over the quarter. And if you can't use the phone book because of a disability or medical condition, you may be able to use directory enquiries free of charge. Call free on 195 for details.

Water and sewerage

The water regulator OFWAT★ has issued each water company with guidelines relating to older customers – for example, bills may be made available in braille or large type or on tape. Registers of elderly people with particular needs may also be kept.

Meters, bills and disconnection

Newly retired people tend to find that they use their heating, cooker and other appliances more than when they were at work all day, so fuel bills are likely to go up.

BASIC UTILITIES

Payment options

If you are newly retired you may find yourself adjusting to life on a smaller income, so careful budgeting is important.

Gas and electricity
There are four main options for paying and budgeting for the gas or electricity you use:

Quarterly bills
Each quarter you receive a bill for energy you have used in the previous three months. This is a good way to pay if you are sure you will have enough money each quarter to meet the bill. If somebody else – for example, your son or daughter – deals with your finances, ask the company to send the bill straight to them. In some cases you pay less if you agree to pay by direct debit.

Monthly payment plans
With a payment plan each month you pay a fixed amount, agreed with the company in advance. The advantages of this are that you don't get big winter bills and you know how much money to set aside. Sometimes, however, the company's estimate of how much energy you're likely to use in a year is wrong and you could find at the end of the year that you still owe them money or that they need to refund some to you. If you're using a payment plan check the figures on the bills you do receive against your meter and let the company know if you think you're using much more or much less energy than was estimated.

Stamps
You can buy stamps to pay for electricity bills from electricity showrooms. You can buy as many or as few stamps as you want, whenever you like, and use them towards your bill.

Pay-as-you-go meters
These meters take special keys, cards or tokens (which you have to buy in advance); coin meters are being phased out. The big advantage of a pre-payment meter is that you don't build up a

debt. A token, key or card meter avoids the problems of having large sums of cash around, but you have to be able to get hold of the tokens (or whatever) easily – ask where you can get them from before opting for one of these meters.

Telephone
Phone bills from BT come every three months – you can pay them by direct debit or at any post office, bank or BT shop. You can also choose to spread your payments by opening a budget account and making monthly payments by direct debit from your bank account, thereby reducing the cost of your line rental. Mercury offers you the choice of receiving your bill every month or quarter. Mercury bills list details of all calls made, while BT is also able to send most customers bills listing all calls.

Water and sewerage
In some areas, you can have a meter installed so that your water bill is based on your actual use of water. But in most cases you pay an average figure based on the total cost of supplying water in your area. Water and sewerage bills are usually issued annually or half-yearly, but you may be able to pay more frequently by direct debit. Contact your local company (or companies – in one or two areas there are different companies for water and for sewerage) for full details of the options.

Estimated accounts (gas/electricity)

The company should call to read your meter every six months. For the quarter when your meter isn't read (you still get a bill every three months) the company will estimate how much energy you have used based on your past consumption, printing a letter 'E' next to the meter reading figure on your bill.

You don't have to pay an estimated bill that is wrong. When you get an estimate check it against the actual reading on your meter. If it's wrong send the bill back giving the actual reading or call the number given on your bill. The company will send you a new bill based on the correct meter reading.

The Gas Consumers Council* has produced a free guide, the

Meter Beater, to help you if you have a query about reading your gas meter. The address and phone number of your local office will be on the back of your gas bill and in the phone book.

If your bill is wrong (gas/electricity)

If you think your bill is wrong, contact the company immediately. If the company doesn't agree with you, but you still think you're right, don't pay the part of the bill which is in dispute. Pay the rest, and ask the company to investigate further. Contact the relevant watchdog (see the last section of this chapter) if you and the company still can't agree on the bill.

If you can't pay your bill

Gas/electricity

If your bill arrives and you can't pay it, don't panic but don't ignore it – tell the company straight away. It is obliged to offer you a chance to pay the bill over time before it can legally disconnect you. Disconnection may be used only as a last resort. If you have difficulty in meeting your bill, you could agree with the company that you'll pay in one of the following ways:

- Pay a set amount each week, fortnight or month towards the debt and the energy you are still using. The company has to set the repayments in agreement with you at a rate you can afford.
- Have a pay-as-you-go meter fitted. The meter will be set so that each time you put in your money or token it will take some money to pay off the debt.
- If you are receiving means-tested benefits, you can have money for your bill deducted from your money before you get it (called Fuel Direct).

Remember these are things that the company *has* to do – if you're not offered a way to sort out your problem that suits you, complain to the company as soon as possible. If that doesn't work, contact the Gas Consumers Council* or OFFER* for help.

British Gas and the electricity companies will not disconnect pensioners who can't pay their bills during the winter months (between 1 October and 31 March for gas, 1 October and 1 March for electricity), so if you and the adults you live with are all pensioners, and you have trouble paying a high winter bill, tell the company straight away and you'll be able to sort out the debt problem without the worry of being left in the cold.

Telephone/water
The phone and water companies don't have any such rule – but they will disconnect people only as a last resort. Once again, contact them as soon as you think you may be struggling to pay the bill, and they will try to sort out some method of payment which you can manage.

Cutting your bill
British Gas and all the electricity companies provide advice on energy efficiency – each runs a special phone line and publishes a leaflet, and many will arrange for an expert adviser to visit your home at no charge to you. The adviser may also be able to help you if you are having difficulty with the controls on your appliances. For example, some gas appliances can be adapted to make the knobs easier to turn. Controls marked in ways to help people with poor sight are also available. These adaptors are free.

If you're receiving certain social security benefits, you may be able to get financial help with the costs of energy efficiency measures such as draughtproofing and insulation.

You may be able to reduce your phone bill if you use the phone very little or, alternatively, a good deal. Ask the company for details of special schemes for low and high use. You might be able to cut your water bill by asking for a water meter to measure your actual use, but note that the initial costs are high. Your local water company should be able to advise you on whether switching would make sense in your particular case.

Breakdowns

If your service is interrupted

British Gas can turn off your supply if it needs to do work on its pipes or in an emergency (if gas is leaking, for example). They should give you ten days' notice that your supply will be turned off, but in an emergency it can happen without warning. If the suspected leak (or other danger) is inside your home British Gas can enter without your permission to stop the leak.

The other utility companies have similar rules about the notice of non-emergency stoppages which they must give customers.

If your supply is interrupted for more than 24 hours (or 48 hours for water, in some cases), you'll get compensation (£10 for water, £20 for gas, £40 for electricity) for each working day until it is restored. You may also get compensation if the company failed to give you adequate notice of the stoppage.

If you need repairs done

All the utility companies should give a high priority to essential repair work for older people (and, in the case of telephone services, if you're immobile and living alone). So, when you need the appliance repaired urgently, remind them that you are a retired person and explain your situation.

Visits by company staff

Checking out callers

With the exception of meter readers, staff will rarely call unannounced. If someone does call at your home saying they are from one of the companies, always ask to see their identity card. If you have poor sight you can agree a confidential password in advance that they will use whenever they call on you. Contact your local office for details or to arrange a password.

Appointments
If someone from British Gas has made an appointment to see you and they don't turn up you are entitled to compensation of £10.

BT promises to pay you one month's line rental for every day that it misses an appointment to install your phone line.

Your water company now has to specify whether your appointment is for the morning (defined as before 1 p.m.) or the afternoon – if they don't turn up, they have to pay you £10.

Similarly, your electricity company has to offer morning or afternoon appointments, but it must give you a more precise appointment if you ask for one. You can request an appointment within a two-hour time-band. If no one turns up as agreed, the company must pay you £20.

Using gas safely

There are special services and rules to ensure that gas is used safely.

Free gas safety check
If you, and anyone who lives with you, are over 60, British Gas will carry out a free safety check on all your gas appliances once a year.

Servicing your appliances
Even if you have had a gas safety check you should still have gas appliances serviced regularly. Appliances such as central heating boilers, gas water heaters and fires should be serviced every year. Always have your gas appliances installed, serviced and repaired by an expert (this is the law, not just good advice). Contact British Gas or a CORGI*-registered installer.

If you smell gas
Turn off the gas at the mains straight away (the lever is usually near your meter – make sure you know where it is). Open doors and windows to let the gas out and then phone the British Gas emergency service – the number is in the phone book under 'Gas'. The first 30 minutes of work in response to an emergency call-out, including small-value parts and materials, is free.

If your gas appliances have to be turned off
If British Gas (or any other gas engineer) finds that one of your appliances is dangerous, by law they must disconnect it and you won't be able to use it again until it is made safe. However, if because of a breakdown in your supply you are left without heating, hot water or cooking British Gas will sometimes be able to help, for example, by lending you an electric heater, kettle and so on.

Complaining

Complain if one of the utility companies doesn't deliver a decent service. They have all set up systems to deal with complaints from customers, and most publish leaflets to direct you to the right person.

Gas
For problems with gas supply or accounts, contact the customer services manager, as shown on the back of the bill. If you're not happy with the reply you get you can take your complaint to a watchdog. Your first contact should be your local Gas Consumers Council (GCC)* – the address and phone number will be found on the back of your gas bill. They are able to take up complaints about any gas matter including disputes about bills, disconnection, broken appointments, repairs and service work. If the GCC can't help you, the regulator, the Office of Gas Supply (OFGAS)*, might be able to intervene. OFGAS can investigate certain types of complaint about the supply of gas (including disconnection).

Electricity/water
Electricity and water companies will consider complaints in writing or by phone (the address and phone number will be on your bill). If you're not happy with their response, contact the relevant watchdog: OFFER* for electricity or OFWAT* for water (the DoE Water Service* in Northern Ireland). They too will accept complaints by phone, although they prefer complicated disputes to be set out in writing.

Telephone

If you've got a complaint about BT, write to your local office or dial 150 (151 for line faults). If this doesn't work, ask for your complaint to be passed to the Appeals Manager. If you're still getting nowhere, go to OFTEL*, the independent industry watchdog. You have to write to OFTEL with your complaint, although if it's an emergency (for example, if you're threatened with immediate disconnection) you can phone. Staff are able to give general advice over the phone.

For queries or complaints about Mercury services, phone the Customer Assistance line on (0500) 500194.

CHAPTER 26

KNOW YOUR RIGHTS

Neighbours

Being good neighbours isn't always easy, especially if you are living close together and like to enjoy very different lifestyles. You may feel this even more acutely when you are newly retired and at home at times of day when previously you would have been out. Legally speaking, you have certain rights and interests in relation to your property and, in turn, your neighbours have rights and interests of their own. Inevitably at times these will conflict, causing tensions or sometimes even a serious dispute.

Needless to say, it's best to try and sort matters out in an amicable way if you can. But if an informal approach fails and you have to take formal action yourself, it will help to keep a written record of specific incidents to back up your case.

Nuisance

The law says that an occupier of property is not allowed to use it in such a way as to interfere with other people's reasonable enjoyment of their property. Loud music or barking dogs may fall into this legal category of 'nuisance', as might an offensive smell or irritating smoke.

But the mere fact that *you* find something a nuisance doesn't mean that the law is being broken. The law accepts that a fair amount of give and take is necessary in everyday living. For example, in a semi-detached property or a block of flats a degree of noise penetration is unavoidable; you have to put up with what's reasonable. And you must react reasonably too, and not, say, turn up the volume on your television to drown the rock music from next-door's stereo.

Someone who is especially sensitive to a particular form of nuisance is not entitled to a legal remedy in respect of behaviour which would not be a nuisance to other people. For instance, if you like to have a nap in the afternoons when children are frequently playing loudly in a neighbouring garden, you have no right to complain if other people going about their various activities would find the noise level tolerable.

Anyone seriously disturbed by noise nuisance can complain to a magistrate's court (sheriff court in Scotland). If the complaint is upheld, the perpetrator of the noise will commit an offence if he or she repeats it. Your local council can also take action to help: contact the environmental health department. Alternatively, if the nuisance continues and is excessive, you can seek an injunction (interdict in Scotland) in the civil courts prohibiting it – you may be awarded compensation too. This civil remedy is available to protect you from other kinds of nuisance too.

It is also important to take into account the type of neighbourhood. If you live in a rural area you must expect to put up with 'country smells' – up to a point, anyway. If, say, a neighbouring farmer chooses to put his manure heap right next to your hedge when there are alternative sitings which would avoid this kind of offence to neighbours, it's reasonable to expect the farmer to take action to improve the situation. In a similar way, if you live close to a factory or industrial site, in an urban area, you must expect to put up with a degree of noise and possibly the emission of fumes or smoke. However, smoke control laws strictly limit what may be emitted from factory chimneys, and in the first place it may be worth contacting the environmental health department of your local council. If noise from an industrial site or roadworks is disturbing you, note that local councils have power under the Control of Pollution Act to serve a notice restricting hours of working and the type of machinery used. It could be that restrictions have been imposed before the works started.

If your neighbours are keen gardeners, they may be in the

habit of lighting bonfires now and again – if the wind is blowing in your direction, this could be rather irritating. In general there are no restrictions on when bonfires can be lit. Whether it's a nuisance depends on whether the fires interfere with the use and enjoyment of your property, and whether they are more frequent than the ordinary person would consider reasonable. If you can't persuade your neighbour to do anything, say by moving the fires to a different part of the garden, you could take the matter up with your local council – keep a detailed diary and get statements from others affected first. Your local council has powers to serve a notice requiring the fires to stop (though this is unlikely) or, for instance, to be lit less frequently. If your neighbours ignore the notice, the council could take them to the magistrate's court, which could impose a fine on them if found guilty. You can bypass the council and go straight to the court to ask for a 'nuisance order' if you wish – but remember that if you do you will need to prove your case.

Neighbours who let weeds and shrubs thrive can be even more of a bane at times, but there is no law which says that people must be tidy. However, your local council has powers to clear up areas within its control, if it considers a highly visible mess is ruining the 'amenity' and beauty of the neighbourhood – you may be able to get the council to shift the rubbish if this is the case (these powers exist in England, Scotland and Wales). If the rubbish attracts vermin the council will certainly act. The council can serve a notice requiring the removal of the mess, and your neighbours could face a considerable fine if they don't comply.

If you are having problems with your neighbour, try contacting Mediation UK* who can put you in touch with local counselling services, which aim to resolve conflicts without having to go to court.

Boundaries

Trespass
Each time they cross over your property without your permission your neighbours are trespassing. If a friendly word doesn't stop this, you are perfectly entitled to bar their way. If

you are faced with repeated acts of trespass you can take them to court, get an injunction and claim compensation. The amount you recover will depend on the amount of inconvenience you have suffered and whether your property has been damaged.

If the next-door neighbour's dog is plaguing you by coming into your garden, you must provide your own fencing to keep it out; as a general rule pet owners do not have to put up fencing to keep animals in. Unless the deeds of the property put the obligation to fence on you, the position is different in relation to farm animals. The farmer must prevent livestock from trespassing, and pay for any damage if it does.

Letter complaining to a neighbour about acts of trespass

Dear

I initially complained to you about trespass on **[date]**, and since then I have told you on a great many occasions that I do not want **[persons involved]** to trespass on my property. Nevertheless you persist in **[describe]**.

If you continue to commit this act of trespass I shall, in accordance with my legal rights, apply to the county court for an injunction restraining **[persons involved]** from so doing. I shall also put in a claim for the considerable distress and inconvenience which you have caused me.

Yours sincerely

Overhanging branches
If branches from a neighbour's tree overhang your property, you are entitled to cut them off at the point where they cross the boundary. Branches laden with ripe fruit may have particular

appeal; however, strictly speaking, the branches and their fruit continue to be your neighbour's property, and so you should either throw them back or provide your neighbour with an opportunity to collect them. A word of warning: before you start chopping make sure that the tree is not subject to a Tree Preservation Order – you can check with your local council (in Northern Ireland, the Department of the Environment). If it is, you will need their authority first. If you live in a Conservation Area, give the council six weeks' notice of any intended action so that they can decide whether to put a Tree Preservation Order on it.

Tree roots

Sometimes tree roots may affect foundations and cause subsidence. Usually it's not the roots themselves which cause damage but the fact that they are absorbing water from the soil, which contracts, causing foundations to shift. The person on whose land the tree is growing will be responsible for the damage as long as this is the cause. If you are insured for this it will be far simpler to claim on your insurance than to pursue a claim against your neighbour.

Boundary in the wrong place

It sometimes emerges from examination of the deeds to a property (the documents which prove ownership) that a boundary wall or fence has been erected in the wrong place. For instance, it may happen that your fence encloses a strip of land that appears on the deeds as belonging to your neighbour. If the true owner has not asserted his or her right to the land over a long period – usually 12 years – it becomes your property. It's not necessary for you to have lived at the property for the entire period: you can take advantage of your predecessor's uninterrupted possession of the land in calculating the relevant period.

A right to light

If trees in your neighbour's garden are blocking out sunshine, and so restricting the natural light you enjoy through your windows, there may well be nothing you can do about it because, generally speaking, there is no right to light. But there

Letter complaining to a neighbour about damage caused by tree roots

Dear

During the last **[period of time]** I have noticed the following problem **[describe]**, which was caused by the roots of the trees **[describe]** in your garden. An independent surveyor's report has confirmed that these roots are to blame; I enclose a copy of that report.

You are legally responsible for the damage to my property.

Please let me know within the next 14 days whether you are prepared to repair the damage, which you are welcome to inspect in advance. If not, I will have the work done by my own contractor and will look to you to pay the cost of the repair in full, as I am legally entitled to do.

Yours sincerely

enc.

---

are two ways in which a right to light can arise. First, it may be expressly granted in the deeds to your property (the documents which prove ownership). Secondly, it may be permanently acquired through long enjoyment over an uninterrupted period of twenty years. It is not the house as a whole which benefits from this but particular rooms. Even if you have acquired a right to light in one of these two ways, and have enjoyed bright sunlight through a window for over twenty years, where a partial obstruction from, say, an overhanging tree as opposed to some artificial structure now partially obscures the light you enjoy, you will probably be without a valid claim.

Ownership of fences
The basic rule is that the person who puts up a fence is the person who owns it. But that won't help on a housing estate where the builder erected all the fences. Where this is the case you'll have to look at the deeds, which may clarify the position.

As a fallback position, there is a legal presumption that close-boarded fences, with supporting posts every so often, and timber lap fences or chain link fences built similarly, are assumed to belong to the owner whose side the supports are on. The reason for this is that the landowner is assumed to put a fence as near the boundary as possible; if the supports protrude over the boundary the landowner will be trespassing on the neighbour's land.

Repairs to a neighbour's fence
If your neighbour's fence is in danger of collapsing and, for instance, ruining your herbaceous border, you cannot automatically require him or her to mend the fence; however, in the case of many estates, where the deeds allocate ownership of a fence, the owner may be responsible for repairs. In any event, if damage actually occurs you can claim the cost of putting it right.

Neighbour's access for repair work
If the side wall, say, of your neighbours' property is close to the boundary between the two properties, they may wish to place a ladder in your garden or on your path in order to paint the side of their house or repair guttering. You are not automatically bound to agree to this unless the deeds to your property specify that your neighbours are entitled to access for such purposes; without such a provision or your express authority they will commit an act of trespass in entering on to your land. However, in England and Wales, the Access to Neighbouring Land Act 1992 gives your neighbours the right to seek a court order permitting them to enter your land for the purpose of carrying out works which are reasonably necessary for the 'preservation' of their property.

Buying goods

Whenever you buy something, whether it's from a shop, market stall, garage or mail order catalogue, you are entering into a contract with the seller. Under that agreement you agree to pay the price, and the seller, in turn, is bound by various obligations towards you.

These are laid down under the Sale of Goods Act 1979, which says that goods must be of the quality a reasonable person would regard as satisfactory – given the price you paid, any description applied to them and all the other relevant circumstances. This means that, for instance, an electrical appliance should be safe, work properly and, if new, look new and be in good condition. Depending on the nature of the goods, they should also last for a reasonable time.

Apart from being reasonably fit for its general purpose, an item must be fit for any other specific purpose, if you make this clear to the sales person and if he or she affirms that the item is indeed suitable for that particular purpose before you buy it. For example, if you're buying new pillows and are assured that they will be suitable for your asthmatic spouse, if you later find they're not, the retailer will be in breach of its legal obligation to you.

Goods must also match any description given, so if an item is wrongly labelled, say, you are entitled to redress. Similarly, if goods are sold by sample – paint chosen from a paint chart, for instance – the product supplied must correspond precisely with that sample.

What exactly are your rights when a supplier lets you down? The Sale of Goods Act says you have a *reasonable* time to reject goods and recover your money when the seller has not complied with any of these obligations. In practice, under existing law, this isn't very long at all. When the engine in Mr Bernstein's new car failed after three and a half weeks, the judge ruled that he wasn't entitled to get his money back because he had had the car too long: he was simply entitled to the cost of repair plus compensation for a spoilt day out. If you elect to reject goods, you must not deal with them as if you own them; you are entitled to ask the seller to collect the goods.

Technically speaking, when you are the victim of a breach of

Letter rejecting goods that are not fit for their specific purpose

Dear

[Reference: make and model]

On **[date]** I bought the above item from your shop. Before purchasing it, I told a member of your staff that I needed it for a specific purpose **[describe]**. He selected the above brand and model as being suitable for my requirements. When I tried to use it for that purpose, it proved unsuitable **[describe problem]**.

Section 14 of the Sale of Goods Act 1979 requires you to supply goods which are of satisfactory quality and fit for their specific purpose if that purpose is made clear to the retailer at the time of purchase. The problem described above indicates that the **[item]** was not fit for the purpose of **[describe]**, despite your staff's assurances. You are therefore in breach of contract, and I am exercising my rights under the Sale of Goods Act to reject the goods and to receive from you a refund of the full purchase price of **[£....]**.

I expect to receive your cheque for that amount within 14 days. If you fail to reimburse me I shall have no alternative but to issue a summons against you in the county court for recovery of the money without further reference to you.

Yours sincerely

contract in this way, the seller is legally obliged to place you in the position you would have enjoyed had the breach of contract never occurred. The compensation you are entitled to will thus often be equal to the cost of repair. Whether or not you are able to reject the goods (assuming you wish to do so), if you have suffered any additional damage or expenditure as a result of the seller's breach, you will be entitled to recover compensation for this as well. Often there will be travel expenses or telephone charges you want to recover. Occasionally, the defect will have caused damage to other items; for example, a leak from your washing machine may have caused damage to the kitchen floor covering; when this happens, you are entitled to recover the cost of putting that damage right as well. But, remember, you must be able to show that your claim is reasonable, so it will be a good idea to get two or three estimates for the cost of repair or replacement in order to demonstrate that you haven't incurred excessive costs.

A few special situations

Private sales
You don't have ordinary Sale of Goods Act protection when you buy goods from someone selling privately so if the goods prove to be faulty after you have bought them, you cannot expect the seller to meet the cost of repair or refund your money – unless the seller was unwise enough to make representations as to the quality of the goods before you purchased them. If, say, you're thinking of buying a second-hand lawnmower advertised through a classified ad in your local paper, or of picking up a cycling machine at a car boot sale, it would be a good idea to ask questions about the reliability of the item in the presence of a witness, who could back you up if a dispute should arise later. Make sure, too, that you get details of the seller's name and address if you decide to buy.

Sale items
Quite often when buying sale goods, people are told they cannot return them. There is no basis for this in law: goods must be of satisfactory quality and match any description given,

Letter complaining to a retailer about damage caused by defective goods

Dear

[Reference: make and model]

On **[date]** I bought the above **[item]** from your shop. On **[date]** it developed a serious fault **[describe]**, causing damage to my property **[describe]**. This cost **[£....]** to repair.

Section 14 of the Sale of Goods Act 1979 requires you to supply goods which are of satisfactory quality. As the **[item]** is faulty and therefore not satisfactory, you are in breach of contract.

I am therefore entitled to financial compensation for the faulty goods. However, while fully reserving my rights, I am prepared to give you an opportunity to repair the **[item]** without any charge to me.

I am also legally entitled to financial compensation of **[£....]** for the **[above damage]** as this cost arose as a direct result of the **[defect]**.

Please inform me within 14 days of your proposals for effecting repairs to the **[item]**. I also look forward to receiving your cheque for **[£....]** within 14 days. If you fail to reimburse me I shall have no alternative but to issue a summons against you in the county court for recovery of the money without further reference to you.

Yours sincerely

in just the same way as if they were being sold at their ordinary price. But sale goods may be marked 'imperfect' or 'seconds', forming part of the description applied to the goods. This description, together with the lower sale price, will affect the quality you are entitled to expect; but that is not to say you should be palmed off with rubbish – unless you paid next to nothing.

Credit notes

If you buy a pair of trousers, say, and decide once you get them home that you really don't like the colour, the shop may be willing to offer you a credit note so that you can buy some other item instead, and be credited with payment up to the value of your earlier purchase. As there is nothing wrong with the trousers – apart from the fact you now don't want them – the shop is under no legal obligation to refund your money, or indeed, to give you a credit note. However, where an item is actually defective in some way – or doesn't match any description applied to it – you are legally entitled to get your money back (or possibly to more limited compensation if you delay) and should insist on your rights rather than accepting a credit note you don't really want.

Gifts

Where an item is faulty but you didn't actually buy it yourself – perhaps a new toaster you were given for Christmas – strictly speaking, you have no right to redress from the seller. This is because you didn't enter into a contract to purchase the item yourself, and therefore don't have the benefit of the rights which arise under the Sale of Goods Act. In this sort of situation, you can very often benefit from the manufacturer's guarantee, which may well operate in favour not merely of the original purchaser, but of later owners as well – check the wording.

Retailer disclaiming responsibility

If you buy an item – a video recorder, say – and find that it is faulty, the retailers may well create the impression – even if they don't expressly say so – that since they didn't make the thing themselves and had no idea it was faulty when they sold it to you, they are not to blame and therefore under no legal obligation to provide you with redress. This is quite simply not so.

Under the Sale of Goods Act, the sellers are strictly liable for defects in goods sold, so that the fact they were not in any way negligent is irrelevant. The existence of a manufacturer's guarantee does not affect in any way your rights against the retailers. Guarantees frequently provide only limited redress over a 12-month period, whereas your Sale of Goods Act rights will normally be wider and last for a period of six years from the date the goods were purchased (naturally, the longer the period that has elapsed since that date the more difficult it gets to prove goods were defective at the date of purchase).

Goods causing injury

If you buy a step-ladder, for example, and a rung gives way while you are using it, causing you injury – say cuts, bruises and a broken wrist – as the buyer you can claim compensation from the retailer on the basis that the goods were not of satisfactory quality under the Sale of Goods Act. By contrast, if your spouse suffered the accident, they would have no claim against the retailer, since they hadn't actually purchased the item, so that no contract would exist between them and the retailer.

However, any person injured due to the faulty nature of the step-ladder would be entitled to claim compensation from the manufacturer of the ladder if they were able to prove that their injury had resulted from negligence on the part of the manufacturer and the fault wasn't such as should have been apparent to the retailer. Significantly, since the Consumer Protection Act 1987 came into force, any person suffering injury caused by defective goods is entitled to claim compensation from the manufacturer without having to prove that the defect has arisen through the manufacturer's negligence. In this sort of situation, where the injury is at all serious, you should seek professional advice from a solicitor.

Mail order goods

What's the position where mail order goods are found to be damaged on receipt – who bears the loss? Surprisingly, the law in this area is not very clear. In general, the owner of the goods whilst they were in transit must bear the loss. One view is that the goods become yours as soon as the seller hands them over to the carrier, which seems rather hard on you as the buyer. However, the seller will normally have insurance cover for the goods and not object either to replacing them or to giving you a refund. It is worth knowing that a Code of Practice has been adopted by members of the Mail Order Traders Association (MOTA)* under which, in these circumstances, members are bound to provide an immediate replacement, if available, and if not, then a full refund.

Delayed delivery
Where you order goods, for instance a new item of furniture, although an estimated delivery date may be given, normally no precise date is specified. Where this is the case, it will be an implied term of your contract that the goods are to be delivered within a reasonable time. If there is unreasonable delay, you should write to the supplier stating this, and requiring delivery to be made within, say, 14 days of the date of your letter (send the letter by recorded delivery and keep a copy). If the supplier does not meet your deadline, you are free to terminate your contract with the supplier and receive a refund of any payment made, together with compensation for any substantial inconvenience or additional expense which reasonably results.

The position is different where it is clear, either from the terms of the agreement reached between you, or from other surrounding circumstances, that the goods should have been delivered by a specific date, or in time for a particular event or occasion. If you order Christmas gifts from a catalogue in reasonable time for Christmas (and have complied with any ordering requirements laid down by the supplier), you will be entitled to your money back and possibly additional compensation if the goods fail to reach you in time.

Getting work done on your home

Most of the problems people experience with building work relate to the **cost**, the **quality of work** and/or the **time** taken to complete it.

Cost

Quotation or estimate?
There is no clear distinction legally, and the fact that one or other term is used need not be decisive. The critical question is whether the price or charge given in the estimate is intended to fix the liability of the customer (making it a quotation), or a rough-and-ready, if informed, guide to the price ultimately to be charged (making it an estimate). Given the difficulty in determining this, it is wise to clarify at the outset whether the figure represents the limit of your liability or merely an informed forecast of the likely cost.

Where no price is specified
If you haven't agreed a price – say, in an emergency when you've been anxious to get the work done as soon as possible – the contractor is entitled to a reasonable price for the job done. If you feel you are being overcharged, you are not bound to pay what the builder asks but can pay a smaller sum in settlement. To ascertain what a reasonable price for the job would be, obtain estimates for the work from other contractors, or contact a trade association for guidance.

If you are going to have any major building carried out, it would be sensible to draw up a contract at the outset to help avoid problems later. The Royal Institute of British Architects Joint Contracts Tribunal produces standard form contracts. You can buy a copy from Riba Publications Limited*.

Quality of the work

When a contractor agrees to do work for you he or she is entering into a contract. Quite apart from the provisions expressly agreed in any contract, for example those concerning price or type of materials, there are various implied obligations the builder must fulfil, which are set out in the Supply of Goods and Services Act 1982 (these are common law obligations in Scotland). Essentially, the contractor agrees to carry out the work to a reasonable standard using materials of satisfactory quality within a reasonable time. If he or she fails to meet any of these obligations, you have a claim for breach of contract.

If the work is defective, you should normally give the contractor an opportunity to put it right, unless circumstances are such that you have reasonably lost faith in his or her ability to do the job properly. If this is the case, you are entitled to get another contractor to finish the work. Before selecting someone else, you should get two or three estimates for the balance of the work – if need be, this will enable you to demonstrate later that you have paid no more than is reasonable. If you are prepared to have the original contractor back, you should send him or her copies of these, stating that unless the job is completed satisfactorily within a specified time, you will be engaging one of these contractors, and will claim from him or her any extra costs you incur as a result.

The time factor

If it is important that you get the work done by a particular date, you should get the contractor's written agreement to this, and also state in writing that 'time is of the essence'. Doing this strengthens your legal position, because in the absence of an agreement of this sort, the law will not regard time of completion as being of critical importance.

Where no date for completion is specified, the work must be completed within a reasonable time; if it isn't, you can claim compensation for any additional expense and inconvenience you are put to as a result (the cost of meals out if you cannot use your kitchen, for example). If, on the other hand, a specific date for completion has been agreed, and you have made time of the essence, you have the option of ending the contract and getting in another contractor if the work isn't completed in accordance with the time specified. Having done so, you are entitled to claim back any extra costs (and compensation for any substantial additional inconvenience) from the original contractor.

Problems with your local council

Your local council has extensive responsibilities for the provision and maintenance of services in your area. When facilities or services are not up to scratch, you may want to complain to those responsible, or even make a formal claim for compensation if you've had an accident as a result.

Litter

The law has recently been tightening up on litter control and has introduced tougher penalties to deter offenders. Local councils can issue a £10 fine for dropping litter. If you don't pay within 14 days you can be prosecuted and fined up to £2,500. What's more, local authorities, transport operators, government departments, schools and other educational establishments now have a legal duty to keep the land they control free from litter and refuse. Local authorities can also designate privately owned land – for example, supermarket car parks – as litter control areas.

If you feel that litter control is inadequate on roadways or other places to which the public has access in your area, take up the matter with your local council. If you are still not satisfied, you may apply to the magistrates' court (sheriff court in Scotland), applying for a litter abatement order against the body under a duty to clear litter from the area concerned – the local council, say, if it's a public road. You must give them five days' notice of your intention to apply for the order before doing so. Similar provisions have recently been introduced in Northern Ireland.

Dog mess

Local councils have a duty to clear dog mess from public places. In addition, in England and Wales local councils can use 'poop scoop' by-laws to designate areas where owners must clean up after their dogs – anyone who fails to do this will face a fine of up to £500. Councils can also use by-laws to set up dog-free zones – children's play areas, for example. Under Scots law, owners who allow their dogs to foul designated areas, for instance public roads and recreation areas, are liable to a fine of up to £500. In Northern Ireland, dog owners permitting their dogs to foul the footpath may be fined up to £100.

Uneven pavements

Local councils are responsible for maintaining the pavement. If you feel the state of a pavement – or road – is a hazard to the public, you should report this to the council (highways department) and ask them to carry out appropriate remedial works.

It doesn't necessarily follow that because you have an accident on a pavement you can hold the council responsible and make a claim against them for any loss or damage you suffer. You will have to be able to show that they were negligent – or careless – in carrying out their duty. This will depend on such factors as:

- how long ago the council did anything to the pavement
- whether the hole or the defect was obvious
- what sort of maintenance and inspection programme the council has
- whether there have been any previous complaints or trouble
- whether you were taking care to look where you were going.

It will often help when making a claim if you have been able to take photographs of the scene of the accident, for instance a close-up shot demonstrating unevenness in a pavement. It is also a good idea if possible to get evidence from a witness who can support your claim; this person need not necessarily have seen the accident – but if he or she can give evidence as to the state of the pavement this may help. If you have suffered injury, it is important to get a medical report from your doctor as soon as possible.

You may not only have suffered injury, but damage to clothing and perhaps additional travel expenses too. You should claim compensation ('damages') for all these things. Don't be surprised if the council (or their insurers) reject your claim at first; more often than not you'll have to persevere – remember, it is for you to prove your claim. Incidentally, you may be told that as the difference in height of the sections of pavement was less than 1 inch or 22mm your claim can't stand. This is not the law – whether the council are liable to compensate you will depend on a consideration of all the circumstances.

If your injuries are at all serious, or the circumstances complicated, you are likely to need help from a solicitor who deals with personal injury cases. In England and Wales ring the Law Society's Accident Line Scheme on Freephone 0500 192939 and you will immediately be put in touch with an Accident Line solicitor in the area. You may also be able to find out if you are eligible to apply for legal aid; if you are not you will be given an estimate as to how much it is likely to cost to fund the case yourself. You may get Legal Aid if your income and savings fall within strict financial limits – and if you can show that you have got a good chance of succeeding.

It is also worth knowing about the Legal Advice and Assistance Scheme – better known as the Green Form Scheme in England, Wales and Northern Ireland. Under the Scheme you can get up to two hours of free advice if your disposable income and capital fall within certain strict limits. In Northern Ireland those ineligible for free advice may qualify for advice on payment of a contribution related to their means. The same is true in Scotland, where assistance is more extensive and may continue until a decision is made to take formal legal action (an application for legal aid would be made at this point). You can find out more about Legal Aid and the Green Form Scheme from leaflets available at solicitors' offices and your local Citizens Advice Bureau.

PART 7

Making the most of your leisure

CHAPTER 27

Getting around

This chapter covers car ownership in retirement, as well as other forms of transport. See also **Chapter 34** for additional information about transport for less able-bodied people.

You and your car

The changes in your routine when you retire may well alter what you require from a car. For example, if you are moving from a town to the country, you are likely to be more reliant on your car than before. Conversely, if you intend to live in a town with good public transport services, you may find a car superfluous most of the time and prefer to hire one occasionally; a mix of public transport, hire-cars and taxis should work out cheaper than running a car if you cover less than 4,000 miles a year.

A couple who have had two cars in the past may find the second unnecessary or may be forced to cut down to one if money is tight; this means finding a car to suit both people. You are also likely to value different features as you grow older: practicalities such as ease of getting in and out will become more important and you may become even more concerned to have a reliable car.

Owning a car is expensive, so you should consider what you can afford if you are budgeting carefully or if you are faced with paying for everything after giving up a company car. Take into account the ongoing running costs as well as the purchase price.

Annual running costs

The major expense of motoring is not petrol or even servicing and repairs, but the basic running costs; those of small and large cars are broadly similar. To calculate the true cost of motoring, add up the following annual expenses:

- servicing and repairs
- fuel – divide annual mileage by average miles per gallon or litre, then multiply by the average price of a gallon or litre over the year
- annual depreciation – check car price guides
- tax – £135
- insurance
- finance costs – add up any annual loan repayments and the amount of cash you put up for the car and work out how much it could have earned if you had invested it instead.

Depreciation

Like any product a vehicle decreases in value over time – a hidden expense which becomes apparent when you decide to replace it. If you intend to change cars every few years, depreciation should figure significantly in your calculations: thousands of pounds can be wiped off a new car in just a couple of years, but thereafter the decline slows dramatically.

Depreciation is generally greatest on large cars. However, each model depreciates in a different way, and some cars hold their value very well. Details for all makes and models are given in car price guides available from newsagents, and the *Which? Guide to New & Used Cars*, published every June, picks out the fast and slow depreciators.

You lose most money if you buy a new car and replace it every two or three years. It makes sound financial sense to buy a second-hand car over two years old and replace it every few years, but if you want a new car consider holding on to it for five years or so to absorb the impact of the initial depreciation.

Insurance

The good news is that insurance premiums generally go down as you get older. However, if you become disabled or have certain illnesses, some insurance companies will refuse to cover you or will ask for an inflated premium. This is by no means the case with all companies, so shop around to find the best price. RICA* keeps comparative quotes of insurance for disabled drivers.

If you have been driving a company car you may encounter problems getting a no-claims discount equivalent to your driving record when you take out your own policy. A letter from the fleet manager should be evidence enough.

Many insurance companies ask for a medical certificate before renewing the policy every year after the age of 70 (or 73, or 75). Most of these rely on self-certification (you declare yourself to be fit to drive), but some require full certification based on a medical examination, for which the driver usually has to pay. The fee recommended by the British Medical Association* for a medical certificate is £30 but many doctors charge less.

Reliability and rust

Despite the financial impact of depreciation you may still prefer to drive a new car if you feel that the extra reliability is worth the cost. If you intend to keep a car for a long time, bear in mind that the older you get, the less reliable the car will become. Car reliability in both the long and short terms has improved since the early 1980s, but rust is still most likely to become a potential problem once cars are over six years old – one in five seven-year-old cars has serious rust.

Buying a new car

If you have been driving a company car, you will need to find a replacement, although it may be possible to buy the car you have been driving. If you have decided that you need a change of car, a lump sum received from a pension on retirement will give you extra leverage when negotiating with a dealer. Ready cash may increase your chances of obtaining a significant discount on the price – up to about 10 per cent or even more – but even if you cannot pay cash you should still be able to get a discount if you shop around.

Buying a car can be arduous, especially if you are determined to get the best price. Do some research before you approach a dealer: look through brochures to familiarise yourself with the various models in a range, the list prices and the prices of optional extras. Decide which features you do and don't want, but try to be flexible about the exact model. Take test drives before you decide what to buy. Monitor motoring magazines to work out when cars are being superseded, as you should then be able to pick up the old model more cheaply (although the car may then depreciate faster than the model replacing it). The make of car you choose will affect the discount available: for example, some Japanese cars are imported in small quantities and, because demand is high, dealers do not need to cut prices to sell cars. Popular cars from manufacturers with a large dealership network offer the greatest opportunity for discounts because you can shop around.

Dealers may be unwilling to quote prices over the phone, but should relent if you persist and make it clear that you know what you want. Some sales staff will be well disposed towards offering a good deal, while others may not be interested, so if you are not happy simply try another dealer. Make it clear if you have cash and how much you intend to spend. Don't let yourself be persuaded to take optional extras or a different model for the list price of the car you are after, rather than a reduction in price, unless the deal is a good one and they are what you want. Remember that the list price is the maximum price of the car, but also bear in mind additional costs such as delivery and number plates which usually add up to around £400.

If you qualify for the higher rate of the mobility component of the Disability Living Allowance or War Pensioners' Mobility Supplement you can use the Motability* car finance scheme. You hand over all or part of your allowance, plus (sometimes) a down-payment, to lease or buy the car. This can work out cheaper than buying conventionally. The Motability scheme can also be used for second-hand cars.

Buying a second-hand car

Buying second-hand is not so much a question of looking for discounts as of making sure you pay a fair price. Do all you can to establish that the car is what it seems: carry out as thorough an inspection as possible (or pay a mechanic or the AA* or RAC* to do one) and satisfy yourself that the documents are in order and that the seller is legally entitled to sell the vehicle.

The price you pay depends not only on the age and condition of the car, but also on where you buy it. The same vehicle will command a higher price if sold by a dealer rather than privately; prices are lowest at auctions. However, your legal comeback is reduced in the two cheaper markets. A private sale does not confer Sale of Goods Act rights, although the car must 'correspond with the description', and an auctioned car is sold 'as seen' – and that is on the basis of the briefest opportunity to inspect it. With a dealer you not only have full Sale of Goods Act rights (see **Chapter 26**), but the car may be sold with a warranty.

Thinking about features

Options and extras

Most car manufacturers offer a range of features which make a car easier to operate. These may be optional extras or may be standard features on the more expensive models in a range. Traditionally the preserve of large luxury cars, these features are increasingly being offered on both smaller cars and less upmarket models.

Automatic transmission (£600 to £1,000 more expensive than a manual gearbox) gives you the benefits of having no clutch pedal to operate and no gear-changing to do in traffic – particularly useful for town driving. It normally has only a small effect on performance and petrol costs. **Power-assisted steering** takes a lot of work out of turning the wheel when moving slowly, so parking and getting round town are far less tiring. It is a standard feature on many large cars, where the need is greatest, but is an option well worth considering on many smaller cars (about £350).

Central locking and **electric windows** save on time, effort and some awkward movements. They are typically featured on upmarket models in most ranges, but are unlikely to be available as an optional extra on basic models. **Height-adjustable seats and steering wheels** may help with getting in and out, but the design of some cars without these features could suit you better. **Adjustable seat height** helps small drivers to improve the all-round field of vision.

Design features

Many older people have difficulty with standard cars, particularly getting in and out. If you want to evaluate a prospective purchase from this point of view, use the checklist below. Also, you may be less tolerant of a car that becomes uncomfortable over the course of a long journey, so be sure to assess leg room and seat comfort in the front and the back and to find out how much noise and vibration the car suffers at speed.

For **access** take note of:

- shape of door catch and effort needed to operate it
- width of door opening and effort needed to open and close door (2-door cars usually have wider doors than 4-door models)
- height of door sill
- height of seat off ground
- obstruction by steering wheel.

For **comfort** and **ease of use** assess:

- seat comfort, angle and height off floor
- seat belt position
- leg room
- distance from driving seat to pedals, height of pedals off floor and pedal spacing
- movement and effort needed to shift gears
- shape and position of handbrake and effort needed to use it
- configuration of dashboard and controls
- access to ignition.

For **ease of using the boot or hatch** look at:

- boot or hatch sill height off ground
- depth from sill to boot floor
- size of storage area
- size of boot aperture
- height of fully opened hatch
- effort to open or close boot or hatch.

RICA★ produces the *Ability Car Park*, which gives detailed measurements of a range of cars for disabled and elderly people. Similar information can be obtained from the Mobility Advice and Vehicle Information Service (MAVIS)★.

Your driving licence

The Driver and Vehicle Licensing Agency (DVLA)* will normally send you a reminder to renew your licence about five weeks before it expires on your 70th birthday. If the address on your licence is not your current address, you can get a renewal form D1 from post offices.

After you reach 70, you must renew your licence every three years. This costs £6 each time. You must declare any physical or mental conditions which may affect your ability to drive safely. These are listed on form D100 available from post offices.

If an entry on the application alerts the DVLA to the possible need for a medical examination, they will send the form to their medical section, who will ask you to complete a medical questionnaire and give consent for them to obtain a report from your GP. Depending on the information given by you on the questionnaire, they may require you to be examined by a local medical officer. The report is paid for by the DVLA, but you will have to pay any travelling expenses.

It is possible that you will then be issued with a medically restricted licence. The medical restriction might be in terms of time, for example a licence issued for only one or two years where a disability is progressive, or restricted to a type of vehicle, such as a car with modified controls.

Fit to drive?

Think seriously about your ability to drive safely as you grow older. Don't give up lightly, but be objective about your capabilities and suit your driving to your skills.

Staying behind the wheel

Many older people unnecessarily give up driving through lack of confidence or because of physical problems such as arthritic fingers and stiffness of the hips, knees, neck and shoulders. Giving up means losing a great deal of independence and, if you live in a rural area, could even mean having to move house. Yet simple conversions and add-on features such as extra-wide mirrors and easy-release levers for the handbrake, as well as manufacturers' options such as automatic transmission and power-assisted steering can make driving possible for years after it becomes difficult to operate a conventionally equipped car.

The Department of Transport's Mobility Advice and Vehicle Information Service (MAVIS)★ can give free advice by letter or phone to any older driver worried about continuing to drive. They can give details of mobility centres where you can have your abilities expertly assessed and try out a range of car adaptations.

Orange badge scheme
If you cannot walk or you have extreme difficulty walking you should be able to get an orange badge from your local social services department (Regional and Island Councils in Scotland, DoE Roads Services Division in Northern Ireland). You need a medical certificate which describes the nature of your disability and makes it clear that the disability severely limits mobility. The badge can be displayed on any car you travel in, whether you are the driver or a passenger. You are entitled to park for up to three hours on single and double yellow lines (except in some parts of central London), and without a time limit in Scotland. You can also park free of charge for any length of time at street parking meters and places where other cars can park only for a limited period.

Danger signs
Eyesight steadily declines from about the age of 50, starting with longsightedness and involving loss of contrast sensitivity, less ability to adapt to the dark and tendency to suffer more from glare. Stiffness in the neck and back leads to difficulty looking around properly and compounds the problems with observation caused by deteriorating eyesight.

Reaction times become longer as you get older and you become more prone to fatigue, which reduces concentration and slows reflexes further. Older people find it harder to make judgements in fast-moving traffic and are less accurate at assessing the speed of other vehicles at junctions. Confusion when faced with complicated junctions and a large number of signs is also more likely.

As the number of people in Britain over 65 increases, so does concern over related road safety issues. While experience counts for a lot, the physical and mental effects of ageing bring with them a higher risk of accidents and greater susceptibility to injury. Studies report that once drivers pass the age of 60 the accident rate per mile driven begins to rise; after 70 the rate then rises quite sharply.

Sensible driving
Let common sense be your guide. If your night vision is no longer too good, restrict yourself to daytime driving. Keep your eyesight at its best by using glasses or contact lenses with an up-to-date prescription. Avoid long journeys or at least take plenty of breaks, and if possible wait for adverse weather conditions to clear – driving in fog or with the wipers running constantly is very tiring. If you are taking any medication, find out from your doctor or pharmacist whether it could affect your driving.

Experience helps drivers stay out of trouble by identifying potential hazards in good time. However, you should assess your abilities as a driver from time to time. You can take a refresher lesson with a driving instructor who will give you a general impression of your driving and offer some useful tips. The Institute of Advanced Motorists* offers members a reassessment test (cost £23) – essentially the same as an advanced driving test but without a pass or fail at the end. The leaflet *Advice for Older Drivers*, available free from the AA Road Safety Unit*, offers plenty of frank advice and useful tips. There are also assessment centres around the country which can advise you on your ability to drive and the type of equipment that might help you. Services and charges vary. The Mobility Advice and Vehicle Information Service (MAVIS)* has produced a free guide to the centres.

As your driving abilities decline, plan ahead for the future, first looking to have a car you can operate easily, and later considering the options open if you finally have to give up driving. For more information see the 'Getting around' section of **Chapter 34**.

Other forms of transport

Air travel

A few airlines offer reduced fares for retired people, so check with your travel agent or airline to see what is available. However, do not leap to the conclusion that these are necessarily the cheapest fares to be had. Provided you book in advance there are a number of cheap tickets you can buy, notably the Advanced Purchase Excursion fares (Apex, Super Apex and so on) and Advanced Booking Charter fares (ABC). Most of these cheap fares have the following conditions attached:

- You must book and pay for both the outward and the return journey at the same time.
- Once the flight is booked you cannot alter the ticket.
- The duration of your stay must be within set minimum and maximum periods.
- You may have to travel on certain days or your stay may have to include certain days – for example, you may need to be away over at least one Saturday night.
- There may be no refund at all for cancellation.

Because of the strictures that are imposed on such tickets, it is imperative that you take out insurance to cover you against the risk of failing to travel on the appointed date.

The discounted fares that are advertised in newspapers are another source of cheap flights. These can be extremely good value, but you should take a more cautious approach than you would if you were buying a ticket direct from an airline. After you have done some phoning around to find the cheapest ticket, take the following precautions:

- Check on the airline that will be carrying you. While all airlines can suffer from delays, the fewer planes an airline has the longer a delay is likely to be. Balancing the saving in fare against the inconvenience caused by a possible delay is a personal decision based on the type of trip, your stamina and your finances.
- Don't pay the whole fare until you have received the ticket

– just pay a small deposit and use a credit card if possible so that you are covered by the Consumer Credit Act.
- Check with the airline's reservation office that your booking is secure and do the same for your return journey as soon as you reach your destination.
- Check on the restrictions on the ticket and if you are not able to change flights take out insurance to cover yourself against an alteration of plans.

Rail travel

British Rail offers a Senior Railcard which costs £16 a year. To obtain one you have to fill in an application form (available from any staffed station) or rail-appointed Travel Agent and provide proof that you are 60 or over in the form of a passport, NHS medical card or birth certificate, for example. The Senior Railcard gives you a one-third discount on First Class Single and Open Returns and on First Class and Standard Singles and Returns, as well as the following fares.

Savers have individual restrictions according to the route; **SuperSavers** cannot be used on Fridays or summer Saturdays. Both have some peak hour restrictions and are valid for one month. **Network AwayBreaks**, available on services in London and the south-east, can be used on any day, with the outward journey on the date shown on the ticket and the return journey within five days. **Cheap Day Singles and Returns** are restricted to offpeak travel, as is the **London One Day Travelcard**. **Leisure First** offers offpeak first-class travel at half the usual first-class fare on most InterCity trains (with a further one-third discount with the Senior Railcard). The numbers of tickets on each train are limited; you must reserve your seats no later than 4 p.m. the day before you travel, and you must stay away over a Saturday night.

The Senior Railcard does not give you a discount on cross-Channel ferries. However, if you have one you can also buy a Rail Europe Senior Card for £5 which will give you a discount, usually of about 30 per cent, on rail and sea travel throughout most of Europe. You can get details from British Rail stations, travel agents or the International Rail Centre (based at Victoria Station)*.

Rail Rovers are restricted to offpeak travel and can be bought for 7 or 14 days with some permutations, such as being available for use over four days within an eight-day timespan.

Coach travel

Coach travel is usually cheaper than rail travel, but it does have the disadvantage that journey times tend to be longer and seating less spacious than on most trains. However, there are now many express coaches that make good time and they tend to have washrooms, toilets and refreshments on board.

The biggest coach company is National Express (known in Scotland as Caledonian Express), which covers well over 1000 destinations in England, Scotland and Wales. However, there are also many independent coach operators with smaller networks; the best way to discover them is to go to a travel agent who handles coach travel and enquire what is available for the destination you have in mind. You can reserve a seat on a particular coach for a small extra charge; if you settle for a 'standard booking' you will be guaranteed a seat on the correct day, but not at any particular time. Make sure you choose the most direct route possible; long-distance coach journeys with multiple stops can be very gruelling. Seats tend to be cheaper midweek, and passengers aged 60 and over get a reduction of approximately one-third on the price.

Bus travel

The concessions available to people travelling by bus vary from area to area and are generally the responsibility of the local transport authority. Senior citizens are nearly always eligible for a reduction, and there may be separate schemes for disabled people. The concessions may take the form of travel tokens of a set value, a pass giving a flat rate for any length of journey in a stated area, a half-fare pass which can only be used at offpeak times or a completely free pass, again limited to offpeak periods. Local bus operators may also have their own schemes for bus passes, and there may be local schemes for passengers with limited mobility. Contact your local transport authority for details of what is available.

CHAPTER 28

Holidays

Types of holiday

Tour operators

'Niche marketing' is the trend nowadays and you'll find it easy to identify some tour operators offering holidays that are suitable for any ages and others that offer special packages for the over-55s – which can include trips down the Amazon or along the Silk Road as well as to more restful destinations. Certain operators also run packages especially for the retired holidaymaker, such as British university and college study breaks, singles festivals, dancing holidays, cruises, wildlife tours, religious tours, garden tours and walking tours, wedding anniversary breaks and winter sun holidays of six months' duration. Many holidays are offpeak to keep costs down, and since offpeak in one country is peak time in another, there is somewhere to go all year round.

For people travelling on their own, the Holiday Care Service* can give ideas and advice on such matters as avoiding cramped rooms and single person supplements.

Touring holidays in Britain

Bed-and-breakfasting can be one of the cheapest types of holiday as well as the most varied. But don't rule out staying in hotels: when hoteliers are faced with empty rooms you are in a strong position to bargain; you may be surprised how easy it is to negotiate quite dramatic reductions in room prices. Consumers' Association* publishes both *The Good Bed and Breakfast Guide* and *The Which? Hotel Guide*, with details of over 1,000 establishments in each Guide.

> **TIPS**
> - You're likely to get bigger discounts if you make your booking on the day. By the afternoon, hotels are anxious to fill their rooms.
> - Pick your season – there are fewer bargains in the busy summer season or at Easter.
> - Hotels often offer deals at weekends. If you're planning to stay for a couple of nights, you may get a discount without even having to ask.
> - The English, Welsh, Scottish and Northern Ireland Tourist Boards* publish free booklets listing short break rates at hotels in the UK. They can also send details of operators offering discounted package breaks.

Self-catering

While staying in a hotel releases the holidaymaker from the burden of shopping and cooking, it does impose certain constraints upon the day, particularly if the evening meal is included in the price. If you want to breakfast at 11, dine at 10 and make yourself fully at home, self-catering is the answer. You should be able to find a holiday cottage in pretty well any part of Britain you wish to visit. There are many companies offering a range of accommodation from the simple and comparatively inexpensive to luxury homes sleeping six to eight with games rooms, videos, dishwashers and freezers – a good option for a family holiday with grandchildren. Most have been checked by the relevant tourist authority and given a grading as to their standard. The best place to look is in the classified columns of the Sunday papers, where you should find a dozen or more companies advertising, along with private advertisements placed by cottage owners themselves.

Self-catering abroad can be booked through most of the major holiday firms, but this can also be done privately; many a British family hope to recoup the costs of doing up a derelict house in rural France, Spain or Italy by letting it out during the periods they are not in residence. The biggest choice is probably in France. An advertisement with a British telephone number attached removes the worry of negotiating conditions and directions on how to get there in a foreign language, but if you prefer to deal through an agency there are various ones specialising in gîtes – rural properties which range from converted barns to grander accommodation. The owner generally lives nearby and will usually help with advice on local services – but not necessarily in English. Various tour operators offer gîte holidays; *The Good Gîte Guide*, published by FHG Publications, contains a broad selection of gîtes and lists of regional offices; and the French national organisation Gîtes de France★ has a London office.

Retreats

A retreat is not, strictly speaking, a holiday: it is a time to spend in quietness and contemplation. For details of over 100 retreat houses in Britain and Ireland, apply to the National Retreat Association★. The Hen House★ offers retreats and various courses (notably, one called 'Growing Old Disgracefully') for women only; or you can simply check in for a general holiday.

Farm holidays

Farm holidays are increasingly popular among town-dwellers anxious for a taste of rural life; you can go as a paying guest in the farmhouse itself or rent a caravan or cottage. Bed-and-breakfast rates are usually good value, and some farms will provide an evening meal as well.

For a choice of over 1,000 farms that have all been inspected by the Tourist Board, buy *The Farm Holiday Bureau Guide: Stay on a Farm* from bookshops, tourist information centres or the Farm Holiday Bureau UK Ltd★.

★*The addresses and phone numbers of organisations marked with an asterisk can be found in the address section at the back of the guide.*

Caravanning

Caravanning is an ideal way of touring without having to worry about what the accommodation at your destination will be like. The Camping & Caravanning Club* offers family membership for £25 plus a £4 joining fee (the latter waived if you join by direct debit). An annual guide called *Your Place in the Country* lists 80 full-facility club sites all over Britain, while the two-yearly *Big Sites Book* contains details of 5,000 sites, 2,500 of which are certificated – that is, they are small sites where only CCC members can go. The Club offers insurance and a foreign touring service, and each new member's pack contains a touring safety guide with advice for beginners. You can also obtain a listing of hire companies for caravans, motor caravans and pop-tops – extendable caravans which are ideal for retired people as they are lightweight and have less wind drag, making them easier to transport.

Timesharing

The activities of some its salespeople have given timesharing a very bad name indeed. The trick is to resist all blandishments, pressure and promises and consider the purchase as coolly as you would with any other large item.

Timeshare should not be regarded as an investment – resale prices can be as little as 40 per cent of the original price and you still have to pay for flights, food and maintenance fees, as well as exchange fees if you want to swap. Do your sums very carefully – you might be better off with package holidays.

The basic idea of timesharing is that you buy the use of a certain property for a certain period at a certain time of year. If you don't wish to use that time yourself you can lend it to friends, sub-let it or swap it for time at another timeshare property elsewhere and, if you have bought the timeshare in perpetuity, you simply leave it to someone in your will as you would any other property.

Depending on location and period a timeshare will cost from four to five figures to buy. Consider buying from a reputable resale agency as this will be quite a bit cheaper. The maintenance charges should be checked very carefully to see exactly what they represent and whether they are linked with a cost of living index. You should also make careful enquiries as to the resale value of the property, which in some cases has been discovered to be a good deal lower than the initial purchase price (the initial marketing costs are often as high as 40-60 per cent of the price); also note that it can be very difficult to resell a timeshare property. In some countries you might become liable for direct taxation as a timeshare owner, so this is another area to investigate.

A reputable timeshare developer will provide a prospectus giving details of the resort, which should include details of the rights and responsibilities of owner and developer, the methods of paying (such as instalments, interest rates, deposit and so on) and a copy of the contract. There are two areas that should be completely independent of the developer. First, the financial and title arrangements should be overseen by an independent stakeholder, such as a solicitor, bank or trustee, to ensure that the developers cannot get their hands on the money until the units are complete and the right to the title has been handed over. Secondly, the owners' association, which takes over the running of the resort once most of the units have been sold, should be made up of owners voted in by the other owners, not the developer's stooges.

One important point to bear in mind is that if you buy your timeshare abroad you are not entitled to a 14-day cooling-off period during which you can change your mind, a safeguard you *will* be covered by if you sign on the dotted line in Britain. This is an extra reason to avoid buying between the beach and your hotel in Mediterranean resorts. (The EC Commission is currently considering a 28-day cooling-off period for timeshare properties bought within the EC.) However, even in Britain you should resist the sort of presentations that are attached to offers of lavish prizes and free holidays and avoid signing any contract until you have had it checked by a solicitor. Never produce your credit card to a sales person as identification – you could come under heavy pressure to use it to put down a deposit.

Most reputable timeshare companies belong to one of two

exchange organisations: Interval International Ltd★ and RCI Europe Ltd★, which give access to over 2,300 holiday resorts in more than 80 countries and offer short breaks, cruises and coach tours.

To obtain *Your Place in the Sun*, a Department of Trade and Industry checklist of points to consider when buying a timeshare, telephone 0171-215 3344.

The Office of Fair Trading★ has produced a report on the industry which can be obtained free of charge by application in writing. The Timeshare Council★ is a self-regulatory body composed largely of developers and marketeers which aims to promote the interests of all legitimate players in the game. It offers potential buyers free advice and provides a free conciliation service to clients of its members.

Holiday peace of mind

No matter what sort of holiday you are planning, there are certain basic guidelines to follow in order to give yourself peace of mind. While you can never completely rule out the possibility of falling victim to a thief or to a bout of illness, you can at least minimise the risk and make sure that if either eventuality occurs it causes as little upset as possible. It's best to contemplate in advance the possibility of things going wrong, take the necessary steps to avoid or mitigate any problems, and then put the whole thing out of your mind and concentrate on enjoying the anticipation and actuality of your holiday.

Money

Never carry more cash with you than you need – and don't be lulled by a holiday atmosphere into being more careless than you would be at home. Don't carry your wallet, passport or indeed anything else of value in your back pocket and never leave a purse invitingly displayed in an open handbag or shopping basket. For preference, use a shoulder bag and sling the strap diagonally across your body, over the opposite shoulder. If you are visiting an area that is particularly notorious for street crime, wear a money belt under your top layer of clothing. Leave jewellery at home or, if you must take it, in the hotel safe or tucked away in your rented accommodation.

If you are unfortunate enough to meet with a mugger, don't play the hero – hand over your money without argument. Pack a copy of your insurance policy so that you can check the procedure if necessary, and keep a list of emergency phone numbers to ring in the event of theft.

Plastic v. traveller's cheques

When you are travelling abroad, it's unwise to rely on just one form of payment. A credit card is the most convenient as you can buy goods and services without having to visit a bank first. It is not necessarily an expensive option – the credit card companies get very competitive exchange rates. But you should also take an alternative like traveller's cheques (which can usually be replaced quickly if lost or stolen), so you will not be left high and dry if your card is lost, stolen or not accepted. These may work out more expensive once you've suffered a poor exchange rate and paid commission on buying and exchanging them, but they may be essential in developing countries, where plastic cards are unlikely to be widely accepted.

Insurance

It's advisable to take out comprehensive insurance appropriate to your needs to cover yourself against things going wrong. Tour operators often insist on insurance as a condition of booking, but note that you do not have to take out the insurance package they offer; you may well be able to find a cheaper one elsewhere that will give you satisfactory cover. However, if you are travelling independently you will not have the compensation that most reputable tour operators should provide for mishaps for which they could be considered liable, so you need to check your insurance especially carefully. Read the small print minutely – there may be a wide variation in terms and conditions between one policy and another. Make sure you will be covered for the following eventualities:

- loss of your deposit or cancellation of the entire holiday
- the cost of curtailing or cancelling your holiday in the event of serious illness or death in your family
- loss of money, baggage and personal effects
- the cost of emergency purchases if your baggage is delayed
- personal liability cover in case you cause injury to another person or damage to property
- compensation for any inconvenience caused by transport cancellations or delays
- medical treatment, hospitalisation, ambulance service, emergency dental treatment, special transport home, the cost of prolonging your stay and that of a companion who may have to stay with you.

The cost of your holiday is easy to establish, and you can calculate the value of the contents of your baggage and your personal effects (your watch, camera, jewellery and so on) accurately enough. In the personal liability and medical categories the sums become astronomical: allow £250,000 for the former (but £1,000,000 in the USA), and £250,000 inside Europe and £1,000,000 for the rest of the world for the latter.

Using a credit card to pay for travel arrangements can provide some medical cover during a journey but not during your stay, so you need extra insurance for that. Gold and charge cards offer more cover, but make sure it's sufficient.

If you've paid for at least part of your holiday by credit card, and things go wrong, under the Consumer Credit Act you should be able to claim from the credit card company as well as the tour operator (though you'll get money only from one). But your holiday must cost more than £100 per person; the credit card slip should be made out to the operator, not the travel agent; and note that debit cards, charge chards and most gold cards do not offer this protection.

Peace of mind while you're away

The Home Office has published a leaflet, *Peace of Mind While You're Away*, giving advice on preventing burglaries while you're on holiday. Free copies are available from police stations.

Health

For travellers abroad, the Department of Health issues a useful leaflet called *Health Advice for Travellers Anywhere in the World* (T5), which gives advice on precautions to take and how to cope in an emergency. You can obtain it by telephoning 0800 555777. This leaflet also contains form E111, which entitles you to free or reduced-cost treatment in the EC countries. You must take this to a post office for processing. However, bear in mind that even within the EC the standard of medical care varies, and claiming refunds can be quite bureaucratic. Nor does the E111 cover repatriation, so it's advisable to take out insurance that will cover medical expenses (see above).

Get medical advice well in advance of your trip, as some courses of vaccinations need to be given over a few months. GPs vary in their knowledge of travel medicine, but their vaccinations are usually cheapest – either free or the cost of a prescription. Alternatively, it is possible to find a British Airways Travel Clinic in a large number of major cities throughout Britain – for details, telephone 0171-831 5333 to hear a recorded message listing various relevant telephone These clinics provide advice, immunisations and a range of first-aid and preventive equipment, such as needle and syringe packs and water purifiers.

The Medical Advisory Service for Travellers Abroad (MASTA)* gives information on immunisation, malaria medication and the latest health advice on journeying abroad. If you telephone MASTA on 0891 221400 and give details of your trip you will receive a printed health brief which costs £5 if sent by post or £7 by fax. Masta also supplies a range of goods, such as mosquito nets and repellents, water purifiers and sterile packs of syringes and dressings.

Don't forget to pack any medication that you take regularly – you may not be able to find it abroad or it may be considerably more expensive. But make sure that it is clearly labelled with both the trade name and generic name, and find out if there are any restrictions on taking it in or out of the UK or the country you are visiting; a back-up letter from your doctor may be useful.

In addition, take a simple first-aid kit with you. If you are going to a hot climate, always pack plenty of high-protection sun screen – and beware of ice-cream, seafoods, salads, fruit (unless you can peel it yourself) and water (which also means ice). Avoid buffets laid out at room temperature – go for foods from the menu that have to be freshly cooked.

Bear in mind that air travel and a sudden change of climate are both debilitating. Travel comfortably in loose-fitting clothes, drink plenty of liquid and remember that alcohol consumed in the air has much more effect than it does on the ground. Allow a couple of days for resting and acclimatisation when you arrive.

Complaints about holidays

The following information covers holidays arranged by a tour operator.

Always try to get problems sorted out on the spot. Speak to the tour rep if there is one. Otherwise, try the manager of your accommodation or the tour operator's office locally or in the UK. If you still aren't satisfied, take it up with the tour operator on your return. Collect names and addresses of witnesses or people who have suffered similar problems, and take photographs if appropriate.

Write to the tour operator as soon as possible. Tell them what went wrong and what sort of response you're expecting. If you're looking for compensation, put a figure on this. The amount will depend on your situation, but here are the three main elements to consider:

- The difference between what you paid for and what you got (for example, the cost of the three-star hotel you booked compared with the two-star hotel you were moved to). If only certain days of your holiday were affected, you should claim just for that proportion.
- Loss of enjoyment, disappointment, inconvenience etc. Take into account what your holiday cost and how much of it was affected.
- Out-of-pocket expenses (for example, the cost of eating out if you aren't given an adequate means to cook on a 'self-catering' holiday.

Only in very extreme cases, when your holiday was such a nightmare that you couldn't enjoy it at all, should you claim back the full cost, with any extra expenses and compensation for loss of enjoyment.

If you aren't happy with the operator's response, write back. If they make an offer you think is too low, keep any cheque they send (but don't cash it) and continue the correspondence until you get a more satisfactory outcome.

If an exchange of letters doesn't get you what you want, consider other ways of settling the dispute. You can go to court, or use the ABTA arbitration scheme if the operator is a member of ABTA. Explain that this is a documents-only procedure.

The small claims procedure is designed to be a fairly quick, straightforward and cheap alternative to the full county court. It is kept informal and you can argue your case in person without having to use a lawyer. It can be used for claims up to £1,000 (£750 in Scotland). These limits apply to the total claim, not each individual's – if, say, you were claiming for a ruined family holiday.

If your tour operator belongs to ABTA, you can use the independent arbitration scheme operated by the Chartered Institute of Arbitrators*. It relies totally on written evidence. You must apply within nine months of your return from holiday, and the decision is binding on both parties, so you can't go to court later if you don't like the decision.

The Association of Independent Tour Operators (AITO)* has launched a scheme for settling customers' disputes with its members, run by an independent mediator. Written evidence is used to reach a decision, and the mediator may phone you.

CHAPTER 29

ENJOYING YOUR LEISURE

When you are a member of the working population, leisure time can often be very limited and the prospect of your days being your own can seem very sweet. Many people dream of all the things they will have time to do when they retire, only to find the reality of all those extra hours to fill something of a shock.

Leisure time needs to be just as planned when there is a lot of it as it does when there is too little; if you don't take a positive stance on structuring your days you may well find yourself expanding the time you spend on everyday chores in order to fill the hours. While it might be nice to wash up at a leisurely pace and stroll to the shops, it's not exactly a fulfilling way to spend the rest of your life. If you have led a very stressful working life you will obviously want to ease off somewhat, but if you don't provide markers of some sort in your life you will look back at the end of a year and be unable to say what you did with those 365 days.

People are living longer and enjoying better health than ever before. Retirement no longer means sitting back and watching the activity of others for the remainder of your life; it is now a period of new beginnings, of learning skills you never had time for before, picking up on education you may have missed out on when you were young and keeping an open mind about the opportunities that may present themselves to you.

People who have worked in occupations that involve dealing with the public, or have been in the kind of office where the companionship of their colleagues played a large part in their enjoyment of their job, are going to find retirement a lonely time unless they find some way of replacing that social activity. Fortunately, this is not hard to do. Most forms of leisure activity bring people together and unless your penchant is for single-handed sailing you'll probably find yourself striking up friendships with a larger range of people than ever you did in the work environment.

Whether you go for energetic outdoor activity or quieter indoor pursuits is of course a matter of personal taste, but ideally you should aim for a mix of the two; if all your leisure activity relies on fair weather you are going to find the winters long and dreary. It's also important to base some of your pursuits in areas where you will mix with other age groups, for while it's helpful to be in contact with people with whom you have the shared experience of retirement, cutting yourself off from the younger generations can lead to an ossification of your outlook on life. The world moves on, and it's infinitely better to move on with it rather than turn into a bystander. An interest in new trends in art, literature, fashion and society as a whole, coupled with a wealth of life experience, makes one good company for people of any age.

You won't find in this chapter anything on sport or exercise – see **Chapter 31** for that – or much on individual hobbies or interests; but there is information on developing existing skills, taking up studying and joining the vast band of volunteers.

Developing skills

Music
At last you've got the time to pick up pursuits you may have dropped as long ago as your schooldays. If you played an instrument in the school orchestra you can begin again, this time with more hours available for practice. It's not hard to find a music teacher – enquire at your local music shop, check the classified advertisements in the local paper or go to the library and ask for the Register of Professional Private Music Teachers (this will also include singing teachers). Playing an instrument is an excellent way of meeting people, and if you have sufficient aptitude you may be able to form your own chamber ensemble.

If singing was your talent, take some singing lessons to tune up your throat muscles and cast around for a choir to join. Some are of very high standard, with strict rehearsal requirements; others are more accessible to all-comers.

Foreign languages
You may already speak some foreign languages, but there's usually room for improvement. If you don't, now is the time to start: a new language gives you access to the culture of another country and a broadening of horizons. You should have no difficulty in finding classes in any of the EC languages, and most local authorities offer a wide range of non-EC languages as well. If you thought that the *en famille* system, where you stay as a guest of a family abroad, was for schoolchildren only, think again: En Famille Overseas* will supply host families in France and other European countries for people of all ages. You can go at any time of year and for any length of time.

Crafts and handiwork
If you've always been good with your hands and have creative flair, you may be able to make some money from selling craftwork. How-to books are available on most forms of craft and local authority classes can be useful. There is a demand for beautiful home-made *objets*, and some people have found that practical talents such as picture-framing or cake-decorating have put them back into the world of full-time work again. Skills such as knitting, crochet and dressmaking are not very remunerative, but having your talent appreciated can be reward enough in itself.

Branching out
While it certainly makes sense to capitalise on existing capabilities and interests, something totally different presents more of a challenge. The Dark Horse Venture* is for the over-55s who wish to take up a new activity, the ethos being that everyone has talents of which they are unaware and it's never too late to discover them. You have to find yourself a teacher who will help you towards an agreed target over the space of a year, and when you have reached it you can apply for an award. These are

given within three categories: giving and sharing; learning and doing; and exploring and exercising. The award is for your own personal best rather than comparing your achievements with other people's, and virtually every activity you could possibly wish to do will fall into one category or another. Best of all, there are no set ideas about what is a suitable activity for a retired person; dark horses have taken up playing steel drums, horse-riding to eventing standard, abseiling at 72 and running in the London Marathon at 60.

A literary life

You'll probably have more time to read in retirement than you've ever had in your life. Adding a little structure to your reading can add to your enjoyment of this essentially solitary activity, so you might want to consider joining (or forming) a book group. These are informal arrangements within which a number of people agree to meet at regular intervals to discuss a particular book. The meetings take place in the homes of the group members.

Perhaps you want to become a writer yourself. You'll probably find that your local authority offers various classes on creative writing, while the National Extension College (see below) offers distance learning courses. *Writers News**, a magazine aimed at new writers, gives details of awards, competitions and markets. As competition is fierce you won't necessarily find a mainstream publisher, but don't let that put you off: a local history group may want someone who can commit their research to paper, or your autobiography might have strong local interest. You could also try approaching your Regional Arts Association; ask your library for the address or write to the Arts Council*.

You may be a keen letter writer, in which case you might like the idea of becoming a penfriend to a prisoner via the Penfriends Scheme, Prison Reform Trust*.

Back to school

Before enrolling on an educational course, decide just how thoroughly you want to explore your chosen subject and what your final goal is. If there are a number of subjects you feel inclined towards, the best bet is to begin with local authority classes; although they have increased in cost as they have diminished in scope, they still offer a good choice of subjects at a reasonable price (sometimes with reductions for retired people). You can usually enrol for just one term, which should be sufficient to give you an idea of how deep your interest in the subject really runs and whether you want to pursue it further.

For more serious study, the Workers Educational Association (WEA)*, operating in all parts of the UK, offers a range of subjects which are usually taught by university lecturers. You don't need any qualifications to enrol and your fellow-students will be of a variety of ages and backgrounds. The study course is usually of 20 weeks' duration in the autumn and spring terms, and there may be further courses in the summer term, with field study courses on local landscapes, wildlife and history a distinct possibility. There are also residential courses. Fees for the courses vary; enquire about reductions for retired people. Ask at the library for the address of your local branch or write to the WEA.

The University of the Third Age (U3A)* is, as you might infer, specifically for the older generation. However, the name is misleading in that no qualifications or diplomas are involved and not all the classes are academic. The study groups may start at any time of year and new members can join in at any point; there may be no long summer break to leave a hole in a new social life. Fees are modest and all the activities are arranged by the members of the particular group, so they tend to be accurately based on local interests. Not only will you make new contacts in your neighbourhood, but there is a national termly newspaper called *Third Age News*, a travel club which organises special interest holidays and a subject network which links up members around the country who have similar interests. You can obtain a list of addresses of U3A groups by sending a large stamped addressed envelope to U3A. However, it is not a good idea to restrict all your social and learning activity to U3A as there will be no opportunity for you to make contact with younger students.

Distance learning
Distance learning provides a greater choice of course than may be available to you locally, but check that the course you are enrolling upon is a reputable one; you can obtain a list of recognised colleges from the Council for the Accreditation of Correspondence Courses*.

The three main providers of distance learning courses are the National Extension College, the Open University and the Open College of the Arts. None of these bodies demands any qualifications for entry and all course material is sent via the post. You can study at your own pace and you will be given a tutor who will give you support. For details of fees and courses contact the individual bodies.

The National Extension College (NEC)* offers a range of opportunities including GCSE and A-Level courses, as well as 'starter' courses designed to ease the way for people who feel unsure of their academic skills. There are also courses for hobbies and subjects such as business skills. Fees are reduced for people on low incomes.

The Open University (OU)* offers a variety of courses, including BA, BSc and Masters degree courses, Community Education courses and Advanced Diploma courses. There are also leisure courses on subjects ranging from art to computing. The demand for degree courses is high, and you may have to go on a waiting list. All new students receive a preparatory package before the course begins and there is a choice of foundation courses in the first year which help to develop learning skills. Some courses call for a week's attendance at a summer school. You should expect the course to cost £2000–£3000 over a period of four to six years. The OU has 13 regional centres which you can visit for advice; look for Open University in the telephone book or contact the Open University, Central Enquiry Service*.

The Open College of the Arts* is an education trust which offers courses on such subjects as art and design, sculpture, textiles, music, photography and creative writing. Some courses require your attendance at group tutorials every few weeks, while others operate by correspondence only. There are no recognised qualifications on completing a course.

Residential courses

The range of residential study courses is vast and growing all the time; the course that interests you may be held at a college, school, field study centre or country mansion in beautiful surroundings. Residential courses are a good way of combining a holiday with your study, and if you go on your own you will find plenty of single companions. The best starting point for researching such courses is *Time to Learn*, a book published twice-yearly by the National Institute for Adult Continuing Education*. Other useful publications are the *Summer Schools Supplement*, available from the Independent Schools Information Service (ISIS)* and *Quality Study Holidays*, available free from the Summer Academy*.

Full-time study

If you feel you want to embark on formal study for a degree, contact your local university. Some have extra-mural departments designed for people who can manage only part-time study, but you may want to be a fully paid-up, full-time student. Most universities are very welcoming to mature students, who often bring to their studies a greater level of commitment than many school-leavers show as well as contributing their life experience. If you have never had a grant you may well be able to obtain one from your local authority, and lack of formal qualifications may not be a bar to entry.

Volunteering

For many people the main benefits of volunteering are the companionship and satisfaction of working towards a particular goal and of knowing that one is making a valuable contribution. The most common voluntary activity for those over 50 is fundraising, but other types of volunteering include visiting sick or housebound people, working for a charity or a political party, getting involved in conservation projects, doing clerical work and so on – contacts for which are beyond the scope of this guide. If you are stuck for ideas your local Citizens Advice Bureau may point you in a suitable direction. Alternatively, the National Association of Volunteer Bureaux (NAVB)* can put you in touch with your local volunteer bureau or council for voluntary services, which acts as a local clearing house for potential volunteers.

REACH* is a charity which finds part-time, expenses-only jobs for retired business or other professional people who want to use their skills to help voluntary organisations. The Scottish Corps of Retired Executives* is similar to REACH.

Grandparenting

These days the image of grandparenting, and particularly grandmothering, is undergoing a change. Far from being at home, knitting needles a-clack and scones baking in the oven, the modern grandmother is more likely to be out at work all day with no more time for domestic duties than her hard-pressed offspring. Consequently, retirement can be seen by both grandparent and parent alike as a time when the approved grandparental role can be fully adopted. If this is what you want, fine – but don't be pressurised into it if it is not. Waves of disapproval can sometimes emanate from parents if grandparents are too involved in social activities, or maybe a relationship with a new partner, to be constantly available as a free babysitting service. It's best to start off on the right foot by establishing the fact that although you have retired you still have your own life to lead; after all, small children soon turn into teenagers with busy social lives of their own and if you have subsumed all your energies into grandparenting you will suddenly find yourself without a role.

Nevertheless, you will have more time in which to enjoy the company of your grandchildren and you might find them enthusiastic companions with whom to embark on some new adventures together.

PART 8

THE GOOD HEALTH GUIDE

CHAPTER **30**

HEALTHY EATING

Most people's eating habits are now very different to those of several decades ago. One of the main reasons, of course, is that a far greater variety of fresh and processed foods is available than ever before. Patterns of health and disease have also changed: people are living longer and are more likely to suffer from what are often referred to as 'diseases of affluence', such as coronary heart disease, strokes, various cancers and diabetes.

Although there has been a welter of apparently conflicting advice in the media over the years on what you should or should not be doing in order to keep healthy, there is a consensus that the key factors are to:

- eat a healthy diet
- exercise regularly
- keep off smoking
- keep alcohol intake to a moderate level.

There is also agreement that these strategies are important at all stages of life. For instance, a recent report by the Department of Health reviewed all the evidence about diet and health for those over 65. They concluded that good nutrition is essential to help maintain health, reduce risk of certain diseases and promote recovery from illness, and that it is appropriate for most people as they get older to adopt similar patterns of eating and lifestyle to those recommended for younger adults.

Another Consumers' Association book, *Which? Way to a Healthier Diet*, contains much more about how to eat healthily, with numerous hints on shopping and preparation of food as well as cooking.

The recipe for healthy eating

Eating for health broadly means focusing on three groups of foods, and concentrating in particular on the first two groups.

Even if you are healthy and active try making changes in line with the following healthy eating guidelines. You don't have to change everything at once. Decide on priorities, make gradual alterations and experiment with different recipes and meals – remember that even small changes can be of benefit.

Fruit, vegetables and salads

Fruit and vegetables provide a variety of vitamins and minerals, and are an especially important source of vitamin C. Eating more fruit and vegetables can help to prevent constipation as they provide dietary fibre; evidence suggests that they may also play a role in reducing the risk of certain cancers. Fruit and vegetables are high in fibre and low in calories, so are ideal for filling up on if you are trying to lose weight.

Tips
Aim to eat **five portions of fruit and vegetables a day**:

- Start the day with a glass of fruit juice.
- Snack on fruit or raw vegetables such as carrots and celery between meals.
- Choose fruit salads, stewed or baked fruit or fresh fruit and yogurt for dessert.
- Use less meat and add extra vegetables, beans and lentils to stews, casseroles and soups.
- Don't overcook vegetables as this destroys some of their vitamins (see the section on vitamins near the end of this chapter).
- Keep a supply of canned fruit and vegetables (but avoid ones which have salt, sugar, or syrup added).
- Keep a supply of frozen vegetables – they are quicker and more convenient to prepare than fresh ones. A survey for *Which? way to Health* magazine found that their vitamin C content was just as good and sometimes better than that of fresh vegetables.

HEALTHY EATING

Breads, cereals, potatoes, rice and pasta

These are sometimes referred to as **starchy** foods or **complex carbohydrates**. Many people think of them as fattening foods to be avoided, especially if you are trying to lose weight. In fact, the recommendations are to eat *more* – this applies especially to older people, who tend to eat only small helpings of them. If you are dieting it is much better to cut down on fatty foods (see the section below on losing weight), which provide approximately twice as much energy (calories) as starchy ones.

Eating more breads, cereals and potatoes has a number of benefits. They provide a variety of vitamins and minerals (such as B vitamins, calcium and iron) and essential fatty acids (types of polyunsaturated fatty acids needed by the body in small amounts). Wholemeal/wholegrain breads are a good source of fibre. Starchy fibre-rich foods are filling and satisfying, so eating more of these will make you less inclined to reach for fatty and sugary snacks and foods.

Tips
- Have thicker slices of bread and eat bread with your meals. Wholemeal bread has more fibre than white but if you do not like it stick to your favourite type – the important point is to eat more.
- Start the day with breakfast. Amongst a group of *Which? way to Health* readers those who started the day with cereal and toast had diets which came closer to the healthy eating recommendations than those who skipped breakfast or had a snack later on in the morning. Choose a low-sugar, high-fibre cereal.
- Don't just rely on bread and potatoes, but try different types of rice and pasta or use other cereals and grains.

Meat, fish and dairy products

In the past everybody was encouraged to eat plenty of these foods because of their high protein content, and many people still consider them to be the most important part of a meal. Studies now show that most people eat far more protein than

than they actually need. Foods high in protein do provide vitamins and minerals but they also tend to be high in fat, and we now know that high-fat diets are associated with increased risks of heart disease and certain cancers (breast, colon and prostate). Fat is also a concentrated source of energy (calories) that can lead to extra weight gain. At the moment in the UK our daily energy intake is about 42 per cent fat; a better target is 35 per cent. Eating more fruit, vegetables and starchy foods will mean that you have less room for high-fat foods anyway.

Tips

- Choose lean meat and remove any visible fat. Poultry contains less fat than red meat but don't eat the fatty skin.
- White fish is low in fat – unless you fry it or add fatty sauces.
- Meat products like sausages, burgers and pâtés often contain large amounts of fat.
- Milk and dairy products are an important source of calcium and vitamins; try using semi-skimmed or skimmed milk and low-fat yogurts and cheeses in place of full-fat ones – they contain just as much calcium and are a good way of reducing fat intake.
- Have a vegetarian meal at least twice a week. Beans, lentils and nuts are good replacements for meat and fish.

Fibre, fat, sugar and salt

Nutritionists agree that we all need to boost our fibre intake, and cut down on fat, sugar and salt.

Fibre

Fibre can be divided into two main types. Most foods contain a mixture of both. **Insoluble fibre** (roughage), found in wholegrain cereals, wholemeal bread, brown rice, wheat bran and the skins of fruits and vegetables, passes through the body unchanged, attracting and holding water on the way. This makes the stools bulky, soft and easier to pass, helping to prevent constipation and diverticular disease and reducing the risk of piles and bowel cancer. **Soluble fibre**, found in peas, beans, lentils, oats and fruit such as apples and oranges, dissolves in water to form a gel and is then broken down further; it also tends to slow down the absorption of sugar, for instance, into the bloodstream. Your appetite is therefore satisfied for longer after a meal.

Although raw bran is high in fibre, adding it to foods is to be discouraged because of its high phytate content. Phytate binds in the gut with certain minerals like calcium, zinc and iron from other foods so that their absorption is reduced. (Other wholemeal foods also contain some phytate but its effect is compensated for by their rich mineral content and the fact that processing reduces the amount of phytates present.)

Tips
- Increase your fibre intake gradually: unpleasant side effects such as wind decrease once your body gets used to having more fibre.
- Drink plenty of fluids.
- Choose wholemeal breads and cereals and have more beans, lentils, fruit, vegetables and salads.

Fat

Butter, margarine and oils all have the same number of calories per 100g. The difference between them lies in their chemical make-up, which gives them different properties and effects; they also contain different proportions of the various fatty acids.

Hard fats, butter, lard, solid cooking fats: these contain mostly **saturated fatty acids**. Saturates raise levels of blood cholesterol, which is a risk factor for heart disease, and are the main type of fat you should aim to cut down on. The fat in meat and dairy products is mainly saturates.

Oily fish, vegetable oils and margarines are mainly made up of **polyunsaturated fatty acids** and contain essential fatty acids. It is a good idea to eat oily fish (mackerel, salmon, herrings, sardines, trout, kippers) two or three times a week as they are the best sources of a particular type of fatty acid, called omega-3, which reduces the stickiness of the blood and therefore helps to stop clots forming. If you do not like oily fish, white fish contains smaller amounts of omega-3 fatty acids, as do a variety of other foods, such as seeds, grains and nuts. Don't take fish oil supplements, unless they are prescribed by your doctor as part of your treatment, as there is not enough information about their effects at the moment.

Olive oil contains mostly **monounsaturated fatty acids**. Mediterranean countries, where olive oil is widely used, have lower rates of heart disease, but whether this is due to the olive oil or other dietary differences (they also have higher intakes of fruit, vegetables and starchy foods) has not been established.

Raised levels of **cholesterol** in the blood are a risk factor for heart disease. Cholesterol is found in certain foods (liver and other offal, eggs and some shellfish) but most is naturally produced in the body. Reducing intake of saturates can help to reduce blood cholesterol levels.

Tips
- Cut down on total fat by limiting saturates, using some polyunsaturates (margarines, oils, oily fish) and having the rest of your fat as monounsaturates such as olive oil.
- Use oils rather than hard fats for cooking as they are low in saturates.
- Change to a low-fat spread or margarine which is low in saturates and high in polyunsaturates.
- Cut down on frying, use less fat in cooking and spread less butter or margarine on bread and toast.
- Go easy on crisps, chocolate, mayonnaise, cakes, biscuits and pastries – all high-fat foods.

Sugar

As some people get older they find they want to add more sugar to their foods and eat more sweetened foods. The problem with consuming lots of sweet foods is that they decrease the appetite for other foods, are not very nutritious, and, of course, cause tooth decay. Sugar provides only calories, no vitamins, minerals, protein or fibre. Avoid sugar and sweet foods if you have diabetes or are trying to lose weight.

Intense **sweeteners** such as aspartame, acesulfame-k and saccharin are much sweeter than sugar and are used in a variety of foods like drinks and yogurts or as a table-top sweetener. Although the government is satisfied that they are safe it is probably not a good idea to eat large amounts of any one type of sweetener. They can help you to lose weight only as part of a calorie-controlled diet.

Tips
- Aim to cut out sugar in drinks and breakfast cereals.
- Use less sugar in recipes.
- Sucrose, dextrose, maltose, invert sugar, syrup and caramel are all forms of sugar – check labels.
- Honey and brown sugar are no better than white sugar.
- Sugary foods are often high in fat as well (cakes, biscuits, chocolates).

Salt

Countries with high salt intakes such as the UK have higher average levels of blood pressure than countries with low salt intakes. Blood pressure increases with age and high blood pressure is a risk factor for heart disease. If you are taking medication for high blood pressure you may have already been advised to eat less salt.

Tips
- Avoid adding salt to foods during cooking or at the table. Some salt is needed by the body but this can easily be obtained from the salt present naturally in foods.
- Season foods with lemon juice, herbs and spices – you will soon get used to the taste of less salty foods.
- Canned and processed foods are often very salty, so choose brands which have less or no extra salt added. At the moment more than half the salt we eat is added by manufacturers during food processing (note that salt = sodium chloride – check labels).
- Salt substitutes still contain some salt.

Special needs as you get older

Your energy (calorie) requirements as you get older will depend on your health and lifestyle. Some people may need to alter the quantities they eat due to changes in these; this does not necessarily mean that you have to eat less, as many people are more active in retirement than they were when working.

Weight gain

Keep a check on your weight. Being overweight is associated with reduced mobility, diabetes and hypertension and puts extra strain on joints. If you need to lose weight set yourself a realistic target, such as one or two pounds a week. Change your diet in line with the healthy eating recommendations, filling up with more fruit, vegetables, salads and starchy foods and cutting down on fatty and sugary ones. Try to increase your level of activity and get plenty of support and encouragement from those around you. Join a slimming group or ask your GP to refer you to a dietitian if you need extra help. Unfortunately, there is no easy way to lose weight; it is much better to lose it gradually and get used to eating a healthy, sensible diet.

Maintaining your weight

Some people lose their appetite and interest in food as they get older, perhaps as a result of illness, depression, problems with teeth, bereavement or certain drug treatments, or because they are living alone. It is not just the amounts that you eat which are important, but the type and variety as well. Poor food intakes over a prolonged period can lead to weight loss, increased susceptibility to infections and illness and nutritional deficiencies. If you have lost your appetite or are underweight, for whatever reason, following the healthy eating guidelines may not be appropriate for you at the moment. It is much more important to ensure that what you do manage to eat is as nourishing as possible. If you experience a sudden loss of appetite or unexplained weight loss check with your GP.

Tips

- Have small regular meals and snacks, using a variety of different foods.
- If you don't feel like cooking, remember that cold meals and snacks can be just as nutritious.
- Choose milky drinks and fruit juices rather than tea, coffee and soft drinks.
- If your appetite is very poor you may need to take a vitamin supplement. Choose a multivitamin and mineral supplement. (Very high doses of some vitamins can cause health problems, so stick to the recommended dosage and take one which provides amounts close to or just below the Recommended Daily Amount (RDA) – it should tell you this on the label.)

Catering for one

Cooking and catering for one needn't be expensive and time-consuming if you plan your meals and shopping in advance. Buying larger quantities is often more economical than buying smaller amounts; some foods can be divided into individual portions and frozen, or you could buy larger quantities with friends or neighbours and divide them between you. Look out for special offers on foods and buy vegetables and fruits which are in season. If you are cooking stews, casseroles and soups, prepare a larger quantity and freeze what you don't need immediately in individual portions.

You may not feel like bothering to cook just for yourself. Quick and/or easy meals like sandwiches, beans or scrambled eggs on toast, jacket potatoes and salads can be just as nutritious as a hot meal, but try to make sure you include a variety of foods. Experiment with new recipes and try different foods.

Stocking up

It is a good idea to keep various storecupboard foods in case you are ill or unable to get to the shops. Useful items include UHT long-life milk, long-life fruit juices, canned fruit and vegetables, dried fruit, canned fish, meat, beans, rice puddings and custards, crackers, breakfast cereals, oats, rice and pasta. If you have a freezer keep some bread, meat, fish, frozen fruit and vegetables and individual portions of meals. Make a regular check on stocks.

Most milkmen will deliver a range of foods to your doorstep, such as bread, eggs, potatoes, yogurt and fruit juices. Local authority social service departments and voluntary agencies often run luncheon clubs, day centres and pop-in clubs – your local library or social services department should be able to provide you with details of these. If you are really not able to cope with cooking you may be able to get Meals on Wheels delivered to your home.

Cooking skills and equipment

Retirement may prove a good time to improve or master new culinary skills. There are plenty of cookery classes available, including ones especially for men. Enquire about adult education classes in your area at your local library.

If you have physical problems cooking or preparing foods a range of special equipment and appliances is available to make things easier. Details are available from the Disabled Living Foundation*.

Vitamins

Vitamin requirements for older people are generally similar to those for younger individuals. However, you should make sure you maintain a good intake of vitamin C, which is found in fruit and vegetables, particularly kiwi fruits and citrus fruits and their juices (oranges, grapefruit, lemons). For most people there is no need to take vitamin supplements; a healthy, varied diet should provide all the vitamins you need.

The vitamin content of fruit and vegetables decreases during storage and cooking (especially vitamins A, C and some B vitamins). To conserve the vitamins as much as possible don't soak vegetables and avoid overcooking them – boil them lightly in a small amount of water and use a saucepan with a lid, or stir-fry, microwave or steam them. Don't add baking soda.

Calcium

Bones become weaker and less flexible as you get older, partly because less calcium is deposited and partly because more is lost from the bones. This loss of bone (see Osteoporosis in **Chapter 33**) is a major problem because it means that bones are more likely to fracture following a fall, for example. Although the role of dietary calcium in the development and prevention of osteoporosis is uncertain, it is known that calcium is important. Make sure you are eating enough calcium-rich foods to ensure that you are meeting the requirements of 700mg per day. All types of cheese and other dairy products are very good sources; other foods such as bread, nuts, pulses, fish with soft bones, green leafy vegetables, hard water and some mineral waters also provide useful amounts.

Most people get all the calcium they need from their diet, but if your appetite is poor or you don't eat any dairy produce, a calcium supplement may be appropriate. Take one which gives at least 500mg per day (there is no advantage in taking extra high doses). If you are already taking a multivitamin and mineral supplement check the label to see if it contains any calcium and, if so, how much.

Vitamin D

Vitamin D is involved in the regulation of calcium absorption and is obtained from exposure to sunlight and a few dietary sources (fatty fish, margarine, eggs, liver, evaporated milk, skimmed milk powder and some breakfast cereals which have extra vitamin D added). Try to expose some skin to sunlight during the summer. Anyone who is housebound or unable to follow this advice may need a vitamin D supplement and should consult the doctor.

Cod liver oil was often taken in the past as it is a particularly good source of vitamins A and D. Most people's diets now provide enough of these vitamins, so it is not necessary to take extra in this way. Both vitamins can be toxic in excess, so if you want to take cod liver oil stick to the recommended dosage and don't take other vitamin supplements which contain either vitamin A or D.

Fluid and alcohol

Drink at least 6 to 8 cups of non-alcoholic drinks a day. It is important to have enough fluid even if you don't actually feel thirsty.

As far as alcohol is concerned, a moderate intake is up to 21 units a week (men) and up to 14 a week (women). A unit of alcohol consists of a half-pint of ordinary beer, a single measure of spirits, a small glass of sherry or a glass of wine. Try to have a couple of alcohol-free days a week, and note that your tolerance for alcohol tends to go down as you get older.

Further information is available in a Drinkwise* leaflet.

Food labels and safety

Food labels

Food labels can be confusing and misleading. Here are some points to watch out for.

- **'Use by' dates** are found on highly perishable foods; don't eat food which is past its 'use by' date unless it has been cooked or frozen to extend its life.
- **'Best before'** means that foods will be at peak quality until this date – after this they are still safe to eat (if stored according to instructions) but their quality may deteriorate.
- Ingredients are listed in order of weight, so that the main ingredient will be listed first.
- Beware of health claims on foods, like 'Healthy' and 'Good for you'. There are currently no regulations controlling the use of these.
- Check foods with claims like 'low fat', 'high fibre', 'sugar-free'. There are no statutory definitions for these claims, so you need to check whether a product that claims to be, for example, low fat, really is what it says by comparing it with similar products.

Convenience foods

This term covers a huge variety of different products. They are not necessarily 'junk foods': products like canned and frozen fruit and vegetables can be just as nutritious as fresh. The vitamin content of frozen vegetables is comparable to that of fresh ones – remember that fresh vegetables may not actually be that fresh. Canned vegetables have lower vitamin contents, but can still provide useful amounts and are often cheaper. Other useful convenience foods include UHT long-life milks and fruit juices, canned fish, beans and pulses.

Storing foods safely

Store foods safely to minimise the risk of illness due to food contamination. Make sure that your fridge and freezer are the correct temperatures, between 0°C and 5°C, and −18°C, respectively. Keep foods covered. Cooked foods should be stored on higher shelves in the fridge and raw ones on the lower shelves. Keep eggs in the fridge.

Food preparation

Follow the basic rules:

- Wash your hands before handling food.
- Don't use the same knife or chopping board for raw and cooked foods.
- Make sure that meat and poultry are properly cooked: when you prick the thickest part of the meat the juices should run clear.
- Follow cooking instructions on food labels – this is especially important for cooked-chilled foods, which must be properly reheated.
- Left-over cooked food should be chilled quickly and then refrigerated or frozen.
- Reheat foods once only.
- Don't eat raw eggs or products containing uncooked eggs.
- Keep pets away from food and food preparation areas.

CHAPTER 31

EXERCISE

What does retirement mean to you? More freedom, more activity – travelling, gardening, visiting new places, getting on with all those things you meant to do but couldn't because you were working?

Or does it mean getting older? An inevitable deterioration? Being unable to cope with everyday tasks which require strength, not being able to keep up with younger people, feeling stiffness in the joints, becoming more dependent on others, not being able to meet up with friends, succumbing to the conditions of old age such as high blood pressure or heart problems? Sounds depressing, doesn't it? Even if you're already suffering from any of these problems, none of them means that you have to succumb to old age and inactivity – some are even reversible. Now is the time to make sure you're still going strong in your nineties.

Do you think you're fit? The chances are that if you've been doing a sedentary job and walking rather than driving, you're not. Nowadays you often don't have to exert yourself physically unless you put your mind to it. Lifts carry you upstairs, cars and buses take you to work. Unless you've been going out of your way to take regular exercise, over the years your muscles have been getting weaker, and your stamina deteriorating. You may not find it so easy to take up the activities you're looking forward to, or keep up the ones you're already doing – but that does not mean you can't, or shouldn't.

What is fitness?

If you're thinking about skipping this chapter because you're too old, too unfit or too unhealthy to consider exercise, or because you've had to give it up because of illness or injury – don't. The benefits of exercise can be enormous, and you don't have to suffer to feel them.

Strength and endurance, stamina and flexibility are all part of being fit. Together these things give you the ability to lift and carry, keep up a fast pace while walking uphill, reach something on the top shelf of a cupboard. Much of what we call ageing is nothing more than the results of being inactive, and losing these aspects of fitness. If your muscles aren't used they shrink, and become less powerful, making it harder for you to do things you could do easily when you were younger. Weaker muscles mean you're more likely to fall, and because bones also get weaker as you age, you're more likely to break something if you do.

You may find you put on weight when you get older, but, more importantly, the proportion of muscle and bone to fat may change, so that there's more fat. Dieting may mean you lose fat, but unless you exercise you could lose muscle and bone as well.

Although fitness tends to decline with age, there's no reason why many older people shouldn't be as fit or fitter than others in their 20s, 30s and 40s, particularly if the younger age groups aren't taking any exercise.

Stamina

This is what we need to walk or run, and keep it up over any distance. Most unfit people can manage to run a short distance – to catch a bus, for example. But muscles need oxygen to keep working, or they will get painful and you'll get tired. Unless you've got stamina your body won't be able to get oxygen to your muscles quickly enough. Aerobic exercise improves the way your body uses oxygen, your cardio-vascular system. People who haven't been exercising aerobically will find they get tired more easily as they get older, but aerobic training can keep your body using oxygen efficiently. Aerobic exercise includes walking, jogging, swimming, dancing, climbing stairs, gardening and cycling. In order to reap the benefits you need to puff a little, and work up some sweat, but not to the extent that you're completely out of breath – you should still be able to carry on a conversation.

Strength and endurance

Strength is what you need to lift – including lifting your own body weight from the chair, for example. Endurance is what you need to carry what you've lifted. Strength training will make your muscles become bigger and more powerful. You don't have to lift heavy weights to do this – even squeezing a tennis ball regularly can help improve your arm muscles so that you'll always find it easy to pull a plug out of a socket. Swimming and gardening are good starting exercises for strength (though be careful of your back at first when digging). This sort of training also helps to strengthen bones. Strength can help protect against back pain (and against falling).

Suppleness

Suppleness means that you can move all your limbs through a full range of movement without difficulty. If you're flexible you'll find it easier to bend your knees to pick something off the floor, and to stretch your arms above your head to reach something off a shelf. Swimming is a good way to get all your joints moving, while keeping them supported, but just moving all your joints around every day will help.

The benefits of exercise

Apart from making sure that you can keep fit enough to live an independent and active life, exercise can have a positive, preventive effect on many of the conditions associated with growing older.

Coronary heart disease (CHD)

If you're physically inactive, you're more likely to suffer from coronary disease. Exercise can prevent the onset of the disease – even a moderate amount reduces the risk. What's more, if you keep up the exercise you're protected for as long as you keep it up. This is a result of improvements in the way your cardio-vascular system works (see Stamina above), and a strengthening of your heart muscle. Exercise can also keep down the build-up of harmful cholesterol in your arteries.

As exercise can also help control your weight, it can influence your likelihood of suffering heart problems related to obesity. If you've had a heart attack you shouldn't necessarily avoid exercise: it has been shown that exercise can have a protective effect. Ask your doctor (and see under Heart attack in **Chapter 33**).

High blood pressure

Exercise can have a similar effect to beta-blocking drugs, although it doesn't work in exactly the same way. Exercising aerobically for 45 minutes three times a week can lower your blood pressure. If you exercise every day there can be an even greater reduction. If you already have high blood pressure you should speak to your doctor before exercising – certain exercises might not be suitable for you, for example those involving lying on the floor.

Respiratory diseases

People with respiratory diseases such as asthma, bronchitis or emphysema often think that their condition means they can't exercise. It's true that the amount of exercise that can be done is limited, but as exercise can improve the conditions it shouldn't be avoided altogether. The amount of exercise you're capable of gradually increases, with the benefit that your capacity for everyday tasks is increases too. Asthma attacks can be brought on by exercise in some cases, but warming up gently and using an inhaler can avoid this. Swimming is less likely to provoke an attack because air breathed is warm and moist.

Back pain

The less physically fit you are, the more likely you are to suffer from back pain. If the muscles in your back are weak, you're more likely to hurt yourself when you attempt to put stress on them – by lifting something heavy, for example. Strengthening stomach and back muscles helps prevent injury. If you already have back pain exercise can help reduce and manage it, depending on the type you have.

Arthritis

Exercise can be of benefit whichever type of arthritis you have. In the degenerative forms of arthritis (*osteoarthritis*) exercise can increase muscle strength and counteract the effect of the wasting of muscles that happens after joint disease and injury. The range of movement in the knee can be improved, for example, making it easier to rise from a chair. For inflammatory joint diseases (*rheumatoid arthritis*) the range of movement in joints can be maintained by exercising while joints are inflamed. When inflammation has gone down, you can work on restoring strength and endurance. Exercise can help correct and reduce the deformities that might occur, and improve everyday activities.

Osteoporosis

Bones get weaker progressively after early adulthood as they lose their mineral content. For women this happens even faster after the menopause. Weaker bones are more susceptible to fracture – older people are more likely to break bones if they fall. One of the reasons for the loss of minerals is physical inactivity. Exercise can help make bones stronger, even after the menopause. Men also benefit, as exercise has been shown to protect against hip fractures. The best type of exercises to do are those for strength, but even regular walking can have a good effect.

Exercise makes you feel good

The main thing to remember is that exercise can be a *fun* part of your life. Look at it as a way to increase your social life, to take advantage of the outdoors and to make sure that you can enjoy life to the full for years to come. Most people who take regular exercise claim they feel better for it.

Apart from the social aspects it seems there is a chemical reaction which can make you feel happier. Substances called *endorphins* released into the brain may help give a sense of well-being, so exercise can help you combat stress, anxiety, tension and aggression. It can help you fight depression and feeling tired, and make you sleep better.

Getting started

One of the most important things you can do to get your body moving and used to exercise is to walk more. If you try to walk, as briskly as you can, for half an hour a day, you're well on the way to improving your stamina and your strength – particularly that all-important strength in your legs which will help protect against falls. Swing your arms too, to help work your upper body. Walking can easily become a part of your everyday routine if you walk rather than drive, or get off the bus a few stops early. Once you've got into the swing of walking you might want to join a walking or rambling club.

Don't try to exercise too hard too soon, as that might easily result in injuries or strains. Before you start exercising it's advisable to do some warm-up exercises to loosen up your joints – particularly because as you get older muscles get stiffer, and tendons and ligaments get weaker. Even before you do some gardening it's advisable to warm up. Try circling your shoulders backwards and forwards, and then circling your whole arm. Stretch your arms out in front of you, and circle your wrists in one direction, then the other. While sitting, bend and straighten first one leg, then the other, in front of you. Lift your feet from the floor, one at a time, and circle them in one direction, then the other. A little gentle marching on the spot, or walking up and down the stairs a few times, will get your cardio-vascular system working.

Exercise includes sports such as bowling, ballroom dancing and golf. Make the most of the advantages of being retired. You'll find that your local leisure centre offers concessions for swimming off-peak, for example.

If you feel very wary of starting exercise, or if you know you're suffering from a particular condition, check with your doctor first. This is especially important if you want to take up any weight-bearing exercising for strength, or exercise involving strenuous aerobic activity. If you really think that your state of health is such that it would be very difficult for you to do any exercise at all, the charity Extend* may be able to help you. They specialise in getting you going whatever your limitations, and have contacts all over the country. Write (enclosing a cheque for £5) for their exercise booklet and details of how you can start and keep exercising.

To make yourself aware of how much you're achieving when you start exercising, make a chart of how you're doing. Monitor how far you walk, and how fast in how long without feeling tired, for example.

A target to aim for is 12 or more occasions of moderate activity, lasting at least 20 minutes, each month, but you can take your time in working up to this. Start by aiming to exercise at least once a week. Table 1 divides activities into light, moderate and vigorous. You should aim to be reasonably fit before you do the more vigorous ones.

Aim to improve all aspects of fitness – stamina, strength and endurance, and suppleness. Table 2 compares different types of exercise for the influence they can have on each area of fitness. The Sports Council* can put you in touch with the governing body of the sport or activity you choose. You can also write to them (enclosing a 10" × 8" s.a.e.) for the leaflet *Exercise – Why Bother?*. Another useful publication is *Mobility is a Must*, specially geared to older people; it is available from the Chartered Society of Physiotherapy* (enclose a 10" × 8" s.a.e.).

Table 1

Light activities	Moderate activities	Vigorous activities
long walks (2 miles plus) at an average or slow pace; lighter DIY (e.g. decorating); table tennis, golf, social dancing and 'exercises' if *not* out of breath or sweaty; bowls, fishing, darts and snooker	long walks (2 miles plus) at a brisk or fast pace; football, swimming, tennis, aerobics and cycling if *not* out of breath or sweaty; table tennis, golf, social dancing and exercises if out of breath or sweaty; heavy DIY activities (e.g. mixing cement); heavy gardening (e.g. digging); heavy housework (e.g. spring cleaning)	hill walking (at a brisk pace); squash, running; football, tennis, aerobics and cycling if out of breath or sweaty

THE WHICH? GUIDE TO AN ACTIVE RETIREMENT

Table 2

Activity	Stamina	Suppleness	Strength	Comment
Aerobics	***	***	**	A lot depends on the teacher; can be pricey
Badminton	**	**	**	Most sports centres have courts
Circuit training	***	***	***	A lot depends on the quality of the routine/class
Climbing stairs	**	*	**	You don't need a gym
Cricket	*	**	*	Sociable; find a club
Cycling (hard)	***	*	**	Wear a helmet
Dancing (ballroom)	*	**	*	Good for co-ordination
Dancing (disco)	**	**	*	Not just for the young
Digging the garden	*	*	***	Mind your back
Golf	*	**	*	Start by taking lessons
Jogging	***	*	*	Use grass, not road; wear proper shoes
Rope-skipping	***	**	*	Not just for boxers
Rounders	**	*	**	Or try soft-ball
Rowing	***	*	**	Mind your back
Soccer	**	**	**	Keep on running
Squash	***	***	**	Wait till you're fit
Swimming (hard)	***	***	***	Best all round
Tennis	**	**	**	Find all-weather courts
Walking/rambling	**	*	*	Hill walks can score ** for strength
Weight training	*	**	***	Make sure you're properly supervised
Yoga	*	***	*	Start in a class

KEY *** very good ** some effect * little or no effect.
Your skill and how hard you play will also affect the rating

CHAPTER 32

YOU AND THE HEALTH SERVICE

GPs

Your GP is a central member of the primary health care team. The team consists of people from various health disciplines who work from the surgery or health centre, and includes practice nurses, health visitors, district nurses, community psychiatric nurses, chiropodists, receptionists, social workers and medical secretaries. The people who make up the primary health care team vary from practice to practice.

GPs carry out most routine diagnosis and treatment of patients in the NHS. They are self-employed and have a contract with the Family Health Services Authority to provide health services within the NHS. There are over 30,000 GPs in the UK, with an average list size of about 2,000 people each. It is estimated that we visit our GP 4.4 times a year.

The GP practice may consist of a single GP or it may be a group practice with two to six partners. This usually means that if your GP is unavailable you can see another one. GPs may also be part of a health centre where one or more group practices are housed; they usually provide a greater range of services such as chiropody and dental care. If your condition needs further treatment your GP will refer you to a specialist or consultant.

In addition to diagnosis and treatment GP practices offer other services. These vary between practices and include health check-up and health promotion clinics, counselling, complementary therapies and minor surgery.

Under the National Health Service and Community Care Act 1990 practices with more than 7,000 patients can apply to the

Regional Health Authority to become fundholders. They control their own budgets, previously held by health authorities. They can purchase some specific hospital services, such as cataract operations, out-patients services, diagnostic services (such as x-ray), physiotherapy, occupational therapy and chiropody. They negotiate directly with hospitals, rather than purchasing services via health authorities. From April 1996 this scheme will be expanded even further to cover more practices. A *Which?* report in 1992 found that by registering with a fundholding GP you are more likely to get extra services at the practice, although not all fundholders provide them. These may include counselling services. Some GPs in the survey also said that you may get better or quicker hospital treatment with a fundholder.

Choosing your GP
You may change your GP for any reason, for example because you are moving, or you want a certain kind of GP such as a woman, or you don't like your current doctor. All you need to do is to turn up at the new practice and register, as long as they are willing to accept you. To make your choice find out about the GP before deciding:

- Get personal recommendations or warnings from friends and neighbours.
- Read the practice leaflet to see what services the GP provides. Since 1990 all GPs have had, by law, to produce a leaflet for patients which describes their practice. These include the doctor's sex, the year he or she qualified, surgery hours, other practice staff and services provided. You can get these leaflets from the GP practice or read them at the local Family Health Services Authority offices (FHSA). (FHSAs are known as Health Boards in Scotland and Social Services Boards in Northern Ireland.)
- Look at the FHSA list of doctors. Since 1990 all FHSAs have had to produce a directory giving the doctor's sex and age or date of qualification, the main services the practice provides and who works there. Contact your local FHSA for a list of GPs in your area. Some give information over

- the phone or you may be able to see the whole directory at the FHSA offices or at your local library.
- Get a pre-registration interview with the GP. GPs should be willing to talk to you before you register to discuss your needs and see if you get on. But remember the doctor may use this time to vet you. If you have a long-term condition that would take up a lot of the practice time or money the doctor may not accept you.
- If there is a problem, contact your local Community Health Council. They are the patients' statutory representative in the NHS. (They are called Local Health Councils in Scotland.)

Your relationship with your GP is crucial as he or she will not only diagnose and treat your problems but control your access to other NHS services. If you want specialist help or a second opinion you'll have to get your GP to agree to it.

When you are making your final decision keep in mind:

- Age: would you prefer an older GP or one who has qualified more recently?
- Sex: would you prefer a male or female doctor?
- Special interests: would you like a GP with an interest or expertise in a particular condition, e.g. diabetes?
- Approach: would you prefer a GP who is trained in some form of complementary medicine, or one who is prepared to be called out in an emergency?
- Access: is it important to have a practice within walking distance or on a certain bus route or with disabled access?
- Services: are there particular services which could be helpful to you, e.g. chiropody?
- Surgery hours: are evening or weekend clinics important for you? Do you prefer an appointment system or an open surgery where you just turn up? Would you like telephone access to a doctor or nurse?

Remember that the GP may turn you down. If you can't find a GP who will take you on contact your local Family Health Services Authority who have a duty to find you one, but you're unlikely to have a choice in the matter.

Just registered
The new GP contract states that all newly registered patients must be offered a check-up within 28 days after being accepted by the GP. All patients between the ages of 16 and 75 who have not been seen by a GP within the last three years may ask to have one. In some practices these checks will be carried out by the practice nurse. If you're not well enough to visit the surgery for the check the nurse can visit you in your home. The new GP contract states that all patients over 75 must be offered an annual check-up, again at home if you can't visit the surgery. This check-up includes assessing your mental and physical condition, mobility, continence and physical environment. The practice nurse may carry it out.

All women between 50 and 60 are invited for breast-screening, possibly in a mobile breast-screening unit. Your GP may also run a 'well woman' and 'well man' clinic for you to have a health MOT.

Community services

Nowadays many of the professionals whose work is summarised in this section are employed by community trusts. You can be referred to them by your GP.

District nurses

District nurses are qualified nurses but are also specially trained to care for people at home. Although most of their time is spent in people's homes, they also work in GPs' surgeries, residential homes and health centres. They carry out a diverse range of duties apart from nursing, such as advising on healthy living. District nurses can also provide further sources of information such as voluntary groups. You are most likely to be referred to a district nurse by your GP although social workers, home helps and relatives can also request help from one on your behalf.

To get in touch with a district nurse ring your GP's surgery or contact the Community Nursing Office (listed under the name of your District Health Authority in the phone book).

Health visitors

Health visitors are trained nurses with an additional qualification. Their main role is to give health advice and monitor the welfare of individuals and families; they don't wear a uniform or carry out routine nursing duties. Health visitors carry out a variety of duties including looking after elderly people who live at home. They can help you get in touch with self-help groups and get welfare benefit advice.

Health visitors are most likely to be attached to your GP's surgery. You don't need to be referred – just phone the surgery and ask to speak to the health visitor. If your surgery doesn't have a health visitor you can contact one through your Community Nursing Office (listed under the name of your District Health Authority in the phone book).

Community psychiatric nurses

Community psychiatric nurses provide counselling, help and support to people in the community who have mental health problems. They are registered nurses, either in mental illness or mental handicap nursing. They can assess the psychiatric needs of an individual and their social and physical requirements. They also provide help and support for family members.

Community psychiatric nurses work with GPs, social workers and hospital doctors who specialise in psychiatric medicine. They operate in regional areas and can be contacted through your GP or the social services. Some work in specialist teams, such as those involved with caring for elderly people with psychiatric conditions.

Chiropodists

Chiropodists treat foot problems such as ingrowing toe-nails and corns. Chiropody is available to everyone under the NHS but priority is given to women over 60 and men over 65, disabled people, pregnant women and children.

Chiropodists train for three years and then become state registered, a requirement for working in the NHS. Because of the long waiting lists many people opt to see a chiropodist privately. You can contact the Society of Chiropodists and Podiatrists* to get details of local practitioners. Members are state registered and have the initials SRCh after their name. Some GP fundholding practices are employing chiropodists to run regular sessions at the surgery.

Care attendants

Care attendant schemes use trained helpers to help elderly or disabled people live in the community, for example helping people get up, wash and dress themselves, prepare meals and go shopping. They work with the primary health care team. Find out from your local social services department or your GP whether there is a scheme in your area.

Specialist nurses

These are qualified nurses who can advise on certain topics such as incontinence. You can be referred through your GP. Specialist nurses sometimes run clinics in the GP practice. Ask your GP what specialist nurses work in your area.

Occupational therapist

Occupational therapists work in the community, visiting patients at home to advise on how to cope with daily living, including giving advice on equipment and aids and their installation. Occupational therapists work for the social services department or in hospitals where they are involved in the rehabilitation of disabled people and preparing patients before they are discharged, for example from elderly care wards.

Physiotherapists

Physiotherapists treat people who have problems with moving, sports injuries and those in pain. They use methods such as manipulation, massage, exercise, ice and acupuncture. They can treat you in your home or at hospital, or at the GP's surgery.

You can be referred to a physiotherapist through your GP or local hospital physiotherapy department. Physiotherapists also practise in the private sector.

Speech therapists

Speech and language therapists work with patients with all types of speech problems, for example as a result of head injuries and strokes. Speech therapists work in hospitals and in the community; you can be referred to one via your GP or district nurse.

Dietitians

Dietitians work in hospitals and in the community, including GPs' surgeries, health centres and homes for the elderly. The dietitian's role is to assess the patient's nutritional status, educate them and help them make informed decisions about their diet. They are especially important in advising patients on therapeutic diets, for example for diabetes.

Other community services

Dentists

Dentists can choose to work privately or to have a contract with the Family Health Services Authority to see patients on the NHS. Some dentists carry out both private and NHS dental work.

There are three main types of dentist:

- general dental practitioners
- dental departments in hospitals, which carry out specialist treatment – you may be referred there by your GP or dentist
- community dentists – based in health centres.

Registering with a dentist
The dental contract means that once you have registered with a dentist you are on that list for two years. When you register with a dentist, the contract with your old dentist ends

automatically. You become entitled to all the dental care you need to maintain the health of your teeth and gums on the NHS. This doesn't include cosmetic treatment. If you are not registered with a dentist, he or she may accept you as an 'occasional patient'. You are then entitled to a limited range of treatment on the NHS. Patient information leaflets should be available from each dental practice.

Family Health Services Authorities maintain lists of dentists in your area if you have problems finding a local NHS dentist.

Paying for dental treatment
You pay 80 per cent of the cost of NHS treatment, unless you are eligible for free or reduced-cost treatment. The most you can be asked to pay for any one course of NHS treatment is £275 (a 'course' is whatever treatments are needed to bring you up to full dental health). The charges for private treatment are far higher with no limit on the costs, so ask for an estimate first.

Certain people get free dental treatment, including those on income support and those who hold an AG2 exemption certificate. Certain war pensioners may be able to get a refund of charges. Other people may get help paying for dental treatment because they are on a low income. Further details are in DSS leaflet D11 *NHS Dental Treatment*. Dentists also provide certain services that are free for everyone when necessary, including home visits and repairs to dentures.

Opticians

Opticians have a contract with the local Family Health Services Authority to provide services on the NHS.

There are four different types of opticians:

- Ophthalmic opticians – sometimes called optometrists, they test eyesight and examine eyes for any medical problems. They prescribe glasses to correct vision but refer any medical problems to your GP.
- Dispensing opticians – they make up your glasses but cannot prescribe them.
- Ophthalmologists – they are doctors specialising in the treatment of eye disorders.

- Orthoptists – they work with ophthalmologists, usually in eye hospital departments.

Eye tests are especially important for older people as they can help detect cataracts and glaucoma. They also give early warning of conditions such as hypertension and diabetes.

Choosing an optician
You can book an appointment with any registered optician for an eye test. You can find a list of registered opticians from a variety of sources, including your local library and the *Yellow Pages* and your local Family Health Services Authority.

Paying for optical services
Since 1989 'free' NHS eye tests have been available only to certain people, including those on income support, people with an AG2 certificate, people registered as blind or partially sighted, diagnosed diabetic or glaucoma patients, anyone of 40 or over who is a parent, brother, sister or child of a person with diagnosed glaucoma, patients in the Hospital Eye Service, people needing complex lenses who would get a voucher for them (see below). If you have an AG3 certificate you may not have to pay the full cost of your eye test. But even this group of people are entitled to a maximum of £12.92.

Vouchers
Even if you qualify for help with eye test costs, you may still have to pay for part of the cost of your glasses. If you need new glasses, you will receive a voucher from your optician which you can use to pay for glasses. The value of the voucher depends on the type of glasses you need. It should be enough to cover the cost of a suitable pair of glasses but if you want more expensive frames you will have to pay the difference.

People who are entitled to a voucher include those on income support, who hold an AG2 certificate or have been prescribed complex lenses. If you hold an AG2 certificate you will receive a voucher with reduced value.

Pharmacists

Pharmacists dispense prescriptions and can give you advice about medicines and a wide range of health problems. They are the most accessible of all health professionals. Most pharmacists work in high-street chemists and some in hospital pharmacies.

Men over 65 and women over 60 automatically qualify for free prescriptions. Exemptions are also made for people with a specified medical condition confirmed by their doctor, those with AG2 certificates and those receiving War or MOD Disablement Pension and who need a prescription for the disability for which they get the pension.

If you have regular prescriptions it might be cheaper to get a four-monthly or yearly prescription pre-payment certificate (£24.60 for the four-monthly one and £67.60 for the yearly one). You can buy these from post offices, pharmacists, Benefits Agencies, or from your FHSA.

Going into hospital

You may be able to claim for the cost of travelling to hospital for treatment as an in-patient or as an out-patient or when you are discharged from hospital. If someone needs to accompany you for medical reasons, their fares may be paid as well.

Your travel expenses will be fully paid if:

- You are automatically entitled to health benefits (e.g. you are on income support) or have an AG2 certificate.
- You live in the area covered by the Highlands and Islands Development Board in Scotland and have to travel at least 30 miles (or more than 5 miles by water) to get to hospital (you can find out about this scheme at your GP's surgery. If you live in the Isles of Scilly and have to travel to the mainland to get to hospital, you should have to pay only the first £5 of your travelling costs (ask at your local health centre before you go to hospital).

If you are entitled to help with your travelling costs, you will receive the payment when you get to hospital. You have to find the cheapest form of transport to the hospital.

YOU AND THE HEALTH SERVICE

If you have an AG3 certificate you may be entitled to some help with travelling costs. The amount you pay will depend on the maximum amount stated on your certificate. To claim, get form H11 *NHS Hospital Travel Costs*.

If you have difficulty travelling to hospital you may be entitled to go by the hospital car service. Ask your GP about this.

NHS ambulance services provide transport for those who are medically unfit to travel by other means. You won't pay for this.

If you receive mobility allowance you can use it to help you with your travel needs. There are also travel passes which allow disabled or elderly people to use public transport free or at a reduced rate. In many parts of the country there are Dial-a-Ride schemes which provide transport for disabled people. Ask your local social services department.

Your pension in hospital

If you are a pensioner, tell your Social Security office if you go into hospital and let them know the discharge date as soon as possible.

If you live in a local council residential home, your retirement pension is reduced as soon as it is to be paid. If you've been in for more than six weeks when it becomes due it will be immediately reduced. If you live in your own home your pension isn't affected until you've been in hospital for six weeks. If you have a dependant your benefit is usually reduced by £11.50 a week. If you don't have a dependant your benefit is usually reduced by £23 a week. After one year in hospital, if you have a dependant, your benefit is reduced by a further £11.50. You can choose how the remainder of your benefit will be paid: all of it can go to your dependant (or someone looking after your dependant); or if you choose not to have any of your benefits paid to, or on behalf of, your dependant, then £11.50 is paid to you.

If you are visiting someone else in hospital you may also qualify for help with travel costs if you are on income support or visiting an MOD Disablement Pensioner who is being treated for the disablement for which he or she is getting the pension. To claim, get form H11 *NHS Hospital Travel Costs*.

Patient's Charter

The Patient's Charter* highlights the rights of all patients. To get hold of a free copy, write to the address at the back of this book.

Private treatment

Some people decide to be treated privately rather than on the NHS. A *Which?* survey in 1992 found that almost half the people who took out private health insurance did so to avoid NHS waiting lists, although most people don't wait long for NHS treatment.

PRIVATE HEALTH INSURANCE: WHAT'S COVERED

Here are the main things you can usually claim for. There may be various limits on the amounts you can claim for in each category:

- Accommodation and nursing charges – often the biggest part of the bill.
- Surgeons' and anaesthetists' fees; operating theatre fees – they can vary a great deal.
- X-rays: dressings and drugs while you're an in-patient.
- Consultants' and physicians' fees.
- Radiotherapy, chemotherapy, physiotherapy and other specialist treatment.
- Home nursing charges if the consultant recommends home nursing and it follows on from in-patient treatment.
- Out-patient and day care treatment, but only if this is linked to a stay in hospital.
- Cash benefits if you stay in hospital as an NHS patient.
- Treatment while travelling abroad, but not if you go abroad specifically to get treatment. (The USA and Canada may be excluded.)

It's important to remember that private health care isn't and doesn't claim to be a complete replacement for the NHS. Don't assume your private health insurance will cover all your needs (see below for points to consider when choosing your policy). The NHS covers all medical and surgical treatments including emergencies, while most private treatment is for straightforward, non-emergency surgery such as hip replacements, varicose vein removal, hernias and piles. These operations can be those with the longer waiting lists, so going private may ensure faster treatment. But NHS waiting lists vary enormously in different parts of the country and you may be able to cut your waiting time by looking around.

Private treatment does have some advantages over the NHS, including choosing your own consultant and sometimes your hospital. The *Which?* survey also found that people were more satisfied with creature comforts in private hospitals than in NHS ones, including food, internal decoration, privacy, visiting arrangements, ward sizes and atmosphere.

What the brochures don't tell you

There are other important issues to consider when deciding whether or not to opt for private health care that won't always be obvious from the brochures.

- The consultants who work in the private sector are usually the same consultants who work in the NHS (most have a part-time contract with the NHS which also allows them to do private work). Private patients will usually always see a consultant. NHS patients are normally in the charge of a consultant but if they have a less serious condition they may be treated by a less senior member of the medical team.
- If you have complications you may sometimes be better off in an NHS hospital, as they are more likely than private hospitals to have the back-up facilities, such as intensive care, though some private hospitals built near NHS hospitals, or on the same site, should have quick access to full back-up facilities.

PRIVATE HEALTH INSURANCE: WHAT'S NOT COVERED

Insurance probably won't cover you for all your needs. Here are some typical exclusions:

- Health problems you've already got or had. You can occasionally be covered for pre-existing (or foreseeable) conditions but only if the insurer agrees to cover them when you apply. Some policies cover pre-existing conditions once you've had no treatment for them for one or two years.
- Chronic and terminal conditions. Insurance covers diseases, illnesses and injuries which can be cured: long-term illnesses such as diabetes are not covered, though initial treatment and relief of acute phases may be. The terminal stages of cancer may not be covered.
- AIDS. Some policies are now specifically excluding AIDS and related conditions. But you may be covered for initial diagnosis and limited stay in hospital.
- Routine treatment, such as dentists' and opticians' services and preventive screening. Some policies entitle you to a discount on the cost of general check-ups.
- Alternative medicine, though some policies pay for osteopaths and chiropractors if your GP refers you.
- Some hospital and nursing home accommodation costs – if you're a patient partly for domestic reasons, for example geriatric care.
- Some out-patient costs, e.g. glasses, hearing aids, medicine.
- The services of your GP (such as the fee for filling in your claim form).
- Renal dialysis.
- Self-inflicted injuries/suicide attempts.
- Alcoholism and drug abuse.
- Cosmetic surgery, unless it's needed after an accident.

- Private hospitals don't always have a resident doctor, so there could be a delay in an emergency – for example, at night if a doctor had to be called to the hospital.

If you are paying out of your own pocket for private health care, ensure that your bill is broken down in sufficient detail for you to see how much you're being charged for each item. Shop around for the best deal for your circumstances.

Paybeds
Some NHS hospitals have private paybeds. Like any other private patient, patients in paybeds pay for both their accommodation and for private treatment, but they have the advantage that NHS back-up facilities are on hand in an emergency. Some of the beds are on private wings, but most are on ordinary wards, so the surroundings may not be as good as in a private hospital.

Community care changes

A report in 1988 by Sir Roy Griffiths, *Community Care: an Agenda for Action*, established the structure for a White Paper and new Act of Parliament which introduced changes to the way community care services would be provided and paid for.

The Griffiths Report recommended that funds which were spent by the Department of Social Security for paying for care in home should be re-directed to local authorities, which should carry out assessments of people needing care. The government responded to those recommendations with a White Paper called *Caring for People* in 1989. This set out the framework for the community care changes. The National Health Service and Community Care Act 1990 established these changes in law.

The White Paper introduced major changes, giving local authorities new powers. These include:

- The power to pay for care in nursing homes, as well as in residential care homes.
- The duty to inspect their own care homes as well as the ones they inspect and register under the Registered Homes Act 1984.
- The duty to carry out assessments of anyone who seems to have a need for community care services.
- The duty to prepare community care plans.

The aims of the White Paper are:

- To encourage the development of domiciliary, day and respite services to enable people to live in their own homes where possible; home-based services will be targeted on those people whose need is greatest.
- To ensure that service providers earmark practical support for carers as a high priority.
- To ensure that the care people get is designed in line with the individual's needs.
- To promote the development of the private sector.
- To clarify the responsibilities of the different organisations involved in community care to ensure it is easier to hold them to account for their performance.
- To secure good value for taxpayers' money by introducing a new funding structure for social care.

Community Care

As from 1993, local authorities have had a duty to assess people who seem to need community care. Local authorities have to state their criteria for eligibility for assessment.

The assessment is in two parts:

- A care assessment – this considers the needs and wishes of an individual and his or her carer, if there is one. If it is decided that care is needed and those needs can be met, the provision of the care is arranged. This 'package care' should be designed to meet the individual's needs.
- A financial assessment to see how much, if anything, the individual has to pay for the services. For care in residential or nursing homes the local authority follows national rules, but for care in the home, the local authority decides its rules.

Residents in care homes that receive public funds have not got special income support since April 1993. Instead they have their own income such as their pension, ordinary income support and also a special residential allowance. The local authority then decides on the arrangements it can afford for that person's care, taking into account the person's own resources. Residents in homes that are run by the local authority are not eligible for the new residential allowance or the full rate of income support.

This whole area is very controversial and fraught with difficulty. One leaflet that may be of interest is available from Benefits Agencies: *Help if you live in a residential care home or nursing home*.

> *The leaflets mentioned in this chapter are available from your local Benefits Agency offices; you should also be able to find them at doctors' and dentists' surgeries, hospitals and post offices.*

> *Under legislation currently before Parliament, Family Health Service Authorities (FHSAs) and District Health Authorities (DHAs) will merge to become Health Authorities with effect from 1 April 1996.*

CHAPTER 33

HEALTH PROBLEMS

Although there are a number of changes in the body that occur as a normal part of ageing, it would be totally wrong to regard ill health, loss of mobility and a decline in mental agility as an inevitable result of growing old. In fact, most people are capable of staying fit and active well into their eighties. Even those who do have to cope with a new health problem, such as arthritis, high blood pressure or heart disease, are usually able, with the correct medication and a few adjustments to their daily routine, to enjoy their retirement to the full.

There is bound to be some deterioration with advancing years, but, in most of us, this natural decline can be slowed right down, simply by staying physically and mentally active.

Stay physically active

As you grow older, you will notice a slight loss of flexibility and muscle strength, as well as a reduction in endurance (stamina). However, taking regular physical exercise should help maintain the heart, lungs, muscles and circulation in the best possible condition, making it easier to perform normal daily activities like shopping and housework without becoming unduly breathless or tired. This exercise routine will also keep balance and coordination in good working order, reducing the chance of a fall indoors or out.

There is no need to push yourself too hard – in fact, it would be dangerous to exercise over-strenuously. Just choose an activity that you enjoy, that gets you moving about, without making you gasp for breath or causing your joints or muscles to become stiff or sore. Also, you should check with your doctor before you start a new activity, and stop exercising at once if you suffer any warning symptoms of heart strain, such as chest pains, dizziness or palpitations.

Even for someone who is housebound, a routine of stretching and loosening-up exercises can do much to stop the joints stiffening up, and help keep you independent and mobile. Ask your doctor, nurse or health visitor to recommend a suitable programme of home exercises, and see **Chapter 31**.

Stay mentally agile

As with physical performance, there also tends to be a slight deterioration in certain mental functions with advancing age. For example, many elderly people notice some difficulties with short-term memory, finding it more difficult to remember a new name or telephone number.

However, a general more serious decline in mental function, known as dementia, is not a normal characteristic of ageing and is always the result of a disease (see the section below on dementia).

To maintain mental vigour, it is important to keep the brain constantly stimulated with a variety of new ideas and activities. The more you use your mind, the more likely you are to remain mentally agile. This is why it is so important to plan ahead before you retire, to ensure your increased leisure time doesn't leave you bored and frustrated.

Preventive measures

Doctors and scientists who have studied the effects of ageing on health and fitness have yet to agree on the exact nature of the biological processes involved. One theory is a progressive decline in the body's immune system so that it is no longer able to defend itself as efficiently against bacteria, viruses and the growth of cancer cells. Alternative mechanisms include the gradual build-up of toxins inside the body; or the wearing down of the templates that control the copying of different types of

SMOKING

People who are trying to give up smoking may have difficulty doing so on their own unless they are highly motivated and have a specific reason for giving up. Not only is nicotine a powerfully addictive drug but many people suffer quite unpleasant side effects from withdrawal. To help overcome these effects there are nicotine substitutes in the form of chewing-gum and skin patches. Counselling and various self-help measures (videos, for instance) may also be encouragements while you are giving up.

cell, allowing errors to occur during tissue regeneration.

What is agreed is the influence of lifestyle factors such as smoking, poor diet, lack of exercise, excessive alcohol consumption and over-exposure to strong sunlight – all of which are known to accelerate the degeneration caused by ageing of body organs and tissues, including the skin, bones, nervous system and circulation.

Although genetic inheritance also influences the ageing process in a way that is obviously beyond your control, adopting a healthy lifestyle can significantly reduce your risk of developing many of the diseases that are more common in older people. The importance of lifestyle is discussed in more detail under each of those health problems where it represents a significant underlying cause.

IMPORTANT NOTE

It is important to seek medical help for any persistent, recurrent or unexplained symptom. Unfortunately, many elderly people suffer their symptoms in silence, blaming their aches and pains, blurred vision, deafness, dizziness, falls – to name just a few of the more common complaints – on getting older.

Do not regard any troublesome symptom as being a normal part of ageing. Often the cause is a particular disease, treatment of which may relieve that symptom, making life a lot more fulfilling.

Health Problems A-Z

Angina

Angina is a transient pain or tightness which occurs in the chest and sometimes spreads to the neck, jaw or arms. Typically, the pain comes on suddenly during exercise, although it may be brought on by stress, extremes of temperature, or eating a large meal.

Descriptions of angina vary from a mild discomfort to a heavy, crushing pain, and sometimes it is mistaken for indigestion or acid reflux. Other symptoms that often accompany an angina attack include sweating, nausea, dizziness and breathing difficulty. The pain usually eases with rest; if symptoms persist this may be due to a heart attack, where the heart muscle is permanently damaged.

Angina is caused by a lack of oxygen and nutrients reaching the heart muscle, usually because the coronary arteries which encircle and supply blood to the heart have become clogged up with fatty deposits – a condition known as atherosclerosis.

This narrowing of the coronary arteries prevents the normal increase in blood flow that should occur when extra demands are placed on the heart, such as during exercise. Atherosclerosis tends to increase in severity with age, which is why angina is more common in elderly people. Women are protected from atherosclerosis by their oestrogen hormones until the menopause, when there is a sudden decline in oestrogen production.

Treatment of angina includes drugs to widen the coronary arteries (nitrates, calcium channel blockers) and drugs to reduce the heart's demands for oxygen by slowing the heart rate (beta blockers). Surgical procedures such as angioplasty (insertion of a catheter with an inflatable balloon tip into the narrowed arteries to flatten the fatty deposits) or bypass grafting (attachment of a blood vessel to divert blood flow around the blockage) are successful in relieving symptoms in many people.

Self-help measures for angina sufferers include stopping smoking to help increase blood flow through the coronary arteries; exercising regularly but only until the symptoms come on; relaxation measures to reduce stress; avoiding exercise on hot or very cold days, or soon after a meal; and losing excess weight to put less strain on the heart.

Anxiety

The main causes of anxiety in older people are worries about health, money, or loss of independence. While anxiety is a perfectly normal reaction to any problem or fear that cannot readily be resolved, it can become a disorder in its own right if it is preventing the individual from thinking clearly or rationally, sleeping properly, or carrying out everyday activities.

Many elderly people live alone and because there is no one to share their worries with on a regular basis, they are more vulnerable to a build-up in anxiety. Therefore, the first step is to find someone to talk things through with, perhaps a friend, a relative, a neighbour, the vicar or your doctor or health visitor.

If there are persistent or recurrent symptoms related to anxiety, such as difficulty falling asleep, loss of appetite, a feeling of suffocation, constant trembling, or a sense of impending doom, it is important to seek professional help. A variety of measures can relieve anxiety, including relaxation exercises, regular physical activities, meditation or counselling. The National Association for Mental Health (MIND)* may be able to offer advice.

Tranquillisers can also be very effective in the short term, but these do not help the individual to overcome the underlying reasons for the anxiety. Also, if they are taken regularly for longer than a couple of weeks, there is a risk of addiction.

Arteriosclerosis

Hardening of the arteries – arteriosclerosis – is a group of disorders which cause a progressive thickening and loss of elasticity of the artery walls. The most common of these disorders is atherosclerosis, a condition where the arteries become clogged by a build-up of fatty deposits.

The risk of atherosclerosis increases with age, but there are a number of lifestyle factors which speed up the development of fatty deposits inside the arteries. These contributory factors include tobacco smoking, lack of exercise, excessive alcohol consumption and eating a lot of foods containing large amounts of saturated fat and cholesterol.

Common disorders which may be caused by atherosclerosis (discussed under their own separate headings) are angina, heart attack, dementia, leg ulcers, stroke and transient ischaemic attacks.

Back pain

The most common cause of back pain in elderly people is osteoarthritis of the spine. In this condition, wear and tear of the joints between the vertebrae (spinal bones) leads to narrowing of the spaces between the joints and overgrowth of bone around them.

As a result of this joint degeneration, the spine becomes painful, stiff and often tender over specific areas. Movements such as bending over or getting out of bed can prove difficult, mainly because of the stiffness that develops in the lower spine.

A sudden attack of severe back pain in someone over the age of 60 is occasionally due to collapse of one or more vertebrae that have been weakened by osteoporosis. In this condition, which mainly affects women after the menopause, the bones lose their normal density and become more fragile. The spine has to carry a considerable load as it is the main supporting column of the body; it is therefore not surprising that vertebrae affected by osteoporosis sometimes compress and crumble.

Anyone with persistent back pain should be careful over their choice of painkillers: they all have their potential side effects which are more likely to develop the older you are and the longer you take them. Codeine and dihydrocodeine are very effective pain relievers, but often cause constipation; aspirin and other anti-inflammatory drugs may cause indigestion, peptic ulcers and a variety of other adverse effects that you should discuss with your doctor; paracetamol is a relatively safe painkiller, but should never be taken in excess because of the risk of liver damage.

For those people with osteoarthritis of the spine, there are a number of important self-help measures in addition to medication. These include exercises to strengthen the supporting abdominal and spinal muscles – swimming is a particularly good activity in this respect; a heating pad to relax any painful muscle spasm; a corset to act as a lumbar support; a firm mattress or a board under the mattress to provide support at night; and a resolve to lose any excess weight if you can to reduce the load on your spine. The National Back Pain Association* may be able to offer further advice.

It is not a good idea to rest your back all the time. Prolonged sitting or lying will only make the discomfort and stiffness due to osteoarthritis worse. Ask your doctor, nurse or health visitor which exercises you can safely do to keep your spine mobile and the supporting muscles firm.

Finally, see your doctor as soon as possible if your back pain is getting worse, or if you develop symptoms of pressure on a spinal nerve, such as weakness, numbness, pins and needles, or problems with bladder or bowel control.

Bereavement

Bereavement, which is a natural reaction to the death of someone you loved or were close to, is a traumatic experience whatever your age. However, because older people are more likely to suffer the loss of their partner or a close friend, bereavement is a relevant issue in any discussion of health problems after retirement.

Although bereavement itself is not a disease, it can cause a variety of symptoms that may be mistaken for the onset of mental illness and, because it is such a stressful life event, it is important to take precautions to prevent any long-term effect on health and well-being.

Symptoms that may occur as the result of bereavement include numbing of emotions, outbursts of grief, feelings of hostility even towards the individual who has died, seeing or hearing the dead person, and guilt about not having done more for the person when he or she was alive. Realising that all these responses are perfectly normal will help in the recovery process as you slowly come to terms with what has happened.

To protect your own health, try not to bottle up your

emotions; keep busy to avoid brooding, but don't take on too much; look to friends and family for comfort and support but don't allow them to overburden you with their grief; and even if you don't feel like it, eat at least one proper meal each day and take some exercise.

For those people who are unable to cope or who become severely depressed or agitated, their GP may prescribe antidepressants or a short course of tranquillisers. A number of organisations offer practical help and advice to the bereaved, including Cruse Bereavement Care*, the National Association of Widows*, and Age Concern England*, all of which have branches all over the UK. They have combined to produce *Survival Guide for Widows* (£3.50 from Age Concern).

Blindness

Blindness may be the result of a variety of disorders; in elderly people the most common causes are damage to the retina due to diabetes (diabetic retinopathy), cataracts (opacities developing in the internal lens of the eye), untreated glaucoma (abnormal build-up of pressure inside the eye), stroke (where the haemorrhage or blood clot damages the part of the brain which responds to visual information) or degeneration of the central part of the retina (macular degeneration).

It is important to consult a doctor as soon as possible in the event of any sudden loss of vision or persistent visual disturbance, such as seeing coloured haloes around lights. However, because loss of vision is usually a gradual process which may pass unnoticed, regular eye checks are essential. Anyone with a close relative who has suffered from glaucoma should mention it to their optician because this eye condition can be inherited; in any case, pressure checks are a routine part of an eye test for an elderly person.

Treatment of blindness will obviously depend upon the underlying cause, for example surgical removal of a cataract which can be replaced by an artificial lens, or laser therapy to seal damaged blood vessels on the retina in someone with diabetic retinopathy.

Anyone who is left with a permanent severe defect in their

vision should ask their GP to register them as blind or partially sighted, which will entitle them to a range of visual aids as well as certain benefits from the DSS. The Royal National Institute for the Blind (RNIB)* can also offer advice.

Bronchitis

A productive cough that brings up sputum (also referred to as phlegm or mucus) may be due to an attack of bronchitis. This condition, which may come on after a cold or flu, is due to inflammation of the bronchi (the main airways inside the lungs). As a result of the inflammation, the normal production of mucus in the bronchi is increased; it often becomes discoloured due to the infecting viruses or bacteria, and the white blood cells that are fighting them.

For an acute attack of bronchitis, the doctor may prescribe a course of antibiotics to deal with any bacterial infection present. To relieve the cough, take an expectorant to make the sputum easier to shift, but avoid a cough suppressant which will only prevent the airways being cleared of excess mucus.

Also, use a steam vaporiser because a moist atmosphere will be less irritating to the airways, and drink plenty of fluids to help thin the mucus.

Chronic bronchitis is mainly a disease of smokers and those who have been exposed to high levels of air pollution. It is defined as a productive cough on most days for three months or more every year. Tobacco smoke and air pollutants have an irritant effect on the bronchi, increasing the production of thick, sticky mucus which clogs up these airways. In addition to the productive cough, there is likely to be wheezing, tightness in the chest and breathing difficulty on exertion.

The problem is mainly due to an increase in the size and activity of the mucus-producing glands and a greater susceptibility to chest infections. Just stopping smoking should improve the situation although the longer the individual has smoked, the more severe the lung damage is likely to be.

Measures to deal with a sudden flare-up of symptoms in chronic bronchitis are as described for acute attacks. In addition, the doctor may prescribe a bronchodilator, usually as an inhaler, to try to open up the obstructed airways, but these don't work as well in chronic bronchitis as they do in asthma.

Anyone with the tendency to develop bronchitis as a complication of a cold or flu should visit their GP for treatment as soon as the symptoms come on in order to reduce the chance of a bad attack. Because older people are more vulnerable to respiratory complications with flu, vaccination each autumn against flu is routinely recommended for everyone over the age of 65.

Cancer

Cancer is not just one disease; there are many different types, each of which starts by involving a specific organ or tissue in the body. If you develop any of the symptoms listed in the box, arrange a visit to your doctor straight away – early diagnosis means that treatment is more likely to be successful.

Unfortunately, many people are scared to report symptoms they think might be due to cancer. This is foolish for two main reasons: their symptoms will often be due to a harmless or non-cancerous condition which will not only respond to treatment, but also allay their fears; and in those few cases where the diagnosis *is* cancer, any delay in treatment reduces the chance of a successful cure.

There have been a number of advances in the treatment of cancer, with improved surgical techniques and a wider variety

---

CANCER WARNING SYMPTOMS

Any of the following symptoms may be an early warning signal for cancer:
- Changes in a mole on the skin.
- A new lump or bump.
- Mouth ulceration lasting longer than one month.
- Persistent change from normal bowel habit.
- Unexplained weight loss.
- Vaginal bleeding after the menopause.
- Hoarseness lasting several weeks.
- Coughing or vomiting up blood.

of powerful anti-cancer drugs available. In addition, doctors are now better able to control the complications that sometimes accompany cancer, such as pain, nausea, constipation, cough or difficulty swallowing.

The cancer screening tests offered to women on a regular basis – cervical smear and mammography (breast X-ray) – are usually only recommended up until the age of 65. However, if any woman has passed this age without having had either of these checks, she should ask her doctor whether the screening test is still advisable. Cancers of the cervix and breast may not cause any obvious symptoms until they have reached an advanced stage.

BACUP (the British Association of Cancer United Patients)* can give further information on general and specific queries to do with cancer.

Colds and flu

For most people, catching a cold or a dose of the flu is no more than a temporary inconvenience. These viral infections may cause a variety of familiar symptoms, including sore throat, fever, dry cough, aches and pains, runny nose, weakness and swollen glands. The main difference between a cold and the flu is that the latter typically makes you feel too ill to do anything other than stay in bed, and lasts a few days longer.

Traditional cold and flu remedies, like paracetamol or aspirin to relieve discomfort and bring down a temperature, plenty of fluids to replace those lost with the increase in sweating, and inhalations to ease nasal congestion, are helpful whatever your age.

However, for older people, a cold or the flu is potentially a lot more serious. Complications such as bronchitis, pneumonia and pleurisy are more likely to develop, and if there is any long-term heart or lung disorder the risks are even greater.

It is therefore advisable for all people over the age of 65 to ask their doctor about receiving an annual flu jab, which is designed to provide immunity against the influenza viruses expected to be around that year. This immunisation is normally given in September or October.

In addition, if cold or flu symptoms do start, it is important to visit the doctor if any complications seem to be developing, such as a productive cough, chest pain, breathlessness or wheezing.

Constipation

Everyone has their own characteristic bowel habit, and for some a bowel movement only once or twice a week is perfectly normal. The proper definition of constipation is either having to strain to open the bowels, or a decrease in the usual frequency of bowel movements.

Although constipation may affect people of any age, it becomes more common with advancing years. One reason for this is the tendency for older people to eat fewer high-fibre foods; another is the influence of physical activity on bowel function – those who take less exercise as they get older are more prone to constipation.

A number of drugs can also cause constipation including iron pills, painkillers and cough medicines that contain codeine, and certain antacids, all of which are commonly taken by older people. In addition, a significant number take a laxative routinely, in the mistaken belief that they need to have a daily bowel movement, and this can lead, paradoxically, to a lazy bowel.

Self-help measures to relieve constipation include taking more exercise – even a gentle stroll can help; eating more fibre-rich foods such as fresh fruit and vegetables, beans and pulses, wholegrain bread and cereal; and drinking six or more glasses of water or soft drink each day. If these remedies don't help, seek medical help.

Deafness

Deafness can be a serious handicap because it acts as a barrier to normal conversation, isolating and depressing the sufferer as a result. However, for many elderly people, it may be possible to improve their hearing significantly, so deafness should not be treated as a normal part of getting old.

The first step is to overcome any embarrassment and admit to the GP that you actually have a hearing problem. Sometimes the cause is simply a build-up in ear wax, and hearing can be restored to a satisfactory level by having the ear canals syringed with warm water.

Your GP may need to refer you to an ear, nose and throat clinic or hearing aid centre for a full assessment of your hearing, and to see whether a hearing aid might help. However, be warned that in some parts of the country there are long waiting lists for this service on the NHS. Also, however sophisticated the hearing aid, it will only be able to amplify those sound frequencies you have difficulty detecting; it will not give you perfect hearing.

Other measures to help you communicate include asking people to speak slowly and clearly, and to avoid shouting at you, which only distorts the words being spoken. Keep any background noise like the television or radio to a minimum. It may be worthwhile taking a lip-reading class to acquire the basic skills. Further advice may be obtained from the British Deaf Association*, the Royal National Institute for the Deaf (RNID)* and the Council for the Advancement of Communication for Deaf People*.

Finally, there has been a lot of adverse publicity about the sale of hearing aids through advertisements in magazines or newspapers. This is because they can be very expensive, and they may not work properly for you if they haven't been designed to suit your particular pattern of hearing loss.

Dementia

Dementia is not a specific type of illness: it is a general term for grossly impaired mental function which may result in loss of short- and long-term memory, altered personality, disorientation and confusion, disruption of speech and comprehension, erratic moods and behaviour, wandering, and an inability to carry out simple everyday activities like washing and dressing.

The most common cause of dementia is Alzheimer's disease, which accounts for about 75 per cent of cases in people over the age of 65. Another common reason for loss of normal mental function is a stroke or series of minor strokes that may not necessarily have caused any physical disability such as paralysis. Parkinson's disease and long-term alcohol abuse may also lead to forms of dementia.

Dementia is not a normal part of ageing and anyone who develops symptoms of mental deterioration should be seen by their GP for a thorough evaluation. Occasionally, these symptoms are the result of a disorder which can be treated successfully, for example certain types of anaemia, an infection or even depression, in which case normal mental function can usually be restored.

Unfortunately, however, there is no cure at present for conditions such as Alzheimer's disease. Research into Alzheimer's has suggested several possible causes, for example the excessive build-up of a protein in the brain, which is actually being produced to stimulate nerve cell regeneration as part of a natural mechanism designed to compensate for the effects of ageing. Other theories put forward include the toxic effects of an accumulation of aluminium inside the brain; or an abnormal response to a viral infection.

New drugs are being developed which may improve memory and intellectual ability in some sufferers, but at the moment their use is still experimental, and clinical trials are under way to establish whether they are really that effective.

For anyone who has to care for someone who is suffering from dementia, here are a few useful self-help measures that may make life a little easier:

- Establish a daily routine with a fixed schedule of events.
- Make sure that clothes are easy to put on.
- Keep doors and windows locked if the sufferer is likely to wander.
- Do not move objects to new places in the home.
- Help the person keep a diary and a daily checklist of tasks.
- Be patient in the event of stubbornness or aggression, and remember that this is due to the condition.
- Claim benefits from the DSS such as attendance allowance.
- Arrange with your GP temporary care in hospital or a nursing home so that you can take a well-earned break.

- Contact the Alzheimer's Disease Association* for support and advice.

There is more about Alzheimer's disease in the next chapter.

Dental problems

With a daily routine of brushing and flossing, most people should be able to keep their natural teeth into old age. However, older people have to take extra care of their teeth as the gums tend to recede with age, exposing the neck of the tooth, which has no protective enamel.

Ask your dentist or dental hygienist to check your brushing technique if you are unsure, or use a disclosing tablet, which shows how effectively the teeth have been cleaned by colouring any plaque left behind. Dental floss can be useful in removing particles of food lodged between the teeth, but take care not to cut into the gums.

If there are large spaces between some of the teeth, try using a toothbrush with a single pointed bristle so that all the tooth and gum surfaces can be reached. Toothpicks should only be used cautiously because of the risk of damaging the gums.

Around one quarter of adults in the UK have lost their teeth, usually because of gum disease that was not treated soon enough. It is also important to take good care of dentures, cleaning them regularly to reduce the risk of a mouth or gum infection.

For older people who still have some or all of their natural teeth, a dental check-up is recommended at least once a year. Dentures should be checked every three years, and sooner if they are no longer fitting properly or causing soreness in the mouth. Because the gums shrink after the natural teeth are lost and the shape of the mouth may also change, it is often necessary to adjust the structure of the denture or make a new one.

Before having any dental treatment, check that the dentist will provide this under the NHS. Your local Family Health Services Authority can supply a list of NHS dentists in the area. Even under the NHS, you still have to pay a proportion of the charges, so ask the dentist to provide an estimate of the likely bill.

Depression

Although older people are more prone to depression, sometimes as a response to treatment of a chronic illness, symptoms of depression should not be accepted as an inevitable part of getting older. Also, it is important not to allow a serious bout of depression to continue without seeking help from the doctor. Depression will not usually disappear on its own and in severe cases there may be a risk of suicide. Treatment with antidepressants is usually very effective.

Warning symptoms of a depression that should be treated if they persist include waking in the early hours of the morning, generalised aches and pain, a sense of despair, being unable to concentrate, and not feeling like eating anything. Confusion, agitation, extreme apathy and drinking more alcohol than usual can each be the result of depression. Often a friend or relative may have to persuade the depressed person to go to the doctor. Any threat of ending it all should be taken seriously and the doctor called out if necessary.

To ward off depression, it is important to avoid becoming isolated. After retirement, build new social contacts, for example by taking an evening class, joining a club or getting involved in voluntary work. Two organisations you might contact for further information are the Fellowship of Depressives Anonymous* and Depressives Associated*.

Diabetes (maturity onset)

Maturity onset diabetes is the form of diabetes that typically only comes on after the age of 40 and usually doesn't require insulin injections to keep the condition under control. Unlike the juvenile type of diabetes, where the pancreas stops producing insulin altogether, in the maturity onset or type 2 form the pancreas does release some insulin into the bloodstream, but not enough to prevent a build-up of sugar in the circulation.

Many elderly people with maturity onset diabetes only

WARNING SYMPTOMS OF DIABETES
- Excessive thirst; frequent urination.
- Fatigue and weakness.
- Numbness or tingling in the feet and hands.
- Blurred vision.
- Impotence in men.

become aware of it as the result of a routine blood or urine test, which reveals abnormally high blood levels of sugar, or the presence of sugar in the urine.

Symptoms to watch out for are listed in the box. In some sufferers, all that may be needed is a diet with fewer refined carbohydrate (sugary) foods and more high-fibre, unrefined carbohydrate (starchy) foods to help slow down the absorption of sugar into the bloodstream, along with cutting down on fatty foods, particularly saturated fats, to help lose any excess weight.

If these measures are not enough, the doctor can prescribe tablets to keep blood sugar levels normal. In rare cases, insulin injections may be required. Regular check-ups either by the GP or hospital diabetic clinic are advisable to detect the onset of any complications such as eye, nerve or skin damage. Most diabetics monitor the sugar level in their blood or urine using a simple testing kit at home in order to ensure that their condition is not going out of control.

The British Diabetic Association* can offer further information.

Emphysema

Emphysema is a serious lung disease which involves extensive damage to some of the millions of tiny air sacs (alveoli) that make up the lung tissues. As a result of the walls of these alveoli ballooning and bursting, with clusters of alveoli merging to form fewer, larger air sacs, the surface area of the lungs (through which gases pass to and from the bloodstream) is reduced. The lungs also become less elastic, making it more difficult to breathe, particularly to breathe out.

Symptoms of emphysema include a wheezy cough and

breathlessness. Because less oxygen reaches the bloodstream, the skin may develop a bluish tinge. There may also be signs of heart failure, with swelling of the ankles, if the heart is unable to cope with the additional workload resulting from blood no longer flowing freely through the lung circulation.

Emphysema is most commonly caused by heavy smoking, as chemicals inhaled within the tobacco smoke have a toxic effect on the alveoli. Another contributory factor may be air pollution, and a few people develop emphysema because of an inherited defect in a lung enzyme.

Drugs to widen the airways, usually in the form of an inhaler, and steroids to reduce lung inflammation, may be helpful for some sufferers. In severe cases, oxygen may have to be provided in the home.

In addition to giving up smoking and avoiding smoky or polluted atmospheres, which will only make the lung damage even worse, an annual flu jab is essential to reduce the risk of a flu-related chest infection. Prompt antibiotic therapy for any chest infection is also essential before it makes the breathing difficulties far worse.

Eye problems

A normal change in the eyes that occurs due to ageing is a gradual loss of elasticity in the internal lens. This condition, known as presbyopia, causes difficulty with near vision. As a result, small print may appear blurred when held at normal reading distance, but can be brought into focus by reading the page at arm's length.

Presbyopia is easily corrected with a pair of reading glasses; it is best to have your eyes checked by an optician to establish the appropriate lens prescription for each eye. Although reading glasses can now be bought over the counter using a do-it-yourself eye chart, the advantage of seeing an optician is to have other more serious eye problems picked up before they cause any permanent damage and loss of vision.

A routine eye test is recommended every two years, and sooner if any loss or disturbance of normal vision occurs. Reading glasses usually have to be changed several times, as the lenses of the eye become increasingly rigid, until all the focusing has to be done by the spectacle lenses.

There may be a charge for the eye test unless the person is receiving income support or belongs to one of the priority groups, which include people with glaucoma themselves (or whose close relative has this condition), diabetics and anyone registered blind or partially sighted.

Apart from presbyopia, the three most common eye problems in elderly people are cataracts, glaucoma and macular degeneration. A cataract is easily remedied by surgery; glaucoma can be treated successfully with eye drops, tablets or surgery, but any damage that has already been caused by the excessive pressure inside the eye ball cannot be corrected.

Although macular degeneration, a condition where the central part of the retina wears out, is not treatable, much can be done to reduce the handicap resulting from the progressive loss of vision it causes (see blindness).

Falls

About one third of elderly people are thought to suffer one or more falls each year, half of which are due to an accident such as tripping, while many of the remainder occur with no obvious cause. Because older people, particularly women, are vulnerable to osteoporosis – a condition which weakens the bones (see below) – these falls may cause a fracture, usually of the femur, wrist or spine.

To prevent accidental falls, there are a number of preventive measures (see box). If falls happen out of the blue, or are preceded by dizziness, weakness or some other warning symptom, a check-up from the doctor is essential.

Many of the medical conditions which can cause recurrent falls may be successfully treated, for example anaemia, heart irregularity or vertigo. The doctor can give advice on the easiest way to get up off the floor after a fall. For anyone who lives alone and does not have frequent visitors, it is a good idea to wear a portable alarm trigger so that help can be summoned if the fall has immobilised them (see pages 311 and 474).

PREVENTIVE MEASURES AGAINST FALLS
- Do not wear loose slippers.
- Electric leads should run around the edge of the room.
- Avoid tables with protruding legs and keep objects out of the way.
- Remove loose mats or rugs.
- Make sure that floors aren't slippery or highly polished.
- Stairs and corridors should be properly lit.
- Fit a handrail to help going up and down stairs.
- Secure loose stair carpets.

Foot problems

Older people are more likely than younger ones to develop calluses and corns on their feet. A callus is a thickening of the outer layers of skin due to pressure or irritation; a corn is a callus found on or between the toes. The reason for the greater susceptibility to these skin changes among elderly people is the higher incidence of foot deformities such as bunions, hammer toes and arthritic joints in this age group. As a result, they often find it difficult to buy shoes that fit comfortably without creating areas of friction when they stand or walk.

All corns or calluses should be covered with tape or a non-medicated corn pad for protection. Try to eliminate the cause of the pressure, for example by changing to a different pair of shoes. Soak thickened areas of skin in warm water to soften them, and then gently rub them with a pumice stone. Do not use non-prescription medicated corn pads, and never attempt to trim calluses yourself.

See a chiropodist if a corn or callus becomes painful, tender or inflamed. For people who suffer from persistent or recurrent calluses or corns as a result of a foot deformity, which can be structural or postural, the chiropodist may construct a specially moulded insole. Occasionally, an orthopaedic surgeon may have to perform some type of corrective surgery, although the chiropodist can operate on a bunion.

Anyone with diabetes or a poor circulation should have chiropody treatment routinely every few months because they are extremely vulnerable to infection of the skin if it becomes irritated or damaged.

Chiropody services are free for people over the age of 60; however, in some parts of the UK there may be a long delay due to a shortage of state registered chiropodists. If you are seeking private treatment, make sure the chiropodist is state registered, shown by the letters SRCh after his or her name. The Society of Chiropodists and Podiatrists* can supply names of state registered chiropodists in your area.

Gout

Gout is a type of arthritis that characteristically attacks one joint at a time, usually the joint at the base of the big toe. It develops as a result of the deposition of uric acid crystals inside the joint, which cause it to become temporarily inflamed, and so extremely painful and swollen with redness of the overlying skin.

Treatment of an attack involves large doses of an anti-inflammatory drug and sometimes colchicine to suppress the inflammation rapidly. If the cause is abnormally high levels of uric acid in the blood and attacks are recurrent, the doctor may prescribe a drug which reduces the production of uric acid in the body or a drug to increase the amount of uric acid passed in the urine.

Occasionally, uric acid crystallises as white deposits under the skin (tophi), which may then ulcerate and have to be removed surgically.

Gout sufferers are advised to reduce their dietary intake of purine, which is converted in the body to uric acid. Foods to avoid because they are high in purine include offal (liver, kidney, heart), game, anchovies, mackerel, herring, scallops, sardines, whitebait and mussels. Foods to eat only in moderation because they contain a fair amount of purine include meat, poultry, fish not mentioned above, peas, green beans, lentils, spinach, mushrooms, asparagus and cauliflower. The Arthritis and Rheumatism Council* produce a free leaflet on the condition.

Hair loss

Gradual, mild thinning of the hair on top of the head is a normal part of ageing; unless the individual has inherited the condition known as male pattern baldness, some hair should remain covering most of the scalp.

In male pattern baldness, which may also affect a few women after their menopause, hair is lost initially from the temples and crown to be replaced by very fine, downy hair. As the affected area of scalp widens, the normal hair line recedes.

There are many other causes of excessive hair loss which may occur whatever your age. Your doctor should be able to tell whether there is some underlying treatable condition by examining the scalp and skin on other parts of the body.

For hair loss that is causing distress or embarrassment, there are a variety of possible measures including wigs, toupees or a hair transplant. Application of a solution of the drug minoxidil (which was originally introduced to treat high blood pressure) may induce regrowth of fine hair in some people, but the results are not impressive.

Heart attack

A heart attack, also known as a coronary thrombosis or myocardial infarction, is a serious condition in which part of the heart muscle dies after interruption of its normal blood supply. In most cases, a heart attack is caused by the formation of a blood clot in one of the coronary arteries which encircle the heart. The clot develops in a section of the artery that is already narrowed by fatty deposits (see arteriosclerosis).

Symptoms of a heart attack may include pain across the centre of the chest, pain spreading into the neck, jaw, shoulders or arms, sweating, nausea, vomiting, palpitations and breathlessness. Risk factors for a heart attack are divided into unavoidable ones, such as getting older, a family history of heart attacks, diabetes and high blood pressure, as well as avoidable ones, such as smoking, drinking too much alcohol, eating foods high in saturated fats and cholesterol, and being overweight.

Anyone suspected of having a heart attack should be seen by a doctor as soon as possible. A new type of medication is available which, injected into the circulation, can quickly dissolve the blood clots that cause most heart attacks. These clot-busting drugs can halt a heart attack and minimise the muscle damage as long as they are injected within a few hours of the onset of symptoms.

After a heart attack, assuming there have not been any serious complications, ask the doctor to recommend an appropriate exercise programme. Taking regular exercise after an attack can reduce the chance of a recurrence.

Hernia

An abdominal hernia is the abnormal protrusion of an internal organ, usually part of the intestine, through a gap or weakness in the abdominal muscle wall. This type of hernia is more common in elderly people because the abdominal muscles tend to lose some of their strength and tone, partly because older people tend to be less active and because they tend to put on weight around the abdomen later in life.

If you notice a bulge on the abdominal wall or in the groin see your doctor. The main risk from an abdominal hernia is obstruction of the intestine or its blood supply as a result of the protruding loop becoming compressed, which in turn can lead to potentially fatal complications such as peritonitis or gangrene.

Surgical repair is recommended in most cases to prevent these complications recurring. The operation is usually relatively easy for the surgeon to perform, keeping the patient in hospital for a few days at the most. Before returning to normal activities, particularly doing any carrying or lifting, it is essential to follow a supervised programme of exercises to stretch and strengthen the abdominal muscles – otherwise the risk of recurrence is much greater.

For those people who are not fit enough to have an operation, a surgical truss or corset may be provided to prevent the hernia from bulging through the muscle wall. To be effective, it must be possible to ease the hernia gently back inside the abdomen; the truss should be put on before getting out of bed and then worn all day.

If a hernia suddenly becomes painful, tender, swollen or inflamed, seek medical attention at once, as these are signs that the intestine is under pressure.

High blood pressure

Blood pressure is the force that pushes blood around the circulation; it is generated by the pumping action of the heart and the natural elasticity of the artery walls. It is when this pressure is too high, a condition known as hypertension, that problems can arise.

Blood pressure tends to increase steadily with age because the arteries in older people are less elastic and often narrowed by fatty deposits (see arteriosclerosis). An excessively high blood pressure at any age usually occurs without any obvious cause, although in a few cases there is an underlying medical reason, for example kidney damage, a blood vessel disease or a hormone disorder.

Most people with dangerously high blood pressure experience no warning symptoms, which is why doctors like to check everyone's blood pressure regularly. The measurement of blood pressure comes as two figures: the higher one is the reading at the moment the heart beats, the lower one is when the heart is relaxed. For people over the age of 60, the ideal blood pressure is 140/90 or less.

If the upper reading is much higher than 140, or the lower reading is 100 or more, your GP will encourage you to take such steps as losing excess weight, taking regular gentle exercise, cutting down on salt and stopping smoking. Relaxation or meditation can also help.

If despite all this the blood pressure remains high, medication is usually recommended. This is because untreated hypertension causes damage to arteries, particularly in the heart, brain, kidneys and eyes, resulting in a greater risk of heart attack, stroke, kidney failure and blindness.

Hypothermia

Hypothermia is a potentially fatal condition in which the body's internal temperature falls to below 35°C (95°F). Elderly people are more vulnerable to hypothermia because as the body ages it becomes less sensitive to the cold. Not only are older people less likely to feel cold when their body temperature drops, but they are also less efficient at generating body heat, for example through shivering.

A number of medical problems that are more common among older people, such as immobility due to arthritis or an underactive thyroid gland, also increase the risk of hypothermia. Death due to hypothermia may occur as a direct result of a low body temperature, which can interfere with normal breathing and the heart beat; or it may be an indirect cause, through making a heart or chest complaint worse or reducing resistance to infections such as pneumonia.

All elderly people should take steps to protect themselves against the cold, for example by living in one warm room if it is too difficult or expensive to heat the whole house, eating and drinking properly, wrapping up in several thin layers of clothing, doing regular arm and leg exercises, if possible, and getting the windows and doors properly insulated.

Help the Aged* run the National Winter Warmth Campaign (telephone Freefone 0800 289404, Mon-Fri, 10am-4pm), which gives more advice on how to avoid hypothermia.

It is also essential for anyone who cares for an elderly person to be aware of the warning symptoms of hypothermia, which include pale cold skin, puffiness of the face, increasing drowsiness and confusion, slurring of the speech and shallow breathing. First aid measures while waiting for medical help are to wrap the person in a warm blanket and if he or she is conscious to give a warm drink. However, it is dangerous to give alcohol, rub the skin, apply a hot water bottle or put the person into a hot bath.

Incontinence

Incontinence of either urine or faeces is not a normal part of growing old. Although it is an embarrassing problem that most elderly people would rather not talk about, incontinence is often curable and so it is important to visit your doctor for advice and treatment.

In older men, incontinence of urine is usually the result of an enlarged prostate gland (see prostate enlargement) and takes the form of dribbling after passing urine, or not being able to get to a toilet in time. Treatment involves a surgical operation, but drugs are being developed that may help by shrinking the prostate, thereby taking pressure off the bladder and urethra.

In older women, incontinence of urine may be due to urinary infection, which should respond to antibiotics; or to a weakness of the pelvic muscles, usually as a result of stretching during childbirth. Pelvic muscle weakness typically causes 'stress incontinence', where a small amount of urine leaks out during coughing, sneezing or laughing.

If the pelvic muscles do not respond to an exercise programme, or if in addition to the muscle weakness there is a prolapse of the uterus which is stretching the neck of the bladder, surgical repair will usually be recommended. For anyone not well enough to have this operation, a plastic ring pessary inserted inside the vagina to hold the uterus in place may be sufficient to relieve the urinary symptoms.

Incontinence of faeces in elderly people is often due to prolonged constipation, the faeces having become compacted inside the rectum and lower colon and the resulting irritation of the bowel wall leading to the formation of a small amount of diarrhoea, which leaks out without warning. Treatment of the constipation, which may in such extreme cases require an enema, should relieve the problem.

In many parts of the UK, there are continence advisers – specially trained nurses – who can explain the practical measures, and give advice on the best aids available, to make it easier to cope with incontinence that cannot be cured. Ask your doctor, health visitor or district nurse whether there is a local continence adviser; if not, one of them should be able to offer support and provide information.

There is also an Incontinence Information Helpline (telephone 0191-213 0050, Mon-Fri, 2-7pm) where you can get advice from health professionals with a special interest and expertise in bladder and bowel control.

Indigestion

When someone complains of indigestion he or she may be suffering from any of a wide variety of symptoms including heartburn, belching, a bloating discomfort, wind, abdominal pain or nausea. The most common reasons for all these digestive symptoms are bad eating habits, such as eating or drinking too much, eating too quickly, not relaxing for long enough after a meal, or eating too soon before going to bed.

If you develop abdominal discomfort or heartburn, you may subconsciously swallow air to try to relieve it, resulting in belching and bloating – flatulence – which makes your symptoms feel much worse.

For an acute attack of indigestion in whatever form, take a dose of antacid. Your pharmacist will be able to recommend one from the dozens of different brands on the market. The antacid should relieve indigestion within an hour or so; however, if the symptoms persist or suddenly get worse, for example an abdominal pain lasting more than four hours, see your doctor.

Recurrent attacks of indigestion should also be investigated by the GP; they may be caused by a peptic ulcer, acid reflux due to a hiatus hernia, irritable bowel syndrome or, rarely, stomach cancer. A physical examination and a few tests can exclude any serious condition; your doctor can then prescribe appropriate medication.

Insomnia

People often seem to need less sleep as they get older. This should not be regarded as a problem as long as the reduced amount of sleep isn't causing tiredness, anxiety or distress. Insomnia is not just being unable to sleep for as long as you want, but sleep may be very fitful, causing the person to wake feeling tired and out of sorts; he or she may take a long time to fall asleep, or wake up in the early hours of the morning and be unable to fall asleep again.

If you are having trouble sleeping in one of the above ways, adopt the following measures to try to alleviate the problem:

- Take some exercise during the day, preferably outdoors.
- Stay up until you feel sleepy.
- Have a milky bedtime drink, but avoid tea and coffee which contain stimulants.
- Don't eat a large meal late in the evening.
- Make sure your bedroom is not too cold or hot.
- Get up at the same time each morning, regardless of how well you have slept.

It is also worth noting that many older people sleep better having had a short nap during the day.

See your doctor if insomnia persists despite these measures. Sometimes the underlying cause is depression, in which case antidepressants will usually help stop the early morning waking that is a characteristic of depression. Sleeping pills which contain a sedative may be prescribed as a short-term measure, but regular use can lead to addiction and unpleasant withdrawal symptoms if you stop taking them suddenly.

Leg ulcers

Leg ulcers are a common problem in elderly people, especially women. Most of them occur in association with varicose veins, because the pooling of blood that occurs in the leg veins in this condition causes the surrounding skin tissues to become unhealthy and vulnerable to relatively minor trauma.

A few leg ulcers are due to disease of the arteries, which interferes with the normal supply of oxygen and nutrients to the skin tissues, again making them unhealthy and at risk of gangrene as well as ulceration. Diabetics are particularly susceptible to leg ulcers, not only because they are more likely to develop arterial disease but also because this disease can damage the nerves in the legs so that minor injuries to the skin may not be noticed.

Ulcers as a result of varicose veins are usually treated with compression bandages and elevation of the ulcerated leg to help reduce blood pooling and allow the skin to heal naturally. Arterial ulcers are cleaned and dressed, antibiotics are prescribed to treat any infection, and drugs may be given to try to improve the circulation, but compression bandages must not be applied because they will make the problem worse by causing further constriction of the arteries.

To reduce the risk of developing a leg ulcer, take regular exercise, don't smoke, eat a healthy balanced diet, lose excess weight if you can, take good care of your skin, protect your legs from accidental knocks and if you suffer from varicose veins it is a good idea to wear compression hosiery.

Medication problems

The main problem for elderly people with regard to their medication is that they may be taking several drugs at the same time. This can be confusing, particularly if doses are being taken at different times of the day and some of the drugs are taken more frequently than others.

Make a chart with each of the drugs and the times of the doses written on it, leaving a space to tick off each time a dose is taken. It is helpful to write what the drug has been prescribed for on the container, for example 'pain', 'dizziness', 'blood pressure'.

Do not put all the drugs for one day in the same bottle, as this can lead to dangerous mistakes over which drug is for which condition.

If you are taking several medications, make sure you tell the doctor about all of them before any new drug is prescribed. Some drugs can be dangerous when taken in combination. For the same reason, check with the pharmacist before starting any new over-the-counter medication.

When a condition such as arthritis makes it difficult to take the childproof tops off the bottles, ask the pharmacist to provide alternative containers; but this makes it even more important to keep all medications out of the reach of children.

Any unexpected symptoms that you think might be a side effect of a drug should be reported at once to the doctor, but do *not* stop the drug abruptly without checking that this is safe to do so. If a drug does not seem to be working, make another appointment with the doctor.

Anyone on long-term medication should ideally have a check-up every three months, certainly at least every six months, to make sure the treatment is still necessary and not causing any hidden complications.

Menopause

The menopause is a normal stage in a woman's life that occurs around the age of 50. While the menopause can be said to be complete once the menstrual periods have stopped, the processes leading up to this point begin several years earlier and symptoms associated with the menopause may continue for several years afterwards.

Hormonal changes are the cause of the various processes and symptoms that occur with the menopause. As the amount of oestrogen being made in the ovaries gradually decreases, ovulation (egg release) may cease and the menstrual cycle becomes very irregular.

A wide variety of symptoms both physical and emotional may be experienced including hot flushes, night sweats, palpitations, vaginal dryness, mood swings, depression and forgetfulness. The reduction in oestrogen levels also accelerates the process of osteoporosis, where the bones become more fragile. There is also a tendency to put on weight, particularly around the abdomen.

Hormone replacement therapy (HRT) can help relieve most of the menopausal symptoms, as well as providing additional protection against osteoporosis and coronary heart disease. A woman may wish to discuss with her GP or at the well-women clinic whether HRT might be suitable for her.

In addition to HRT, other measures that can help minimise some of the unwanted effects of the menopause include regular exercise to tone up the muscles, a sensible diet to avoid gaining weight, using moisturising cream or an emollient to counteract dry skin and stopping smoking, which is a major risk factor for both osteoporosis and coronary heart disease.

Finally, if menstrual bleeding occurs after the menopause, it is essential to have this checked by a doctor, as post-menopausal bleeding can be a warning symptom of cancer.

Obesity

Energy requirements, in the form of calories provided by our food, gradually decrease with age, partly because the body requires less energy for cell processes at rest, partly because older people tend to take less physical exercise during the day and therefore burn up fewer calories overall.

However, most elderly people do not adjust their calorie intake to match these changes. As a result the excess calories are laid down as fatty tissue, causing a steady increase in weight that can progress to obesity. In addition to the undesirable effect of being overweight from the point of view of appearance, obesity is bad for long-term health because it increases the risk of developing high blood pressure, diabetes, osteoarthritis and even cancer.

To avoid obesity, you should follow a diet which restricts high-calorie foods such as biscuits, cakes, chocolate, sweets and cuts down on fatty foods like butter, full-fat cheese and fried meals, while continuing to eat foods high in vitamins, minerals and fibre.

The ideal daily diet should include fresh fruit and vegetables, wholegrain bread and cereals and lean meats such as poultry. To ensure you get sufficient calcium without too many calories, choose low-fat milk, cheeses and yoghurts. For more on healthy eating, see **Chapter 30**.

Osteoarthritis

Wear and tear of the cartilage surfaces inside a joint, resulting in pain, stiffness and swelling, is the cause of the most common form of arthritis, known as osteoarthritis. This wearing out of the joint tends to occur gradually with advancing years, so that most people in their sixties have osteoarthritis in at least some of their joints.

The joints most commonly affected are those that have taken

the most punishment over the years, like the hips, the knees and the joints at the base of the neck and lower back. Factors which increase the risk of osteoarthritis include being overweight, overuse of a joint playing a particular sport, or a serious or recurrent injury to a joint when younger.

There is no cure for osteoarthritis but symptoms can usually be controlled with painkillers or anti-inflammatory drugs taken by mouth or applied to the affected joints as a gel. Exercises to strengthen the muscles around an arthritic joint, under the guidance of a doctor or physiotherapist, can help to protect the joint against further damage. The Arthritis and Rheumatism Council* produce a leaflet on the subject.

In severe cases, where the arthritic joint has become very painful or stiff, it may be necessary to be referred to the hospital for a joint replacement operation.

Osteoporosis

In osteoporosis, the bones become brittle and fragile as the result of a gradual loss of minerals, including calcium, from their internal structure. Affected bones are more likely to break as a consequence of relatively minor trauma, such as falling over in the street.

As part of the normal ageing process, almost everyone experiences a reduction in their bone density. After the age of 35, the amount of new bone being formed to replace the continuous degeneration of old bone is reduced and the body also becomes less efficient at absorbing calcium from digested food and storing it in the bones.

The gradual decline in bone mass speeds up in women after the menopause because of the loss of the protective effect of oestrogen. Other factors that may accelerate the onset of osteoporosis include smoking and drinking too much alcohol, as well as inactivity such as prolonged bed rest.

To avoid osteoporosis, it is important to build up strong bones earlier in life by taking regular exercise, particularly activities that put stress on the bones; by eating adequate amounts of calcium, especially during pregnancy and breastfeeding, when calcium requirements go up, by not smoking, and drinking alcohol only in moderation. Hormone replacement therapy taken for at least 12-18 months during the menopause can also protect against osteoporosis.

Even when osteoporosis is already established, it is still worth increasing calcium and vitamin D intake and following a gentle exercise programme. Particular care must be taken to avoid any accidental falls by making the home extra safe (see under falls earlier in the chapter) and not going outdoors in icy weather, if possible.

In severe cases, a drug may be prescribed to try to halt the continuing loss of minerals from the bones. However, as yet, no medication is available that can restore bone strength to normal, which is why prevention of this disease is so important.

More information can be obtained from the National Osteoporosis Society*.

Parkinson's disease

Parkinson's disease affects the part of the brain which controls all body movements. The exact cause is unknown, but symptoms occur as a result of depletion of one of the brain chemicals – dopamine – in this area, which in turn interferes with the transmission of nerve impulses involved in the co-ordination of muscle action.

The incidence of Parkinson's disease increases significantly in elderly people, rising to 1 in 100 over the age of 65, and 1 in 50 over the age of 80. Symptoms tend to come on gradually and typically include a coarse tremor in the hands, muscle stiffness, difficulty starting and stopping movements such as walking, and a fixed facial expression with staring eyes. Sufferers tend to stoop forward and walk with a shuffling gait.

Several different drugs may be tried before the symptoms are brought under reasonable control. The amount of drug and the timing of each dose have to be adjusted carefully to suit the individual's response. A great deal of research is under way to develop more effective treatments and one day to find a cure.

Physiotherapy and occupational therapy can help improve mobility and maintain independence to a limited extent but, unfortunately, the condition tends to become more severe with time. For details of a self-help group in your part of the country, write to the Parkinson's Disease Society*.

Peptic ulcer

In older people, a common reason for developing an ulcer in the stomach or duodenum – popularly referred to as a peptic ulcer – is long-term treatment with an anti-inflammatory drug to relieve the symptoms of a painful condition such as arthritis. Another medication that can also cause peptic ulceration when taken on a regular basis is a corticosteroid such as prednisolone.

Warning symptoms of a peptic ulcer include recurrent attacks of abdominal pain, nausea and vomiting, belching and feeling bloated. Vomiting material that looks like coffee grounds or passing black tarry stools are signs that a peptic ulcer is bleeding.

To reduce the risk of developing a peptic ulcer, try to take an ordinary painkiller such as paracetamol or codeine rather than anti-inflammatory drugs which include aspirin and ibuprofen. Doctors now sometimes prescribe a drug to protect the lining of the stomach and duodenum at the same time as prescribing an anti-inflammatory.

Because a peptic ulcer can cause serious complications, such as profuse bleeding or perforation leading to peritonitis, it is essential to visit the doctor if you develop any of the warning symptoms described above.

Pneumonia

Pneumonia is a condition where the lungs become inflamed; it is usually as a result of an infection from bacteria or viruses, although there are other causes, such as accidental inhalation of a piece of food or a poisonous gas. Symptoms of pneumonia include a productive cough, discoloured or blood-stained sputum, fever and chills, chest pains and breathlessness.

In elderly people, pneumonia can be extremely serious, either because the immune system which defends the body against infections doesn't work as efficiently later on in life, or because the pneumonia aggravates an underlying chronic disorder such as heart failure or chronic bronchitis.

Antibiotics will be prescribed for a bacterial pneumonia and also in many cases of viral pneumonia to prevent a secondary bacterial infection of the inflamed lung tissues. Hospital admission may be necessary so that oxygen can be given and, in extreme cases, mechanical ventilation initiated until the infection is brought under control.

Because pneumonia is a fairly common complication of flu in elderly people, an annual flu jab is recommended for everyone over the age of 65, especially anyone with a chronic heart or lung condition.

Prostate enlargement

An enlarged prostate gland is a very common problem among older men, although why it should affect some men more than others is not known. The prostate sits at the base of the bladder and surrounds the urethra, which is the narrow tube that carries urine and, in men, semen to the tip of the penis. The function of the prostate is to produce most of the seminal fluid, secretions which transport and nourish the sperm after ejaculation.

Enlargement of the prostate closes off the upper part of the urethra and, as a result, may cause a variety of urinary symptoms such as difficulty starting the flow, a poor stream, dribbling after urination, having to get up to pass urine during the night and rushing to the toilet frequently during the day.

Embarrassment causes many men to delay seeing their doctor until these symptoms become intolerable. However, treatment is usually successful at restoring near-normal urinary function. The usual procedure is a surgical rebore, where a narrow instrument with viewing and cutting devices is passed up the urethra and the obstructing tissue pared away.

New forms of treatment under investigation include the inflation of a tiny balloon inside the urethra to relieve the constriction, the use of a microwave beam to heat up the prostate gland and a drug which, by preventing hormonal stimulation of the prostate, shrinks the gland and improves the flow of urine as a result.

Rheumatoid arthritis

Rheumatoid arthritis (RA) affects roughly one million people in the UK. It is a severe form of arthritis and, although the exact cause is unknown, is believed to be an autoimmune disease where the body's immune system starts to attack the joints. The resulting inflammation causes pain, tenderness, swelling, redness and warmth in many joints, usually in a symmetrical pattern on either side of the body.

Other symptoms of RA include severe joint stiffness which is typically worse in the early morning, loss of grip strength and sometimes fever, generalised weakness and malaise.

Although RA is popularly thought to be a disease of old age, it usually strikes people first in their thirties. The condition then commonly flares up intermittently, with periods of remission which may last several months, even years. Also, many sufferers develop only a mild disability and are able to remain mobile and independent.

In the past, RA used to cause severe joint deformities in those people who were seriously affected by the disease. By the time they reached their sixties and beyond, even though the arthritis often seemed to burn itself out, they would be left housebound and possibly in a wheelchair. However, with the development of powerful drugs, which can slow down the disease and limit the amount of damage to the joints, the risk of permanent handicap in these more severe cases has been reduced considerably.

Various aids are available to help the arthritic cope with everyday tasks. Artificial joints can now be used to replace knees, fingers and shoulders as well as the hips, if they have been left very stiff or uncomfortable. The Arthritis and Rheumatism Council* can supply more information; and see also **Chapter 31** on exercise.

Sexual problems

A common myth about growing older is that an active sex life should end at 60. However, for many couples, love-making actually improves once they become free from the pressures of work and the menopause has removed the worry of an unwanted pregnancy. Some couples may prefer to cease their love-making, while others would like to continue demonstrating their mutual love in a physical way, but encounter some difficulty such as discomfort or impotence.

For any sexual problem, the first step is to talk opening with your partner. The family doctor is usually the best person to consult next. There may be an underlying medical reason which can be corrected, for example a change in medication if a particular drug is thought to be the cause of impotence; or application of a vaginal lubricant or oestrogen cream, if discomfort is due to post-menopausal inflammation of the vaginal lining.

If a medical disorder such as heart failure or osteoarthritis is causing love-making to be uncomfortable because of breathlessness or joint pain respectively, the doctor may be able to recommend alternative positions for sexual intercourse which are less stressful. Referral to a professional counsellor, usually through the organisation Relate*, can help a couple learn to communicate better and resolve any sexual fears or anxieties. An excellent publication from Age Concern* that deals with issues related to sexuality in older people is *Living, Loving and Ageing: Sexual and Personal Relationships in Later Life*, by Wendy and Sally Greengross.

Skin problems

Older people who have been regularly exposed to the ultraviolet radiation of strong sunlight earlier in life without taking appropriate precautions, such as wearing a broad-brimmed sunhat, putting on a sunscreen and keeping out of the midday sun, are much more likely to develop the three characteristic changes that occur in the skins of older people: severe wrinkling, thickened and roughened skin and large numbers of brown spots (also known as age spots) that typically appear on the face and the backs of the hands.

To treat skin-ageing, there is now an effective cream which contains retinoic acid (a derivative of vitamin A). Retinoic acid, which is available on prescription, can reduce wrinkling and roughening of the skin, as well as causing the age spots to fade. A new form of laser therapy has also been developed to remove unsightly age spots from exposed areas of skin.

WARNING
See your doctor if you develop any new blemish on your skin; or if a mole or blemish changes size, colour or shape, itches, bleeds, crusts over or becomes painful. This may signify a skin cancer and the earlier it is treated, the greater the chance of a successful cure.

Stroke

A stroke is caused by the interruption of the normal blood supply to part of the brain, resulting in damage to those brain cells deprived of oxygen for more than a few minutes. The three main types of stroke are a cerebral thrombosis, where a blood clot (thrombus) obstructs one of the main arteries in the brain; a cerebral embolism, where a fragment of blood clot that has broken off from a thrombus elsewhere in the circulation blocks a brain artery; and a cerebral haemorrhage, where a blood vessel in the brain ruptures.

Symptoms from a stroke depend primarily on which part of the brain has been damaged, as each brain area controls specific functions related to particular parts of the body. Typical symptoms may include sudden onset of numbness or weakness (usually on one side of the body), loss of speech or slurring of words, a sudden severe headache, unexplained dizziness, a sudden fall, or blurred vision.

Measures to reduce the risk of a stroke include not smoking, drinking alcohol only in moderation, cutting down on foods high in cholesterol and saturated fats and taking regular exercise. Also, have your blood pressure checked regularly as a high level that goes untreated may cause a stroke without any warning symptoms.

If a stroke has occurred, the main part of therapy is a rehabilitation programme that may need to include speech therapy, as well as physiotherapy and occupational therapy. Recovery is unpredictable, but progress may continue to be made for over a year or even longer. For information and practical advice, contact the Stroke Association*.

Transient ischaemic attacks

A transient ischaemic attack (TIA) is a mini-stroke which causes similar symptoms to a normal stroke, but, because there is no permanent damage to the brain, these symptoms resolve completely within 24 hours, leaving no additional disability.

Even if the TIA symptoms disappear within minutes, it is still essential to see your doctor for a full check-up as a TIA is a warning signal that a major stroke could be on the way. Around 10 per cent of strokes are preceded by one or more TIAs, with perhaps a few days or even several months between them.

For some people who have had a TIA, the doctor may recommend aspirin or anticoagulant therapy, or surgery to remove fatty deposits from one of the brain arteries, as a way of reducing the chance of a future stroke.

Varicose veins

Around 20 per cent of the population suffer from varicose veins – bulging, twisted swollen veins usually confined to the lower legs. For most sufferers, the symptoms they cause are only mild and can be eased by wearing elastic support hosiery and not standing still for long periods. The typical symptoms are aching legs, swelling of the feet and ankles and a few visible swollen veins on the calves and thighs.

Varicose veins are generally caused by damaged valves inside the veins, which allow a backflow of blood down the leg and from the deep veins out into the superficial veins that run just under the skin. This pooling of blood in the veins causes them to swell under pressure.

Anyone with mild varicose veins should take various precautions to try to avoid making them worse, such as wearing elastic support stockings or socks, not crossing the legs or ankles, not standing for a long time, and never putting on a garter or elastic stocking top that presses into the thigh and obstructs the circulation. In addition to keeping weight within normal limits, you should ask your GP to recommend a programme of leg exercises to help the circulation through the veins.

Complications from more severe varicose veins include thrombophlebitis (painful tender swelling along a vein) and leg ulceration, both of which should be treated as soon as possible by your doctor.

CHAPTER 34

CARING FOR ELDERLY PARENTS

While retirement can bring the bonuses of more leisure and, one hopes, sufficient income to enjoy it, problems may be lurking in the wings. Very many people in middle age find that their parents (or other relatives) increasingly need help as their health and strength diminish. Sometimes this can happen suddenly as illness strikes or one parent dies, leaving the other unable to cope. At worst the situation may arise when, for example, you yourself have family worries, expenses with older children, a difficult menopause or other health problems.

Although it would be misguided to try to cross all the bridges before coming to them, a certain amount of forward-planning would be prudent, and could save time, money and problems later on, whether you are already a carer or suspect that you might one day become one.

Taking decisions
You and your partner should decide how much time you could devote to looking after elderly relatives if the need arose. It may be that you are working and will be for some time to come, or you may have to take into account your own health and ability to cope with any stress that might occur as a consequence of becoming a carer. The temptation to try to 'take over' your parents' lives may be difficult to resist, but as far as possible the decisions should be theirs.

Which home?

If your parents are considering moving discuss with them in some detail where they go, whether it is to be nearer to you or not. This decision, at least, should certainly involve you even if they are still very active.

The availability of local social services and of public transport, the helpfulness of neighbours, ease of access to doctor, dentist and shops, and aspects such as whether hills have to be climbed regularly – all need to be considered, particularly if your parents will not be living near you.

If your parents move in order to be closer to you, your involvement will clearly become more immediate and you will need to consider your commitment carefully. If one parent is widowed there will be a particular need to keep an eye on the survivor, if he or she is determined to stay on at home. But even if your parents are still together, you will probably find an increasing amount of time will be spent visiting them and lending a hand. Unless there is a big job to be helped with, frequent short visits are probably best if they live nearby – and, of course, whenever possible, *they* will want to help *you*.

David Bookbinder's comprehensive book, *Housing Options for Older People*, published by Age Concern*, is well worth reading before coming to any decision.

Staying put

Many elderly people are anxious to remain in their own homes, particularly if they have lived there for a long time, know the district and have friendly neighbours, a sympathetic doctor, and so on. But with increasing age and infirmity it is important to help them make the right provisions for doing so. It is surprising how much *can* be arranged if necessary. See the section on General safety and convenience later in this chapter.

There are various schemes designed to help people stay in their own homes. Help the Aged have a 'Gifted Housing Plan', for example, which allows you to donate your home to them

---

*The addresses and phone numbers of organisations marked with an asterisk can be found in the address section at the back of the guide.

while continuing to live there. The charity is responsible for the maintenance of the property during your lifetime. More information is available through Help the Aged Housing Division*; and see also **Chapter 20**.

Some areas have home improvement agencies, usually for older people, run by voluntary organisations, housing associations or the local authority, who can advise on how to get a home surveyed and how to apply for the appropriate grants and loans to fund the improvements. The organisation Care & Repair* has national and local groups which provide advice and practical help on house repairs, improvements and adaptations. The Anchor Housing Trust* also offers information and leaflets.

Another option may be to raise money on the home to provide an annuity or capital, while the owner continues living in it. Home income plans or home reversion schemes might be considered, but it is essential to take good legal and financial advice before making any commitment; for more details see **Chapter 6**.

Age Concern* has a free fact sheet (No.12) called *Raising an Income from your Home*.

Living under the same roof

It may be that you consider your elderly parent(s) would be better living with your family – or that you should move to their home. This should be a family decision taken jointly after a long, hard look at all the options.

An existing house could be extended: one of the provisos for successful integration between different generations is plenty of living space, so that they can be independent from one another while having, say, an alarm bell installed in case of need. This option depends on finances or on the parent(s) being willing and able to put their own money into it and planning permission being obtainable. Building on an extension could improve the value of the house; it could be designed for maximum convenience, taking into account any existing or possible future disabilities. You might wish to investigate the possibility of grants for such work: the Department of Environment* produces a booklet (No. 90 HOU 08) called *House Renovation*

Grants, or ask your local authority housing department for up-to-date information about these grants, as well as renovation grants and minor works assistance grants. The Age Concern* Factsheet No. 13 *Older Home Owners: Financial Help with Repairs* may also be of use (it covers home improvements too).

It could be worth pooling resources – money from your own house and that of your parents – to buy a bigger property with amenities to suit everyone. Or, if your parents live in a big house and the area is convenient to jobs, schools and so on, consider moving in there if they agree, and doing a certain amount of conversion.

If accommodation is tight, the situation can be that much more difficult. You may be in a position where you feel you *have* to offer a home to a widowed mother or father and it can produce poor reactions from the rest of your family. Not only might there be physical considerations to cause resentment – children having to share a room, for example, when they have been used to their own space – but emotional ones, too. For example, your son or daughter and their friends could come in for open criticism in their own home.

Parents moving in with you should bring some of their own furniture, especially the bed. Any small possessions which mean 'home' should also be included and an electric kettle and ring would enable them to make a snack or drinks without always having to use the main kitchen (make sure that these are safely sited to eliminate the risk of scalds and burns and that a fire blanket is readily available).

No one of any age likes to feel useless, so if there is something parents can contribute – perhaps helping to prepare meals or doing some gardening or shopping, it is a good idea to involve them. Not only is it beneficial for their morale, but can also be a help to you, to set against the extra work of having another family member living with you.

Sheltered housing

Sheltered housing usually consists of a group of self-contained bungalows or flats where elderly people who are still active can live independently, yet the development is under the care of a warden who keeps an eye on the properties, any communal rooms and the welfare of the residents. This is particularly reassuring if your parents live some distance from you. The housing department of the local authority or Age Concern* should be able to provide appropriate addresses and information on the requirements which have to be met in order to qualify for their schemes, costs and so on.

In the private sector, many property developers and some housing associations and councils build sheltered houses or flats for sale. There is a service charge to cover the cost of a warden and maintenance. Further information can be obtained from Age Concern's free factsheet No. 2 *Sheltered Housing for Sale* or their book *A Buyer's Guide to Sheltered Housing* (£2.50 including p&p). Or contact the Anchor Housing Trust*, the Elderly Accommodation Counsel*, the New Homes Marketing Board* or Sheltered Housing Services Ltd*. See also **Chapter 20**.

Another option, if the developer agrees, is to buy a 'life share' in a sheltered housing scheme – that is, the purchaser buys sheltered housing at a percentage of the asking price and lives in it for life, after which the entire value of the property reverts to the finance company putting up the money. This option requires good legal advice.

Abbeyfield supportive care houses are another possible choice nationwide. These accommodate up to ten elderly people in individual bed-sitting rooms with their own furniture; residents have a great degree of independence. The aim is to create a happy family atmosphere with some meals taken communally but also with plenty of privacy, overseen by a resident housekeeper. Although Abbeyfield homes are normally for active people, there are now some extra care schemes which cater for the more infirm. With all charitable housing associations offering a licensee arrangement, any proposed contract should be carefully checked by a solicitor, particularly with regard to security of tenure, so that your parent fully understands his or her rights as well as those of the housing association. More details are available from the Abbeyfield Society*.

Residential and nursing homes

There may come a point where a parent needs so much help and supervision that you have to consider giving up work or finding suitable residential care. This is an extremely difficult decision. The carer may enjoy working and make a significant financial contribution – to exchange this for the confining task of nursing an elderly person is not a decision to be taken lightly. It could be a bad option not only for the carer, but for the person being cared for.

Very often in such a situation it is a good idea to involve someone outside the family to help and advise. A talk with a social worker or someone at Age Concern* or from a local branch of the Carers National Association* could help in coming to a decision acceptable to everyone. It might, indeed, be better for all concerned, not least the elderly person, if he or she went into residential care close by, if a suitable place were available and financially viable, where visits and outings with the family could be frequent. However, this may not always be acceptable, certainly at first, by the person who has to make the move.

Such charities as Age Concern* and the Elderly Accommodation Counsel* or some private organisations offer useful leaflets and advice on choosing a home and financing a place, or you could consult the local authority or the social services for information about homes in the area. The local telephone directory gives a list of local homes under Social Services – Homes for Adults. Or try the Community Health Council for information (address in the phone book). Age Concern's factsheet No.29 *Finding Residential and Nursing Home Accommodation* is helpful. Voluntary organisations such as the Salvation Army also run homes; more information is available from the *Charities Digest*, which you should be able to consult at a local library. See also page 423–5 on financial help for people living in a residential care home or a nursing home.

Look round at several residential homes and try to take your parent to visit when you have narrowed down the selection. A place may not be available in the home your parent likes most, but if second best is accepted, a move may be possible later on when a vacancy occurs.

Everyone will have their own priorities, but points to note are:

- Situation – is the home within safe and easy walking distance of shops, post office, doctor's surgery, bank, library, etc.?
- Are there any hills to climb en route and is the site level? Is it in a pleasant area with not too much noise from main road, factories, etc.?
- Is public transport readily available? How frequent are the services and where do they go? Is there a concession for elderly people on local transport and what are the fares?
- Do the other residents seem congenial? Is it a mixed-sex home (these can often have a better atmosphere)?
- Are the staff pleasant? What is the quality of the catering? Is the home well-maintained, pleasant and clean?
- Are outings and other social activities arranged?
- Are pets allowed, and can residents bring some of their own possessions?
- Is there a guest room, and can visitors obtain meals? What is the cost? How available is the room?
- Is the home near enough for your parent's own doctor to visit?

If your parent has a great degree of disability, a move to a nursing home will probably be necessary as residential homes normally cater for reasonably active clients. Try to talk to some of the residents privately; look at the lavatories and kitchens; find out how regimented the home is: do the residents have to get up and go to bed at particular times?

General safety and convenience

Whether your parent lives with you or on his or her own, look together at safety precautions and general convenience. The tidier a house can be kept the safer and more convenient it will be.

- Could a change be made from a coal fire to gas or electric central heating? (Budget schemes are available for paying installation and running costs.)

- Special care should be taken with gas appliances, open fires and the guarding of cookers and kettles.
- Bathing or showering should be made as easy as possible, with grab rails and aids for getting in and out (the social services can advise on and fit these).
- Install a smoke alarm to alert your parent in case of fire (obtainable quite cheaply from DIY shops).
- Ensure that there are non-slip backings on mats and rugs, adequate lighting on stairs and landings, and a fire extinguisher or safety blanket ready to hand.
- Adequate locks on doors and windows, a door peep-hole and/or some form of alarm (see below) could provide reassurance (always assuming that the locks can be easily undone in the case of fire).

RICA* has produced a free booklet called *Equipment for an Easier Life*, and a free leaflet produced jointly by the Royal Society for the Prevention of Accidents and Age Concern called *Home Safety: Care of Elderly People for Families* (available from Age Concern*) lists useful hints for all areas of the home.

Practical Ways to Crack Crime (phone 0181-569 7000 for a free copy) has a special section called 'Help for the Elderly', with many pointers on how to ensure as far as possible that older people continue to be safe in their homes as well as out of doors. For example, the police are always ready to help with advice on security, perhaps with a home visit – contact the crime prevention officer at the local police station. It may be possible to get financial assistance to help with the cost of door and window locks, door chains and so on once a need has been identified; get in touch with the housing department of the local council. Age Concern* and Help the Aged* also give advice and offer leaflets on security problems: Help the Aged's leaflet *Security in Your Home* is generally useful and *Be Sure Who's at the Door* covers aspects of doorstep selling and visits to the home. Write, or telephone their free national information service on 0800 289 404.

An elderly person living alone is likely to welcome a social alarm system as a means of getting help quickly and easily whenever it is needed. Many local councils run schemes, usually through their housing or social services departments, for both council tenants and home owners. The user needs to wear a small pushbutton on a neckcord or wristband or clipped to clothing. When pressed this sends a radio signal to a unit (plugged into the mains and a modern telephone socket), which then automatically dials out to programmed telephone numbers. With the council schemes, the call will go through to a 24-hour control centre where, depending on the service offered, the operator will try to speak to the user through the system (most of the units have loudspeakers built in). If the user needs someone to go to him or her, the operator will send one of the scheme's staff or will contact the user's local friends or relatives.

Most councils charge for the service and have eligibility rules, but if your parent is, say, 75 and lives alone, he or she is very likely to qualify if there is a scheme in the area. If not, there are other options: commercial schemes that operate in a similar way to that of councils; or you can buy alarms that can be programmed to dial friends' numbers direct; or many councils will take on people who live outside their area and have bought a compatible alarm – Help the Aged* can tell you about these.

Which? (October 1992) has a report on 18 different alarm systems and the results are given in more detail, along with advice about using systems, in a booklet available from RICA* (£1.95 inc. p&p). The Information Department of the Disabled Living Foundation* can also advise.

Financial and legal matters

Your parent may appreciate help and advice from you about his or her financial affairs. The first step is to see exactly what money is available. See the main section **Your finances in retirement** earlier in the book to help you work out your parent's situation in terms of pension and tax. He or she may be entitled to the higher tax allowances for older people whose incomes are less than a certain amount – the 'age-related allowance' – see **Chapter 15**. Other tax allowances may also apply. When your parent has listed current expenditure on food, heating, clothes, repairs and so on, prepare a budget together, writing down and totalling basic expenses and seeing how much is left over for other items such as holidays, newspapers, TV and video rental.

Certain benefits may be claimable, such as disability living allowance, and although your parent may be reluctant to apply, thinking of financial aid from, say, the DSS as 'charity', you will have to be persuasive that he or she has a right to receive it. Age Concern* produces an inexpensive booklet, *Your Rights: A Guide to Money Benefits for Older People*, which lists all the welfare benefits to which elderly people are entitled. Also see leaflet FB.2 *Which Benefit* from the DSS, which contains a useful summary of all the social security benefits. The Citizens Advice Bureau, too, can advise on money matters.

Power of attorney?

You might like to think about taking out an Enduring Power of Attorney so that you would be able to manage your parent's financial affairs and property in the event of his or her becoming mentally incapable of doing so. Although a sensible measure, this may be psychologically unacceptable to your parent, who may still feel in full control. However, it may be an acceptable solution, at least for a time, to enter into an arrangement where cheques are signed jointly and your parent does not therefore need to feel so threatened by the idea of being 'taken over'. The deed must be drawn up while your parent still has all his or her faculties and it can be modified, if preferred, to take effect only if and when he or she can no longer cope. You can find out more detailed information from the Public Trust Office, Protection Division*.

Wills

It is also advisable to ensure that your parent has made a will. You may feel reluctant to bring up the subject, but many elderly people feel easier in their minds when a will has been made and they know that their property will be disposed of according to their wishes. Once done, the matter can then be forgotten until the will is needed. See **Chapter 35** for more information.

Getting around

Different cities, authorities and voluntary bodies offer their own individual schemes for elderly people who require help to get about because they are disabled or have no means of transport, so get in touch with an organisation such as Age Concern★ to see what is available in your parent's particular area.

Short distances
- *Door to Door: A Guide to Transport for People with Disabilities* is published by the Department of Transport★ (together with Tripscope – see next page) and covers many forms of transport, including local buses, trains, taxis, cars, etc. For instance, the 40 towns in Britain participating in a shop mobility scheme (wheelchairs on loan in shopping areas) are listed.
- Orange badges are available, giving parking concessions to disabled or blind people or their drivers. Enquire about these at the local social services department (Regional and Island Councils in Scotland, DoE Roads Services Division in Northern Ireland). To qualify for an orange badge the person must fulfil certain criteria which these departments can outline. The badge is given to the *person* rather than the vehicle, so it can be displayed on a friend's car, taxi, etc. if the disabled person is travelling in it. Conditions will vary locally, but these will be explained when the badge is issued.
- RADAR★ has produced *A Guide to British Rail for Disabled People*, which gives information on access to over 500 principal stations; or you could ring Customer Care Service at the stations you want to use.
- Concessions are available for elderly and disabled people on public transport. These vary regionally: local transport authorities will tell you about their schemes. Ask at the information desk of railway stations for details of the Disabled Person's Railcard as well as the Senior Citizen's Railcard, which enables concessionary fares to be purchased.
- Many councils issue concessionary tokens for use on public transport and sometimes these can be used towards the cost

of a local taxi fare. Find out details from your Social Services Department or your County Council public transport information officer. In some areas there are Taxicard schemes for disabled residents – contact your local authority (regional council in Scotland).
- Voluntary car drivers and ambulances run by the social services department are available to take elderly people to lunch clubs, and day care and local doctors' surgeries can usually provide a 'hospital car' for visits to the surgery or hospital.
- Some Age Concern* offices in cities have wheelchairs on loan for a few hours so that an elderly person can be wheeled to the shops if they find walking too difficult.

Longer distances and general information
- The Bus and Coach Council* offers a free booklet, *Getting around by Bus and Coach: A Guide for People with Disabilities*, listing members of the council who hire out special vehicles for disabled people and advising how to get the best from other bus and coach services.
- Motability* can help with leasing or buying a car or electric wheelchair for people receiving the higher rate of the 'mobility' part of the disability living allowance.
- Tripscope* is a nationwide telephone-based travel and transport information service for people with a mobility handicap. It can tell you how to get from A to B, no matter where A and B are, taking into account your disability. It also offers assistance with any aspect of travel in the UK and abroad and can answer any transport-related questions, from wheelchair hire to accessibility of lavatories. It can supply a free information pack explaining the scope of the organisation.
- Autohome* (the Disabled Travellers Motoring Club), the AA*, National Breakdown* and RAC Response* offer special roadside assistance and recovery for disabled motorists.

When one parent dies

A parent left alone by the death of a spouse has certain problems to face – just as a carer trying to cope on his or her own does.

In the case of a widow or widower, the spouse's death has often been the major factor in dictating a change of lifestyle. However, this is a decision which should not be taken hastily and any new long-term arrangements should be carefully organised. Once the funeral and sorting out of legal and financial matters are over, there is often a feeling of flatness or restlessness as well as grief – just the wrong time to move or make radical rearrangements, although a holiday or period of staying with a son or daughter could be a good idea.

The problems may not be the same for widows as for widowers who decide that they want to continue living in the marital home. An elderly woman left alone may find herself worrying about filling in official documents or forms, sorting out household and garden maintenance problems (especially if they require some strength), and all the many tasks that her husband may have been responsible for. It will be necessary to make sure that she can manage the practical tasks around the house and that all the installations are safe. An accident to someone living alone could be that much more serious than with a partner in the house.

If she does not drive, this could be very confining, particularly if she lives in an isolated area. There could be volunteer transport available, or a kindly neighbour willing to offer lifts to the nearest town. It may be possible to organise some volunteer or paid-for gardening help, which would give her a little company as well as keeping everything tidy.

The problems for a man on his own are slightly different. He may not have been used to doing any housework or cooking – and he may not feel like bothering with meals. You may be able to arrange domestic help, either through the social services or privately, which would have the advantage of providing someone to keep a discreet eye on his welfare as well as giving him a helping hand. It is preferable, if you can pop in quite often, not to take over the domestic side of his life entirely as his wife did. You will probably not have time, and the activity will be good for him and give him something to do, especially at first when he is probably feeling very lost. Practical advice on how to organise things may, however, be appreciated.

Help with cooking and planning nutritious meals will be essential for his continuing good health, and a well-filled cupboard of canned and packaged foods will be an invaluable back-up to easily prepared fresh food. He may have a freezer, so he could stock up with a few ready-prepared meals for when he does not want to cook. If he also has a microwave, keeping himself fed should be fairly simple. Remember that the milkman can deliver basic foodstuffs as well as milk – a boon in bad weather or if your parent is ill.

Men *or* women can feel that catering for themselves and eating alone has no pleasure in it, so this is an area which needs watching if a daily regime of biscuits and scrappy snacks is not to take the place of well-balanced meals. If you live at a distance, it may be necessary to enlist the help of a neighbour or home help to keep an eye on things. There may be a lunch club that your parent could go to once or twice a week or a friend nearby who might like to take a turn-and-turn-about lunch every week. Lunch clubs, as well as being provided by social services departments, are often run by voluntary organisations. Age Concern* has its own clubs, sometimes providing transport with provision to take wheelchairs. They can supply a list of all clubs in your parent's area.

Before the situation arises when one parent is left alone, it is a good idea to suggest tactfully activities and interests which are *not* joint ones, so that when the time comes, there is a ready-made group of friends and acquaintances to offer company and something to do. The social life of couples can be very different from that of a single partner; surprisingly, old friends may appear not to want to meet a widow or widower, either because the constant reminder of death depresses them or because they feel that three is an awkward number. For all these reasons individual hobbies and interests are a good investment for the future.

Passing the time at home can sometimes be difficult for someone living alone and the days may hang heavily. Make sure that your parent's radio and television work properly, and that newspapers and magazines are available. Joining the local library if it is not too far away is a must if your parent is not already a member. A neighbour may be able to change books if it is difficult to get there. If your parent has a tape recorder, this is a good way to record letters for distant friends and relatives and many elderly people also enjoy recording their reminiscences. An active elderly parent will probably want to continue gardening and there is a useful leaflet from Help the Aged* on gardening for older people. There is also a guide to gardening equipment for disabled people available from the Disability Information Trust*.

Even if your parent seems fit and well, it is prudent to plan in case of sudden illness. If you can, pack a bag with hospital requirements such as pyjamas or nightdress, dressing gown and slippers, toilet articles and change for the telephone, and put it away. Ask a neighbour to keep it if you live some way away. It could save a great deal of trouble in case of hospital admission.

Being a carer

Whether or not your parent lives with you it is important to be on the alert for health problems. In any case you may have to ensure that physical check-ups – at optician, dentist, chiropodist and so on – take place regularly and that your parent is having an adequate and nutritious diet.

Remember that some symptoms which are often put down simply to 'getting old' are, in fact signs of treatable illness which can be, if not cured, at least alleviated. This applies more if the symptoms appear gradually rather than suddenly; in the latter case, medical advice should be sought immediately.

If symptoms persist, encourage your parent to have a thorough check-up. In some cases a change in personality such as irritability, rudeness and difficult behaviour or extreme withdrawal and gentleness may indicate the onset of illness, particularly if such behaviour is uncharacteristic. Such infections as bad colds or flu can be serious in elderly people and sudden lack of energy or extreme tiredness should be taken seriously. It is better to call the doctor if in doubt, rather than dismissing such manifestations as minor ailments.

Medication

If medication is prescribed, make sure, unobtrusively, that your parent is taking it regularly (and not taking proprietary medicines at the same time) and that he or she can undo bottle caps easily. Discreet inspection of the medicine cabinet may reveal a variety of prescribed and over-the-counter pills and potions, some of them completely out-of-date.

There are various memory aids to help elderly people take their medication at the right time. Ask the pharmacist for more details and see also Medication problems in **Chapter 33**. It is particularly important to ensure the correct and correctly spaced dosage if your parent has been in hospital and has been given new medication with which he or she is unfamiliar.

Incontinence

If your parent is incontinent the problem can be partially alleviated. Help may be available via the social services in the way of laundering bed linen, and a local continence adviser or district nurse can offer practical advice on obtaining a commode, other types of appliance available, incontinence pads and protection of bedding, and so on.

There are also ways of helping to control incontinence and the district nurse or adviser should be able to suggest these. Sensible measures would be to make sure that the lavatory or commode is easily accessible and, while not cutting down on the *amount* of fluid drunk over 24 hours, to offer drinks in the morning rather than before going to bed. Age Concern* produces a comprehensive range of leaflets on incontinence for both men and women. You could also contact the British Association for Continence Care* or the Disabled Living Foundation*.

Alzheimer's disease

Mental problems can be more difficult to deal with than physical ones, but they are now much more widely recognised

*The addresses and phone numbers of organisations marked with an asterisk can be found in the address section at the back of the guide.

WHERE TO GET HOLD OF WHAT
Aids and appliances for people who need them are available from different sources, depending on where you live. For example, you might get grab rails and bath aids from your local social services, incontinence pads and walking frames from the GP via the district nurse and the physiotherapist attached to the practice respectively, and commodes from the British Red Cross* or your health authority. This type of equipment is on show at over 30 centres in the UK – contact the Disabled Living Centres Council* for details. Contact your GP or the social services in the first instance, or telephone the local branch of Age Concern*. See also *Equipment for an Easier Life* (a guide to products and where to get them), available from RICA*.

---

than they used to be and there are many more sources of information and help, such as MIND* (the National Association for Mental Health). Again, **Chapter 33** has more information about dealing with these problems but Alzheimer's disease is a very common problem in elderly people and deserves a special word in this chapter as it is the cause of so much worry and stress to carers.

Although obviously this does not apply to all elderly people who occasionally become muddle-headed and less 'sharp' than they once were, early signs of Alzheimer's disease can be confusion, forgetfulness (not being able to remember the right word, not recognising familiar faces, becoming mixed up over dates or times, for example), wandering off, and having fixed delusions and changes in personality. These pointers, especially if they happen gradually, can alert a carer or relative as to what may be happening and the parent's GP should be contacted so that a diagnosis and specific advice can be obtained, perhaps from a geriatric specialist or psychiatrist.

Symptoms that occur suddenly signal a need for urgent medical attention. If your parent is going to need protracted care, it is important to find out at an early stage what support would be available from the social and medical services and to have a frank discussion with everyone concerned over how much – or how little – care you are in a position to give in these circumstances.

Do your best to simplify life for your parent. Make sure that clothes are easy to put on – trousers and skirts with elasticated waists, sweaters which can be worn either way round and loose dresses. If your parent lives with you, you could lay the clothes out in order ready for putting on each morning. Cut down on the number of pots, pans and crockery in use to avoid confusion, and ensure that medication is easily checked and taken.

If wandering off is a problem, make sure that your parent carries a card with your name, address and telephone number, and a back-up number of someone else for extra reassurance.

If your parent is very confused, he or she may not recognise the difference between night and day and may get up and even dress at any time of the night. Instituting a regular routine during the day with set hours for meals, bathing and going out can provide a framework within which both carer and parent can work – not the least important being regular exercise so that the parent is more likely to be tired and sleep well. Remember that a change – going on holiday, moving house – can cause extra disorientation and confusion in an elderly sufferer, and be ready with extra support if possible.

Alzheimer's disease can, more than almost any other problem for carers, cause immense distress. Not only are the physical manifestations trying and wearing, but the psychological ones too. To see a parent on whom one has relied and whom one loves become a different person, who may not even recognise close members of the family, is enormously upsetting. However, it is essential for carers to protect their emotional state by, first of all, doing everything practical to help the parent, and then accepting that the present condition is brought about by illness and that the *real* affectionate, loving and competent parent is the person they remember before the illness struck. Nevertheless, carers will need all the emotional as well as practical support that can be called upon.

Minimising stress

Not the least of the problems attached to being a carer is the stress it can bring because you yourself may be at a stage where you may have family, health or financial problems. Causes of stress can be very small – irritating mannerisms and reactions in your parent which, repeated on a day-to-day basis drive you mad – or far more serious if your parent is ill or disabled and needs constant physical help and emotional support.

It is most important to try to cut down the stress factors on you and your family in order to avoid possible damage to your own health and disruption of daily life. In some cases, stress can have potentially serious consequences.

Local social services departments

These can be extremely helpful; consider involving them at an early stage. A social worker can be consulted direct, either by phone or in writing, and will be able to advise on a particular problem or point you in the direction of the right person to deal with it. There is usually an emergency service in case of need. Although they will vary from district to district, some of the services on offer for elderly people or those caring for them at home, if people qualify and circumstances warrant it, are:

- **Meals on Wheels** – on a five-day-a-week basis (usually for people who have no one to provide lunch for them and are incapable of getting it for themselves).
- **Home helps** (usually for elderly people living in their own homes).
- **Laundry service** for linen.
- Installation of an **alarm system** – see above.
- **Installation of a telephone** free of charge if it is deemed to be vitally necessary.
- **Aids** to make the home more manageable, such as ramps, rails, bath aids – see page 482.
- Provision of **respite or short-term residential care**.
- **Care attendants**, who can take over from a carer who is looking after someone at home.

Local social service departments (social work departments in Scotland, health and social services boards in Northern Ireland) will provide information on all the services they offer and also about other services in the area which can help elderly people or their carers.

Sitting service schemes
Such schemes may be available, depending on the area, and could be provided by the district health authority, local authority or voluntary organisations, or jointly. Your health visitor or social worker will be able to advise you. Not much help is available for night-time, but a friend or relative might relieve you for the occasional night. Private care might also be a possibility, although this is expensive.

Respite care
All carers should be able to enjoy breaks from the responsibility of caring. Carers need not only annual holidays but regular shorter breaks each week. Respite care for elderly people can provide time for holidays, and voluntary organisations as well as official ones should be able to help on a week-by-week basis.

Holidays
Such organisations as BREAK* are able to provide holidays for people, whatever their degree of disability, although there is a charge; this gives carers the opportunity to take their own holiday. The Holiday Care Service* gives free information on which holidays would best suit elderly or disabled people, according to their needs. It also runs a Holiday Helpers scheme, providing a volunteer helper to accompany the disabled person. Normally you pay for the volunteer's holiday, but if there is difficulty over finance, the Service can suggest possible sources of help.

Local carers' association
There might be a carers' association in your area, probably a branch of the Carers' National Association*, which will provide much support and helpful advice on alleviating strain.

The addresses and phone numbers of organisations marked with an asterisk can be found in the address section at the back of the guide.

Looking ahead

Carers naturally become depressed sometimes and bogged down in the everyday business of caring. They may feel resentful that the rest of the family are not doing enough to help, and see themselves in a situation that can only get worse. Many dread the death or increasing illness of their parent and wonder how they are going to cope.

It cannot be emphasised enough that not only must carers have free time but peace of mind in the knowledge that their parent is being kindly and safely cared for by someone else. The cultivation of a good self-image is important too – after all, giving compassionate care to another human being is a very important job and should be recognised as such.

Sport and exercises can be a great release for a carer under stress, and you might think of joining an adult education class. It is also a good idea to prepare for the time when you will no longer be a carer, either by taking up some form of retraining for work or a leisure activity which will be enjoyable later on.

PART 9

WILLS AND INHERITANCE

CHAPTER 35

MAKING YOUR WILL

Over half the adults in Britain do not bother to make a will. Often people do not want to think about it, and even if they do they don't know where to start. However, it may be very important to make one if you are likely to be adversely affected by the inheritance tax limits or by the 'intestacy' rules (see below).

Throughout this chapter, leaving somebody 'money' includes leaving them particular possessions or property, unless specified otherwise. Similarly, where giving someone 'property' or 'possessions' is mentioned, this includes gifts of money. Note that this Chapter is based on the rules in England and Wales; see page 504 for the main differences in Scotland.

Why should you make a will?

The first purpose of writing a will is to ensure that your possessions go to the people you want. If you do not write a will this may not happen. Instead, your property will be divided among relatives according to the 'intestacy' rules – see Chart 1. However, the wife or husband always gets the personal effects, such as furniture or the car, as well as any money they are entitled to. For how joint property is treated, see page 496.

The Chart shows that if you do not make a will your property will not necessarily go to the people you want. For example, if you are married with children you may well want to leave everything to your spouse. But under current rules, if you personally owned more than £125,000 this would not happen.

THE WHICH? GUIDE TO AN ACTIVE RETIREMENT

Chart 1: Who your money would go to if you died without making a will (in England and Wales)

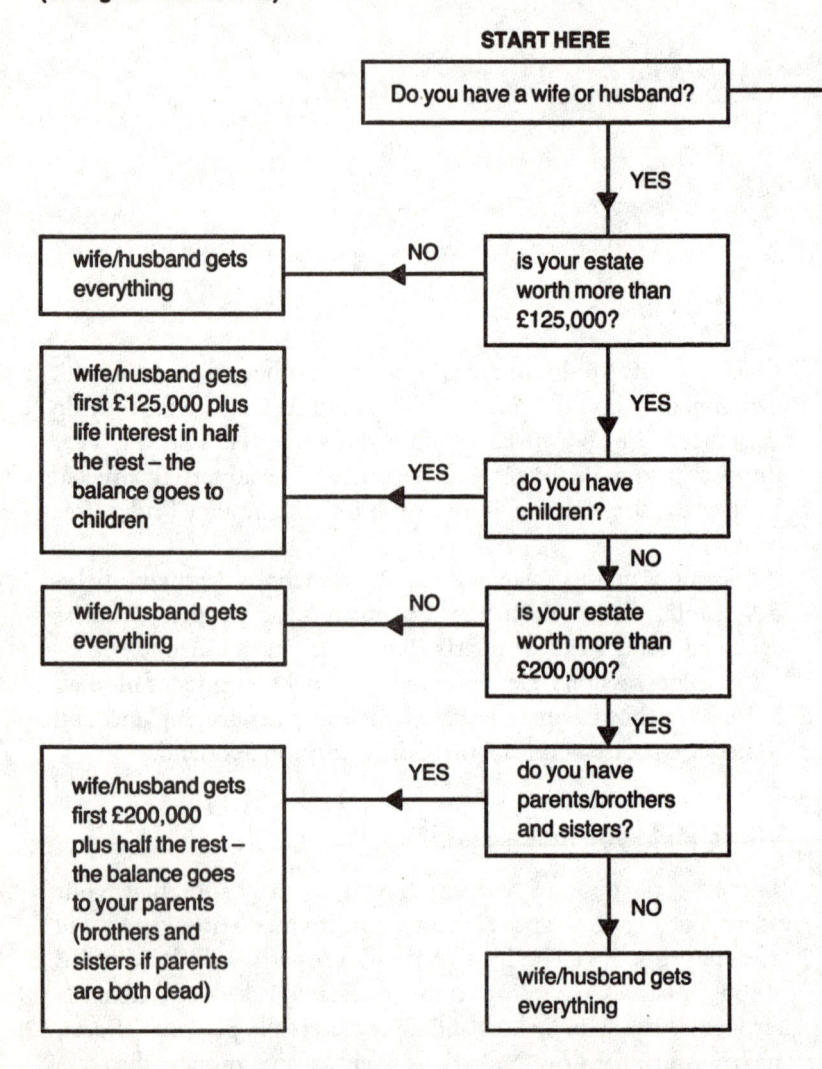

```
                            START HERE
                    ┌──────────────────────────┐
                    │ Do you have a wife or    │
                    │ husband?                 │
                    └──────────────────────────┘
                              │ YES
                              ▼
┌──────────────────┐   NO   ┌──────────────────┐
│ wife/husband gets │◄──────│ is your estate  │
│ everything        │        │ worth more than │
└──────────────────┘        │ £125,000?       │
                            └──────────────────┘
                                     │ YES
                                     ▼
┌──────────────────┐        ┌──────────────────┐
│ wife/husband gets │ YES   │ do you have     │
│ first £125,000   │◄──────│ children?       │
│ plus life interest│       └──────────────────┘
│ in half the rest- │                │ NO
│ the balance goes  │                ▼
│ to children       │        ┌──────────────────┐
└──────────────────┘   NO   │ is your estate  │
┌──────────────────┐◄──────│ worth more than │
│ wife/husband gets │       │ £200,000?       │
│ everything        │       └──────────────────┘
└──────────────────┘                │ YES
                                     ▼
┌──────────────────┐ YES    ┌──────────────────┐
│ wife/husband gets │◄──────│ do you have     │
│ first £200,000    │       │ parents/brothers│
│ plus half the rest│       │ and sisters?    │
│ - the balance     │       └──────────────────┘
│ goes to your      │                │ NO
│ parents (brothers │                ▼
│ and sisters if    │       ┌──────────────────┐
│ parents are both  │       │ wife/husband gets│
│ dead)             │       │ everything       │
└──────────────────┘       └──────────────────┘
```

Notes:

1. Adopted and illegitimate children count as legitimate. Relatives who are descended from the same pair of ancestors as the deceased will inherit before any relative who only shared one common ancestor, e.g. half-brothers and sisters.
2. As a general rule, if a relative who would have inherited dies before you, his or her share is divided equally between his or her children, e.g. if you had a son and a daughter and the son predeceased you, his children – your grandchildren – would inherit his share.

MAKING YOUR WILL

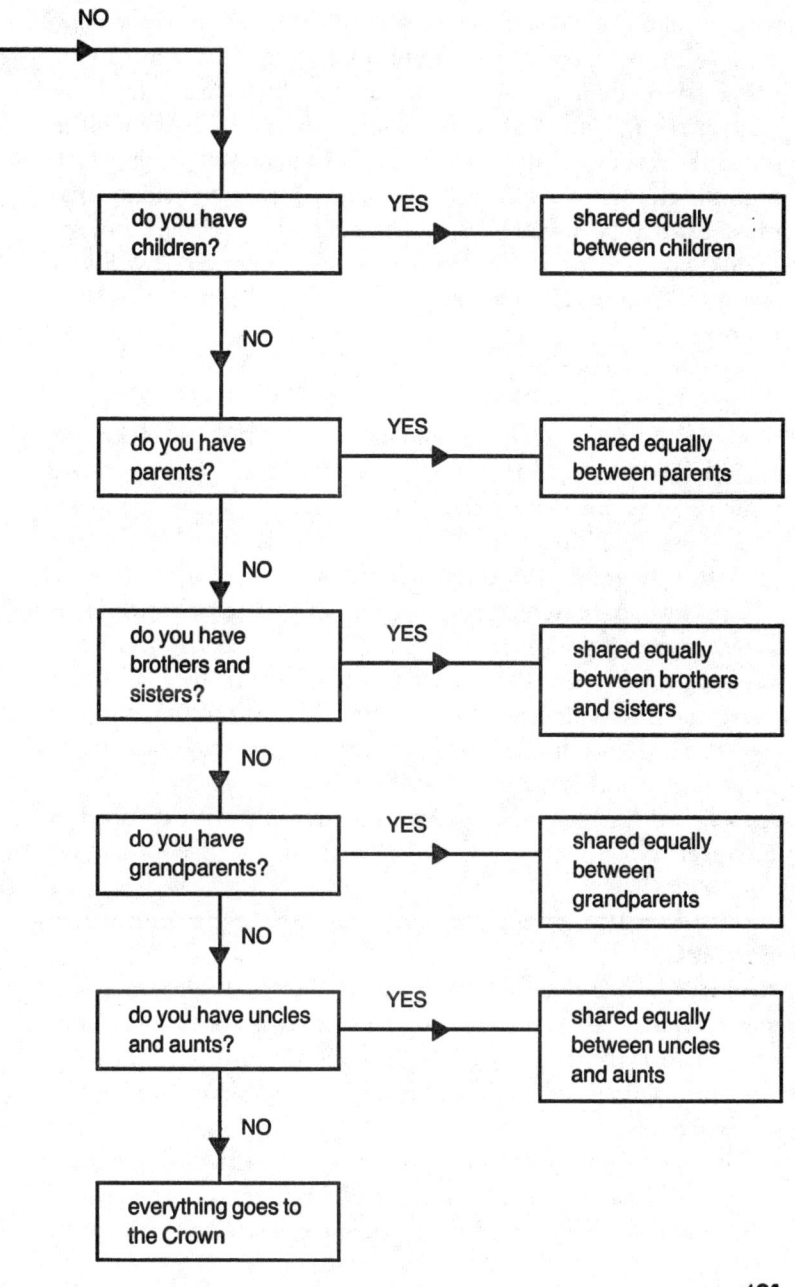

NO →

- **do you have children?** — YES → shared equally between children
- ↓ NO
- **do you have parents?** — YES → shared equally between parents
- ↓ NO
- **do you have brothers and sisters?** — YES → shared equally between brothers and sisters
- ↓ NO
- **do you have grandparents?** — YES → shared equally between grandparents
- ↓ NO
- **do you have uncles and aunts?** — YES → shared equally between uncles and aunts
- ↓ NO
- **everything goes to the Crown**

Instead your property would be divided between your spouse and your children.

A second reason for making a will is that it allows you to specify who you would like to sort out your affairs after your death. This is especially important if you might leave money or property to children under eighteen, in which case it must be held in trust. This means that someone named in the will is given the responsibility of looking after the money or property until the children are old enough to inherit. Money held in trust must usually be invested in a limited range of secure investments, such as British Government stocks, but in your will you can give the trustees freedom to invest in whatever way they choose.

A will provides a suitable opportunity to express wishes about who you would like to act as guardians for your children. You can also say how you would like to be buried, whether you would like to be cremated or whether you would like to donate your body to medicine. These wishes are not legally binding, even if expressed in a will. However, a will is probably the best place to state your views on such matters.

One further reason to make a will is that it may help you avoid paying more inheritance tax than you need. If you leave behind property worth more than £154,000 (in the 1995-6 tax year), the Inland Revenue can take up to 40 per cent of anything over the £154,000 limit. However, certain gifts (including those to your husband or wife) are tax-free. A will can help you make the best of these tax exemptions. Inheritance tax is explained in **Chapter 36**.

EXAMPLE 1

Bridget's husband Tom died aged 62: they had two grown-up sons. Bridget and Tom owned their home in Suffolk as joint tenants so it passed directly to Bridget, as did their joint bank account. Tom also left around £175,000 in shares and other investments.

There was no will so Bridget, with the help of a solicitor, valued the assets in the estate and applied for a grant of administration from the court of probate. With this legal authority she contacted Tom's stockbroker (who held his shares) and the life insurance company and had the assets transferred to her as administrator.

Under the intestacy rules, the first £125,000 of Tom's investments went to Bridget. The remaining £50,000 was divided in two: half was split between the children (£12,500 each) and under the intestacy rules the remaining £25,000 had to be held in trust for Bridget. She has a 'life interest' in this, which means that she can spend the income, but must leave the capital for the children. The inconvenience of setting up a trust and paying money to the children could have been avoided if Tom had written a will.

Who should make your will?

You can have a will written by a solicitor, by a will-writing company, or through a bank. Alternatively, you may be able to do it yourself, if your financial and family affairs are not too complicated.

Writing your own will
You should not write your own will if any of the following apply:

- you have been married more than once
- you want to do more than simply divide your property among your friends or relatives
- you will be providing for someone with a physical or mental disability
- you own a business or a farm
- you want to pass on your home intact to someone other than your spouse
- you were born abroad or are likely to be considered 'domiciled' abroad (i.e. where you have your permanent home and are likely to end your days)
- you are involved with family trusts.

If you are likely to be liable for inheritance tax, you might also benefit from professional advice.

If none of these applies to you, it is a fairly straightforward matter to write your own will. However, you will need some help and advice to do it correctly. Do not just write out your will on a sheet of paper or one of the will forms available from legal stationers. There are a number of technical phrases you will need to know about to make sure that your will makes proper legal sense. Consumers' Association* publishes *Make Your Will*, an action pack which explains what you should do and provides you with the necessary forms, if you live in England or Wales. There are also a number of books available on the subject.

Solicitors

The lowest charge for a simple will from a solicitor will be in the region of £30, including VAT. For most people a will costs around £50 but, if your circumstances require a particularly complicated will it can cost as much as £200.

There is no sure-fire way of picking a good solicitor. Ask your friends if they can recommend one. Alternatively, try contacting a few local solicitors from your phone book. Many are willing to give an introductory interview for free, or to give a rough estimate of how much they expect it will cost to draw up your will.

Legal aid is available for some people aged over 70 or with disabilities, if they have a low income.

Will-writing companies

There are a number of companies which specialise in making wills. They usually charge a fixed fee of around £30. Many specialist will writers have formal legal training and can provide a service as good as going to a solicitor. However, some do not have sufficient legal training. They may know enough to make simple wills, but not enough to recognise when they are out of their depth. In general, if you are not sure where to go, you will be safer going to a solicitor than to a specialist will-writing company.

Banks

Banks can arrange to have your will written, but are probably best avoided. They usually insist on being the executor of the will, for which they charge very high fees.

Witnessing and storing your will

When your will is written it must be witnessed. This means that at least two people must see you sign the will, and then must sign it themselves attesting to the fact that they saw you sign it. They do not have to read the will.

If you leave anything to the people who witness your will or to their spouses, they will not be allowed to accept your bequest, so make sure you do not ask anyone to witness your will to whom you might want to leave something. If you have your will written by a solicitor, the solicitor and a colleague will usually volunteer to witness the will.

Keep your will in an obvious place where people will find it, or tell someone where it is. There are many stories of wills only coming to light months after the estate has been divided up on the assumption that no will existed.

You should review your will regularly. If your circumstances change you may need to write a new one. For example, if you get married your will is automatically revoked and you will need to make a new one.

Revoking and changing your will

Never write anything on your will. Any amendments to a will are assumed to have been made after the will was signed and will therefore be ignored. If you make too many changes to a will it may not be possible to tell what your original intention was, in which case the entire will may be considered invalid.

There are two ways to change a will. You can draft a codicil, which must be witnessed and signed in the same way as a will (though not necessarily using the same witnesses) and then kept with the will. Alternatively, you can start from scratch and write a new will.

A will is usually entirely revoked if:

- you write a new will which includes the standard phrase stating that you revoke all other wills

- you get married
- you destroy the will, with the intention of revoking it, or if someone else destroys it at your instruction and in your presence.

Divorce does not invalidate the entire will; however, all gifts to your ex-spouse, and the appointment of ex-spouse as executor, will be automatically revoked.

Dividing up your property

When deciding who to leave your possessions to, the first thing to work out is how much you own – known legally as your 'estate'. Things to think about are:

- the market value of your home, less outstanding mortgages, and of any other homes or land
- any money, including interest earned, from all sources (the bank, National Savings, building society accounts, other deposits)
- any investments (stocks, shares, unit trusts, PEPs etc.)
- any amounts to be paid out on your life insurance policy, including any bonuses (unless they are written in trust)
- the value of any antiques, jewellery, furniture and other effects
- the value of your car and other possessions, such as caravan, dinghy etc.
- the amounts of any loans you are owed
- the value of any business or farm that you own
- any interests you may have in trusts or settlements (i.e. rights you have to income, capital or property held in trust).

You need to deduct from the total of your money and effects any outstanding loans that you owe (apart from mortgages, which you took into account when assessing the value of your home); also deduct an amount for your funeral expenses. You will then be left with the current value of your estate.

Jointly held assets can be held in two different ways – either as joint tenants, or as tenants in common. In England and Wales it is assumed, in the absence of any other arrangement, that jointly owned property is owned by joint tenants. This means that both owners have an equal interest in the whole property. In the event of one joint owner dying the entire property automatically belongs to the other joint tenant, regardless of any will, and regardless of the intestacy rules. It does not form part of the deceased person's estate for the intestacy rules. (This is particularly confusing as it does form part of the estate when calculating inheritance tax.)

Alternatively, it is possible to own property as tenants in common. This means that each owner owns a share of the property absolutely. They are free to do with this share as they see fit. So, if you and your spouse owned your home as tenants in common, you would each be free to leave your portion of the house to whomever you chose. This can prove useful for reducing your liability to inheritance tax (see page 518). In Scotland, it is assumed that property is owned by tenants in common, rather than joint tenants, in the absence of any other arrangement.

If you wish to switch from owning property as joint tenants to owning property as tenants in common, it is very straightforward. All the owners simply need to sign a declaration to the effect that they own the property as tenants in common, and specifying the shares held by each. It is more complicated to switch from being tenants in common to joint tenants. Consult a solicitor if you need to do this.

Who to leave things to?

You can leave property to people and organisations such as companies, charities, hospitals, schools, universities or political parties. You can leave property to children but it must then be held in trust for them, usually until they reach eighteen. You can also leave money to be held in trust for adults or unborn descendants – for example, you could leave money to be held in trust and paid, say, to your great grandchildren or the first woman to land on the moon. You can even leave money to be held in trust and used for certain purposes – for example, to pay for a party once a year on your birthday. You cannot leave money to pets or other animals, however, and if it is unclear whom you mean the gift to go to, it will be treated as intestate.

You are free to leave your money and property to whomever you like, but under the Inheritance (Provision for Family and Dependants) Act 1975 certain people have the right to challenge your will. Your spouse, your children, any ex-spouses and anyone who was financially dependent on you at the time of your death are entitled to 'reasonable financial provision' from your will and can go to Court if they do not get it. If you do not want to leave anything to the people listed above you should seek advice from a solicitor.

What sorts of gifts can you give?

Legacies/bequests
When specifying a particular possession to be given to someone make sure you use entirely unambiguous phrases. For example, don't leave someone your 'favourite' clock, as it will be impossible to decide for sure which was your favourite. You can make gifts which are unspecific so long as your intention is clear. For example, you could say in your will that certain friends are allowed to come and select items of your jewellery, or choose their favourite picture. But if it is not clear what you intended, the gift will 'fail'. This means that the relevant money or property will go to the residuary beneficiary (see opposite). If the residuary legacy fails it will be treated as if no will had been written (see above). Also make sure that all your legacies and bequests come to less than your estate.

It is normal to make legacies 'free of tax'. This means that all the inheritance tax to be paid will fall on the residuary legacy (see below). If the residuary legacy was not large enough to cover the tax bill, then recipients of any gifts would still have to pay some tax. If you do not make legacies free of tax then, providing your estate is large enough for you to pay inheritance tax, the recipient of the gift will have to pay the necessary tax.

Residuary legacy
You will not be able to know for certain how much your estate will be worth when you die, so you will have to name a bene-

ficiary who is to receive the 'residue' – i.e. everything which is left after all the other legacies have been made. Normally, the residuary legacy is the largest part of the estate. For example, if you are married, it is common to leave a few gifts to relatives and friends, but the residue – your home and most of your wealth – to your spouse.

Gifts for life

Normally, if you leave somebody something in your will, it is an 'absolute' gift. This means they are free to do with the gift as they please. However, it is possible to give somebody a sum of money, or a possession, for them to have only as long as they live, after which the property must go to someone else – known as the 'ultimate beneficiary'. This might happen if, for example, you had children from a first marriage, remarried but had no further children. Your will might leave all your property to your second spouse for his or her lifetime, after which your children would inherit.

If you leave someone money or property for life, trustees (see below) will control the property until the ultimate beneficiary or beneficiaries inherit. If you have left someone a particular possession or your house for life, they will be able to use it until they die. If you have left someone a sum of money for life, the trustees will invest the money, and the lifetime beneficiary will receive the income earned by the investments, but the capital will be passed on to the ultimate beneficiary.

Executors and trustees

Executors

In your will you must specify who is to take charge after your death and make sure that all the wishes expressed in your will are carried out properly. This person is your executor and has the power and the duty to pay off any debts, pay any inheritance tax you owe, and then distribute the remaining property according to your will. If you don't write a will, or if your will doesn't name an executor, your next of kin will usually act as administrator.

You can appoint up to four executors. It's sensible to appoint at least two, in case one cannot act. Someone who is named as executor in a will is free to refuse to take on the responsibility, so make sure that whoever you name is willing to do the job. If more than one person acts as executor they must act together and none can act without the agreement of the others.

You can appoint either friends and relatives or professionals, such as solicitors, as your executors. The safest course of action, wherever possible, is to appoint lay executors, such as friends and relatives. They will be free to hire professional help and can charge the costs to the estate. They can also charge their own expenses to the estate. If you appoint professionals as executor, they will insist on a clause being added to the will allowing them to charge their fees to the estate. (This is because the law does not allow any executor to profit from being an executor, unless the will specifies otherwise.)

If possible, you should appoint the people who will inherit most under your will as your executor. They can then make sure that the cost of sorting out your will is kept to a minimum. However, you should not appoint as executors people who are likely to argue, or who live very far apart and would not be able to work together conveniently.

Trustees
If a trust might arise from your will you will need to appoint trustees. The most common reason for a trust arising is that one of your beneficiaries is under eighteen, in which case the inheritance must be held by trustees until the beneficiary is old enough to inherit. You will also need trustees if you make a gift for life (see above), or if you set up a discretionary trust (see **Chapter 36**). It is usual to name your executors as trustees.

Powers of executors and trustees
The law sets strict limits on what trustees and executors can do but you can extend these powers in your will if you wish. The most common reasons for extending the powers of executors and trustees are as follows.

Appropriation
Normally, where property is being divided between people,

executors have the power to give specific items instead of money only with the beneficiary's consent. However, you can alter your will to allow your executors to do this without the beneficiary's consent.

Investment
The law limits trustees to investing only in very safe, but possibly poorly performing, investments. It is common to alter this and allow trustees to invest in a wider range of investments.

Advancement
If money is held in trust for children, the trustees are allowed to use up to all the income and half the capital to pay for maintenance and education of the child. You can extend this so that all the money can be used for the child's benefit. If money is held in trust for adults you can also give the trustees extra powers.

Problems with wills

At the moment, after someone dies it is extremely difficult to dismiss their professional executors such as solicitors and banks. If you are dissatisfied with the way you are treated by the professional executors or trustees of a friend's or relative's will, for example you feel they are not giving you enough information, there is little you can do except complain. However, if you feel there has been maladministration, fraud or negligence, there are some things you can do – although they may well not solve your problems.

If you are dissatisfied because of the maladministration of a will, complain to the Banking Ombudsman★ (if the executor is a bank), or the Solicitors Complaints Bureau★ (if the executor is a solicitor). If you're not satisfied with the outcome of a complaint to the Solicitors Complaints Bureau, you can take it to the Legal Services Ombudsman★, who will review the Bureau's handling of the complaint.

If an executor or trustee fails to carry out the terms of the will, or loses money through neglect or fraud, consult a solicitor. Although it is expensive, you can go to court to get compensa-

EXAMPLE 2
After Albert's wife died without making a will, Albert decided to get his own will written. He went to a nearby solicitor who wrote his will, leaving everything to be distributed among his three children, Rachel, Cathy and William. When Albert died the solicitor who had written the will took over the work of valuing Albert's estate, applying for probate and dividing the estate. After two months little appeared to have happened so Rachel contacted the solicitor to ask how long it would take to sort out the will. The solicitor said he was still checking the value of all the assets.

Two months later Rachel, Cathy and William had still not heard anything. Rachel called the solicitor a second time. The solicitor said he was waiting for the Inland Revenue to confirm payment of inheritance tax. A month later still nothing had happened so in the end Rachel called the Inland Revenue herself and managed to get the tax agreed within days. In the end it took the solicitor seven months to sort out the £120,000 estate for which he charged a bill of £5,340. Rachel wishes her father had just named her and her brother and sister as executors since they could have carried out the work without delay and without great expense.

---

tion and ask the court to oversee the estate's administration. However, it is hard to prove that someone has been negligent, rather than simply doing a bad job.

If you are unhappy with a bank's charges as executor, there is nothing practical you can do, unless the bank as executor has broken the terms of the will. If you are unhappy with a solicitor's fees, you can ask them to have the bill checked by the Law Society*; if they refuse, contact the Solicitors Complaints Bureau*. Solicitors' clients can ask the Law Society to make a solicitor reduce unreasonable bills. But beneficiaries of wills do not count as clients.

Making a 'lifetime will'

Your will determines who is to sort out your affairs after you have died. So long as you are of 'sound mind' at the time you make a will, it will be valid. However, you may wish to appoint someone to look after your affairs in the event of your becoming unable to do so, through mental incapacity. In England or Wales you can do this by appointing an 'enduring power of attorney', sometimes referred to as a lifetime will. There is no way of doing this in Scotland.

Note that an enduring power of attorney is quite different from a normal power of attorney. A normal power of attorney is used to allow someone to sort out your affairs while, say, you are abroad. It would lapse if you became mentally incapable and unable to appreciate the significance of it. An enduring power of attorney works in the opposite way. It comes into effect only in the event of your becoming mentally unable to conduct your own affairs.

Under normal circumstances, if you become mentally ill and unable to manage your own affairs, the Court of Protection* – an office of the High Court – will either manage your affairs itself or else will appoint someone who volunteers, such as a relative or close friend, to do this. By giving someone an enduring power of attorney you effectively specify whom you want to look after your affairs.

Setting up an enduring power of attorney

You need to complete a legal document, not unlike a will, to give someone an enduring power of attorney. There is a standard wording for doing this – a form is available from the Court of Protection*. The form must be signed by both the 'donor' – the person giving someone power of attorney – and the attorney. The signing of the document must be witnessed by at least one person, who must then also sign the document. Anyone can act as witness though it is best to avoid your or your attorney's spouse.

The person you name as your attorney must be over eighteen when they agree to act and must not be a bankrupt. As with executors of wills, you can name a friend, relative or professional, such as a solicitor, to act as your attorney. If you appoint a solicitor they will charge for their services. If you appoint friends or relatives, they will be able to charge for all reasonable expenses – including the cost of hiring professional help from, say, a solicitor – incurred in administering your affairs.

When the attorney believes that the donor is becoming mentally ill and incapable of looking after his or her own affairs, the 'enduring power' must be registered with the Court of Protection*. There is a small fee for this. The attorney does not have to produce medical evidence that the donor is mentally ill, but the donor and certain relations must be informed that the application for power of attorney has been made. They can then object if necessary.

When the Court of Protection receive the application for enduring power of attorney, they will first wait to see if any objection is made. If so, the court will consider the objection and can refuse the application, if it considers that the donor is not becoming mentally ill, or if it considers that force or undue pressure was used to make the donor give the power in the first place. The Court can also refuse an application on the grounds that the attorney is unsuitable or because the Court has already appointed someone else to look after the donor's affairs.

If the Court accepts the application the power of attorney is registered. From this point, the attorney has powers to do almost anything on the donor's behalf, including completing tax forms, operating bank accounts, buying and selling property and collecting benefits from the Department of Social Security. The donor cannot revoke the power of attorney and the attorney cannot cease to act as attorney without application to the Court of Protection. The attorney must act at all times in the interests of the donor. The Court has the power to inspect the attorney's activities and, if necessary, remove an unfit attorney.

The law in Scotland

In Scotland the law on wills varies in many important respects from the law in England. Below are the main differences.

Joint property

This is almost always held as a tenancy in common rather than as a joint tenancy, so a husband would not automatically inherit the wife's share of jointly owned property. In practice, though, the title deeds usually state that the spouse should inherit the entire home, unless overruled by a will. Similarly, with joint bank accounts, the money is assumed to remain the property of whoever deposited it.

Intestacy

If you are married, your spouse will automatically inherit a proportion of your estate known as 'prior rights'. These are:

- your share of any joint home, up to £110,000 – the remainder is distributed as part of the 'legal rights'. If you have a mortgage on your property your spouse's share of the home will only be the net value of the home – i.e. after deduction of debts. This is the case even if you have a life insurance policy designed to pay off the mortgage on your death
- furnishings, up to £20,000 (this does not include cars or jewellery)
- a cash sum of £30,000, if there are surviving children, or £50,000 if there are none.

The remainder, known as 'legal rights', is divided between your spouse and other relatives according to a complicated formula. Basically, if there are no children your spouse will get at least half the remainder, and if there are children, your spouse will get at least one third of the remainder and at least another third will be divided among the children.

If you leave children but no spouse the estate is divided equally among the children, or among their children if they do not survive you.

If you leave neither a spouse nor children your estate is divided among more distant relatives in the following order:

- parents
- if no surviving parents, brothers and sisters, or, if they do not survive you, their children, your nephews and nieces

- if no brothers and sisters, uncles and aunts, or if they do not survive you, their children (i.e. your cousins)
- if no uncles and aunts, grandparents
- if no grandparents, great uncles and aunts or if they do not survive you, their children.

Witnessing your will

In Scotland, you can write a holograph will, which does not have to be witnessed. A holograph will is one written entirely in your handwriting. Alternatively, you can type out your will and then write, by hand, 'adopted as holograph' at the bottom before signing it. If the validity of a holograph will is challenged it will be assumed to be invalid unless proved otherwise. With a witnessed will, the challenger must prove that a will is not valid.

Provision for family and dependants

The Inheritance (Provision for Family and Dependants) Act 1975 does not apply in Scotland. However, the system of 'legal rights' for spouses and children ensures that your spouse has a right to at least a third of your moveable estate (roughly everything except lands and buildings), as have your children.

Note that you can still effectively disinherit your children if your estate is small enough to fall completely within the limits for the 'prior rights'. If you don't write a will in these circumstances, your spouse will be entitled to all 'prior' rights before distribution of legal rights.

Revocation of wills

In Scotland, marriage does not revoke your will, and divorce does not automatically invalidate gifts to your ex-spouse. If you have a child after you have made your will, it is assumed that you would have wanted to write a will including the child. The child (and only the child) can therefore apply to have the will set aside, in which case the estate will be divided according to the rules of intestacy. In Scotland, a will destroyed at your instruction but not in your presence will be revoked.

CHAPTER 36

INHERITANCE TAX

Inheritance tax is a tax on what you leave when you die – your estate – and on certain gifts you make while you are still alive. The tax is complicated, and avoiding it can be complicated. This chapter sets out to explain the bare essentials. If, as a result of reading this, you think you need to take action, you may be best advised to get professional advice and help, especially where large sums of money are involved. Accountants and solicitors often specialise in estate planning.

Three rules to remember

Anyone who has money, property or other assets to pass on should remember three important rules. The first rule is that you don't have to be a duke to worry about 'death duties' – or inheritance tax, as the modern equivalent is called. The seriously rich usually have accountants and other advisers to make sure they keep their tax bills to a minimum. It is often relatively modest estates which are stung most heavily by inheritance tax. However, there are some straightforward ways of reducing the tax.

Rule number two: using tax-free ways to pass on your wealth will not, in most cases, save *you* a penny in tax. With a few exceptions, any inheritance tax due is paid after you have died. Estate planning – i.e. finding ways to avoid inheritance tax – is a way of saving your heirs tax. It is of no real benefit to you. On the contrary, you actually incur a risk. Estate planning may mean you lose control over your own assets. You could end up a loser in your old age.

The third rule is that the regulations on inheritance tax can be changed – usually in the annual Budget. Some Budgets make few or no changes, but a wholesale reform of the tax cannot be ruled out. This is a hazard which can make any estate planning ineffective. The rules described in this chapter apply to the tax year which runs from 6 April 1995 to 5 April 1996.

WARNING
In trying to avoid one tax, you may be confronted by another. Capital gains tax is a tax on the increase in value of things (less an allowance for inflation) during the time you have owned them. You can be taxed on an increase in value when you dispose of an asset – and disposal includes giving something away.

For example, you may have a holiday cottage which you would like to give to your grandchildren – to help keep down the value of your estate when you die. Before giving it away, check what, if any, capital gains tax you might incur. You might still decide that a small capital gains tax bill now is preferable to a potentially larger inheritance tax bill. Capital gains tax is covered in **Chapter 17**.

How inheritance tax is levied

There are a few types of gift – mainly gifts to companies and some types of trust – on which inheritance tax may be due immediately, though this is payable at only half the rate applying on death. But inheritance tax is most likely to be due only after you have died, on:

- your estate – what you leave when you die
- some gifts you make in the seven years before you die. These may be gifts which are taxable only if you die within seven years of making them (known as 'Potentially Exempt Transfers' or PETs), or gifts which were taxable at the time you made them, on which further tax may be due.

The rate of tax

Some gifts, plus part of what you leave on death, may become chargeable to inheritance tax when you die. This applies to gifts both of cash and of non-cash assets, such as a house. Whether tax is payable depends on the 'running total' of chargeable gifts you have made in the seven years before each gift, or before you die as far as your estate on death is concerned.

There is no tax on the first £154,000 (known as the 'nil-rate band') of the running total of chargeable gifts. Above £154,000, the tax rate on death is 40 per cent. However, tax on gifts you make in the last seven years of your life may be reduced on a sliding scale – see Table 1.

The key word here is chargeable. A distinction needs to be made between what is chargeable but on which no tax need be paid because it falls within the £154,000 band, and what is exempt (tax-free). A range of gifts – or transfers, as the Inland Revenue calls them – which you make while you are alive and part or all of what you leave on your death could be exempt. Transfers which are exempt do not count towards the £154,000 nil-rate band.

Table 1 The sliding scale of tax

Years between gift and death	Tax rate
Up to 3 years	40 per cent
More than 3 years, up to 4 years	32 per cent
More than 4 years, up to 5 years	24 per cent
More than 5 years, up to 6 years	16 per cent
More than 6 years, up to 7 years	8 per cent
More than 7 years	Tax-free

Chargeable – or tax-free?

Gifts you make while you are alive
These may fall into one of three categories:

- transfers which are exempt whenever they are made during your lifetime

- transfers which are chargeable to tax at the time you make the gift
- transfers which will be exempt if you live at least seven years after making them, but otherwise become chargeable – known as potentially exempt transfers.

Tax-free lifetime gifts
Small gifts
In each tax year, you can make any number of gifts with a value of £250 or less to different people. But you cannot claim this exemption for gifts which exceed £250, not even for the first £250's worth.

Gifts out of expenditure
Gifts which form part of your regular expenditure and come out of your income are tax-free so long as they really do come out of your income, not your capital, and don't affect your ability to maintain your normal standard of living. For example, you might pay the regular contributions on a savings plan taken out for your grandchildren.

Wedding gifts
Wedding gifts are tax-free within limits. Each parent of the bride and groom can make gifts worth up to £5,000; grandparents can each make gifts worth up to £2,500; others can make gifts worth up to £1,000.

Gifts within the family
Gifts to your husband or wife are tax-free, unless the spouse receiving the gift is 'domiciled' outside the UK, in which case only the first £55,000 given is tax-free. Your country of domicile is not necessarily where you currently live, but depends on where you have your permanent home and where you are likely to end your days.

Gifts for the maintenance of your ex-spouse are tax-free, as are transfers of property to an ex-spouse under a divorce settlement. Also tax-free are gifts for the maintenance of your or your spouse's children if they are under 18 or still in full-time education or training and gifts to meet the regular needs of old or infirm relatives who cannot support themselves.

INHERITANCE TAX

Yearly exemption
In each tax year you can make other gifts worth up to £3,000 which are not covered by any of the above exemptions. Any unused part of this tax-free £3,000 can be carried forward just one year, but can be used only if the following year's £3,000 exemption is used up first.

Public bodies
A number of gifts to public bodies are tax-free, including: gifts to charity; gifts to many museums, art galleries, universities; gifts to national and local government; gifts to the National Trust and a number of other bodies; gifts of property and possessions of outstanding national interest made to approved non-profit-making bodies; gifts to political parties; gifts of land to a registered housing association; gifts of shares or securities to a trust which holds them for the benefit of employees, if the trustees hold more than half the ordinary shares of the company and have voting control.

Gifts which are partly tax-free
Where tax-free gifts have limits – such as wedding gifts – gifts in excess of the limit do not incur an immediate tax bill. But they will become chargeable if you do not live at least seven years after making them.

Lifetime gifts immediately chargeable to tax
A small number of gifts are immediately chargeable to tax. These are mainly gifts to companies and to discretionary trusts (see page 516).

Where gifts are immediately chargeable, any inheritance tax due depends on what other chargeable gifts you have made in the previous seven years. The first £154,000 worth of chargeable gifts in any seven-year period falls within the nil-rate band, and there is no tax. Tax on gifts in excess of the £154,000 nil-rate band is due at only half the rate on death, i.e. at 20 per cent. But if you die within seven years of making a chargeable gift, extra tax may be due – see below.

The recipient is normally liable to pay any tax on these gifts. But if you agree to pay any tax due – i.e. make a 'net chargeable transfer' – then the tax itself counts as part of the gift and is added to the running total. Example 1 shows how this affects the tax bill.

EXAMPLE 1
Henry has already made chargeable transfers of £154,000 within the last seven years, so any further chargeable transfers will be taxed. He makes another chargeable transfer of £50,000 and agrees to pay the tax due. In this case, he doesn't pay tax of 20 per cent on £50,000. Instead he needs to work out what figure, after deducting tax at 20 per cent, would leave a net (after-tax) gift of £50,000.

To do this, Henry 'grosses up' the £50,000 gift, i.e. divides it by 0.8. He comes up with an answer of £62,500. £62,500 minus £50,000 is £12,500. So the total gift is worth £62,500, tax of 20 per cent on £62,500 is £12,500 and the net gift is £50,000. When it comes to working out Henry's running total for any future chargeable gifts, this gift is worth £62,500.

Lifetime gifts which may be taxed
Any lifetime gift which is not tax-free or immediately chargeable will be exempt if you live for more than seven years; if you die less than seven years after making the gift it will be taxed according to the sliding scale shown in Table 1 (though it won't be taxed if it falls within the £154,000 nil-rate band).

Inheritance tax on death

There is no tax on some transfers when you die including:

- transfers to your husband or wife (up to £55,000 only, if your husband or wife is not domiciled in the UK – see 'Gifts within the family' on page 510)
- transfers to public bodies and charities (see 'Public bodies' on page 511)
- the estate of someone whose death was caused by active military service
- lump sums paid at their discretion by trustees of your

employer's pension scheme or a personal pension plan if you die before reaching retirement age.

On death, two things happen. First tax on any chargeable gifts made in the previous seven years, i.e. PETs and gifts which were chargeable immediately you made them, is worked out. Tax at 40 per cent (or whatever the death rate then applying is), reduced if appropriate by the sliding scale shown in Table 1, is due on them, minus any tax paid at the time of the gift.

An important point to note here is that the tax due on gifts which do become chargeable on your death is determined by the running total of all chargeable gifts in the seven years before the gift is made (including those gifts which become chargeable only on your death). That means that chargeable gifts made up to 14 years before your death could affect the tax bill on gifts made in the seven years before your death.

Secondly, any chargeable gifts, including potentially exempt gifts made in the seven years before death are added to the value of your estate. The £154,000 tax-free slice is then deducted before tax on your estate is calculated.

Planning to avoid the tax

If you want to save your heirs a tax bill, how do you go about doing it?

Make lifetime gifts

Make tax-free gifts, or gifts which are potentially tax-free as soon as you can, if you can afford to do so. If you die between three and seven years after making a potentially tax-free gift, the tax rate will be reduced (see Table 1), and after seven years no tax will be due at all. Even if you die within seven years, there may be no tax on some or all of the potentially tax-free gifts if they fall within the £154,000 nil-rate band.

Use your will

If you are married, there will be no tax if you leave everything to your husband or wife – but when your husband or wife dies,

WARNING
If you don't properly give something away, but continue to benefit from it in some way, you may be making a 'gift with reservation'. This is as good as making no gift at all, as far as inheritance tax goes. Such a gift will still count as being part of your estate when it comes to totting up the value of your estate. For example, if you gave your house away but continued to live in it you would probably be making a gift with reservation – though the Inland Revenue might be persuaded that the gift was without strings attached if you paid a full market rent for it.

---

there may be tax on his or her estate. Rather than leave everything to your husband or wife, you can use your will to make gifts to other members of your family (assuming that leaves enough for the surviving spouse to live on). There will still be no tax to pay if the gifts fall within the £154,000 nil-rate band, and there will be less tax when your husband or wife dies.

Share your wealth with your husband or wife

If one of you has fewer assets than the other, you could try to 'equalise' your wealth. This just means the richer partner giving assets to the poorer. Gifts between husband and wife are normally tax-free, but you can then both 'use your will' as described above. Don't forget that there may be income tax implications, too – see page 238.

Look for gifts which will rise in value

Give away first those assets which are likely to grow fastest in value – that way, any increase in value will be outside your estate and outside the inheritance tax net. One way to put assets outside the inheritance tax net is to put investments 'in trust' for children or grandchildren – see below.

Make use of trusts

Planning to avoid inheritance tax may mean considering the use of trusts – although there are other reasons to use trusts. A trust (which you may also come across as a form of 'settlement') is a legal arrangement which allows you to give away assets to one or more 'beneficiaries' but restrict or direct how and when they can be used.

Trusts come in various forms. Here is an outline of the sorts of trust people mainly use. Anyone who thinks they might benefit from setting up a trust ought to get professional advice on whether a trust makes sense, what the income tax and capital gains tax implications are, and how to set one up.

Interest in possession trusts

With this type of trust, one or more people has a right to the income from the trust's assets, or a right to use the assets, such as a house. One or more people will eventually become the owner of the assets at, say, a specified date, or when a specified event has taken place.

Sometimes, the person with the 'interest in possession', who is entitled to the income from or use of the asset, may be the same as the person with the 'reversionary interest', who is entitled to eventual ownership. For example, you might put a portfolio of shares in trust for each of your grandchildren, allowing them outright ownership when they reach a certain age.

Equally, the different types of beneficiary may be different people. For example, you may put assets in trust, for your spouse to benefit from the income, but for your children to acquire the assets when your spouse dies.

This sort of trust allows you to reduce the value of your estate without passing (immediate) control of the capital to the people who will benefit from the income. A trust like this can also be set up in your will not to avoid inheritance tax but, for example, to allow your husband or wife to be provided for during his or her life while ensuring that your wealth is eventually passed on to your children and grandchildren.

If you make a gift to this type of trust while you are alive, it will be exempt from inheritance tax if you live for seven years after making it. But the trust may have to pay some income and capital gains tax, and the person with an interest in possession will usually be counted as making a 'potentially exempt transfer' when the interest passes to the reversionary beneficiary.

Discretionary trusts
Unlike interest in possession trusts, discretionary trusts allow the trustees to decide who, amongst a number of named or defined beneficiaries, will benefit from the assets in the trust. They allow you to transfer assets while you are alive in order to lower the value of your estate, but maintain flexibility over who will benefit. The potential beneficiaries could be wide, for example your husband or wife, your children, grandchildren, and great-grandchildren.

It is gifts to this sort of trust which are chargeable while you are still alive (see page 511) – except for some special types of discretionary trust, and except for gifts which fall within one of the tax-free exemptions listed on pages 510 and 511 or within the £154,000 nil-rate band (see page 509). Discretionary trusts are liable to a 'periodic tax charge' every ten years. This tax is worked out according to a formula which produces a maximum tax rate of six per cent every ten years. For some people, this is a price worth paying for the benefits of using this type of trust.

Accumulation and maintenance trusts
These are a version of discretionary trust often used to benefit children and grandchildren, while lowering the value of your estate. The trustees can use their discretion to pay out for the maintenance, education or benefit of children who are the beneficiaries. Transfers into this sort of trust are not immediately chargeable to inheritance tax, and will be exempt from the tax once you have lived for seven years after making the gift.

But these trusts are subject to a number of rules:

- At least one of the beneficiaries must be alive when the trust is made. So if you set up the trust in favour of your grandchildren, you must have at least one grandchild living when you make the trust (it doesn't affect the trust if he or

she then dies). You can, of course, name specific beneficiaries rather than a class (e.g. 'my grandchildren') of beneficiaries.
- At least one of the beneficiaries must have a right to at least part of the trust's property by the age of 25.
- The trust must not last more than 25 years, unless all the beneficiaries have at least one grandparent in common.

Trusts through life insurance
The proceeds of a life insurance policy 'written in trust' do not form part of your estate so there will be no inheritance tax to pay. And because the proceeds do not form part of your estate, they can be paid to the beneficiaries of the trust without the need to get probate. Insurance companies can usually arrange for a policy to be written in trust fairly easily.

You can also use a life insurance policy written in trust to pay for an inheritance tax bill. For instance, you could take out a policy written in trust, with the proceeds going to people to whom you have made gifts, so that they will be able to afford a tax bill if you die within seven years of making the gift. Or you could take out a 'whole of life' policy (explained on page 118) to pay any inheritance tax bill on what you leave when you die.

Premiums paid into a life policy written in trust will not count as chargeable gifts if they fall within one of the tax-free gifts on pages 510 and 511 – they may well be classed as coming out of your normal expenditure.

What to do with your home

Some people have few assets in the way of stocks and shares or cash in the bank, but they own a valuable property which would land their estate with an inheritance tax bill. Simply giving your home away to your children while you continue to live in it may not save inheritance tax – see 'Warning' on page 514. But there is another option.

It might make sense for a married couple or other joint owners of a home to become tenants in common rather than joint tenants. Property which is held as a joint tenancy automatically becomes the property of the remaining joint tenant(s) when one joint tenant dies. Tenants in common, however, can choose who inherits their share of a property. (See page 505 for the position in Scotland.)

As tenants in common, a husband and wife could each leave their share of a property to a child or grandchild. Half the house would be passed on when one of you dies, half when the other dies. In this way, both husband and wife could make use of the £154,000 nil-rate band. Without this sort of arrangement, the whole house might pass to the surviving husband or wife. There would be no inheritance tax on the first death, because transfers between husband and wife are exempt. But on the second death, there could be tax if the house were worth more than the £154,000 nil-rate band.

For more on different types of ownership see page 496. But anyone thinking of entering this sort of arrangement should think very carefully about who will inherit half the house when the first one dies. Things can go wrong even in the most amicable of families.

Business and agricultural property and certain share-holdings

Provided you have owned business assets for at least two years before they are transferred (or, possibly, if you owned the assets for less than two years but they replaced other property acquired more than two years before), you will get 100 per cent relief (i.e. there is no tax to pay) on gifts of:

- unincorporated businesses (i.e. if you are a sole trader or a partner in a partnership)
- unquoted shares or loan stock which on their own or with other holdings belonging to you or your husband or wife give a controlling interest
- unquoted shares which on their own or with other holdings belonging to you or your husband or wife give 25 per cent of the voting rights of a company.

Shares on the Unlisted Securities Market count as unquoted. You pay only half the tax on:

- land, buildings, machinery or plant you own used mainly or wholly by a business controlled by you or a partnership to which you belong
- unquoted shares which do not qualify for 100 per cent relief.

The relief is not usually available in respect of businesses dealing in shares or other securities, land or buildings or businesses which make or hold investments.

A similar relief is available for agricultural land or buildings if certain conditions are met. You get 100 per cent relief if you have vacant possession or can get it within 12 months; 50 per cent if the land is tenanted (though for disposals of let farmland after 31 August 1995, the relief is 100 per cent). You must have owned the land for seven years if someone else farmed it, or you must have farmed it yourself for two years.

The point to bear in mind about business property relief and agricultural property relief is that although you may pay less or no tax when you pass on business or agricultural property, this may affect the planning you may need to do for the rest of what you own. But the detailed rules on how these types of relief work can be complicated. Get professional advice if you think they apply to you.

Who pays the tax?

Any tax due on what you leave when you die comes out of your estate. The estate will also pay the tax due (if any) on gifts you make in the seven years before you die if the recipient does not pay it. But the tax is normally due from the person who received the gift. The timing of your gifts can affect the tax bill.

For example, suppose you give £50,000 to each of your four children when they reach their 30th birthdays, an age they all reach in the seven years before you die. For the sake of this example, the only other transfers you make while you are alive are tax-free (such as wedding gifts to your children). Now, the first three children will have no need to worry about a tax bill, because their gift falls within the £154,000 nil-rate band. But the youngest child, who received £50,000 one year before your death, faces a tax bill on the £46,000 of the gift which exceeds the nil-rate band. Tax of 40 per cent of £46,000 comes to £18,400.

To avoid this problem, you could take out life insurance policies, written in trust for the benefit of any of your children who risk a tax bill. Alternatively, you could state in your will that any tax should be paid by your estate – though that will mean less for whoever receives the 'residue' of your estate – what's left after tax and all other gifts.

The pitfalls of estate planning

It is important to reiterate that estate planning will benefit your heirs, not you, and it could lead you into difficulty.

Complicated schemes
Some tax-saving schemes on offer are complicated. They can be too clever for their own good and could be nullified by Inland Revenue rules and rulings. Some may become pointless as a result of subsequent unforeseeable changes in tax legislation. It is usually sensible to get professional help on estate planning, especially where large sums of money are involved.

Off-the-peg schemes
Insurance companies and other providers of financial services sell off-the-peg schemes to save inheritance tax. Before entering one of these arrangements, it is sensible to get a second opinion from someone outside the company selling the scheme. Is it right for you? What are the administrative charges involved? And will it do the trick of saving inheritance tax? The fact that a scheme is on sale from an insurance company does not mean that the Inland Revenue will accept that it saves inheritance tax.

Leaving yourself short
One school of thought says that the coming decades will see a generation of inheritors, as people inherit homes (if nothing else) from home-owning parents and grandparents. But others reject this scenario. Medical science, they say, is allowing people to live longer lives, but people will need all their wealth to pay

for nursing and other services – as well as general living costs. So don't be too hasty in giving away assets you may need to finance extra expenses as you grow older.

Changing family circumstances
There is a danger in devising schemes which rely on the goodwill of children or grandchildren. Even the closest family can find itself falling apart. And even if you remain on good terms with your heirs, there are other pitfalls. If they were to die before you, or to get divorced, you could find that your erstwhile wealth is in the hands of people who do not have your interests at heart.

Saving tax, but incurring other costs
Efforts to avoid inheritance tax may save less money than you would expect if, for instance, you incur a capital gains tax bill instead, or if you are sacrificing investment performance.

Postponing your planning

It is possible for your heirs to do some estate planning after you have died. So, for example, if you were to leave everything to your husband or wife there would be no inheritance tax to pay – and you would not risk giving too much away to other people and leaving your husband or wife short. But this could result in a much larger tax bill when your surviving husband or wife dies. He or she could choose, however, to make transfers of wealth after you have died as if you had made them in your will, in order to make use of the £154,000 nil-rate band. Re-arranging an estate has to be done within two years of death and must have the approval of everyone who is affected. There is also the risk that the rules which allow wills to be 'varied' in this way are changed in future, a proposal floated (but rejected as unworkable) by the Government in 1989.

Addresses

AA Road Safety Unit
Norfolk House, Priestly Road,
Basingstoke, Hants. RG24 9NY
01256 493038

Abbeyfield Society
53 Victoria Street, St Albans,
Herts. AL1 3UW
01707 644845

ACAS (Advisory, Conciliation and
Arbitration Service)
27 Wilton Street,
London SW1X 7AZ
0171-210 3000

Action: Employees in the
Community
8 Stratton Street,
London W1X 5FD
0171-629 2209

Age Concern England
Astral House, 1268 London Road,
London SW16 4ER
0181-679 8000

Alzheimer's Disease Association
Gordon House, 10 Greencoat Place,
London SW1P 1PH
0171-306 0606

Anchor Housing Trust
Anchor House, 269A Banbury
Road, Oxford OX2 7HU
01865 311511

Arthritis and Rheumatism Council
Copeman House, St Mary's Court,
St Mary's Gate, Chesterfield,
Derbys. S41 7TQ
01246 558033

Arts Council
14 Great Peter Street,
London SW1P 3NQ
0171-333 0100

Association of British Insurers
51 Gresham Street,
London EC2V 7HQ
0171-600 3333

Association of Consulting
Actuaries
1 Wardrobe Place,
London EC4V 5AH
0171-248 3163

Association of Independent Tour
Operators (AITO)
133A St Margaret's Road,
Twickenham TW1 1RG
0181-744 9280

Association of Private Client
Investment Managers and
Stockbrokers (APCIMS)
112 Middlesex Street,
London E1 7HY

Association of Relocation Agents
Premier House,
11 Marlborough Place,
Brighton BN1 1UB
0131-558 3060

Association of Temporary and
Interim Executive Services
Federation of Recruitment and
Employment Services,
36-38 Mortimer Street,
London W1N 7RB
0171-323 4300

Autohome (Disabled Travellers
Motoring Club)
202-204 Kettering Road,
Northampton NN1 4HE
01604 232334

BACUP (British Association of
Cancer United Patients)
3 Bath Place, Rivington Street,
London EC2A 3JR
0171-613 2121
0800 181199 (freephone)

USEFUL ADDRESSES

Bank of England
Threadneedle Street,
London EC2R 8AH
0171–601 4540
(0800 616814 for free leaflet on gilts)

Banking Ombudsman
70 Grays Inn Road,
London WC1X 8NB
0171–404 9944

BREAK
20 Hooks Hill Road, Sheringham,
Norfolk NR26 8NL
01263 823170

British Assoc. for Continence Care
The Basement, 2 Doughty Street,
London WC1N 2PH
0171–404 6821

British Association for Counselling
1 Regent Place, Rugby,
Warks. CV21 2PJ
01788 578328 (information line only)

British Association of Removers (BAR)
3 Churchill Court, 58 Station Road,
North Harrow HA2 7SA
0181–861 3331

British Deaf Association
38 Victoria Place,
Carlisle CA1 1HU
01228 48844

British Diabetic Association
10 Queen Anne Street,
London W1M 0BD
0171–323 1531

British Executive Service Overseas
164 Vauxhall Bridge Road,
London SW1V 2RB
0171–630 0644

British Franchise Association
Franchise Chambers,
Thames View, Newtown Road,
Henley-on-Thames,
Oxon. RG9 1HG
01491 578049

British Insurance and Investment Brokers Association
14 Bevis Marks,
London EC3A 7NT
0171–623 9043

British Medical Association
Tavistock Place,
London WC1H 9JP
0171–387 4499

British Red Cross
National Headquarters,
9 Grosvenor Crescent,
London SW1X 7EJ
0171–235 5454

British Venture Capital Association
Essex House, 12–13 Essex Street,
London WC2R 3AA
0171–240 3846

Building Society Choice magazine
Riverside House, Rattlesden, Bury
St Edmunds, Suffolk IP30 0SF
01449 736287

Bus and Coach Council
Sardinia House, 52 Lincoln's Inn
Fields, London WC2A 3LZ
0171–831 7546

Camping and Caravanning Club
Greenfields House, Westwood
Way, Coventry CV4 8JH
01203 694995

Care and Repair
Castle House, Kirtley Drive,
Nottingham NG7 1LD
0115 979 9091

Carers National Association
20–25 Glasshouse Yard,
London EC1A 4JS
0171–490 8818

Charity Recruitment
40 Rosebery Avenue,
London EC1R 4RN
0171–833 0770

Chartered Association of Certified
Accountants
29 Lincoln's Inn Fields,
London WC2A 3EE
0171–242 6855

Chartered Institute of Arbitrators
24 Angel Gate, London EC1V 2RS
0171–837 4483

Chartered Insurance Institute (CII)
20 Aldermanbury,
London EC2B 7HY
0171–606 3835

Chartered Society of Physiotherapy
14 Bedford Row,
London WC1R 4ED
0171–242 1941

Commission for Racial Equality
Elliott House, 10–12 Allington
Street, London SW1E 5EH
0171–828 7022

Companies House

(England and Wales)
Crown Way, Cardiff CF4 3UZ
01222 380801

(Northern Ireland)
Registry of Companies and
Friendly Societies, IDB House,
64 Chichester Street,
Belfast BT1 4JX
01232 234488

(Scotland)
100–102 George Street,
Edinburgh EH2 3DJ
0131–243 4061

Consumers' Association
2 Marylebone Road,
London NW1 4DF
0171–830 6000

Council for the Accreditation of
Correspondence Courses
27 Marylebone Road,
London NW1 5JS
0171–935 5391

Council for the Advancement of
Communication for Deaf People
School of Education, University of
Durham, Durham DH1 1TA
0191–374 3607

Council for Registered Gas
Installers (CORGI)
4 Elmwood, Chineham Business
Park, Crockford Lane,
Basingstoke, Hants. RG24 8WG
01256 707060

Court of Protection
Public Trust Office, Stewart
House, 24 Kingsway,
London WC2B 6JX
0171–269 7000

CRUSE (The National
Organisation for the Widowed and
Their Children – Bereavement
Care)
Cruse House, 126 Sheen Road,
Richmond, Surrey TW9 1UR
0181–940 4818

Dark Horse Venture
Kelton, Woodlands Road,
Liverpool L17 0AN
0151–729 0092

Data Protection Registrar
Water Lane, Wilmslow,
Cheshire SK9 5AF
01625 535777

Department of Environment
2 Marsham Street,
London SW1P 3EB
0171–276 0900

Department of Social Security
Longbenton Central Office
(Overseas Branch),
Benton Park Road, Longbenton,
Newcastle upon Tyne NE98 1YX
0191–213 5000

USEFUL ADDRESSES

Department of Trade and Industry
Ashdown House, Victoria Street,
London SW1 6RB
0171-215 5000

Department of Transport
Mobility Unit, 2 Marsham Street,
London SW1P 3EB
0171-276 0800

Depressives Associated
PO Box 1022, London SE1 7QB
0181-760 0544 (information line only)

Disability Alliance ERA
Universal House,
88-94 Wentworth Street,
London E1 7SA
0171-247 8776

Disability Information Trust
Mary Marlborough Lodge,
Nuffield Orthopaedic Centre,
Headington, Oxford,
Oxon. OX3 7LD
01865 227592

Disabled Living Centres Council
286 Camden Road, London N7 0BJ
0171-700 1707

Disabled Living Foundation
380-384 Harrow Road,
London W9 2HU
0171-289 6111 (telephone first)

DoE Water Service
Northland House,
3 Frederick Street,
Belfast BT1 2NS
01232 244711

Drinkwise
Health Education Authority,
Hamilton House, Mabledon Place,
London WC1H 9TX
0171-383 3833

Driver and Vehicle Licensing
Agency (DVLA)
Swansea SA6 7JL
01792 772151

Elderly Accommodation Counsel
46A Chiswick High Road,
London W4 1SZ
0181-995 8320/742 1182

Employment Agency Standards Offices
(Dept. of Employment)

Exchange House, 60 Exchange
Road, Watford, Herts. WD1 7HH
01923 210706

Cumberland House,
200 Broad Street,
Birmingham B15 1TD
0121-608 9744

City House, New Station Street,
Leeds LS1 4YU
0113 283 6539

En Famille (Overseas)
The Old Stables,
60B Maltravers Street, Arundel,
W. Sussex BN18 9BG
01903 883266

English Tourist Board
Thames Tower, Blacks Road,
London W6 9EL
0181-846 9000

Equal Opportunities Commission
Overseas House, Quay Street,
Manchester M3 3HN
0161-833 9244

Extend
22 Maltings Drive,
Wheathampstead, Herts. AL4 8QJ
01582 832760

Farm Holiday Bureau UK Ltd
National Agricultural Centre,
Stoneleigh Park, Warks. CV8 2LZ
01203 696909

Federation of Recruitment and
Employment Services
36-38 Mortimer Street,
London W1N 7RB
0171-323 4300

Fellowship of Depressives
Anonymous
36 Chestnut Avenue, Beverley,
Humberside HU17 9QU
01482 860619

Gas Consumers Council
Abford House, 15 Wilton Road,
London SW1V 1LT
0171-931 0977

Gîtes de France
178 Piccadilly, London W1V 9DB
0171-493 3480/408 1343

Help the Aged
St James's Walk,
London EC1R 0BE
0171-253 0253

Help the Aged Seniorline
0800 289 404

Hen House
Hawerby Hall, North Thoresby,
Lincs. DN36 5QL
01472 840278

Holiday Care Service
2 Old Bank Chambers,
Station Road, Horley,
Surrey RH6 9HW
01293 774535

IMRO (Investment Management
Regulatory Organisation)
Broadwalk House,
6 Appold Street,
London EC2A 2AA
0171-628 6022

Incorporated Society of Valuers and
Auctioneers (ISVA)
3 Cadogan Gate,
London SW1X 0AS
0171-235 2282

Independent Schools Information
Service
56 Buckingham Gate,
London SW1E 6AG
0171-630 8793

Inland Revenue (Publications
Section)
Somerset House,
London WC2R 1LD
0171-438 6420

Institute of Actuaries
Staple Inn Hall, High Holborn,
London WC1V 7QJ
0171-242 0106

Institute of Advanced Motorists
359-365 Chiswick High Road,
London W4 4HS
0181-994 4403

Institute of Chartered Accountants
in England and Wales
PO Box 433, Chartered
Accountants' Hall, Moorgate Place,
London EC2P 2BJ
0171-920 8100

Institute of Chartered Accountants
in Ireland
Chartered Accountants House,
87-89 Pembroke Road, Dublin 4
00353 1 6680400

Institute of Chartered Accountants
of Scotland
27 Queen Street,
Edinburgh EH2 1LA
0131-225 5673

Institute of Directors
116 Pall Mall, London SW1Y 5ED
0171-839 1233

Institute of Personnel and
Development
IPD House, 35 Camp Road,
London SW19 4UX
0181-946 9100

Institute of Public Loss Assessors
14 Red Lion Street, Chesham,
Bucks. HP5 1HB
01494 782342

USEFUL ADDRESSES

Insurance Brokers Registration Council
15 St Helen's Place,
London EC3A 6DS
0171–588 4387

Insurance Ombudsman Bureau
City Gate One, 135 Park Street,
London SE1 9EA
0171–928 7600

International Rail Centre
Victoria Station,
London SW1V 1JY
0171–834 2345

Interval International Ltd
4 Citadel Place, Tinworth Street,
London SE11 5EG
0171–820 1515

Investment Ombudsman
(contact via IMRO)

Investors Compensation Scheme
Gavrelle House, 2–14 Bunhill Row,
London EC1Y 8RA
0171–628 8820

Law Society
113 Chancery Lane,
London WC2A 1PL
0171–242 1222

Law Society of Northern Ireland
Law Society House,
98 Victoria Street, Belfast BT1 3JZ
01232 231614

Law Society of Scotland
Law Society Hall,
25 Drumsheugh Gardens,
Edinburgh EH3 7YR
0131–226 7411

Legal Services Ombudsman
22 Oxford Court, Oxford Street,
Manchester M2 3WQ
0161–236 9532

Life Insurance Association
Citadel House, Station Approach,
Chorleywood, Rickmansworth,
Herts. WD3 5PF
01923 285333

Local Investment Networking Company Ltd (LINC)
4 Snow Hill, London EC1A 2BS
0171–236 3000

Mail Order Traders Association
100 Old Hall Street,
Liverpool L3 9TD
0151–227 4181

Mediation UK
82A Gloucester Road, Bishopstone,
Bristol BS7 8BN
0117 924 1234

Medical Advisory Service for Travellers Abroad (MASTA)
Keppel Street, London WC1E 7HT
0171–631 4408
0891 224100 (healthline)

Mobility Advice and Vehicle Information Service (MAVIS)
Department of Transport, TRL,
Old Wokingham Road,
Crowthorne, Berks. RG11 6AU
01344 770456

Money Management
Financial Times Magazines,
Greystoke Place, Fetter Lane,
London EC4A 1ND
0171–405 6969

Motability
Gate House, Westgate, The High,
Harlow, Essex CM20 1HR
01279 635666

National Association of Estate Agents (NAEA)
Arbon House, 21 Jury Street,
Warwick, Warks. CV34 4EH
01926 496800

National Association of Goldsmiths
78A Luke Street,
London EC2A 4PU
0171–613 4445

National Association for Mental
Heath (MIND)
Broadway, London E15 4BQ
0181–519 2122

National Association of Volunteer
Bureaux
St Peter's College, College Road,
Saltley, Birmingham B8 3TF
0121–327 0265

National Association of Widows
54–57 Allison Street, Digbeth,
Birmingham B5 5FH
0121–643 8348

National Back Pain Association
16 Elmtree Road,
Teddington TW11 8ST
0181–977 5474

National Extension College
18 Brooklands Avenue,
Cambridge CB2 2HN
01223 316644

National House Building Council
Chiltern Avenue, Amersham,
Bucks. HP6 5AP
01494 434477

National Institute for Adult
Continuing Education
21 De Montfort Street,
Leicester LE1 7GE
0116 255 1451

National Osteoporosis Society
PO Box 10, Radstock,
Bath BA3 3YB
01761 432472

National Retreat Association
Liddon House,
24 South Audley Street,
London W1Y 5DL
0171–493 3534

National Savings
Dept. for National Savings,
Blackpool FY3 9YP
01253 697333
(Recorded messages giving current NS rates)
Helpline 0645 645000

New Homes Marketing Board
82 New Cavendish Street,
London W1M 8AD
0171–580 5588

Northern Ireland Tourist Board
1 St Anne's Court, 59 North Street,
Belfast BT1 1NB
01232 231221

Occupational Pensions Advisory
Service (OPAS)
11 Belgrave Road,
London SW1V 1RB
0171–233 8080

OFFER (Office of Electricity
Regulation)
Hagley House, 83–85 Hagley Road,
Edgbaston, Birmingham B16 8QG
0121–456 2100

Office of Fair Trading
Field House, 15–25 Bream's
Buildings, London EC4A 1PR
0171–242 2858

OFGAS (Office of Gas Supply)
Stockley House, 130 Wilton Road,
London SW1V 1LQ
0171–828 0898

OFTEL (Office of
Telecommunications)
Consumer Representation Section,
Export House, 50 Ludgate Hill,
London EC4M 7JJ
0171–634 8888

OFWAT (Office of Water Services)
Centre City Tower, 7 Hill Street,
Birmingham B5 4UA
0121–625 1300

USEFUL ADDRESSES

Ombudsman for Corporate Estate Agents (OCEA)
Beckett House, 4 Bridge Street,
Salisbury, Wiltshire SP1 2LX
01722 333306

Open College of the Arts
Houndhil, Worsbrough, Barnsley,
S. Yorks. S70 6TU
01226 7303495

Open University
Walton Hall,
Milton Keynes MK7 6AA
01908 274066

Parkinson's Disease Society
22 Upper Woburn Place,
London WC1H 0RA
0171–383 3513

Penfriends Scheme, Prison Reform Trust
2nd Floor, The Old Trading House, 15 Northburgh Street,
London EC1V 0AH
0171–251 5070

Personal Insurance Arbitration Service
Chartered Institute of Arbitrators,
24 Angel Gate, City Road, London EC1V 2RS
0171–837 4483

Personal Investment Authority (PIA)
7th Floor, 1 Canada Square,
Canary Wharf, London E14 5AZ
0171–538 8860

Personal Investment Authority Ombudsman Bureau
Centre Point, 103 New Oxford Street, London WC1A 1QH
0171–240 3838

Pre-Retirement Association
Nodus Centre, University Campus, Guildford,
Surrey GU2 5RX
01483 39323

Proshare Association
Private Investor Services,
PO Box 1, Hastings TN35 4SE
01424 755755

Public Trust Office, Protection Division

(England & Wales)
Stewart House, 24 Kingsway,
London WC2B 6JX
0171–269 7000

(Northern Ireland)
Office of Care and Protection,
Royal Courts of Justice, Chichester Street, Belfast BT1 3JF
01232 235111 (ext. 2348)

(Scotland)
Account of Court, Parliament House, Parliament Square,
Edinburgh EH6 6DT
0131–225 2595

RCI Europe Ltd
Kettering Parkway, Kettering,
Northants. NN15 6EY
01536 310101

REACH
Bear Wharf, 27 Bankside,
London SE1 9DP
0171–928 0452

Reaction Trust
Clerkenwell Green, St James Walk,
London EC1R 0BE
0171–336 7477

Registrar of Pension Schemes
Occupational Pensions Board,
PO Box 1NN,
Newcastle upon Tyne NE99 1NN
0191–225 6393

Relate
National Headquarters, Herbert Gray College, Little Church Street,
Rugby, Warks. CV21 3AP
01788 573241

Retired and Senior Volunteer
Programme
237 Pentonville Road,
London N1 9NJ
0171–278 6601

Retirement Pensions Forecast and
Advice Service
Room 37D, Central Office, Benton
Park Road, Longbenton,
Newcastle upon Tyne NE98 1YX
0191–213 5000

Revenue Adjudicator's Office
3rd Floor, Haymarket House,
28 Haymarket, London SW1Y 4SP
0171–930 2292

Riba Publications Limited
66 Portland Place,
London W1N 4AD
0171–580 5533

RICA
2 Marylebone Road,
London NW1 4DF
0171–830 6000

Royal Association for Disability
and Rehabilitation (RADAR)
12 City Forum, 250 City Road,
London EC1V 8AF
0171–250 3222

Royal Institution of Chartered
Surveyors (RICS)
Information Centre, Surveyor
Court, Westwood Way,
Coventry CV4 8JE
01203 694757

Royal National Institute for the
Blind (RNIB)
224–228 Great Portland Street,
London W1N 6AA
0171–388 1266

Royal National Institute for Deaf
People (RNID)
105 Gower Street,
London WC1E 6AH
0171–387 8033

Rural Development Commission
Dacre House, 19 Dacre Street,
London SW1H 0DH
0171–276 6969

Securities and Investments Board
(SIB)
Gavrelle House, 2–14 Bunhill Row,
London EC1Y 8RA
0171–638 1240

Scottish Corps of Retired
Executives (SCORE)
c/o Peter Lewis, Scottish Business
in the Community, Romano
House, 43 Station Road,
Edinburgh EH12 7AF
0131–334 9876

Scottish Tourist Board
23 Ravelston Terrace,
Edinburgh EH4 3EU
0131–332 2433

SFA (Securities and Futures
Authority)
The Cotton Centre, Cottons Lane,
London SE1 2QB
0171–378 9000

Sheltered Housing Services Ltd
8–9 Abbey Parade, North Circular
Road, London W5 1EE
0181–997 9313

Society of Chiropodists and
Podiatrists
53 Welbeck Street,
London W1M 7HE
0171–486 3381

Society of Pension Consultants
Ludgate House, Ludgate Circus,
London EC4A 2AB
0171–353 1688

Solicitors Complaints Bureau
Victoria Court, 8 Dormer Place,
Leamington Spa,
Warks. CV32 5AE
01926 820082

USEFUL ADDRESSES

Sports Council
16 Upper Woburn Place,
London WC1H 0QP
0171–388 1277

Stroke Association
CHSA House, 123–127 Whitecross Street, London EC1Y 8JJ
0171–490 7999

Summer Academy
School of Continuing Education,
The University,
Canterbury CT2 7NX
01227 470402

Third Age Network
Friary Mews, 28 Commercial Road, Guildford, Surrey GU1 4SU
01483 440582

Timeshare Council
23 Buckingham Gate,
London SW1E 6LB
0171–821 8845

Tripscope
The Courtyard, Evelyn Road,
London W4 5JL
0181–994 9294

University of the Third Age (U3A)
1 Stockwell Green,
London SW9 9JF
0171–737 2541

Welsh Tourist Board
2 Fitzalan Road, Cardiff CF2 1UY
01222 499909

Workers Educational Association (WEA)
Temple House, 17 Victoria Park Square, London E2 9PB
0181–983 1515

Writers News Ltd
PO Box 4, Nairn IV12 4AU
01667 54441

INDEX

accidental falls 314–15, 444, 445
accountants 143, 190, 234
actuaries 88, 143
age spots 462–3
air travel 362–3
Alzheimer's disease 439–40, 481–3
anaemia 439, 444
angina 429–30
annuities 91–2, 140, 205–6
anxiety states 430
arteriosclerosis 430–1
arthritis 404, 432, 456–7, 462

back pain 404, 431–2
banks
  charges 22, 68
  interest rates 126–9
  investment accounts 121–8
  investment advice 142–4
  overdrafts 68
  and wills 493, 494–5, 501–2
bereavement 432–3
blindness 433–4
borrowing
  0 per cent finance 68
  credit cards 22, 68
  credit insurance 25, 27
  dealing with creditors 68–9
  fixed-term loans 68
  loans secured on your home 68
  overdrafts 68
  see also mortgages
British Government stocks (gilts) 122, 131, 132, 133, 136–7, 140–1
broker bonds 135
bronchitis 434–5
building societies
  Building Society Monthly Income Accounts 139
  interest rates 128, 129
  investment accounts 123, 126–8
  investment advice 142, 145
  Permanent Interest-Bearing Shares (PIBS) 137
bus travel 364, 477
business, starting your own
  accounting year 228–9
  bank accounts 186
  business licences 186
  business name 183
  Business Start-Up Scheme 188–9
  confidential data 187–8
  employees 231–2
  franchises 180–2
  guarantees and security 189–90
  insurance cover 187
  keeping records 185–6
  limited companies 180, 181, 182, 232–3, 234
  National Insurance contributions 38, 183–4
  partnerships 180, 181, 182, 224, 230–1, 233
  raising finance 188–90
  sole traders 179, 180, 181, 182
  sources of advice 190
  taxation 185–6, 223, 224–6
  Value Added Tax (VAT) 184–5, 186
  who should know 191
  working from home 191–2, 226
buying goods
  credit notes 342
  defective/unsuitable goods 338–42
  delayed delivery 344
  gifts 342
  good causing injury 343
  mail order goods 343–4
  private sales 340
  retailer's responsibility 342–3
  Sale of Goods Act 338, 339, 340, 341, 342, 343
  sale items 340, 342
buying and selling a property
  bridging loans 293
  change of address, notifying 294–7
  conveyancing 281–2
  estate agents 276–8, 279, 283–6
  flats 268–9, 276, 280–1
  gazumping 281
  house hunting 276–8
  house-buying chain 293–4
  making/accepting an offer 279, 281, 286
  mortgages *see* mortgages
  moving abroad 292
  moving to a new area 267–8, 278
  relocation agents 278
  removal arrangements 290–2
  in Scotland 287
  selling privately 285–6
  services, dealing with 294–6
  sheltered housing 270–1, 469–70
  stamp duty 279
  surveys 279–81

INDEX

calluses 445–6
cancer 435–6, 463
capital gains tax
   calculating 236–7
   on gifts 245, 508
   on the home 250–2
   indexation allowance 241
   on investments 235, 238, 239–40, 241, 242, 243, 244–5
   payment 243
   rate 242
   rented property 251–2
   tax-free gains 236–7
cars
   buying new/second-hand 355–7
   depreciation 354
   features 357–8
   insurance 44, 354–5
   ownership 46, 353
   reliability 355
   running costs 46, 354
cataracts 444
charitable gifts 206, 224
Citizens Advice Bureaux (CABx) 68–9, 143
coach travel 364, 477
cold weather payments 66
colds and flu 436–7
community care 423–5
community health services
   care attendants 414, 484
   chiropodists 413–14, 445–6
   community psychiatric nurses 413
   dentists 415–16
   dietitians 415
   district nurses 412
   GP practices 409–12
   health visitors 413
   occupational therapists 414
   opticians 416–17
   Patient's Charter 420
   pharmacists 418
   physiotherapists 414–15
   prescriptions 66, 418
   specialist nurses 414
   speech therapists 415
constipation 437
corns 445
coronary heart disease (CHD) 403
corporation tax 232–3
Council Tax Benefit 66
council tenants 269–70
covenants 206

deafness 437–8
debt 68–9

dementia 427, 438–40
dental problems 440–1
dentists 415–16
Department of Social Security (DSS)
   information for those on law incomes 67
   notification of retirement date 202
   pension forecasts and advice 20, 40, 41
depression 441
diabetes 441–2, 453
divorce/separation
   maintenance payments 207, 213
   and pension rights 87–8, 108
   tax allowances 213, 214
driving
   assessing your abilities 361
   disabled drivers 476–7
   driving licence 359
   fitness to drive 359–60
   orange badge scheme 360, 476
   road safety 360–1
   sensible driving 361
   see also cars

early retirement
   on health grounds 25
   pensions and 24–5
   redundancy 25–7
educational courses 379–82
elderly parents
   adapting houses for 468–9
   aids and appliances 482, 484–5
   Alzheimer's disease 438–40, 481–3
   caring for 466, 480–6
   death of a spouse 478–9
   eligibility for benefits 475
   financial affairs 474–5
   health problems 480–3
   holidays 485
   home income plans 59–60, 250, 468
   home reversion schemes 59–60, 468
   incontinence 451–2, 481
   living alone 478–80
   living with 468–9
   local services 484–5
   medication 481
   power of attorney 475
   residential and nursing homes 49–50, 64–5, 66, 471–2
   respite care 484–5
   safety in the home 472–4
   security in the home 473–4
   sheltered housing 270–1, 469–70
   sitting service schemes 485

533

social alarms 311, 473–4
staying in their own home 467–8
transport schemes/services 476–7
wills 475
electrical appliances 315
emotional implications of retirement 22
emphysema 442–3
employer pension schemes
Additional Voluntary Contributions (AVCs) 21, 83–4, 85
average pay schemes 73–4
boosting 21, 57–8, 83–4
contracting out of SERPS through 78–81
contributions 81–2
death after retirement 114–15
death before retirement 111, 114
dependants' benefits 70, 76, 111, 112–13, 114–17
divorce and pension rights 87–8
early leavers 16, 83
early retirement, ill health and 25, 82
early retirement, voluntary 26–7, 82–3
equal treatment of men and women 82
final pay schemes 71–2, 78–9, 82–3
flat rate schemes 74
forecasts 20, 88
free-standing AVC (FSAVC) schemes 20, 21, 84–5
Guaranteed Minimum Pension (GMP) 78–9
hybrid schemes 73, 74
Inland Revenue limits 14, 24–5, 76–8, 81–2, 83–5, 114–15
life insurance 117, 118
lump sum payments 75–6, 77, 111–14
money purchase schemes 72–3, 79–80, 82–3
non-contributory 81
pension age 24–5, 82–3
revalued average earnings schemes 73–4
risks 85–6
salary grade schemes 74
tax advantages 70
tax relief on contributions 224, 227
taxation 199–201
transferring 83, 162
working in retirement 58, 82, 159–62

exercise
benefits 400–6, 426–7
for fitness 400–2
getting started 405–6
levels of activity 407
types of activities 408
expenditure
health-related 47–50
house and car insurance 44
household expenses 45
income and expenditure: Calculator 52–6
life insurance 44
reducing 22
travel 46–7
work-related 42–3
eye problems 443–4
eye tests 66, 443–4

financial advice
best advice rule 153
best execution rules 152
commission and fees 155
compensation scheme 154
complaints 152–3
conduct of business rules 150–2
cooling-off period 152
Financial Services Act protection 142, 143, 145, 149–52, 154
getting the best from 153–6
independent advice 150
know the customer rule 154
portfolio management 144
regulatory bodies 106, 108, 149–50
sources of 142–8
financial publications and telephone services 146
fitness
stamina 401–2
staying mentally active 427
staying physically active 426–7
strength and endurance 402
suppleness 402
see also exercise
foot problems 445–6
friendly societies 122, 138
funeral costs 66

gilts *see* British Government stocks
glaucoma 444
gout 446
GP practices
choosing 410–11
newly registered patients 412
services 409–10, 412

INDEX

grandparents 383
guaranteed income bonds 139–40

hair loss 447
health *see* community services;
    exercise; health insurance; health
    problems; healthy eating;
    hospital, going into
health insurance
  exclusions 422
  extent of cover 420
  long-term care insurance 50
  tax relief on premiums 48, 204–5, 207
health problems
  ageing process 426–7
  lifestyle factors 428
  preventive measures 427–8
  seeking medical help 428
  see also specific problems
healthy eating
  catering for one 395
  cholesterol levels 392
  convenience foods 399
  cooking skills and equipment 396
  fats 391–2
  fibre intake 390–1
  fluid and alcohol 398
  food groups 388–90
  food labels 398
  food storage and preparation 399
  key factors 387
  salt intake 393
  storecupboard foods 395–6
  sugar 392–3
  vitamins 396–7
  weight control 394
hearing aids 437–8
heart attacks 403, 447–8, 449
heart irregularity 444
Help the Aged gifted housing scheme 267, 467–8
hernias 448–9
high blood pressure 403, 449
high-interest cheque accounts 127
holidays
  complaints 374–5
  credit cards and travellers' cheques 371
  crime and security 370–1
  expenditure 47
  health advice 373–4
  insurance 371–2
  special deals 366
  timeshares 368–70
  travelling alone 365

varieties of 365–70
home
  adapting 266–7, 468–9
  assessing present home 265
  building work 344–6
  insurance *see* house insurance
  letting rooms 58, 63, 248, 251–2
  letting the house 248–9, 251–2
  loans secured on 68
  mortgages *see* mortgages
  moving 58, 267–71
  moving abroad 271–2
  renting 287–9
  sheltered housing 270–1, 470–1
  staying put 265–7
  taxation and 244–52, 517–18
  working from 43, 191–2, 252
  see also buying and selling a
    property; safety in the home;
    security in the home
home helps 485
home income plans 59–60, 250, 468
home reversion scheme 59–60, 468
hormone replacement therapy 455
hospital cash plans 48
hospital, going into
  effect on income support 65–6
  effect on pensions 48, 419–20
  NHS treatment 421, 423
  Patient's Charter 420
  private treatment 420–1, 422–3
  transport needs 418–19, 476–7
  waiting lists 420–1
house insurance
  all-risks insurance 301
  amount of cover 298–300
  buildings 300, 301
  claims 304–6
  complaints 306
  contents 301–2
  discounts 44, 305
  exclusions 304
  extent of cover 300–4
  indemnity cover 299
  new-for-old 299
  valuations 299–300
  while moving house 302
housing benefit 66
hypertension 449
hypothermia 450

income
  boosting 57–61
  effect of inflation 16–17, 33–4
  of the elderly retired 31–2
  and expenditure: Calculator 52–6

535

help for those on low incomes 60–7
for income support purposes 63–4
sources 31
of those retired now 31–2
income bonds 139–40
income support 60–7
income tax
  allowances 207–14
  basics of 195–6
  calculating 196–8
  Pay-As-You-Earn (PAYE) 195, 199, 200, 201, 202, 215, 216–19, 223, 224, 232, 233
  payment 199
  on pensions 199–201
  rates 196, 198
  reducing your tax bill 204–13
  on redundancy payments 202
  on savings and investments 120–2, 125, 126, 128, 129, 130, 131–3, 134–5, 136–8, 139–41
  tax codes 202, 216–18
incontinence 451–2, 481
Independent Financial Advisers (IFAs) 145–6
indigestion 452
inflation 16–17, 33–5, 60
inheritance tax
  business and agricultural property 518–19
  chargeable gifts 508, 509–12, 513
  on death 512–13
  estate planning 507–8, 520–1
  and the home 517–18
  interest on loans to pay 206
  persons who pays 519–20
  rates 509
  reducing liability 492, 507–8, 513–18
  tax-free gifts 509–11, 512–13
Inland Revenue
  appeals 262
  correspondence with 258–61
  general enquiries 254
  Notice of Assessment 258
  notice of coding 216–18, 256–7
  notification of retirement date 202
  tax claims 256
  tax collection 254
  tax offices 253–4
  tax overpaid/underpaid 258–61
  tax rebates 259.
  tax returns 255–6
  taxpayer's charter 254–5
insomnia 452–3
instant access accounts 126

insurance
  business 187
  car 44, 354–5
  credit insurance 25, 27
  health 48, 205, 207, 420, 422
  holiday 371–2
  hospital cash plans 48
  house *see* house insurance
  Insurance Premium Tax 303
  life *see* life insurance
  long term care insurance 50
  removals 292, 297
  when working from home 192
insurance brokers and advisers 146
insurance companies
  annuities 140
  financial advice 146–7
  guaranteed income bonds 139
investment managers 147
investment trusts 123, 131–2, 133–4, 135
investments
  after retirement 122–3
  balanced portfolio 123
  before retirement 121–2
  British Government stocks 122, 123, 132–3, 136–7, 140–1
  chance of capital gain or loss 120, 130–5
  commission and charges 135
  compensation schemes 108, 125, 153
  Enterprise Investment Scheme (EIS) 133, 134, 238
  fixed interest schemes 129–30
  guidelines 120, 123–5
  income-producers 123, 139–40
  index-linked investments 119, 122, 140–1
  joint holdings 238
  long-term savings plans 137–8
  main types 119, 126–41
  professional portfolio management 144, 148
  regulatory bodies 149–50
  selling 125
  tax credits 121, 204, 237
  tax-free 121, 122, 201–2, 203, 235, 236–7, 238–40
  taxation of income 120–1, 125, 126, 132–3, 199–201, 235–45
  variable interest schemes 126–8
  Venture Capital Trusts (VTCs) 133, 134

Jobseeker's Allowance 28

INDEX

leg ulcers 453–4, 465, 466
leisure
    crafts and handiwork 378
    educational courses 379–82
    foreign languages 378
    higher spending on 47
    literary interests 379
    music 377–8
    new activities 378–9
    planning for 376–7
    voluntary work 166, 382–3
life insurance
    choosing 18, 117
    employer pension schemes 111, 115, 117
    endowment policies 117, 239
    family income benefit insurance 117
    friendly society policies 137, 138, 239
    regular-premium policies 239
    savings plans 122, 137–8
    single premium insurance bonds 123, 131, 134–5, 140, 239
    taxation and 138, 239
    term insurance 117, 118
    unit-linked policies 103–5, 138
    whole life insurance 118
    with-profits policies 138, 239
local council services
    dog mess 347
    litter control 347
    uneven pavements 348–9

macular degeneration 444
Meals on Wheels 484
medication problems 454–5
menopause 455–6
mortgages
    endowment mortgages 21–2, 273–4
    fixed/variable rates 275
    home income plans 59–60, 250, 468
    interest-only mortgage 275
    MIRAS system 205, 247
    more than one home 251
    mortgage certificate 275
    mortgage interest relief 21, 205, 213, 246–7, 248–9
    paying off 21–2, 246, 247, 248
    pension mortgage 274
    repayment mortgage 273–4
    types 273–4
    valuations 279–80

National Health Service (NHS) *see* community health services;
    hospitals, going into
National Insurance contributions
    contribution types 38
    credits 28, 38–9
    Home Responsibilities Protection (HRP) 39
    National Insurance rebate 79, 94–6
    reduced-rate 38
    self-employed 38, 183–4
    and state basic pension 36, 37
    voluntary 38
    working in retirement 160
National Savings Capital Bonds 129–30
National Savings Certificates 123, 129, 140–1
National Savings FIRST Option Bond 130
National Savings Income Bonds 139
National Savings Ordinary and Investment Accounts 128–9
National Savings Pensioners Guaranteed Income Bonds 129, 139
National Savings Stock Register 137
Neighbourhood Watch schemes 313
neighbours
    access for repair work 337
    boundaries 333–7
    nuisance 331–3
    overhanging branches 334–5
    ownership of fences 337
    repairs to a neighbour's fence 337
    right to light 335–6
    tree roots 335, 336
    trespass 333–4
notice accounts 127
nursing homes 49–50, 64–5, 66, 471–2

obesity 456
Occupational Pension Advisory Service 20, 145
opticians 416–17
osteoarthritis 431–2, 456–7, 462
osteoporosis 404, 444, 457–8
overseas
    moving 271–2, 292
    pensions 201, 272
    taxation 272

Parkinson's disease 439, 458–9
Pay-As-You-Earn (PAYE)
    on benefits 219–21
    changing jobs 218
    codes 215–18, 256–7
    on expenses 222–3

income from several sources 218
new employee 218
pensions and 199–201
sick pay 219
temporary or casual work 219
pensions
  adequacy of 14
  divorce and 87–8, 108
  forecasts 20, 35, 41
  from abroad 201
  living abroad 272
  pension age 24
  regulatory bodies 86
  taxation 199–201
  see also employer pension schemes; personal pension plans; state retirement pension
peptic ulcers 459
Permanent Interest-Bearing Shares (PIBS) 137
personal allowances
  additional personal allowance 209, 210–12
  age-related 208, 209–11
  basic 207–8, 209
  blind person's allowance 208
  claiming 209
  divorce/separation and 213, 214
  married couple's allowance 208, 209, 210–12, 213–14
  special personal allowance 211
  widow's bereavement allowance 208, 209, 213–14
Personal Equity Plans 122, 133–4, 275
personal pension plans
  annuity rates 90–1, 92, 93, 108
  benefit statement 20, 107
  bonuses 103–4
  boosting 21, 101
  carry back rule 98, 102
  carry forward rules 101–2
  cash or deposit funds 21, 105
  charges 101, 106, 107
  choosing 91–2, 106
  contracting out of SERPS 78, 80–1, 94–6
  contributions 96–9
  death after retirement 116–17
  death before retirement 111–14
  deferring 108, 161–2
  dependants' benefits 115–17
  divorce and pension rights 108
  early leavers 101
  early retirement 24–5, 90–2, 100, 101
  early retirement, ill health and 25, 99

employer contributions 97
flat-rate pension 91
how much pension 90–1
Inland Revenue limits 93, 96–8
investment choices 103–5
life insurance 116, 117–18
lump sum contribution plans 96
lump sum payments 93, 116, 117
new-style plans 93, 96–8, 99, 108, 116
old-style plans 93, 96–8, 99, 108, 116
open market option 91, 108
pension age 24, 99
plan performance 15–16, 20–1
plan providers 106, 108
risks 106–8
for the self-employed 89, 98
tax advantages 89, 93
tax relief on contributions 98, 224
taxation of 199–200, 201
transferring 101
unit-linked basis 105, 107
with-profits basis 103–4
women 91, 95–6
working in retirement 58, 159–60
pneumonia 459–60
postal-only accounts 126
pre-retirement courses 19, 22–3
presbyopia 443–4
prescriptions 66, 418
property: income from letting 204, 249–50
prostate enlargement 451, 460
public transport 46–7

rail travel 46–7, 363–4, 476–7
redundancy
  compulsory 25–6
  defined 25
  employee rights 26, 176
  negotiating terms 27
  pay in lieu of notice 202
  statutory redundancy pay 26, 202
  taxation of redundancy payments 201–2
  unfair dismissal 27, 176–7
  voluntary 26–7
Registrar of Pension Schemes 20
regular savings accounts 127
removals
  choosing a firm 290
  complaints 292
  insurance 292
  moving abroad 292

INDEX

rented accommodation
  eviction 289
  rent 288–9
  tenancy agreements 288–9
residential homes 49–50, 64–5, 66, 471–2
respiratory diseases 403
Retail Prices Index 33, 241–2
retirement age 13
rheumatoid arthritis 461

safety in the home
  elderly parents 472–4
  electric blankets 317
  electrical safety 315
  fire extinguishers 316–17
  fire safety 316–17
  gas safety 315
  heaters and fires 316
  preventing falls 314–15, 445
  smoke alarms 316
security in the home
  awareness 307, 312–13
  burglar alarms 310–11
  exterior lighting 312
  fire security 310, 316–17
  leaving the house 307, 311, 372
  letting people into your home 312–13, 327–8
  locks and bolts 308–10
  Neighbourhood Watch schemes 313
  security advice 308
  social alarms 311, 473–4
  spare keys 308
  storing valuables 312
  Victim Support Schemes 312
self-employment
  advice, sources of 190
  National Insurance contributions 38, 183–4
  personal pension plans 96–8, 99
  self-employed status 215–16
  taxation 185, 224–34
  work-related expenses 43
  working from home 43, 191–2, 252
  see also business starting your own
SERPS 36
  calculating 39–40, 78–80
  contracting out 39, 78–81, 85, 94–6
  forecasts, 20, 40
  maximum pension payable 39, 40
  opting back in 14
  taxation of 200
services
  breakdown in service 327

complaints 329–30
difficulties in paying bills 325–6
electricity 294, 322, 324–6, 329
estimated accounts 324–5
gas 294, 315, 321, 324–6, 328–9
local council 346–8
meters 323–4, 325
moving house 294–5
payment options 323–4
reducing bills 326
repairs and safety checks 315, 327, 328
special services for the retired 321
telephone 45–6, 295, 322, 324, 326, 327, 330, 484
visits by company staff 327
sexual problems 461–2
shares 131–2, 133, 135, 243–4
sheltered housing 270–1, 469–70
single-premium insurance bonds 123, 131, 134–5, 139–40
skin problems 462–3
smoking 429, 434, 443, 447, 449
social fund 66
solicitors 147–8, 493, 494, 495, 501–2, 504
state benefits
  Benefits Enquiry Line 25
  cold weather payments 66
  disability living allowance 25
  for exceptional expenses 66
  income support 60–7
  incapacity benefit 25
  social fund 66
  unemployment benefit 26–8, 166
  widows and widowers 109–11, 112–13
  and working in retirement 166
State Earnings Related Pension Scheme *see* SERPS
state retirement pension
  adequacy of 14
  adult dependency allowance 200
  basic pension rates 36
  deferring 57, 160–1
  early retirement 24
  forecasts 20
  graduated pension 40, 200
  inflation-proofed 35
  information 41
  NI contributions 36, 37
  non-contributory pension 200
  and periods in hospital 48, 419–20
  qualifying for 36–7
  rates 36
  SERPS *see* SERPS

539

taxation 199–200
  working life 36–7
stockbrokers 135, 148
stress 28
strokes 463–4

taxation
  allowances 207–14
  divorce and 213
  investments 121–2, 125, 126,
    133–4, 199–200, 201, 203, 235–45
  life insurance policies 138, 236–7
  marriage/remarriage and 214
  pensions 199–201
  self-employment 185, 224–34
  working in retirement 160, 215–34
  and your home 246–52, 517–18
  see also capital gains tax; income
    tax; inheritance tax; Inland
    Revenue
term accounts 127
TESSAs (Tax Exempt Special
  Savings Accounts) 121, 127–8
thrombophlebitis 465
transient ischaemic attacks (TIAs) 464
transport
  concessionary travel schemes 46–7,
    362–4, 476–7
  see also cars; driving
trusts 515–17

unemployment benefit 26, 27–8, 166
unit trusts 123, 131, 132, 133, 135

varicose veins 464–5
Victim Support Schemes 312
voluntary work 166, 382–3

water boards
  difficulties in paying bills 325–6
  payment options 324
  services for retired people 322
water rates 294
widowers
  personal allowances 213, 214
  state financial support 112–13
widows
  personal allowances 209, 213–14
  state financial support 109–11,
    112–13
  widowed mother's allowance
    109–10
  widow's bereavement allowance
    213–14
  widow's payment 109

widow's pension 109–11
wills
  appointing guardians 492
  challenging 498
  enduring power of attorney
    (lifetime will) 503–4
  estate 496–7
  executors and trustees 499–501
  gifts for life 499
  and inheritance tax 492, 514
  intestacy rules 489, 490–1
  jointly held property 496–7
  legacies/bequests 498–9
  necessity for 18, 489, 492–3
  problems 501–2
  residuary legacy 498–9
  revoking and changing 495–6
  in Scottish law 504–6
  using a bank/solicitor 494–5, 501–2
  who to leave property to 497–8
  will-writing companies 494
  witnessing and storing 495
  writing your own 493–4
women
  divorce and pension rights 87–8
  reduced-rate National Insurance 38
  state retirement pension 36–7
  see also widows
working life: defined 36–7
working in retirement
  career consultancies 170
  CVs 171–3
  disability or health problems 58,
    171
  effect on benefits 166
  effect on pensions 160–2
  employee rights 173–8
  employment agencies 169–70
  Employment Service 170–1
  financial factors 159–63
  freelance or consultant basis 164
  job applications and interviews
    167–8, 172–3
  job-share arrangements 163
  NI contributions 160
  network organisations 171
  part-time 164, 165, 177–8
  pensions and 58, 82–3, 161–2
  sources of vacancies 169–70
  and state benefits 166
  taxation 160, 215–34
  voluntary work 166, 171
  work possibilities 165
  see also business, starting your own;
    self-employment